Africana Studies

Africana Studies

Philosophical Perspectives and Theoretical Paradigms

**Edited by Delores P. Aldridge
and E. Lincoln James**

Washington State University Press
Pullman, Washington

WASHINGTON STATE
UNIVERSITY

Washington State University Press
PO Box 645910
Pullman, Washington 99164-5910
Phone: 800-354-7360
Fax: 509-335-8568
E-mail: wsupress@wsu.edu
Web site: wsupress.wsu.edu

Library of Congress Cataloging-in-Publication Data

Africana studies : philosophical perspectives and theoretical paradigms
/ edited by Delores P. Aldridge and E. Lincoln James.
    p. cm.
  Includes bibliographical references.
  ISBN 978-0-87422-294-4 (alk. paper)
  1. African Americans--Study and teaching. 2. Blacks--Study and teaching.
3. Africa--Study and teaching. I. Aldridge, Delores P. II. James, E. Lincoln.
E184.7.A317 2007
960.07--dc22

WSU PRESS
Fine Quality Books from the Pacific Northwest

Contents

Foreword

TALMADGE ANDERSON

Professor Emeritus, and Founding Editor,
The Western Journal of Black Studies

T*he Western Journal of Black Studies* was initiated to provide mostly Black scholars and professional writers with an opportunity to publish empirical and theoretical articles on the life and history of African Americans and Africans.

Prior to the Supreme Court's *Brown v. Board of Education* decision in 1954, few Black scholarly periodicals treating exclusively with the African American experience existed. The *Journal of Negro History, Journal of Negro Education*, and *Phylon* were among the limited number of established academic journals.

The desegregation era in higher education of the 1960s incited a spirit of intellectual liberation among Black scholars and academic professionals. The development of Black/African American Studies programs and departments, concomitant with the hiring of African American faculty at predominately white colleges and universities, caused the need and demand for research and articles on the Black experience authored by Blacks to increase dramatically.

Traditional white scholarly journals would not generally accept for publication articles on Black life and history by African American writers. If a work by an African American author was accepted, it could not contradict prevailing white scholarly assumptions or be racially sensitive regardless of its research quality or theoretical profundity. For the most part, a form of "domestic intellectual imperialism" prevailed relative to scholarship of African American life, culture, and history.

The Black Scholar published by Nathan Hare in the late 1960s may have been the first significant journal of its kind to offer publishing opportunities for the emerging new Black intellectualism. *The Black Scholar* provided a forum of Black thought, philosophy, and dialogue free from Euro-American filtering, sanctions, and constraints. For a similar reason, *The Western Journal of Black Studies* and *The Journal of Black Studies* were founded in the 1970s.

Because of the excellent quality of the articles published and good promotion strategy, *The Western Journal of Black Studies* gained rapid acceptance and circulation at major colleges and universities, especially at institutions having Black/African American programs and departments. A key element in the early success of the *Journal* was the support that it received from the WSU College of Liberal Arts and the Washington State University Press.

It is important to emphasize the necessity of having scholarly journals that treat almost exclusively the Black/African American experience. First, each identifiable collective race or ethnic group experiences different socio-cultural, politico-economic, and psychological realities. Different ontological belief systems and cultural characteristics reflect each group's distinct approach in conceptualizing and experiencing universal reality or worldview.

Second, because of different collective experiences, Afrocentric social scientific theory is philosophically and ideologically distinct from Eurocentric social scientific theory. Whether minute or substantial differences exist, the Black or African American scholar may be the appropriate or leading one to formulate new or alternate research paradigms toward the study of African American and African peoples. Moreover, the primary purpose or rational for Black/African American Studies is to analyze and study comprehensively the factors and conditions that have affected the sociological, political, economic, and psychological status of peoples of African descent.

The two editors of this volume have selected some of the most salient, profound, and provocative articles and essays published in *The Western Journal of Black Studies* since its inception in 1977. The book includes papers that are theoretically and empirically analytic, descriptive, prescriptive, and critical of the Black/African American past and present experience.

The writer of this Foreword is the founding editor of *The Western Journal of Black Studies*; the succeeding editor has continued the scholarly tradition consistent with the original intent.

Introduction

DELORES P. ALDRIDGE

Emory University

Africana, Black, African-American, Afro-American, Africology, Pan-African, and Afro-Caribbean studies are but different names for academic units that focus on the systematic investigation of people of African descent in their contacts with Europeans, their dispersal throughout the diaspora, and the subsequent institutionalization of racism and oppression as means of economic, political, and social subordination. Africana Studies/Black Studies are the terms increasingly used interchangeably by those who identify the new or emerging discipline. Because of the recent and evolving nature of Africana Studies as an intellectual enterprise, there continues to be debates about whether Africana Studies is a discipline in the traditional sense, or an area of inquiry to which one brings tools from selected disciplines and applies them to a particular subject matter.

While debate continues over its status as a discipline, there is consensus that Africana Studies/Black Studies began as a systematic field of study in the late 1960s in the wake of the civil rights movement and in the midst of pervasive campus unrest. From the outset it had both an academic and social mission. Although contemporary Africana/Black Studies as an interdisciplinary curriculum is a product of the 1960s, it draws much of its academic content from earlier times. Today's academic units vary in size, structure, emphasis, and resources, but there is common understanding of the human predicament that resulted in the transformation of African people into an enslaved people.

In reflecting over the more than three decades of its existence, it is important to make many assessments about the nature of Africana/Black Studies and the evolution of its scholarship that will guide its future. There have been numerous specialized journals and other research outlets. These include but are not limited to the *Journal of Black Studies, Western Journal of Black Studies, International Journal of Africana Studies, Black Scholar,* and the *Journal of African American Studies.*

Interest in the compiling of this particular book published by the WSU Press is an outgrowth of much inquiry about theory and method in the discipline following the release of *Out of the Revolution: The Development of Africana Studies* (Lexington Books, 2000), edited by Delores P. Aldridge and Carlene Young. For several decades, *The Western Journal of Black Studies* has served as a major outlet for publishing works focusing on issues and concerns in the discipline of Africana Studies. Because of the journal's longevity and broad reach to faculty and academic professionals, a compilation of its articles was pursued for inclusion in *Africana Studies: Philosophical Perspectives and Theoretical Paradigms*, which here focuses on more than a quarter-century time span with representative essays on philosophical perspectives and theoretical paradigms. This volume brings together selected works that have been printed in *The Western Journal of Black Studies* from its inception in 1977 and into the new millennium. The goal is to examine the development of the discipline by presenting the perspectives and theoretical paradigms that emerged in this time period as found in this major journal, which, itself, has changed over the years.

While more than 500 articles have been published in the journal since 1977, emphasis was placed on selecting essays (27 in number) focusing on "perspectives and theories," which resulted in the elimination of some otherwise very good work that did not tightly fall under the major themes being addressed in *Africana Studies.*

Perspectives are seen as evaluations with proportional importance given to the component parts. Theoretical paradigms are ideas or mental plans of the way to do something, or systematic statements of principles involved. Hence, the field of Africana Studies in its evolution over three decades or more should have developed many evaluative lenses of phenomena, as well as mental plans of ways to understand African people and their many experiences. Conjointly, perspectives and theoretical paradigms undergird methodological approaches in a variety of substantive areas in Africana Studies. Hence, it is envisioned that this book will be instructive in efforts designed to examine the discipline's past and contemporary scholarship, as it relates to perspectives, theoretical paradigms, and methodology.

* * *

Africana Studies is divided into four parts. Part One provides "Philosophical Perspectives on Africana Studies in the 1970s." Part Two, "Developing Theoretical Paradigms in Africana Studies in the 1980s," devotes attention to different theories set forth to explain substantive areas. Part Three focuses on "Africana Paradigms in Practice since 1990." In this latter section, works that demonstrate how theory can be applied to substantive areas is an attempt at uncovering methodological approaches. Part Four, "Africana Studies in the New Millennium," outlines the possibilities for the development of the discipline by suggesting new and refined paradigms as well as highlighting two major issues for the early 21st century, namely, gender relations, and resources for further development of the undergraduate curriculum.

Taking one periodical, *The Western Journal of Black Studies*, to assess the discipline's growth over a quarter-century can serve as a beginning to examine other journals and communication outlets to determine how major theoretical and methodological approaches have developed since formal entry into the academy in the late 1960s, and the possibilities for further growth and development.

It is essential to note that each author's brief biographical description presented in *Africana Studies* outlines the contributor's academic status at the "time" their essay appeared in *The Western Journal of Black Studies*. Importantly, the reader is presented with an author's intellectual and career development at a given moment in the past.

Study Guide

Chapter 1: "The University of Sankore at Timbuctoo: A Neglected Achievement in Black Intellectual History," by John Henrik Clarke.

1. What were the two most notable empires of Africans in the Western Sudan prior to the end of the 16th century?
2. Why does Clarke call Ahmed Baba "the greatest Sudanese scholar of [his] day"?
3. What were major themes in Baba's books? What was the subject of *El Ibtihadj*, and why is it especially significant for scholars?
4. What does Clarke call "one of the great tragedies in African history"?
5. Why is it important to introduce this work at the beginning of the volume?

Chapter 2: "Historical Dialectics of Black Nationalist Movements in America," by James E. Turner.

1. What does the Black Nationalist tradition perceive as freedom?
2. How does Turner define the "push-pull" syndrome?
3. Name an important event, movement, or Black Nationalist leader from each of the five periods described by Turner, and describe how this event, movement, or person contributed to the evolution of Black Nationalism.
4. What was the American Colonization Society? Who were the society's members and what were the society's goals? How did free Blacks in the United States react?
5. In 1857, what did the Dred Scott decision tell free Blacks about the future of race relations in America?
6. How did the Civil War disrupt the plans of the National Emigration Conference and Henry Highland Garnet's African Civilization Society?
7. What was Edward Wilmot Blyden's attitude toward indigenous Africans, and what relationship did he seek with them?
8. Why were the Liberian Exodus Company and the Oklahoma Black Settlement effort not successful?
9. What did Marcus Garvey feel was one of the main problems for Black people? How did he attempt to address this problem? What strategy of Garvey's is now called "Third World Politics"?
10. What was the long-term goal of Malcolm X's memorandum and address at the Second Summer Conference of the OAU in Cairo?

Chapter 3: "Toward the Evolution of a Unitary Discipline: Maximizing the Interdisciplinary Concept in African/Afro-American Studies," by Karla J. Spurlock.

1. According to Spurlock: "What *were* and *are* the benefits of interdisciplinarity" in Black Studies?

2. How does Spurlock define "discipline" and "interaction"? How does she distinguish between the terms "multidisciplinary" and "interdisciplinarity"?
3. In discussing the problem of creating an interdisciplinary Black Studies program, what are two of the curricular remedies that she suggests?
4. Spurlock offers a program at the State University of New York at Albany as an example of how to correctly approach an interdisciplinary curriculum: (a) What twelve major disciplines did this program consider to be minimally essential to their African American Studies program?; (b) What other measures does the program take to "circumvent the multidisciplinary fate" she predicted earlier in this essay? How are these measures useful?
5. What are some other "extracurricular strategies for maximizing interdisciplinarity in Black Studies?

Chapter 4: "An Ideology for Liberation: A Response to Amiri Baraka and other 'Marxists,'" by Betty J. Collier and Louis N. Williams.

1. What is the difference between direct control and indirect control? Why can no system of suppression be maintained by direct force alone?
2. What are the three basic components of all ideologies?
3. What is Baraka's position? What does he see as the source of Black oppression? What does he suggest as a solution?
4. What are two kinds of inequalities, and what are some characteristics of each?
5. What two separate systems of oppression do the authors mention, and what is the basis for each?
6. What are the possible negative consequences of Baraka's Marxist view?
7. What two oppression-maintaining behavioral sets do the authors discuss, and how are each related to the victim?
8. Why are marriage and the family important for social change?
9. What steps toward social change do the authors suggest?
10. What is the essence of the "ideology for liberation"?

Chapter 5: "Historical Consciousness and Politics in Africa," by Lansiné Kaba.

1. How does Kaba define "historical consciousness"?
2. Kaba states: "Therefore, historical consciousness tends to have a class character." Explain this statement. Why might different groups within a society develop a different historical consciousness?
3. To what historical event or period does Kaba trace the origins of "the derogatory image associated with the African peoples"?
4. How did anthropology contribute to the problem?
5. Why does Kaba object to the terms "tribe" and "tribalism"?
6. Kaba states: "At the core of this positive consciousness lie four main principles reclaiming Black cultural and historical values and having direct political implications." What are the four principles?

Chapter 6: "The Intellectual Foundations of Racism," by Chukwuemeka Onwubu.

1. How does Onwubu define the term "intellectual"?
2. How does W.E.B. Du Bois define race? Do you agree or disagree with his definition? If you disagree, how would you change or modify it?
3. What "two major facets to race" are proposed by Fairbanks and Smith?
4. How does Rex distinguish between the concepts of "race" and "racialism"?
5. According to Onwubu, what is one of the primary tasks of a genuine student of race relations?
6. According to van den Berghe, in what context should race-relations studies be undertaken? Why is it inappropriate to approach them from the angle of an experiment or the scientific method?
7. Why is Gordon against school integration and affirmative action in hiring? Do you agree or disagree with his arguments and why? What flaws does Onwubu see in Gordon's arguments? What does he see as the "crucial question" that Gordon should be reminded of?

Chapter 7: "The Ideology of European Dominance," by Dona Richards.

1. What does Richards say that white social theory represents? How does it view African civilization?
2. How does she define the term "ethos," and what does it indicate?
3. What does the conception of the "Great Chain of Being" hold, and where did it originate? How is this concept significant for Western European scientific thought and for the Western view of Africans?
4. What does Richards call "a new morality," and what did it do for Western European ideology?
5. Richards states that Europeans were "precisely the wrong people to formulate the so-called universal laws of human nature." Explain this position.
6. Richards explains several theories that "form the white Western European frame of reference." What do they have in common? What are Africanists obligated to do regarding these theories?
7. For European social theorists of the 18th and 19th centuries, what was the "problem of race"? How did the monogenists and polygenists attempt to answer this "problem"? What was racial craniology?
8. Edward Tylor, the "Founder of Anthropology" saw a dichotomy where? According to Tylor, differences in cultures were due to what?
9. How are the social sciences related to Darwin?
10. What do Western Europeans generally assume, according to Richards? What does this view of social history not allow for?
11. What does Richards say that Black anthropologists and other African social scientists must do?

Chapter 8: "Black Studies and Sensibility: Identity, the Foundation for a Pedagogy," by Johnnella E. Butler.

1. How does Butler define "pedagogy" for the purpose of her work?
2. What does Butler say are "the organizing principles for a pedagogy" of Black Studies?
3. Butler says that "the Black person's experience is shaped basically by two forces constantly interacting with one another and never operating separately." What are they?
4. In Levine's discussion of culture, what does he say we must be sensitive to? What does Butler say is "paramount" to understanding culture?
5. What does Redfield offer as an alternative, better term for "culture"? What term does Butler prefer, and what does she say culture is a product of?

Chapter 9: "Notes on an Africentric Theory of Black Personality," by Joseph A. Baldwin.

1. According to Baldwin, what does African psychology take as its conceptual framework?
2. How are the concepts of race and cosmology defined? How are the concepts of race, cosmology, culture, and collective survival thrust related?
3. What four basic assumptions about the relationship between race and psychological experience does Baldwin discuss?
4. How is personality conceptualized, and how should it be analyzed, according to Baldwin?
5. What three fundamental propositions are deducible when the basic principles about personality outlined are applied to the concept of Black personality?
6. How are the "African Self-Extension Orientation" and "African Self-Consciousness" defined? How are they related?
7. What is "the most important aspect of African Self-Consciousness," and what does this include under normal conditions?
8. What seven basic traits of Black personality have been most widely recognized in the literature?

Chapter 10: "Toward a Theory of Popular Health Practices in the Black Community," by Clovis E. Semmes.

1. Why are popular health practices essential components of culture?
2. How is popular medicine defined by Spicer? How is popular medicine different from folk medicine?
3. Why does Semmes say that the term "health practices" is more appropriate than "medical practices" for his theory?
4. What is the author's purpose in writing this article?
5. What were the two central components of the plantation slave diet? How did this gain cultural significance?

6. How did urbanization in the South and the North transform traditional eating patterns? What dietary aspects remained unchanged? What further changes did the post-urban period bring?
7. According to Semmes, conjure, voodoo, hoodoo, or root doctoring all have to do with what belief?
8. What is the difference between a natural illness and an unnatural illness? What are their causes? What is the unifying concept behind treatments for both types of illnesses?
9. Why is the power of the word significant?
10. What are some forms of collective healing, and where are they usually found? The author states that they are not reactions to poverty, racism, or oppression. What are they instead?
11. What dimension remains central to popular post-urban health practices?
12. What important change was brought about by Elijah Muhammad and the Hebrew Israelites of the 1960s? What did Muhammad's teachings challenge, and how did this affect the significance of "soul food"?
13. What were some of the key dietary changes that these groups advocated? What were some resulting health issues?
14. What is the theory that is ultimately proposed for understanding health practices among Black people in the United States?

Chapter 11: "Theories of Black Culture," by Amuzie Chimezie.

1. In the debate over Black culture, what is at "the heart of the issue"?
2. What are the names of the three affirmative theories, and what is the common bond among them?
3. What is African-Heritage Theory? What are its three major components?
4. What cultural elements have been used as examples of remnants from Africa?
5. What are the "three hurdles" that African-Heritage Theory faces?
6. How does Affirmative New World-Experience Theory differ from African Heritage Theory?
7. What is Biculturation Theory? How does Chimezie criticize Biculturation Theory (as it is presented by Charles A. Valentine)? Why does Chimezie say that it could be seen as eclectic?
8. What is the Eclectic View (or Eclectic Theory), and how does it differ from the theories discussed above?
9. What do negative theories of Black culture argue?
10. What is Negative New-World Experience Theory, and how is it different from Affirmative New World-Experience Theory?
11. What two factors seem to underlie some of the Affirmative and Negative New World-Experience Theories? How are each of these factors used to explain Black cultural distinctiveness?
12. What is Lower-Class Theory? Why does Chimezie state that the assumption that middle-class Black culture is *the* Black culture would not be valid, as compared to the same assumption of white culture?

13. What is the Pathology Theory of Black culture? How has this theory been fostered by white, middle-class social scientists?
14. What theory(ies) does Chimezie propose as most significant for understanding Black culture?

Chapter 12: "Toward an Understanding of Black Male-Female Relationships," by Delores P. Aldridge.

1. Aldridge calls for an increased amount of research in several areas. What are they?
2. How does the Black female-headed family operate in the eyes of critics? How can it be seen from the general systems perspective?
3. What theme unites the work of the researchers on Black male/female relationships listed by Aldridge?
4. What two problems threaten Black male/female relationships as presented by the author?
5. What five facts serve as a "point of departure for any serious analysis of Black men, Black women, and their relationships," according to Karenga and Aldridge?
6. "American society is defined by and derived from four major structural and value systems." What are they, and how are they defined?
7. What four factors shape the interactive nature of communication between Black males and Black females?
8. What are the "grave consequences" of the scarcity of Black men?
9. What conflicting signals do Black men receive about their role as men, and how does this affect their relationships?
10. What is the differentiation between a "connection" and a "quality relationship"?
11. How does the author explain the relationship between courtship and sex to capitalism?
12. Why did many Black men and women speak out against feminism and the women's liberation movement? What is the author's stance on this?
13. Is the reader left with a conceptual understanding or explanation of Black male/female relationships?

Chapter 13: "Conceptual and Logical Issues in Theory and Research Related to Black Masculinity," by Clyde W. Franklin II.

1. Franklin says that there is a dearth of literature relating to what?
2. What major factors are significant influences in male role assumption? What does this mean?
3. David and Brannon have delineated and defined several dimensions of masculinity that are congruent with the MSRI paradigm. What are they?
4. What does sex role strain analysis (as suggested by Pleck) imply?
5. To what three different, although related, sets of role expectations must Black men conform, according to Franklin?
6. What factors have resulted in the "institutional decimation" of Black men?

7. According to Franklin, what two factors are critical to point out when examining the Black masculine role?
8. What important contributions did Wallace make with her book, *Black Macho and the Myth of the Superwoman*? What logical problems does Franklin see in her book?
9. What is the "crucial omission in theory and research on Black masculinity"?

Chapter 14: "Race and Raceness: A Theoretical Perspective of the Black American Experience," by Jacqueline E. Wade.

1. What is the purpose of the work according to the author?
2. How does Wade differentiate between the concepts of "race" and "raceness," and what determines each?
3. According to Franklin and Blumer, what do the concept of race and racial prejudice do for the "wretched" or "low-status" individual from the dominant group?
4. What does the author see as the source of racial degradation and exploitation for other racial groups in society (e.g., Native Americans and Asians)?
5. Wade provides descriptions of several empirical studies as evidence of "White-Race Centeredness." Briefly explain those findings.
6. According to Wade's reinterpretation of Blumer's perspective on racial prejudice, what four basic types of feelings, attitudes, and/or beliefs are always present in white/Black interactions? How does each of these perceptions refer to a unique race status positioning in the white/Black encounter?
7. What do white Americans do as a consequence of "on the average, truly believ[ing] that they are unprejudiced about Blacks in terms of their sense of group responsibility for the problems that Blacks face"?
8. What does Wade say is perhaps "the most poignant example of a medium that fosters the perception of white-raceness as normal and Black-raceness as deviant"? Explain how this example fosters this perception.
9. Explain Goffman's concept of management of "stigma identity" as it relates to white/Black interactions. What are the various identity management techniques that Blacks use according to Wade?
10. What does Wade mean by the "schizophrenic existence" faced by Blacks?
11. According to Chestang, what is the greatest toll of the task that Blacks face "to demonstrate *intrinsic* equality, competence, and humanity"?
12. What does Wade mean in saying that Blacks know that they are "on" in the company of whites?
13. Explain Chestang's suggestion; "The Black man is not a marginal man but a bicultural man."

Chapter 15: "Consensus and Neo-Conservatism in the Black Community: A Theoretical Analysis of Black Leadership," by Richard A. Davis.

1. According to Davis, the controversy surrounding Black leadership touches upon what three different concerns?
2. What definition of a Black leader does Davis provide? What three considerations can be turned to next, if one accepts this definition?
3. What did the National Urban League conclude about the schism between Black leaders and the Black community? Their concern centered around what issue?
4. Davis states that the second main concern in this controversy "centers around the apparent emergence of a new type of Black leader." Who are these new Black leaders and how do they contrast to traditional Black leaders?
5. To what does Sowell attribute the growing split among Black leaders? Explain.
6. How does Converse explain the difference between the opinions expressed by most groups and their leaders?
7. According to Max Weber, leadership is based on what three forms of authority? What are each of these forms of authority themselves based upon?
8. The Civil Rights Movement gave precedence to what kind of leaders? Why does this kind of authority tend to ultimately give way to a different form of authority?
9. What two things tend to happen during the "routinization of charisma" phase that explain the divide among Black leaders?
10. During the consolidation period, the apparent lack of diversity of opinion in the Black community might have been due to what?
11. What does Davis mean by "a shift in the institutional basis of Black leadership"?

Chapter 16: "The Emerging Paradigm in Black Studies," by Terry Kershaw.

1. The methodology suggested in Kershaw's work is a synthesis of what two types of methodologies?
2. Several definitions are offered for the term "paradigm." How does the author define paradigm for the purpose of this work? What will a paradigm of Black Studies determine?
3. Kershaw says that, "The basic assumptions of the field of Black Studies revolve around the concept of Afrocentricity." How does he explain this term?
4. What are the three basic assumptions of the Black Studies discipline?
5. How does the author use two predominant sociological theories to illustrate the need for the discipline of Black Studies?
6. Compare and contrast positivist and critical research methodologies.
7. Moynihan's study is an example of which methodology—positivist or critical? How do you know?
8. How does the role of the researcher differ between positivist and critical methodologies (in regards to relationship between researcher and subjects, bias, objectivity, etc.)? Which approach does the Black Studies method emphasize?

9. Why is it important to study past empirical research along with historical analysis?
10. Does Kershaw advocate quantitative or qualitative methods?

Chapter 17: "Re-examining the Black on Black Crime Issue: A Theoretical Essay," by Robert L. Perry.

1. According to Perry, where does the "law and order hysteria" have its roots? What belief is implicit to this hysteria? How do law and order advocates perpetuate it?
2. What does the author tell us about the police forces in most urban Black communities? How do the police view the residents of these communities, and how do the residents view the police?
3. An understanding of Black on Black crime needs to be understood in what context? Where does a study of the origins of Black on Black crime need to begin?
4. The author says that the legacy of slavery "defined interactions between Black and White America." Explain.
5. Within American culture, legislation puts more of an emphasis on what kind of rights? Who defines criminal behavior, and how is this definition used? How do American laws do more to protect the interest of the powerful than less powerful groups?
6. What were the three reasons that Blacks migrated North following the Civil War and Reconstruction? What kind of treatment did they receive there?
7. Perry says that Black on Black crime is a "*victim on victim* crime." What does he think ultimately needs to be the cure?
8. How is frustration different for Black Americans and white Americans, according to Perry? Frustration usually is acted out upon who?
9. What is the relationship between drug and alcohol use and crime? Why does Perry caution against asserting causation?
10. According to Perry, why do drug addict criminals commit most of their crimes in Black communities?

Chapter 18: "Afrocentricity and the Critique of Drama," by Molefe Kete Asante.

1. What are the three principal metaphors in the critique of drama according to Afrocentric theory? How does Asante define/explain each?
2. Why is it important for the dramatist and the critic to operate from a similar location?
3. What is the principal question that must be answered by the critic of a dramatist's work?
4. According to Asante: What must African American writers and critics consider and address in their writing?
5. What is the relationship between culture, economics, politics, and writing?
6. What is the real substance of relationships for African Americans? How does it relate to the circle of memory and the writer?

Chapter 19: "Africentricity in Social Science," by Gordon D. Morgan.

1. Morgan talks about the cleavage along age lines in Black American social science scholarship. Who were some of the leading scholars or organizations during the first generation?
2. Why does Morgan say the tradition of these older scholars was essentially assimilationist? What did self-improvement mean for these scholars?
3. Why were Paul Cuffee, Martin Delany, Alfred Sam, and Marcus Garvey notable proponents of the Africentric orientation?
4. What changes began to happen in the Africentric orientation during the 1960s? How were these changes manifested in universities?
5. What model of research has traditionally held the most sway in social science scholarship? Why did this model start to fall under attack by the Black scholars of the 1960s?
6. Who formed the two opposing sides of the Africentric debate "in its classic phase"? What did they argue?
7. What caution does Morgan give regarding the need to develop Africentric methodological and theoretical guidelines?
8. Historically, why was so much positive Black scholarship never published?
9. Morgan says that "Africentric knowledge comes from many sources," but it is especially what?
10. Why is debate so important in the Africentric tradition?
11. Who was the most prominent spokesperson for Africentrism at the time of this writing? What does this spokesperson believe and call for? What does he fail to provide in his writings?
12. According to Morgan, what did the Renaissance prove? What role did Isaac Newton play in this?
13. "In the diaspora, and especially in North America, the ultimate expression of Africentricity" was what? How does Morgan describe this concept?
14. Compare and contrast the ways that Arabs and Europeans approached the African continent (their goals and tactics).
15. Who "kept the idea of Africentricity alive"? How did their social status affect them?
16. Morgan says that whether "there is or is not an Africentric view is immaterial." What is important instead?
17. What is Morgan's perspective on racial and ethnically comparative research?

Chapter 20: "Beyond Afrocentrism: Alternatives for African American Studies," by Perry A. Hall.

1. What four reasons does Hall give for why "the African American Studies discipline should be conceptualized as a set of theoretical perspectives, rather than as a single theoretical perspective"?

2. What two theoretical perspectives are being compared in this work, and which is most strongly advocated by the author?
3. Hall points out that most Black Studies programs are housed by Eurocentric institutions. What consequences does this have for Black scholarship?
4. Hall contends that "Afrocentrism, while necessary, is of itself insufficient as a theoretical base from which to address the complete set of issues facing Black Studies scholars." Explain.
5. How does Hall define culture? What is the danger of a static view of culture from a Eurocentric perspective?
6. In contrast, what does a dynamic view of culture focus upon?
7. What are the bases of the framework of the transformationist perspective, and what is its basic analytical principle?
8. According to Hall, what is Afrocentrism's seminal objective? How does transformation differ from this view?
9. How do a static view of culture and a dynamic view of culture differ in their perspective on words and language?
10. Why does Hall feel that Afrocentrism is failing to adequately reach and instruct Black youth?
11. How would the two theoretical perspectives outlined in this paper differ in their treatment of rap and Malcolm X in university Black Studies courses?

Chapter 21: "A Blueprint for African American Economic Development," by Robert E. Weems.

1. Which two complimentary doctrines have historically "coalesced in the promotion of greater (internal) African American economic development"?
2. According to Weems, what is perhaps "the most noteworthy work associated with the anti-Black business scholarly tradition"? What criticisms of this work does Weems present?
3. During the late 19th and early 20th centuries, how did most non-Anglo-Saxon Americans view internal economic development? How has this changed for European Americans and African Americans since that time?
4. What concept does Weems suggest is the "key element in a potential, mass-based revitalization of the African Community"? How is it defined, and who brought it to the United States originally?
5. According to Light, the advantage of this economic strategy depends on what? Why has this made it difficult for African Americans to utilize this strategy, and why does Weems suggest that African Americans may have difficulty in implementing it in the future?
6. What are two ways that the "fruitless debate as to what represents the 'best' means by which African Americans can achieve economic self-determination" have had a negative impact on Black economic empowerment?
7. What does Weems see as the "ideal vehicle" to promote his proposed economic strategy, and what other locales does he also suggest? Why?

Chapter 22: "Perception of Power/Control among African Americans: A Developmental Approach," by Rudolph A. Cain.

1. How does Cain explain the variable "locus of control"?
2. In the study, were study participants more inner-directed or outer-directed overall? What impact did racism have?
3. What noteworthy findings of previous research (Gore, Rotter, Gurin, Epps, and Bullough) does Cain mention?
4. What is the focal theoretical assumption of the Levinsonian model of eras and stages of adulthood? What are the three levels of life structures in this model?
5. How does Cain explain the role of the Mentor and the Dream in this theory?
6. What hypotheses does Cain make about his expected findings?
7. What are the weaknesses and limitations in Cain's participant sample design? What does he say outweighs these limitations?
8. As young adults, were individuals more internally or externally oriented?
9. In what ways did the roles of prejudice, discrimination, and racism in the data surprise researchers (go against expectations)?
10. What does Cain find particularly noteworthy about the Mid-Life Transition stage?
11. Were Cain's hypotheses supported by his findings? Explain.

Chapter 23: "Towards an Africological Pedagogical Approach to African Civilization," by Victor Oguejiofor Okafor.

1. According to the author, what are the two objectives of this work?
2. What was the major contention of the debate on the topic of African Civilization that the author took part in?
3. What evidence does Okafor provide against the notion that "Africans of the pre-colonial era hibernated in closed-off clan or ethnic enclaves and remained unaware of Africans based in other regions of the continent"?
4. What evidence does the anthropological school of thought offer in support of the idea of "Western Civilization"?
5. What two major historical epochs does Davidson identify as the origins of Pan-Africanism, and how does each of them account for the diversity in modern African societies?
6. In what way does Asante criticize the anthropological Africanist view of African civilization and the origins of this view?
7. What two major constituent parts of African History are identified by Diop?
8. What four time periods does Keto outline in his "*time map of Africa*" in which Africans excelled in history, and what modification does Okafor make to this time map?
9. What distinction does Okafor make between the subjects of African History and African Civilization?
10. Why does Okafor argue for the title of "African Civilization" instead of "African Civilizations"? Where does he say the anthropological preference for "African

Civilizations" stems from? Why does a holistic pedagogy reject the traditional title of "African Civilizations"?

11. Describe some of the linguistic and cultural evidence provided by Okafor in support of the ideas of African civilization and unity.

12. What are the three major definitions of Africology provided by Okafor, and who proposed each? What is the common thread that binds these definitions together?

13. What is Diop's two-cradle theory? How did the resources available in the Northern and Southern cradles influence the culture and human nature that developed in each?

Chapter 24: "Towards a Grand Theory of Black Studies: An Attempt to Discern the Dynamics and the Direction of the Discipline," by Arthur Lewin.

1. According to Lewin, what is the "pivot around which the discipline [of Black Studies] revolves"?

2. How are the inclusionist and nationalist schools similar, and how are they different?

3. How do these schools view each other? What departments are given as examples of each school?

4. According to Lewin, "How can a comprehensive theory of Black Studies resolve the ideological struggle without taking sides"?

5. When and why did the multicultural movement and the "third world" liberation struggles emerge?

6. According to Lewin, how is it that the emerging homogenous global culture is heavily influenced by African American culture?

7. How did the age of Empire lead to the development of Eurocentricity and Afrocentricity? According to Lewin, why is Afrocentricity potent? Why is it flawed?

8. Why are both inclusionists and nationalists necessary to the field of Black Studies?

Chapter 25: "Africana Womanism: The Flip Side of a Coin," by Clenora Hudson-Weems.

1. According to Hudson-Weems, Africana Womanism became an antidote to what?

2. What was the "true catalytic event" of the modern Civil Rights Movement of the 1950s and 1960s?

3. How does Hudson-Weems define Africana Womanism?

4. How do the priorities of Africana women differ from those of white women feminists? How do they differ in the way they view their male counterparts?

5. Why does white feminist Aptheker say that addressing race issues for Black women is a prerequisite for addressing gender concerns?

6. What were the original goals of feminism and the Woman Suffrage Movement? What caused a shift in the goals and attitudes of participants in these movements?

7. Hudson-Weems says that because "Africana men have unfortunately internalized the patriarchal system to some degree," what must they now do?
8. A quote from Steady says that "Women belong to different socio-economic groups and do not represent a universal category." How might this affect the way Black women view the middle-class dimension of the women's movement?
9. How did American slavery negate traditional notions of male or female roles for African American slaves?
10. What does Hudson-Weems perceive to be the number one priority of Africana women around the world? To what models does she trace the roots of Africana Womanism?

Chapter 26: "Africana Studies and Gender Relations in the Twenty First Century," by Delores P. Aldridge.

1. Africana womanist scholars urge the redefinition of what?
2. According to Aldridge, what would increase the likelihood of gender political cooperation? What is the most powerful force for group positive action and complementarity?
3. What caused the shift away from the original movement, in which both men and women fought "side by side for the liberation of Black people"? Why has the move to Women's Studies resulted in tension and disappointment for a number of Black female scholars?
4. How does Aldridge apply the phrase, "It takes a village to raise a child" to Africana Studies? Explain.
5. How does Aldridge describe her own perspective of Africana womanism? What does she say that men and women scholars must do to advance this perspective?
6. What common ground do Black men and women share that may be obscured by gender tension?
7. What role did African American women play in the various "Black Power" movements of the 1960s, which eventually led to the development of Black Studies programs in colleges and universities? What reception did they receive after these programs were started?
8. What was novel about the book, *Out of the Revolution: The Development of Africana Studies* by Aldridge and Young (2000)?
9. Aldridge says "our fate is inextricably connected with the structure and functioning of the global economy, for there are external forces impinging upon the destiny of African peoples and their scholarship." What external forces does she discuss? Why are these external forces especially relevant in illustrating her argument for gender cooperation among Black scholars?
10. How does Walker define a "womanist"?
11. What does Aldridge advocate should be built into Africana Studies programs?

Chapter 27: "Will the Revolution be Digitized? Using Digitized Resources in Undergraduate Africana Studies," by James B. Stewart.

1. What does Stewart imply with the title of this work?
2. Why will using digitized resources serve students in Africana Studies courses in particular? And/or how will using digitized resources serve the long-term individual and collective social survival and empowerment objectives of Africana Studies?
3. In the 1960s and 1970s, what factors hampered the development of field specific introductory Africana Studies texts?
4. Stewart lists and briefly describes four of the first Africana Studies introductory texts published. What were they, and how did they differ in their approach to presenting material?
5. According to the NCBS Interdisciplinary Curriculum Model, an Introduction to Black Studies course typically provides the foundations for further study in what three possible areas of concentration?
6. According to Stewart, what do websites such as "African Timelines," "West African Kingdoms," and "The Atlantic Slave Trade and Slave Life in the Americas: A Visual Record" provide that is lacking in the Anderson and Karenga texts?
7. In studying the antebellum and postbellum time periods, why is digital information about free Blacks resistance to slavery, and efforts to form all-Black towns, especially valuable when compared to traditional texts for these courses?
8. Stewart emphasizes that social and behavioral science courses within Africana Studies "should be designed to impart an understanding of the information conveyed by various social indicators and by trends in the value of such indicators over time." Why might on-line resources be especially valuable compared to traditional texts for these courses?
9. Why does Stewart call attention to the fact that most of the websites mentioned in the article were not produced by Africana Studies specialists, or with Africana Studies-specific instructional objectives in mind?

Part One: Philosophical Perspectives on Africana Studies in the 1970s

1

The University of Sankore at Timbuctoo: A Neglected Achievement in Black Intellectual History

John Henrik Clarke

John Henrik Clarke is Advisory Editor for the African-American Scholar and Professor, Department of Black and Puerto Rican Studies, at Hunter College, New York; Past President, African Heritage Studies Association; and Founding Member, Black Academy of Arts and Letters. He is a prolific writer of articles on African and Afro-American history and culture appearing regularly in journals in the United States and abroad.—The Western Journal of Black Studies, *June 1977, Vol. 1, No. 2*

In the Mali Republic in West Africa today, the ruins of some of the buildings that once housed the University of Sankore and the Grand Mosque of Timbuctoo can still be seen. Therefore this subject is both topical and historical. Most Black Americans are just beginning to hear about the University of Sankore and the grandeur of the Songhay Empire during Africa's third and last Golden Age.[1] Western historians have either ignored this period in African history or attributed it to the influence of the Arabs and Berbers.

The intellectual history of Africa has not been written. It is a history that is long, strong, and rich, and the holocaust of the slave trade did not destroy it. Contrary to misconceptions that still prevail, in spite of historical evidence that can dispel them, the Africans were producers of literature and art, and a philosophical way of life, long before contact with the Western world.

Before the destruction of the Empire of Songhay by the Moroccans and European mercenary soldiers at the end of the sixteenth century, the Africans in the Western Sudan (inner West Africa) had been bringing into being great empires and cultures for over a thousand years, the most notable empires being Ghana and Mali. The Songhay Empire and the University of Sankore, at Timbuctoo, was in existence over a hundred years after the slave trade had already been started along the west coast of Africa.

During this period in West African history—from the early part of the fourteenth century to the time of the Moorish invasion in 1591—the city of Timbuctoo and the University of Sankore in the Songhay Empire were the intellectual centers of Africa. Black scholars were enjoying a renaissance that was known and respected throughout most of Africa and in parts of Europe. At this period in African history, the University of Sankore was the educational capital of the Western Sudan.[2] In his book, *Timbuctoo the Mysterious*, Felix DuBois gives us the following description of this period:

> The scholars of Timbuctoo yielded in nothing, to the saints in their sojourns in the foreign universities of Fez, Tunis, and Cairo. They astounded the most learned men of Islam by their education. That these Negroes were on a level with Arabian Savants is proved by the fact that they were installed as professors in Morocco and Egypt. In contrast to this, we find that the Arabs were not always equal to the requirements of Sankore.[3]

I will speak of only one of the great Black scholars referred to in the book by Felix DuBois. Ahmed Baba was the last chancellor of the University of Sankore and one of the greatest African scholars of the late sixteenth century. His life is a brilliant example of the range and depth of West African intellectual activity before the colonial era. Ahmed Baba was the author of more than forty books; nearly every one of these books had a different theme. He was in Timbuctoo when it was invaded by the Moroccans in 1591, and he was one of the first citizens to protest this occupation of his beloved hometown. Ahmed Baba, along with other scholars, was imprisoned and eventually exiled to Morocco. During his expatriation from Timbuctoo, his collection of 1,600 books, one of the richest libraries of his day, was lost.

Now, West Africa entered a sad period of decline. During the Moorish occupation wreck and ruin became the order of the day. When the Europeans arrived in this part of Africa and saw these conditions, they assumed that nothing of order and value had ever existed in these countries.

Western scholarship, in most cases, has ignored the great wealth of information on intellectual life in the Western Sudan. The following details on the subject were extracted from the pamphlet,[4] "Literacy and Scholarship in Muslim West Africa in the Pre-Colonial Period," by John O. Hunwick (1974).

In sixteenth-century Timbuctoo, during the relatively settled and prosperous period of the Askias of Songhay, there was an important concentration of scholars around the famous Sankore Mosque and University. There were many celebrated families of scholars in Timbuctoo and throughout the Songhay Empire. Ahmed Baba came out of such a family. This family, and others, produced numerous scholars during the fourteenth and fifteenth centuries, and an illustrious dynasty of judges. In his book Professor Hunwick tells us:

> The scholars of Timbuctoo were not wholly wrapped up in their theoretical studies and the preservation and handling of knowledge, important as this was...many went on pilgrimage to Mecca and while there took the opportunity to hold discussions with, or acquire knowledge from scholars from other parts of the Muslim world. On the way home, some stopped in Egypt and studied under the leading scholars in Cairo. Some also visited other African towns in the course of their travels such as Kano, Katsina, and Takedota and Walata, studying if they found teachers, and teaching if they found pupils.

In *Timbuctoo the Mysterious*, Felix DuBois tells us:[5]

> Timbuctoo was not merely the great intellectual nucleus of the Sudan, but also one of the great scientific centers of Islam itself.

The University of Sankore had established relationships with similar institutions in Cairo, Cardova, Fez, and Damascus. The collection of ancient manuscripts found in the library at Sankore leaves us in no doubt on this point. These manuscripts give us the opportunity to reconstruct the life of the intellectual community at Timbuctoo and to see how this community related to the Muslim world of its day. According to DuBois:

> An entire class of the population was devoted to the study of letters, being called fakirs or sheiks by the old manuscripts, and marabuts (holy men) of the Sudanese of today...these pious and cultured families of Timbuctoo lived within the precincts of the mosque of Sankore...they were held in high esteem by both dignitaries and people. The Songhay kings pensioned the most celebrated, and they received many gifts, especially in the month of Ramadan.

The great scholar, Ahmed Baba, belonged to one these families. When the Moroccan expeditionary force, composed largely of Andalusian renegades and other white mercenaries, occupied Timbuctoo in 1591, an attempt to revolt led to the deportation of the leading scholars, including Ahmed Baba.[6]

The story of Ahmed Baba is part of the story of the Songhay during the years after the death of the great ruler that is known in African history as "Askia the Great." After the death of Askia, in 1528, the Songhay Empire began to lose its strength and control over its vast territory. When the Songhay Empire collapsed after the capture of Timbuctoo and Gao by the Moroccans in 1591, the whole of the Western Sudan was devastated by the invading troops. The Sultan of Morocco, El-Mansur, had sent a large army with European firepower across the Sahara to attack the once-powerful Empire of Songhay. When the army reached Timbuctoo in 1591, the prosperous city was plundered by the army of freebooters and a state of anarchy prevailed. The great Sudanese scholar of that day, Ahmed Baba, was among those exiled.

Timbuctoo provides the most appalling example of the struggles of the West African states and towns as they strove to preserve what was once their Golden Age. The Arabs, Berbers, and Tuaregs from the North showed them no mercy. Timbuctoo had previously been sacked by the Tuaregs as early as 1433, and they had occupied it for 30 years. Between 1591 and 1593, the Tuaregs took advantage of the situation to plunder Timbuctoo once more. One result of the plundering was the destruction of the great University of Sankore and the exiling of its leading teachers and scholars.

The following information on this sad period in West African history is extracted from DuBois' *Timbuctoo the Mysterious*:

> However regrettable this exile may be from its consequences to the Sudan, it does not lack great historical interest. It is the touchstone which enables us to test the Eulogies concerning Sudanese science and learning contained in the native documents, for we now see the scholars of Sankore confronted by the highest developments of Arabian civilization. How will they stand the ordeal? The test proves entirely to their advantage.
>
> Among the exiles was a learned doctor, Ahmed Baba by name, born in 1556 at Arawan, of Sehnadjan. In spite of his youth, he enjoyed a considerable reputation in Timbuctoo at the time of the Moorish conquest, and his brethren gave him the title of "The Unique Pearl of his Time." His renown increased in Morocco and became universal, spreading from Marrakesh to Bougie, Tunis and even to Tripoli. The Arabs of the north called this African "very learned and very magnanimous," and his gaolers found him "a fount of erudition." At the request of Moorish scholars the doors of his prison were opened a year after his arrival (1596). All the believers were greatly pleased with his release, and he was conducted in triumph from his prison to the principal mosque of Marrakesh. A great many of the learned men urged him to open a course of instruction. His first thought was to refuse, but overcome by their persistence he accepted a post in the Mosque of the Kerifs and taught rhetoric, law and theology. An extraordinary number of pupils attended his lectures, and questions of the greatest importance were submitted to him by the magistracy, his decision always being treated as final. With a modesty worthy of his learning, he said concerning these decisions: "I carefully examined from every point of view the questions asked me, and having little confidence in my own judgment I entreated the assistance of God, and the Lord graciously enlightened me." The ancient histories of Morocco relate many other interesting details, and the author of the *Bedzl el Nousaha* reports the following utterance of Ahmed Baba: "Of all my friends I had

the fewest books, and yet when your soldiers despoiled me they took 1600 volumes." The Nozhel el Hadj gives the following instance of the courage and the pride of the African sheik: "After he was set at liberty Ahmed Baba presented himself at the palace of El Mansour, and the sultan gave audience to him from behind a curtain. "God has declared in the Koran," said the sheik, "that no human being can communicate with Him hidden behind a veil. It is your wish to speak to me, come forth from behind that curtain." When El Mansour raised the curtain and approached him Ahmed Baba continued, "What need had you to sack my house, steal my books, and put me into chains to bring me to Morocco? By means of those chains I fell from my camel and broke my leg." "We wish to establish unity in the Mussulman world," replied the sultan, "and since you were one of the most distinguished representatives of Islam in your country, we expected your submission to be followed by that of your fellow-citizens." "If that is so, why did you not seek to establish this unity amongst the Turks of Tiemcen and other places nearer to you?" "Because the Prophet says, Leave the Turks in peace so long as they do not interfere with thee." "That was true at one time," responded Ahmed Baba, "but since then Iba Abbas has said, Leave not the Turks in peace even though they should not interfere with thee." El Mansour, being unable to reply to this, put an end to the audience.

Although apparently free, Ahmed Baba was detained in Morocco for twelve years; the sultan had only released him on that condition, fearing the effect of his influence on his fellow-citizens. It was not until after the death of El Mansour that permission was obtained from his son for the learned man to return to the Sudan. Ahmed Baba then set out for the country to which he had so ardently desired to return, and of which he never spoke without tears, in his eyes. The following verses were written by him in his exile:

"O thou who goest to Gao, turn aside from thy path to breathe my name in Timbuctoo. Bear thither the greeting of an exile who sighs for the soil on which his friends and family reside. Console my near and dear ones for the deaths of the Lords, who have been entombed."

The principal marabuts of Marrakesh formed him a guard of honour at his departure, and, at the moment of farewell, one of them seized Ahmed Baba by the hand and saluted him with the following sura from the holy book: "Certainly he who has made the Koran for thee shall lead thee back to the point of departure"—a customary address to a traveller in wishing him a safe return. On hearing these words, the sheik abruptly withdrew his hand, exclaiming, "May God never bring me back to this meeting, nor make me return to this country"

He reached Timbuctoo in safety, and died in 1627. A man of great learning and a prolific writer, the names of twenty of his books have been handed down to us. Except for an astronomical treatise, written in verse, and some commentaries on the holy texts, his books are chiefly elucidations of the law and the sciences he professed, and prove that he was above everything a jurist.

Two of his books alone possess general interest; they have been preserved, happily… One is entitled the *Miraz*, and is a little book upon the different West African peoples, written by Ahmed Baba in exile, with a view to making the Sudanese populations known to the Moors. The other is *El Ibtihadj*, a large biographical dictionary of the Mussulman doctors of the Malekite sect; in it Ahmed Baba carried on the famous work of Ibn Ferhoun, and made it a continuation of the latter's *Dibadje*. The learned biographer added to it the lives of all the scholars whom Ibn Ferhoun had not mentioned. Ahmed Baba completed his book in 1596, and it had such a great success in both Northern and West Africa that the author was obliged to publish a popular edition containing the principal biographies only.

It is partly owing to the *Ibtihadj* that it has been possible to reconstruct the intellectual past of Timbuctoo, and for this reason the name of Ahmed Baba deserves to be held in pious memory by our savants, as it is by those of the Arabian countries of Northern Africa. To this day his name represents to the letter every effort made by the Sudan to attain the intellectual level of the Mussulman word; so much so, in fact, that any Sudanese work of unknown parentage is attributed to him.

The family of Ahmed Baba is not yet extinct…One of his great-great-grandchildren, Ahmadou Baba Boubakar, was kadi, and enjoyed a considerable reputation for learning; the other, Oumaro Baba, lived by making copies of books, which he executed in a very beautiful handwriting. The family religiously preserves a chair which had belonged to their glorious progenitor, to whom it had been presented by his liberator, the Sultan El Zidan. A curious family tradition is connected with this venerated piece of furniture. On the occasion of the marriage of a member of the family, the bridegroom is permitted to seat himself in this chair on the day of his nuptials. It is hoped, they told me, that some of the great qualities of the illustrious sheik will fall upon the husband and his descendants.

The sixteenth century, which we saw and so disastrously for the marabuts, formed the apogee of Timbuctoo's scientific and literary grandeur. The wholesale arrest and exportation of her scholars proved a fatal blow to the University of Sankore. The decline of learning, as of everything else, set in with the Moorish occupation, and yet the greatest work of all the literature of the Sudan was produced in the first days of its twilight, namely, that *Tarik and Sudan* (the History of the Sudan) which we have so often had occasion to mention.

Ahmed Baba lived in the part of inner West Africa that is now the Republic of Mali. The story of this great Black scholar has been handed down from one generation to another.[7]

There is no way to separate the name of Ahmed Baba from the University of Sankore at Timbuctoo during its last days before the Moroccan invasion. The destruction of this great institution, and the wreck and ruin of the Western Sudan, is one of the great tragedies in African history.[8]

Notes

1. "Africa in Early World History," by John Henrik Clarke, *Ebony*, August 1976. Also see: "Africa: The Passing of the Golden Age," by John Henrik Clarke, *The National Scene*, August-September 1975, Vol. 4, No. 4.
2. "The Origin and Growth of Afro-American Literature," by John Henrik Clarke, *Journal of Human Relations*, Vol. 16, No. 3, 1968.
3. *Timbuctoo the Mysterious*, by Felix DuBois, Longmans, Green and Co., New York, 1896, 352–353. Reprinted by Negro Universities Press, Greenwood Publishing Co., Westport, Conn., 1969.
4. "Literacy and Scholarship in Muslim West Africa in the Pre-Colonial Period," by John O. Hunwick, an "Occasional Paper" Publication, the Institute of African Studies, University of Nigeria, Nsukka, Nigeria, West Africa, 1974.
5. *Timbuctoo the Mysterious*, by DuBois, 275–281.
6. "Literacy and Scholarship in Muslim West Africa," 29–34.
7. "Ahmed Baba, A Scholar of Old Africa," by John Henrik Clarke, *Black Books Bulletin*, Chicago, Ill., Vol. 2, No. 1, 1974. Also see: "Time of Troubles," by John Henrik Clarke, in the *Horizon History of Africa*, ed. by Alvin M. Josephy, American Heritage Publishing Co., New York, 1971, 355–358.
8. A large portion of the information for this article was drawn from the new research on the life of Ahmed Baba by John O. Hunwick, who is presently Chairman of the History Department, University of Ghana. The following works by Professor Hunwick are recommended: "Ahmed Baba and the Moroccan Invasion of the Sudan, 1591," *Journal of the Historical Society of Nigeria*, Vol. 2, No. 3 (1962), 311–328; "Further Light on Ahmed Baba Al-Timbukti," Centre of Arabic Documentation, Institute of African Studies, University of Ibadan, Nigeria, West Africa; "Religion and State in the Songhay Empire, 1464–1591," in *Islam in Tropical Africa*, ed. by I. M. Lewis, Oxford University Press, New York, 1966, 296–314.

Other References Regarding Sankore and Ahmed Baba

Africa Before They Came, by Galbraith Welch, Morrow and Co., New York, 1965, 271–278.

Africa in History, by Basil Davidson, Macmillan and Co., New York, 1968, 173.

"Africa the Wonder and the Glory," by Anna Melissa Graves, originally printed in 1942 as "Foreword" to her book *Benvenuto Cellini Had No Prejudice against Bronze, Letters from West Africans,* Waverly Press, Baltimore, Md., 1966, 37–40.

Black Africa, from Pre-History to the Eve of the Colonial Era, by Russell Warren Howe, Walker and Co., New York, 1965, 63.

Discovering Our African Heritage by Basil Davidson, Ginn and Co., Boston, Mass., 1971, 101, 102.

(The) Golden Trade of the Moors, by E. W. Bovell, Second Edition, Oxford University Press (paperback), New York, 1970, 66, 89, 186–187.

History of West Africa, Volume One, edited by J. F. Ada Adjayi and Michael Crowder, Longman, London, 1971.

(An) Introduction to African Civilizations, with Main Currents in Ethiopian History, by Willis N. Huggins, Avon House, Publishers, New York, 1937. Reprinted 1969 by Negro University Press, a Division of Greenwood Publishing, New York, 111–112.

Introduction to African Civilizations, by John G. Jackson, University Books, Secaucus, N. J., 1970, 21, 217, 300–301.

North African Prelude, by Galbraith Welch, Morrow and Co., New York, 1949, 352–353.

Realm of the Evening Star, A History of Morocco and the Lands of the Moors, by Eleanor Hoffman, Chilton Books, Philadelphia and New York, 1965, 125–145.

Travels and Discoveries in North and in Central Africa, By Henry Barth, Harper and Brothers, New York, 1859, Vol. 3.

A Tropical Dependency, by Lady Lungard, Frank Cass and Co., Ltd., London, 1964, 156, 204.

2

Historical Dialectics of Black Nationalist Movements in America

James E. Turner

James E. Turner has been a member of the Cornell University faculty since 1969. He is an Associate Professor of Afro-American Studies and Director of the Africana Studies and Research Center. His field of teaching and research is sociology: social change and Black social movements; politics and national integration in Africa; and political economy of development in African states and Afro-America. He has published articles in several of the major Black professional journals.—The Western Journal of Black Studies, *September 1977, Vol. 1, No. 3*

Introduction

This paper presents a socio-political analysis of the dialectical pattern of African consciousness movements. It is a survey of two hundred years of African-American history, examining a corpus of political views in Black political thought with a continuous history. This study seeks to understand the sociological environment and its dynamics that are related to the contours of social forces as a context in which Black nationalist movements develop and persist.

Black nationalism has much in common with the nationalism of other oppressed people: it involves, for example, the effort to invoke a common national(istic) consciousness, ethnic/racial loyalty and cultural pride, and shaping of a sense of national identity to develop a collective movement for sovereign territory and political participation in self-government. However, the Black nationalist tradition in the United States has been nurtured in a peculiar environment of political oppression and racial proscription, and has developed unique qualities of its own. Black nationalists often have envisioned redemption of Africa as imperative for the liberation of African people in both America and Africa. Freedom, in its various dimensions, has been perceived as successful emigration to Africa and the establishment of an independent political base on the continent.

The Black nationalist doctrine in America is at once both a means of protest within the American political framework, and at the same time a force for the disruption of, or potential release from, that framework. Black nationalist movements within the context of growing monopoly capitalism of the American state (in a stage of imperialism, propagated on the exploitation of slavery and afterwards the labor of Black workers, and exploitation of land and resources of Africa, Asia, and the Americas) engendered paradoxes and dilemmas for their major leaders. Although radical in their premises, these movements often attracted men of conservative views, many of whom were religious ministers with a curious commitment to Christian chauvinism and ideas of the superiority of Western civilization; the settler-state of Liberia was not a happy or progressive intrusion for the indigenous people of the country.

I have divided the development of Africa-oriented social movements into five periods. There is of course some overlapping, but each period contains distinctive manifestations of the general theme. The first period (1790–1840) begins with Paul Cuffee after American independence. The American Colonization Society is formed during this period. The second period (1845–1861) is more concerned with Black emigration schemes, independent of white aid; although Edward Wilmot Blyden worked with the American Colonization Society for expedience in pursuit of his objective of settlement in Africa. However, the most outstanding feature of this period is the formation and articulation of a definite Black nationalist ideology. The third period (1870–1915) reflects the disappointment and disillusionment of American Blacks after Reconstruction. During this time, more independent Black schemes to emigrate were formed than ever before. The first Pan-African Conference was held during this period. The fourth period is dominated by the Garvey Movement (1916–1930), the largest mass return-to-Africa movement to date. Garvey stands out because of his ability to integrate the Black nationalist theme into the life of a large segment of the Black working class. The fifth period (1960–) includes the more recent resurgence of Black nationalism and Pan-Africanism since Garvey and Du Bois, respectively. The most outstanding figure of this period is Malcolm X. The central importance of Malcolm X's contribution to the profusion of Pan-African Black nationalism among Black students and intellectuals and at the grassroots level in the Black community has been recorded in the literature, but has not been systematically analyzed. Instead, the importance of political and cultural linkages has been stressed more than the actual physical return to Africa. However, this period as none before speaks of separation and Black nationalism in terms of revolution.

Throughout this paper, I have sought to understand the meaning and reasoning behind the back-to-Africa movement. In many instances I have looked at specific individuals. I have developed my analysis in terms of a "push-pull" syndrome. The "push" effect is the social, political, and economic climate of America; the "pull" effect is the attraction to Africa. Black people who have responded mainly in reaction to the "push" of America are those Harold Cruse calls the "rejected strain." These Black people, for the most part, felt that they could neither fulfill their aspirations nor realize their potentiality within a racist American society. However, they were chiefly reacting to American oppression. When a situation arose, such as the Civil War or World War II, when there was hope for equality and integration into white American society, this "rejected strain" abandoned their emigration schemes. On the other hand, there was another segment of Black nationalist thought that felt more greatly the "pull" of Africa rather than the "push" from America

The Genesis of the Return to Africa Movement: 1790–1840

The first dying that is to be done by the Black man in the future will be done to make himself free. If we have any charity to bestow, we may die for the white man. But as for me, I think I have stopped dying for him.—Marcus Garvey

It is widely acclaimed that Crispus Attucks, a Black man, was the first to die in the American Revolutionary War. In fact, more than 5,000 Black people fought to secure the independence of a nation that would continue to enslave the masses of its African population. It is therefore not surprising that the first return-to-Africa movement should begin at the end of the Revolutionary War.

The first major American-born Pan-Africanist was Paul Cuffee. Cuffee, who became interested in navigation at an early age, "became owner of one brig, afterwards of two; then he added a ship, two brigs, and several smaller vessels, besides considerable property in houses and land."[1] Cuffee was an industrious, ambitious, and very independent Black man who "built a wharf and a storehouse…a schoolhouse with his own funds on his own farm and offered its use to the public."[2] In 1808, Cuffee was turning his interest toward Africa as an economic market and a Pan-African base. "The travail of my soul is that Africa's inhabitants may be favored with reformation."[3] At this time Cuffee saw the most potential in Sierra Leone, whose trade and other affairs were managed by the African Institution in London. In 1811, he visited Sierra Leone and England to persuade the officers of the African Institution of the need for "good sober steady characters to hasten prosperity."[4] Cuffee volunteered to carry Black farmers, artisans, and mechanics from the United States while at the same time obtaining trading privileges at the colony. When the African Institution had agreed to his plan, Cuffee, also a Quaker, formed a Friendly Society at Sierra Leone under the leadership of John Kizell, a Sierra Leone merchant and former slave. By the time Cuffee visited Sierra Leone, the colony already had 2,000 Black inhabitants.[5]

On returning to the United States, Cuffee talked to free Blacks in Baltimore, Philadelphia, and New York, urging them to emigrate from America and return to Africa. Daniel Coker, a teacher in the African school in Baltimore, James Forten, a prosperous sailmaker in Philadelphia, and the Reverend Peter Williams, Jr., of New York organized miniature African institutions in each place.[6] Cuffee's plans were to take the emigrants to Africa annually, but the War of 1812 delayed his sailing. Undaunted by this war, Cuffee petitioned Congress for special permission to trade with the enemy's colony, but the House killed the bill 72 to 65, and Cuffee had to wait until the end of the war to carry out his scheme.[7] In late 1815 at his own expense, amounting to some $4,000, Cuffee sailed to Sierra Leone carrying 38 Black repatriates.[8]

Cuffee died in 1817, thus bringing to an end his scheme for annual emigration. However, Cuffee's success gave impetus to the creation of the American Colonization Society, an organization of prominent whites. The American Colonization Society, mostly slave-owners, wanted to send all free Blacks back to Africa—thus removing an important resistance element to the institution of slavery in America. As Cuffee had done earlier, they petitioned Congress for aid, but in their case, Congress was more receptive.

In 1819, a slave trade act was passed to suppress the trade and also to create an African agency with the power to return rescued Africans. The broad powers of this act allowed President Monroe to "establish an African agency, send carpenters to prepare shelters, protect and support the station, organize a government for the resettled Africans and send free Negroes from the U.S. if such a course was essential to the 'safe and comfortable removal' of the rescued Africans."[9] A three-ton freighter, the *Elizabeth,* served as the supply ship, equipped with government-bought "wagons, wheelbarrows, plows, iron work for a sawmill and a grist mill, two six-pound cannons, one-hundred muskets, twelve kegs of powder, a fish seine, and a four-oarred barge."[10] The government agent, who in reality was a representative of the American Colonization Society, hired free Black carpenters and laborers.

Of the eighty-eight who sailed on the *Elizabeth* in 1820, only one-third were men—the rest being their wives and children. The woman posed as seamstress, nurses, and laundry women, but all regarded themselves as emigrants—"as pioneers in a venture which would change the status of African peoples everywhere." Of this group was Daniel Coker who acted as both government and society agent in Africa. By December 1821, the American Colonization Society had seized a foothold in Africa. The small colony was called "Liberia" and its first permanent settlement was named "Monrovia" in honor of President Monroe, and federal government aid.[11] Outstanding among these early settlers were Daniel Coker, Elijah Johnson, Lott Cary, Colin Teague, John B. Russwurm, Hilary Teague, and Joseph Jenkin Roberts, who was elected first president of Liberia in 1848.

Black people in America have never been united in their thinking about Africa. Many Blacks rejected the idea of returning to Africa and they vociferously opposed the American Colonization Society, whose membership included white slaveholders. These Blacks did not feel the pull of Africa—they did not regard Africa as the "motherland." They felt entitled to equality in America and directed their energies toward bringing that about. In January 1817, under the chairmanship of James Forten, a meeting of Philadelphia Blacks at Bethel Church adopted the following resolutions without dissent:

> 1. Through the blood and sweat of our ancestors, we are entitled to participate in the blessings of America.

> 2. Any measure to banish or exile Blacks is cruel and violates the principles upon which America is founded.[12]

A mass meeting of New York City Blacks on January 25, 1831, under the leadership of Samuel Ennals resolved:

> Differences of color is not a difference of species…We are content to abide where we are. We do believe that things will always continue the same…This is our home, and this is our country.[13]

Also, many free Blacks felt united with their brothers in bondage; they could not leave America knowing that the masses of their people were enslaved. The 1817 meeting of the Philadelphia Blacks, mentioned earlier, resolved:

> That we will never separate ourselves from the slave population in this country; they are our brethren by the ties of consanguinity, of suffering, and of wrong; and we feel that there is more virtue in suffering privations with them, than fancied advantage of a season.[14]

James Forten, who was the chairman of this Philadelphia meeting, illustrates the ambivalence felt towards Africa. Just one year earlier, Forten had met with Paul Cuffee and had endorsed Black emigration. In 1816, Forten told the British African Institution: "We consider ourselves as merely instruments for the furtherance of your views," and he volunteered to serve as an emigration agent and sought "any exemptions…made in favor of this Institution [in Philadelphia] provided it should embark in any commercial enterprise desirable for the purpose of civilizing Africa."[15]

Whereas Forten could work with Paul Cuffee, he completely rejected working with the American Colonization Society. Cuffee himself had turned down a job with the American Colonization Society, and he warned other Blacks to be wary of the intentions of this white group. This fact also may have been a reason for Forten's change of attitude.

On the other hand, for many Blacks, returning to Africa was appealing on the basis of offering a practical alternative to a life of continual discrimination. Well-educated and ambitious Blacks could neither develop their potential worth nor fulfill their aspirations to achieve in a racist society. The racial/caste restrictions pushed some Black men and women from America's shores to Africa. During the early period of the emigration movements, John Russwurm stands out as a man disillusioned with American "democracy." Russwurm, a graduate of Bowdoin College and the editor of *Freedom's Journal,* the first Afro-American newspaper, had criticized emigration. He felt "we are all, to a man, opposed in every shape to the African Colonization Society."[16] But by early 1829, Russwurm had changed his views and was prepared to go Liberia. When he announced his conversion, a "violent persecution" set upon him and old friends disowned him. Russwurm's belief in the hopelessness of American society is well reflected in his farewell statement to all Black people in America. Russwurm declared that full citizenship in the United States was "utterly impossible in the nature of things" and all Blacks who "pant for this, must cast their eyes elsewhere."[17] A few months later, Russwurm landed in Monrovia and started the *Liberian Herald* to promulgate the message of "Pan-Africa." In Liberia, Russwurm also was superintendent of education and the secretary of the American Colonization Society branch there.

Daniel Coker, who had been a Baltimore teacher and minister, was one of the first settlers in Liberia. His strong race pride had led him to play an important role in breaking away from the Methodist Episcopal Church to become co-founder of the African Methodist Episcopal Church in 1816. Although elected as the first bishop of the AME church, Coker declined the honor in order to go to Africa. He felt the greater pull of Africa—to help lay the foundation of a strong Black nation.

Lott Cary, a former minister in Richmond, Virginia, felt a sense of duty to Christianize the Africans. Paul Cuffee also continually wrote about the importance of bringing Christianity to the African people. Even so, Cary felt that all American Blacks should return to Africa, and he stated that neither honors nor position could lure him back to America.

Another example of the push from America can be seen in the letter written by Abraham Camp, an Illinois free Black, to Elias B. Caldwell, secretary of the American Colonization Society. Dated July 13, 1818, this letter states that a "large collection of free Blacks living on the Wabash...are all willing to leave America whenever the way shall be opened...freedom is partial, no hope of change...rather leave then suffer hunger and nakedness for years."[18]

In December 1829, a group of Baltimore free Blacks met at the Sharp Street African Church and praised Liberian settlers as "the pioneers of African Restoration."[19] These Blacks had no illusions as to their place in society. They considered themselves a "distinct caste" who were "natives and not yet citizens; surrounded by the freest people and most republican institutions in the world, and yet enjoying none of the immunities of freedom."[20]

Even so, there remained other Blacks who felt thrust out of American society, but who felt no ties to Africa. This group expressed a strong desire to create a separate colony of their own, but they preferred to live "in the most remote corner of the land of our nativity" rather than "exiled to a foreign country." On January 24, 1817, a large meeting of Blacks in Richmond, Virginia, under the chairmanship of William Bowler, expressed these views:

Resolved…submit to Congress…an act of charity to grant us a small portion of their territory, either on the Missouri River, or any place that may seem to them most conducive to the public good and our future welfare, subject, however, to such rules and regulations as the government of the United States may think proper to adopt.[21]

There always has been a bipolarity in the historical development of Black political thought. There were/are those African Americans who are assimilationist/integrationists and whose political objectives seek to resolve the difficulties of Black oppression through participation and adjustment to the constraints of this nation-state while seeking social change in the status prescribed to Black people in America. There were/are other Black people who preferred/prefer to seek freedom from the imposition of the American nation altogether. The inspiration for nationalist or emigrationist movements springs from the exclusion of Africans from the original conventions of American nationality, and from a position of marginal citizenship and social status as a consequence of racial oppression. Such conditions produce among an oppressed people the quest for a political base (which under such circumstances means a territorial base) to establish a new nationality as a method of freedom and self-determination.

The Quest for Nationality, Africa or America: 1845–1861

Nationality is an ordinance of Nature. The heart of every true Negro yearns after a distinct and separate nationality.—Edward Wilmot Blyden

During the decade and a half between 1845 and 1861, life for Blacks in America became increasingly intolerable. The passage of the Fugitive Slave Law in 1850 indicated to Black people that the U.S. government not only sanctioned slavery, but also safeguarded it. The Kansas-Nebraska Act of 1854 allowed individual state legislatures in the West to accept or reject slavery in their respective states. This legislation also proved a victory for slaveholders. However, in 1857, the Dred Scott decision did much to exacerbate the feelings of Black men who had optimistically awaited "a new day" in America's race relations. This decision, passed by the highest court in the land, stated that a slave was property and therefore could not even file suit in the federal courts; it also stated that residence in a free state did not necessarily free a slave. Free Blacks were emphatically told that the U.S. government had no intention of freeing their brothers in bondage.

Life for free Blacks in Northern states was precarious, even dangerous, without legal protection or political redress. The free Blacks were being steadily pushed out of American society; the "Black Laws" in the northwest and social custom in the northeast regulated their behavior. Then one by one these states disfranchised Black voters, while at the same time they enacted universal white manhood suffrage. Black people were victims of American racism—victims of inhumane segregation, unemployment, and in many instances, victims of white terrorists and violence. During the 1830s and 1840s, riots occurred in Philadelphia, New York, Cincinnati, Pittsburgh, and other places.[22] Consequently, to those Africans who felt alienated from the ever-increasingly racist American society, there remained the lure of Africa—this time in the enticing form of Liberian political independence in 1847. Between 1850 and 1860 emigration from America reached an all-time high. In one decade Liberia had settled the unprecedented total of 5,029 emigrants—almost as many people as had been settled over the past three decades.[23]

The most outstanding Pan-African spokesman and intellectual of this period was Edward Wilmot Blyden. Although West Indian by birth, Blyden considered himself African in nationality. Thus, on December 21, 1850, Blyden left the West Indies and arrived in Monrovia on January 26, 1851.[24] Like Coker, Russwurm, and some of the other Pan-African nationalists, Blyden also worked with the American Colonization Society. As was the case with these earlier emigrants, Blyden did not concern himself with the motives of the society. Blyden was a nationalist in the strongest sense—his goal was African liberation for all African people. Unlike Forten, Blyden firmly believed that Blacks would never be equal to whites in America. The American Colonization Society was therefore a tool to the greater end of a united Black race. Blyden made many trips to the United States as an emigration agent for the American Colonization Society. For almost forty years Blyden served Africa in the form of missionary, teacher, and founder of educational institutions.[25] He was active in the politics of Liberia and finally became chief justice there. Working closely with Blyden in Liberia was also Alexander Crummell. Crummell, a graduate of Cambridge University, found the doors of opportunity closed to him in America because of his color. "Restless still and unsatisfied, he turned toward Africa, and for long years, amid the spawn of the slave smugglers, sought a new haven and a new earth."[26] Crummell, an educator and clergyman, lived in Liberia for twenty years (1853–1873) before resettling in the United States.

Although the majority of outstanding Black leaders prior to 1854 had not favored emigration, there was "no dearth of champions for this cause" between 1845–1861.[27] Sons of prominent anti-emigration leaders were now seeking fortunes in Liberia and the Caribbean. Through the concerted efforts of Black people in the years between 1845 and 1861, independent back-to-Africa schemes developed; many of these Black leaders were dissatisfied with Liberia because of its connection with the American Colonization Society. In part, the Black leaders of this period are distinguished by their strong belief in "nationalism," i.e., a nation created and controlled by Black people. Also, Black assemblies and national conventions, while not a new phenomenon, were now more inclined to discuss independent Black ventures.

In 1847, the National Negro Convention at Troy, New York, met to consider a commercial venture between Black people in Jamaica, the United States, and Africa. "This company was to be owned and operated by African descendents."[28] Closely tied to this commercial, triangular trade was a project to return New World Blacks to Africa. In September 1848, S. S. Ball, representing interested Illinois Blacks, returned from Liberia favorably impressed.[29] Delegations of Blacks from Ohio and Kentucky also returned from Africa to report on life in the continent.[30]

Henry Highland Garnet, a graduate of Oneida Institute and advocate of militant resistance and radical political action in America, had now reassessed and changed his views on emigration. By January 1848, Garnet recognized back-to-Africa schemes as "legitimate means to wealth and power insofar as it benefited Africa."[31] He urged that those doubtful of their opportunity for advancement in America should emigrate. In the early 1850s, Garnet was not decisive as to the particular place for Black emigration: California, Haiti, and Mexico were all prospects. By 1858, he favored the African Civilization Society, which was founded with Garnet as president. The goal of this society was to establish in West Africa "a grand center of Negro nationality from which shall flow the streams of commercial, intellectual, and political power which shall make colored people everywhere respected."[32] In July 1852, a state convention of Maryland Blacks also met to consider repatriation to Africa.[33]

There also were many Blacks who met to consider the formation of a nation within the western hemisphere. Cincinnati Blacks, convening in 1852, were chiefly concerned with emigration to Canada. The minority sentiment in this convention is reflected in the speech of John Mercer Langston. Langston spoke of the "natural repellency between the races, and paradoxically the loss of identity if Negroes were to remain in the United States."[34]

Blacks of Trenton, New Jersey, held a series of meetings to purchase land in Canada.[35] Black people, meeting in Toronto in 1851 and at Amhersburgh in 1853, declared militantly that American Blacks "owed no loyalty to the U.S.... that if emigration did not take place, revolution would."[36] In August 1854, a convention of Blacks led by Martin Delany, James M. Whitfield, and James T. Holly met in Cleveland, Ohio, to discuss the possibility of a Black polity in the Caribbean.[37] This group set up a National Emigration Board and scheduled another conference in Cleveland in 1856. In the meantime, these leaders were to begin negotiations with the various governments of South America, Central America, and Haiti. By 1858, at the third National Emigration Conference, Delany and his supporters had turned their eyes to Africa.[38] The geographical base for an all-Black nation seemed more realistic and practical in Africa. With this objective in mind, Delany and Robert Campbell, a young Jamaican chemist, traveled to West Africa to explore the Niger Valley. Delany and Campbell traveled as far as Abeokuta, and on December 27, 1859, they signed a treaty with chiefs and the

Oba, which assigned to them as "commissioners on behalf of the African race in America, the right and privilege of settling in common with the Egba people on any part of the territory belonging to Abeokuta, not otherwise occupied."[39] This treaty was hoped to be the beginning of a "progressive West African nation." In May 1861, the National Emigration Conference joined forces with Garnet's African Civilization Society in an attempt to raise adequate funds to promote colonization in the Niger Valley.

Unfortunately, these schemes were to end abruptly after the start of the Civil War. To an African nationalist such as Blyden, the Civil War had little meaning; he saw "no reason why it should delay plans for emigration to Africa." Characterizing the civil rights efforts of Blacks in America, Blyden said "half the time and energy that will be spent by them in struggles against caste…if devoted to the building up of a home and nationality of their own would produce results immeasurably more useful and satisfactory."[40] On the other hand, to American-born Blacks such as Garnet, Delany, and John Mercer Langston, the Civil War became a symbol of hope—hope for significant social change in general, and for the conditions and status of Black people in American society in particular. That is why John Mercer Langston felt it opportune to join in Republican party politics. It is also the reason Delany accepted an officer's rank in the Union Army. These Black leaders put aside their dream for a Black nation and united instead for the immediate goals of destroying slavery and the Confederacy.

Nonetheless, the most outstanding and significant contribution to Pan-Africanism during this period (1845–1861) is the crystallization and articulation of a definite Black nationalist ideology. This advancement is most clearly seen in the writings of Martin R. Delany and Edward Wilmot Blyden.

Delany spoke of the cultural uniqueness of American Blacks as a "nation within a nation—as the Poles in Russian, the Hungarians in Austria, the Welsh, Irish and Scotch in the British dominions."[41] However, he contended that, as an oppressed nation of minority position in American society, "we have been despoiled of our purity and corrupted in our native characteristics, so that we have inherited their vices and but few of their virtues, leaving us in character, really a broken people."[42] Obviously Delany realized the difficulty and the frustration of retaining a Black consciousness/Black group-identity within the larger and opposing white society. Even during exploration of the Niger Valley, Delany criticized the Christian missionaries' habit of changing the names of their African converts, "on the grounds that this would lead to a loss of identity."

Blyden also recognized the uniqueness of Black people. He believed strongly in the importance of preserving the unique characteristics of African people. Blyden went one step further than Delany; Blyden spent an important part of his life in Africa studying, writing, and teaching about Africanity. Blyden felt that one could find the soul of the race "through the careful study and appreciation of African customs and institutions."[43] Blyden studied the great past achievements of Africans in order to dispel the racist myths about Black people. Blyden felt that each Black man should strive to project himself in a distinctive African personality; this personality represented the softer aspects of human nature.[44] He believed that the special contribution of the African to civilization would be a spiritual one. To Blyden, the European personality was the antithesis to the worldview of the African. The European was considered harsh, individualistic, and combative.[45] In contradistinction there was a natural and wholesome quality in African culture that Blyden felt should be preserved. He spoke of the African social system as "socialistic, cooperative, and equitable—an ideal for which Europe was desperately striving as the answer to the ills created by individualism and unscrupulous competition."[46] Blyden concluded that Christianity, which focused on changing African values, had a disruptive and deleterious influence on Africans. He considered Islam more appropriate to the basic African lifestyle. Blyden was referred to as the "vindicator of the race."

All of these factors guided Blyden in developing his political ideology. Blyden believed that the "object of Liberia was the redemption of Africa and the disenthralment and the elevation of the African race."[47] Unlike many of the emigrant Blacks, Blyden regarded the indigenous African as the source of authenticity and essential kindred connection. He stated: "Ours is a fraternal connection";[48] it was no "mere commercial relation like that of the Europeans who reside upon the coast." Thus, in order to facilitate Pan-African unity, Liberia "should have regular intercourse with the Mohammedan states of the interior with the aim eventually of incorporating them into the Negro Republic."[49] Blyden learned Arabic and taught this language to his students in order for them to be emissaries to these Moslem states. Blyden was dedicated to the creation of a unified Africa for Black Africans. Perhaps it was/is this very race pride, this ability to define oneself clearly in relation to Africa that pulled men like Blyden to Africa rather than those like Delany, who felt compelled to leave America.

The Roots of Pan-Africanism: Africa for the Africans at Home and Abroad, 1870–1915

Every people should be the originators of their own design, the projectors of their own schemes, and creators of the events that lead to their destiny—the consummation of their desires.—Martin R. Delany

Over 186,000 Black soldiers had fought valiantly in the Civil War. The institution of slavery was abolished, and, for the first time, Blacks were participating in the politics of the South. However, in 1877, the Republican Party betrayed Black people. The Compromise of 1877, which ensured the election of Rutherford B. Hayes, resulted in the removal of federal troops from the South and thus brought an end to Reconstruction. Southern Bourbon Democrats took over the reins of power, to be succeeded by the spokesmen of the Agrarian Revolt. In either case the result was the same—white supremacy was reinstituted. It was not long before the Black man was again without the ballot. The Mississippi Plan, the South Carolina Eight-Box Plan and the Constitution of 1895, and the Louisiana "grandfather clause" were all "legal" methods to castrate Blacks politically. Between 1898 and 1908, North Carolina, Alabama, Virginia, Oklahoma, and Georgia had adopted similar policies.[50] New state constitutions required poll taxes, literacy tests, and property qualifications. The state primary elections also excluded the Black man. At the same time, there were extra-legal means to keep the Black man in line. The Ku Klux Klan was founded in 1867, and throughout the period violence and intimidation were rampant.

To make matters worse, the Supreme Court sanctioned the racist activities of the various states. In 1883, the Civil Rights Act of 1875 was declared unconstitutional by the Supreme Court.[51] In 1896, the Court went further and sanctioned segregation laws enforced by the police power of the states, on the basis of the separate-but-equal doctrine. In 1898, the Court upheld literacy and poll tax qualifications for voting. Whatever Blacks had gained in the Fourteenth and Fifteenth Amendments was certainly lost now with the Supreme Court's reinterpretation of the Constitution. The Black man's century-long struggle for constitutional rights had in reality been systematically subverted with the support of the U.S. government.

Furthermore, the economic condition of Blacks proved even more disheartening as the sustaining basis of oppression. There were no "forty acres and two mules" for the Black man at the end of the Civil War. In fact, the subordinate and dependent status of the Black farmer had been clearly defined under the new labor and tenancy arrangements. The crop-lien system, which kept the Black man in perpetual debt to unscrupulous landlords and merchants, proved to be another form of economic peonage. Even the few Blacks in skilled professions were losing out. For example, the onetime Black monopoly of the barbershop was gone. Disfranchised and without political influence, the Black man, by the end of the century, had no hope for political redress of his grievances.

Disillusioned and disappointed with American society, many Black people once again tuned their eyes to Africa. Between 1870 and 1915, dozens of short-lived companies and organizations were formed for Black repatriation. Among these were the Freedman's Emigration Aid Society and the Liberian Exodus Company of South Carolina. In the mid-1870s, Shreveport, Louisiana, reported 69,000 men and women who wished to emigrate to Africa. In 1887, the Kansas Emigration Association declared its goals as the establishment of a "United States of Africa for the elevation of Africa."[52] From 1897 to the 1920s, Albert Thorne, of Barbados, tried unsuccessfully to take American Blacks to Central Africa.[53] Even Booker T. Washington, while not supporting physical removal to Africa, encouraged commercial links with the continent. In 1912, Washington called a conference at Tuskegee Institute to discuss Black American business ventures in Africa. One such business already was the African Union Company, a carefully organized scheme for promoting trade between Black Americans and the Gold Coast.[54] In states where racism and violence were especially outrageous, many Black people burned with the "Liberia Fever." One such state was South Carolina, where Black emigration movements were reported in the counties of Abbeville, Laurens, Oconee, Pickens, Newberry, Lexington, Marlboro, Georgetown, Colleton, Barnwell, Aiken, Edgefield, Beaufort, and Charleston.[55]

Perhaps one of the most outstanding back-to-Africa efforts during this period was the Liberian Exodus Company of South Carolina. This company was led by men who had held political positions during Reconstruction, but who had been subsequently pushed out of office in 1877. The Liberian Exodus Company was founded initially by H. N. Bourney, a Black Republican judge until 1876, and the Reverend B. F. Porter, pastor of Morris Brown A.M.E. Church. After meeting with African professor J. C. Hazely, they became extremely interested in emigration. On July 26, 1877, these men called a mass meeting in Charleston to honor Liberia's 30th year of independence. The day climaxed with a parade of over 4,000 Blacks; it proved to be the start of the Liberian Exodus Joint Stock Steamship Company.[56] Martin Delany, recently appointed trial judge in Charleston, renewed his faith in African nationalism and joined the company. In a short time the Liberian Exodus Company acquired capital ($6,000) through the sale of stocks, and bought the ship *Azor*.[57] By April 21, 1878, the *Azor* sailed out of Charleston with 206 emigrants aboard, 175 being left ashore since the boat was overloaded.[58] To accommodate those Blacks left ashore, the company purchased a plantation on the Wando River for them to occupy until the *Azor* returned. More adequate planning on the part of the directors may have prevented certain hazards on the journey. During the trip to Africa there was a water shortage, 23 died, and unforeseen expenses were incurred at Sierra Leone. To make matters worse, the *Azor* was stolen, and by 1879 the Liberian Exodus Company had collapsed.

The Liberian Exodus Company, just as the other emigration schemes of the period, was not successful in its long-range goals for various reasons. Prospective emigrants in many instances encountered white hostility. Afraid of losing a cheap supply of labor, whites used various tactics to discourage Blacks from leaving the South en masse. Another problem facing Black independent schemes was that of raising adequate funds. In many instances, Blacks were charged unreasonable prices for ships and other equipment. Inexperience on the part of the directors of many of these companies resulted in a mismanagement of funds—even when intentions were sincere.

While some Blacks sought freedom in an African nationality, there were others who sought equality of opportunity in separate Black enclaves in America, which was not a new concept. As in earlier periods, some Blacks felt pushed from American society and yet felt no strong pull to Africa. The outstanding movements of this type are interesting because although they are separatist in nature, they are not nationalistic. For example, in 1885, S. H. Scott, an attorney in Fort Smith, Arkansas, tried to encourage support for an all-Black state in America.[59] Another example of the formation of a separate Black community was Mound Bayou, Mississippi, founded in 1887 by Isaiah Montgomery.[60] In 1889, Edwin P. McCabe undertook a plan to transform Oklahoma Territory into an all-Black state. McCabe envisioned a Black created and governed state, sending Black senators and representatives to the U.S. Congress.[61] Between 1891 and 1910, about twenty-five Black towns were created.[62]

The deterioration of the Oklahoma Black settlement epitomizes the insurmountable obstacles purposely created to thwart the efforts of Black people endeavoring to control their destiny within the framework of the U.S. government. Black migration to Oklahoma resulted in limited control over some areas of life during the pre-statehood era. Life was relatively good in the all-Black city of Boley. In Boley, Black people had the vote, and a certain amount of economic independence. When Oklahoma was admitted to the Union as a state, however, the power of Blacks in all-Black communities was looked upon as a threat by the ever-increasing white population. Whites tried to prevent the further immigration of Blacks to Oklahoma. Ballot-box stuffing and other fraudulent voting practices were used by whites. In order to remove the threat of Black voting blocs, Okfuskee County, in the Black-belt of Oklahoma, was gerrymandered in such a way as to remove any consolidation of influence for the Black vote.[63] Finally, Blacks were disfranchised—a testimony to the expulsion of Blacks from the American "dream."

It is no wonder, then, that the Black residents of Oklahoma rallied around Chief Sam's back-to-Africa movement in 1914. At the end of 1913, an Okemah paper reported that a Black man, Chief Sam, claiming to be an Ashanti chief, was in Okfusee County hard at work among the local Blacks.[64] Chief Sam had organized the Akim Trading Company, Ltd., which was dedicated to Black repatriation as well as commercial shipping. For the purchase of a $25 share in stock, the buyer and his family could return to Africa. Chief Sam had great appeal to Blacks, who felt let down for the final time by American society. Chief Sam clubs appeared in Oklahoma, Texas, and Arkansas. Approximately $100,000 was raised in order to buy the ship *Curityba,* later renamed the *Liberia,* and camps were set up to accommodate emigrants who had gathered from all parts of Oklahoma. By the end of July 1914, some 500 people had gathered in these camps. On August 20, 1919, the *Liberia* departed with provisions for only sixty people, "weeded out of the mass of persons desperately anxious to be included in this first voyage."[66] However, the voyage to Africa was not without hardship and disappointment. By 1915, *Liberia* had to encounter the harassment of the wartime (World War I) navies of both Britain and Germany. In Ghana, adequate provisions had not been completed, and the colonial government of the "Gold Coast" tried to prevent these Blacks from immigrating into the country. Nevertheless, the Chief Sam movement offered an escape from a life of degradation in America. Boley, Clearview, and the other Black communities in Oklahoma had been experiments in modest self-determination—experiments that were pushed to failure in America.

After serving as a major in the Civil War, an agent of the Freedman's Bureau, and a school principal in Charleston, Martin Delany once again found his only hope in African nationalism. But the most outstanding emigrationist throughout this period was Henry McNeil Turner, bishop of the AME Church. Serving in the Union Army as a chaplain and afterwards elected to the Georgia House of Representatives in 1868, Henry Turner was pushed out of politics in the early 1870s.[67] By 1874 he had become a staunch advocate of returning to Africa. Turner's alienation from American society and his bitterness over the souring of the American "dream" can be seen in his writing:

> I used to love what I thought was the grand old flag and sing with ecstasy about the stars and stripes, but to the Negro in this country today the American flag is a dirty contemptible rag…Hell is an improvement upon the United States when the Negro is involved.[68]

On another occasion Turner wrote:

No man hates this nation more than I do.[69]

Thus Turner, who had at one time put faith in American democracy, had come to realize that this democracy had never intended to include the Black man. Turner had endured "the great American let-down" for the last time. His message now contained a sense of urgency that told Black people never to delude themselves with America's promise of freedom. Like his predecessors, Turner believed that a people seeking freedom would not be respected if they did not create and control a government of their own. Turner made four visits to Africa: he went three times to Liberia and Sierra Leone in 1891, 1893, and 1895; in 1898, he traveled to South Africa to consolidate branches of the African Methodist Episcopal Church.[70] During the period 1870–1915, Turner proved to be the most eloquent and flamboyant spokesman for Africa as a base for Black nationality.

Taking all this data into consideration, it is important to note that during this third period of return-to-Africa movements, the ideology for emigration was now more than ever advocated by the masses of Black people; i.e., the ordinary people. This period is different from the ante-bellum era when many articulate, educated Blacks had been the most outstanding supporters. In fact, the more well-educated Blacks who showed interest in Africa now expressed their views in the Pan-African Congresses.

In 1884, the Berlin Conference had partitioned Africa between European countries. Black men such as W.E.B. Du Bois and Henry Sylvester Williams protested European colonialism through the medium of the Pan-African Congress. However, their activities were not directed towards an effort to return physically to Africa; at most, they expressed common concern and political solidarity with Africa—it was the "idea of one Africa to unite the thoughts and ideals of native peoples of the dark continent…Here various groups of Africans, quite separate in origin, became so united in experience and so exposed to the impact of new cultures that they began to think of Africa as one idea and one land."[71] Thus, the union of Africans and African Americans was to be a mutual exchange of culture and cooperation.

The first Pan-African Conference, organized by Henry Sylvester Williams, was held in London in 1900. The Conference sent a memorandum to Queen Victoria protesting the treatment of Africans in South Africa and Rhodesia and succeeded in eliciting from the Prime Minister of England, Joseph Chamberlin, a pledge that "Her Majesty's Government will not overlook the interests and welfare of the native races."[72] The Pan-African Congress of 1900 also protested the exploitation and inferior status of Black people everywhere and demanded "as soon as practicable the rights of responsible government to the Black Colonies of Africa and the West Indies" as well as full civil rights for Blacks living in predominantly white societies.[73] There were six Pan-African Conferences in all—1919, 1921, 1923, 1927, and 1945.* However, results from all of the conferences were weak because they sought, futilely, the good will of their colonial oppressors. (*Note: There is confusion and debate in the literature about the number of Pan-African Congresses. The 1900 meeting is considered the first Pan-African Conference, though the first formal Pan-African Congress is usually identified with the meeting in 1919 organized by Dr. W.E.B. Du Bois.)

In order to understand fully the reactions of Africans in America to racial subjugation in America, we must look at the changing social conditions and their consequences for the Black population. It must be noted that the peaks of interest in African emigration among Blacks between 1870 and 1915 occurred concomitantly with Black migration within the United States. Thus Blacks, now freed, could move about more easily than before. Besides the desire to return to the African motherland, or even to set up separate Black states, there was also another alternative open to Blacks. For the many who previously had been slaves, or who were daughters and sons of slaves seeking to better their condition in America, the urban centers of the South and especially of the North began to symbolize a new hope.

Seeking economic opportunity and hoping for improved race relations, the urban Black population grew phenomenally during this period. The Black population of the "New South" cities like Birmingham grew by 215 percent and Atlanta by 45 percent.[74] Also Northern cities grew rapidly in terms of their Black constituency. By the 1910 census, two cities, Washington and New York, had over 90,000 Blacks, while New Orleans, Baltimore, and Philadelphia over

80,000; of these five cities, only one was in the Deep South.[75] Blacks would move northward in greater numbers than ever during World War I, only to find a new variation of racism to contend with in the urban and Northern environment.

The Modern Mentor of Black Nationalism: Marcus Garvey, 1916–1930

✳   *The eventual Negro exodus must take place; young Negro leaders would arise who would catch the spirit of the future and place themselves in accord with it.*—Edward Wilmot Blyden

Racism and economic crisis drove thousands of Southern Blacks to Northern urban areas. Northern industry solicited skilled and unskilled Blacks in order to meet wartime demands; the great migration of the World War I era resulted in an exodus of over one-half million Blacks.[76] Full of hope, Black people crossed over the Mason-Dixon line as though crossing over the River Jordan into "the promised land" of freedom and social equality. But the North was far from the "promised land," and Blacks were soon to realize that racism was a national phenomenon rather than merely a Southern way of life. Besides the obvious and inevitable difficulties in adjusting to a strange, urban setting, these Southern migrant Blacks encountered police brutality, unemployment, Jim Crow laws, cold winters, and poor and limited housing.

Although over 400,000 Black soldiers had served to "make the world safe for democracy," it was obvious that Black lives were not safe in America. The year 1915 witnessed the rebirth of the Ku Klux Klan as a national organization. Within ten months after the war's end, the Klan had chapters in 27 states, including New England, New York, Indiana, Michigan, and Illinois.[77] Lynching also took an upward turn during the war years with 38 Blacks recorded lynched in 1917, and 57 in 1918.[78] By 1919, over twenty cities across the nation witnessed race riots. Riots ranged from Washington, D.C., to Elaine, Arkansas, and from Longview, Texas, to Chicago, Illinois, during that year's "Red Summer."[79] To make matters worse, as the troops were demobilized at the end of the war, Blacks were the first to lose their jobs. Into this climate of oppression and despair came Marcus Garvey with a new hope and a new dream for the future.

During his early years in Jamaica, Garvey had lost his job as master printer because he had led the striking Printers' Union. In search of work, Garvey traveled to Costa Rica, Panama, Ecuador, Nicaragua, Honduras, Colombia, and Venezuela. In 1912, Garvey went to London, where he was greatly influenced by African nationalists such as Duse Mohamed Ali. In all of these countries, Garvey observed one basic social fact: the color bar existed everywhere, with Black people being the object of racial discrimination and economic exploitation. Garvey became determined that: "Blacks would not continue to be kicked about by all other races and nations of the world." Garvey's dream was "of a new world of Black men, not peons, serfs, dogs, and slaves, but a nation of sturdy men making their impression upon civilization."[80] Garvey felt that one of the main problems for Black people was their disunity and their disorganization. With this thought in mind, he formed the Universal Negro Improvement Association (UNIA) with the goal of uniting "all the Negro peoples of the world into one great body to establish a country and government absolutely their own."[81] This country was to be Africa, a unified Africa with the motto: "One God! One Aim! One Destiny!" However, the immediate goal of the UNIA was the establishment of industrial schools and colleges in Jamaica.

Garvey first planned to come to the United States to raise funds for the UNIA and hoping to meet Booker T. Washington. Washington's philosophy of the separation of the races and especially his advocacy of independent Black businesses appealed to Garvey. Although Washington died shortly before Garvey was to make his trip, he was still determined to visit America in order to broaden his knowledge of the Black world.

Soon after his arrival in the United States, Garvey began listening to and organizing the most discontented people. His message of self-pride and African nationalism offered an alternative hope to those Blacks who felt completely alienated from American society. In fact, the real appeal of Garvey's message can be seen in the eagerness with which people joined the UNIA. The Harlem branch could boast of over 2,000 members only two months after its inception in 1917.[83] By 1919, the UNIA was composed of thirty branches in the United States as well as in the Caribbean, Latin America, and Africa.[84] Although the exact number of Garvey's following is unknown, it is generally estimated at over one million. On August 20, 1920, the Universal Negro Improvement Association held a week-long mass conference in Harlem. Over 25,000 Black people were present, including delegates from twenty-five countries in the West Indies, Central and South America, and Africa.[85] The highlight of the convention was a huge parade through the streets of a proud and applauding Harlem. In the keynote speech on the second day of the conference, Garvey best articulated the feeling of his followers: "We are descendents of a suffering people; we are determined to suffer no longer." Giving Blacks a sense of purpose and direction, he said:

> We shall organize the…Negroes of the world into a vast organization to plant the banner of freedom on the great continent of Africa. If Europe is for the Europeans then Africa is for the Black peoples of the world.[86]

Marcus Garvey stands out above all Pan-African leaders because of his ability to project the return-to-Africa theme to a level and degree of acceptance by vast numbers of Black people never achieved before or after him. Realizing the importance of "organization," Garvey developed an economic, social, and political program to weld Blacks into a conscious, united group for effective mass action.

Marcus Garvey's economic program was based on Booker T. Washington's philosophy of independent, Black-owned businesses. Garvey put this program into effect by the establishment of Black business ventures and of regular commercial links through a shipping line with various part of the Black world. In its first year of existence, the Black Star Line (which included three ships) raise $610,860 in capital through stocks sales and subscriptions.[87] To further boost the sale of Black Star stocks, Garvey early in 1921 made a five-month tour of the West Indies and Central America.

In addition to the Black Star Line, Garvey also established the Negro Factories Corporation. Capitalized at $1,000,000 under a charter from the State of Delaware, the Corporation offered 200,000 shares of common stock to the Negro race at par value of $5 per share.[88] The purpose of the company was to "build and operate factories in the big industrial centers of the United States, Central America and the West Indies, and Africa to manufacture every marketable commodity."[89] Among the businesses developed by the corporation were a chain of cooperative grocery stores, a restaurant, a steam laundry, a tailor and dressmaking shop, a millinery store, and a publishing house.

In examining Garvey's economic policy, it is important to note his attitude toward capitalism and communism. Although his was basically a capitalistic program, Garvey's motivation for profit was for the redemption of Africa. Liberia was considered as the main base of operation; Garvey set the goal of raising $200 million for construction work in that country—"where colleges, universities, industrial plants and railroad tracks will be erected; where men will be sent to make roads and where artisans and craftsmen will be sent to develop industries."[90] Garvey already had sent fifteen technical experts and much equipment to Liberia.

Although he believed "capitalism to be necessary to the progress of a nation," Garvey did not agree with the idea of unlimited individual acquisition. He felt that no individual should control more than $1 million, while no corporation should control over $5 million.[91] "Beyond this all control, use and investment of money should be the prerogative of the State with the concurrent authority of the people."[92]

Realizing the importance of self-help and self-reliance for the race, the UNIA encouraged Blacks to provide employment for each other and to seek out good business opportunities. It even offered its members a loan of initial capital from a cooperative fund established through the sale of stock. Like a mutual aid society, the UNIA also realized the importance of giving sick and death benefits. "This was the easiest means of reaching the common man, who wanted security in his distress; hand him this first, then tell him of the spiritual, racial benefits that would come in time."[93]

Garvey's philosophy of economics excluded pure Communism and trade unionism. In Garvey's mind, the question of race superseded all others. The theory of class struggle and alliance with white workers was pointless to Garvey in a racist country, where Blacks would always be in the minority. "The danger of Communism to the Negro in countries where he forms the minority of the population is seen in the selfish and vicious attempt of that party…to use the Negro's vote and physical numbers in helping to smash and overthrow by revolution, a system that is injurious to them as the white underdogs, the success of which would put their majority group or race still in power, not only as communists, but as white men."[94] Garvey's nationalism and concepts of racial solidarity never would have allowed him to put class struggle in the forefront.

The social program of the UNIA was geared toward the psychological need for Black self-pride and dignity. The *Negro World,* the UNIA newspaper, exalted Black standards of beauty and would not advertise such items as hair strighteners and bleaching creams. The Universal African Legion, the Black Cross Nurses, the African Motor Corps, the Juvenile, and the Black Flying Eagles (all equipped with officers and uniforms) provided a fulfilling social outlet for Black people. However, one of the most interesting social aspects of Garvey's program was the African Orthodox Church. Garvey believed that the worship of a white God reinforced white superiority. Religion, like every other aspect of Garveyism, was a tool to bring about African nationalism. Reverend George Alexander McGuire, a prominent former Episcopalian from Boston, headed the African Orthodox Church. He told his congregation to erase the white gods from their hearts and minds and "go back to the native church, to our true God."[95] Black artists were encouraged to paint pictures of a Black Madonna and Black Christ.

Garvey's political program, just like other aspects of his movement, was directed toward the redemption of Africa. Garvey referred to men such as Du Bois and Roi Otley, editor of the *Chicago Defender,* as integrationists who wanted social and political equality with whites in America. However, Garvey felt that this kind of thinking was foolish because "reason dictates that the masses of the white race will never stand by the ascendancy of an opposite minority group to the favored positions in a government, society and industry that exist by the will of the majority."[96] Garvey also knew that Black people would never redeem Africa through moral persuasion or petition. Unlike Du Bois and the Pan-African Conferences, Garvey felt that verbal protest was useless; "what influences is brought to bear against the powers opposed to Negro progress must contain the element of force in order to accomplish its purpose."[97] In other words, it was by force that Europeans and Euro-Americans continued to enslave and dominate the Black man throughout the world.

Like Blyden, Garvey clearly defined himself as African. Garvey identified the problems of Blacks in America with the problem of colonialism in Africa. Blacks living in America were not Americans—on the contrary, they were Africans colonized in America. These Blacks would not be free until Africa itself was redeemed from colonial oppression:

The U.N.I.A. studied very seriously this question of nationality among Negroes—American nationality, British nationality, French…it counts for naught when that nationality comes in conflict with the racial idealism of the group that rules. When our interests clash with those of the ruling faction, then we find we have absolutely no rights. Negroes have a hard time, wherever we go, wheresoever we find ourselves, getting those rights that belong to us, in common with others whom we claim as fellow citizens; getting that consideration that should be ours by right of the constitution, by right of law, but in the time of trouble they make us all partners in the cause, as happened in the last war, when we were partners, whether British, French or American Negroes. And we were told that we must forget everything in an effort to save the nation.[98]

[During peacetime, racial tension was greatest, Black frustration and alienation was highest, and return-to-Africa emigration plans increased in number. When the Civil War began, emigration plans were abandoned, but after the war, Black people were left with the unfulfilled promise of freedom.] During World War I, Du Bois had told Black soldiers to "close ranks" and fight shoulder to shoulder with their American compatriots. But Garvey continued to say:

We have allowed ourselves for the last 500 years to be a race of followers…in the direction that would make them more secure.

The U.N.I.A. is reversing the old time order of things. We refuse to be followers any more. We are leading ourselves. That means, if any saving is to be done, later on, whether it is saving this one nation or that one government, we are going to seek a method of saving Africa first.[99]

In other words, Garvey was telling Black people all over the world that they were Africans first. Garvey continuously spoke of there being 400 million Africans: he continuously emphasized the numerical strength of Black people. Garvey's strategy is what we now call "the concept of Third World politics." Today, Blacks emphasize that two-thirds of the world are people of color who must unite against the common racist and imperialist enemy. Garvey called out to this "Third World" when he said:

The dark Spaniards, Italians, and Asiatics are colored offsprings of a powerful Black African civilization and nationalism. When we speak of 400,000,000 Negroes we mean to include several of the millions of India who are direct offsprings of that ancient African stock that once invaded Asia.[100]

It is no wonder, then, that England and France banned the *Negro World* from their African colonies and likewise pressured Liberia into refusing Garveyite emigrants. It is also not surprising that African nationalist leaders such as Nkrumah, Azikiwie, and Kenyatta derived inspiration from the message presented by Garvey.

But eventually, mismanagement and incompetence on the part of the directors of the Black Star Line placed Garvey in a vulnerable position to be destroyed by his enemies. Although convicted of mail fraud, it was beyond doubt that Garvey's intentions had been sincere. Garvey was sentenced to jail in 1925 and deported to Jamaica two years later. It was not long thereafter that the organizational structure of his movement fell apart. Even so, Garvey had planted the seed of Black nationalism, to blossom in another period of history.

In the final analysis, Garvey must be considered a race-conscious nationalist whose pride in Africa was founded on his knowledge of Africa's great history and culture. The UNIA newspaper, the *Negro World,* was used to promulgate this knowledge to the masses. Garvey felt that Black people needed to honor their heroes and great achievements, instead of vicariously identifying with the achievements of another people who were also the enemy. To Garvey, "Africa was our guiding star—our star of destiny." However, his was not a mystical return to Africa, nor did Garvey think that a return to Africa would automatically free Blacks. By the 1920s, colonialism was at its peak. European counties had partitioned Africa and controlled it through a system of military force and oppressive colonial governments. It was at this time that many Blacks considered the physical return to Africa as merely the transfer to another oppressive situation. But yet Garvey strongly felt the pull of Africa; he was called to Africa in order to redeem it. To Garvey, African redemption entailed struggle, sacrifice, and bloodshed. "How in the name of God, with history before us, do we expect to redeem Africa without preparing ourselves—some of us to die."[101]

Consequently, Garvey's philosophy demanded a totally self-sacrificing dedication to Africa. The pushing and alienating features of American society were of far less importance. To Garvey, America was a white man's country and it was useless for the Black man even to expect to better his condition "under the dominance of another, inherently hostile race." Thus, Garvey felt that the Black man must never forget his African racial and cultural background. Turning his back on America, the Black man must direct his total attention and effort toward African redemption, so that "in the twentieth century we see a new civilization and a new culture shall spring up from among our people, and the Nile shall once more flow through the land of science, of art, and of literature, wherein will live Black men of the highest learning and the highest accomplishments."[102]

Malcolm X and Black Liberation in the Context of International Linkage: 1960–

In the soul-life of the land he is today, and naturally will long remain, unthought of, half forgotten; and yet when he does come to think and will and do for himself—and let no man dream that day will never come—then the part he plays will not be one of sudden learning, but words and thoughts he has been taught to lisp in his race—childhood.—W.E.B. Du Bois

The decade of the 1960s has symbolized most dramatically the ambivalence and the dilemma of Black people in American society. In this decade, Black people evolved from the advocacy of integration and non-violent protest to that of militant resistance to racial oppression by any other means necessary. As we stand in the middle of the 1970s, behind us is a legacy of sit-ins and the 1963 march on Washington on the one hand, and the concept "Black Power" and urban riots on the other. The reason for all of this upheaval is obvious: despite the many civil rights acts and Supreme Court decisions, the basic fabric of American society remains unaltered.

The Kerner Commission has stated: "Our Nation is moving toward two societies, one Black, one white—separate and unequal…Discrimination and segregation have long permeated much of American life."[103] The Kerner Commission, set up by the Federal Government in reaction to the riots, further states that "white racism is essentially responsible for the explosive [conditions]."[104] This report reveals the present plight of Blacks in America in terms of:

1. Pervasive discrimination and segregation in employment, education, and housing which has resulted in the continuing exclusion of great numbers of Negroes from the benefits of economic progress.

2. Black in-migration and white exodus, which have produced the massive and growing impoverished Negroes in our major cities, creating a growing crisis of deteriorating facilities and unmet human needs.

3. The Black ghettos where segregation and poverty converge on the young to destroy opportunity and enforce failure. Crime, drug addiction, dependency on welfare and bitterness and resentment against society in general and white society in particular are the results.[105]

During the last decade, there has been critical assessment of social progress over the past century for people of African descent in America. The fundamental conclusion drawn by many political activists and a broad section of the Black masses and young intellectuals was that the essential social position for Black people vis-à-vis all strata of white America had not changed. The system of social relations (of slave to master, of tenant to landlord, of consumer to producer, of the colonized to the colonizer, and of the exploited to the privileged) remained the basis for social conditions, leaving Blacks a dependent, marginal, and landless people powerless to affect even small decisions that control their lives. Malcolm X unrelentingly denounced the racism and hypocrisy of America, while at the same time revealing race pride to the people. Through the American news media, masses of Blacks could see the violence being perpetrated on nonviolent integrationists. While Malcolm preached self-defense, they saw civil rights workers being beaten by policemen and bitten by dogs. While Malcolm called for Black political self-determination, they saw Black Mississippians turned away from the Democratic

National Convention in Atlantic City in August 1964. Many grew weary of non-violence and moved toward the idea of "Black Power." Although Malcolm was assassinated, he managed to reintroduce the concept of Black Nationalism as a political ideology. This ideology became dominant among the most alienated and defiant sectors of the Black population, which Du Bois described as: "Tired of begging for justice and recognition from folk who have no intention of being just, and do not propose to recognize Negroes as men."[106]

First as a black Muslim minister in Harlem, Malcolm preached the doctrine of separation from "White America." Even after his break from Elijah Muhammad, Malcolm had continued to define this separation as "going back home to our own African homeland."[107] However, he saw this move as a long range program, while in the meantime, "22 million of our people who are still here in America need better food, clothing, housing, education, and jobs right now."[108] Malcolm stressed the need for the sovereignty of the Black community. This independence could only be achieved when Black people controlled their communities economically, politically, and socially.

Malcolm's trips to Africa in the spring and later in the summer of 1964 were to have a profound effect on his thinking. They would cause him to define even more clearly the ideology of Black nationalism in terms of Pan-Africanism. Malcolm was to feel the pull of Africa more strongly than ever before. He saw a new image of Africa emerging as African nations gained independence and strong leaders became the heads of states. Malcolm looked with pride at the great strides Egypt had made under Nasser. Under Nkrumah, Ghana had become the "Mecca of Pen-Africanism." The warm reception that Malcolm received in each of the fourteen countries he visited revealed to him that Africans were truly concerned with the plight of their brothers in the diaspora. Consequently, Malcolm never hesitated to portray the actual conditions under which the Afro-American lived, "suffering the most inhuman forms of physical and psychological tortures imaginable."[109] He adamantly spoke out against the propaganda and trickery used by the U.S. Central Intelligence Agency to keep all Africans divided. Malcolm saw the Organization of African Unity (OAU) as a sincere effort towards a unified Africa. It was the OAU that served as the inspiration and guideline for the formation of the Organization of Afro-American Unity (OAAU) on June 28, 1964.[110]

During the week of July 17–21, Malcolm served as the official representative of the OAAU at the Second Summer Conference of the OAU in Cairo. At the conference, he submitted an eight-page memorandum and also addressed the African nations, referring to them as the "shepherds" of African peoples everywhere. He urged that they bring the United States before the United Nations and charge her with violating the human rights of 22 million African-Americans. By so doing, Malcolm sought to internationalize the Black man's struggle for freedom, and thus elevate it from the subordinated position of an American domestic problem. With this idea in mind, Malcolm also formed chapters of the Organization of Afro-

American Unity in Ghana and in France to function as pressure groups against America's domestic colonialism and neo-colonialism abroad.[111]

As a result, the OAU passed a resolution expressing deep concern for discrimination in the United States. Malcolm's influence can be seen again in the UN debates over the Congo in 1964. Several African delegates, in denouncing American policy in the Congo, also referred to the racist treatment of Afro-Americans. Finally, John Lewis and Donald Harris of the Student Non-Violent Coordinating Committee attested to Malcolm's influence in Africa. In their tour of Africa during the same summer, they noted:

> Among the first questions we were continually asked was, "What's your organization's relationship with Malcolm's?" We ultimately found that this situation was not peculiar to Ghana; the pattern repeated itself in every country. After a day of this we found that we must, immediately on meeting people, state our own position in regard to where we stood on certain issues—Cuba, Vietnam, the Congo, Red China and the UN…In every country he was known and served as the main criteria for categorizing other Afro-Americans and their political views.[112]

It is important to note that Malcolm's work and his impact on Africa was based on his understanding of the nature of the Black liberation struggle. He obviously was not convinced by the limited progress of Black people in America. Like so many race pride nationalists before him, he realized that Black people would continually be pushed out of America as long as they looked to this country to ameliorate conditions. He was an astute observer of history, and noted that any changes or trends toward progress were never brought about by the internal good will of America, but rather by external pressures. The migration of Blacks to the Northern cities during World War I and later World War II, was not an attempt by the United States to open the job market and offer Black people economic opportunities; rather, it was a situation which arose simply out of a desperate wartime need for manpower. When the war was over and stability returned, many Black people were left jobless, most were underpaid, and all had to endure the continual abuses of racism in this country.

> It was the pressure that Uncle Sam was under. The only time that man has let the Black man go one step forward has been when outside pressure has been brought to bear upon him. It has never been for any other reason. World pressure, political pressure, military pressure: When he was under pressure he let you and me have…[I]t has never just been on our own initiative that you and I have made any steps forward.[113]

Consequently, organizations like the NAACP and the Urban League, which make appeals to the conscience of America, and which try to change the system from within, have proven a failure in their endeavor to bring true freedom to Black people. They have ultimately failed because they have looked to the leaders of the dominant white population and the powerful elites in American government, the very source of their oppression, in order to find a solution. According to Malcolm, Black people must therefore see their problem from a new perspective—a perspective which makes them the majority and not the minority. The solution to the problem must thus be found outside of America:

> When you find people outside America who look like you, getting power, my suggestion is that you turn to them and make them your allies. Let them know we all have the same problem, that racism is not an internal American problem, but an international one.[114]

Malcolm saw this power base as Africa, and he saw in the ideology of Pan-Africanism the linking force between African people all over the world. It was not the intention of the Organization of Afro-American Unity to transport the masses of Black people to Africa physically. The Basic Unity Program of the OAAU spoke of the need for Afro-Americans to establish communications with Africans through independent national and international newspapers, publishing ventures, personal contracts, etc.[115] Another goal was to reorient people to become informed that the Black struggle is worldwide, and that even though Blacks remain in America and fight for their human rights, they must "return to Africa philosophically and culturally and develop a working unity in the framework of Pan-Africanism."[116]

The education of youth was also a priority and would be accomplished through independent educational systems—experimental schools, liberation schools, and child care centers.[117] Finally, the OAAU saw the need for an industrialized Africa in a highly technical world. Therefore, it planned to set up a Technician Pool so that "the newly independent nations of Africa can turn to us who are their Afro-American brothers for the technicians they will need now and in the future."[118] However, the assassination of Malcolm put an end, for the most part, to the newly formed Organization of Afro-American Unity. Although Malcolm never lived to implement the actual organization of the masses, he helped to lay down the ideological framework which would serve as the basis for this organization in the future.

Malcolm realized that the continent of Africa was far from free of European colonialism and imperialism. Despite progress, there were millions of Africans still held in the throes of white colonial governments. Malcolm constantly spoke about the strategic importance of the Congo in the destruction of the oppressive racist regimes of southwest Africa, southern Rhodesia, and South Africa. In speaking of the Congo, he said:

> If it were to fall into the hands of a real dyed-in-the-wool African nationalist he could then make it possible for African soldiers to train in the Congo for the purpose of invading Angola…then it would mean Angola would fall, Southern Rhodesia would fall, South-west Africa would fall and South Africa would fall.[119]

One such "real dyed-in-the-wool African nationalist" had been Patrice Lumumba, who, Malcolm unequivocally stated, was murdered by Moise Tshombe and other paid agents of Western imperialism. Malcolm was not alone in his condemnation of the assassination of Lumumba; there were other Afro-Americans who realized how the United States had engineered the suppression of the people's struggle for freedom in the Congo. In February 1961, immediately following the death of Lumumba, they protested vehemently at the UN building. Reporting on the demonstration, John Henrik Clarke speaks of this Afro-American nationalism:

> The demonstrators in the United Nations gallery interpreted the murder of Lumumba as the international lynching of a Black man on the altar of colonialism and white supremacy. Suddenly to them, at least, Lumumba became Emmett Till and all of the other Black victims of lynch law and the mob. The plight of the Africans still fighting to throw off the yoke of colonialism and the plight of the Afro-Americans still waiting for a rich, strong, and boastful nation to redeem the promise of freedom and citizenship became one and the same.[120]

Considering this evidence, it was also clear that most of the African states had attained only nominal independence—still being politically controlled and economically exploited by Western powers. Kwame Nkrumah describes neo-colonial control in terms of economic investment in Africa with foreign capital being used for exploitation rather than development. "Aid to a neo-colonial state is merely a revolving credit, paid by the neo-colonial master, passing through to the neo-colonial state and returning to the neo-colonial master in the form of increased profits."[121] Voicing this same concern, Malcolm continued to politicize Black people in America so that they would neither condone nor participate in any way in the further exploitation of Africa.

> Now the raw materials are taken from Africa, shipped all the way to Europe, used to feed the machines of the Europeans, and make jobs for them, and then turned around and sold back to the Africans as finished products.[122]

Malcolm warned of the pitfalls of Western neocolonialism which entraps Africa with "economic aid, Peace Corpism, and Crossroadism." Thus, he consistently cautioned the African heads of state not to fall victim to American "dollarism." With the deposition of Nkrumah from power in Ghana only one year after Malcolm's death, the Western powers and their conservative African faction had struck another costly blow to Africa in defense of neo-colonialism.

Africa's wealth gives her the potential to produce substantial improvements in the social welfare of her people, and to be an area of strength and influence in international affairs. However, precisely because of its material wealth, a divided Africa is vulnerable to European imperialism. Realizing this fact, Malcolm referred to the wealth of minerals found in Africa—the gold, diamonds, bauxite, cobalt, etc.—as necessary for the survival and maintenance of Western industry. He voiced the urgency for Africans to industrialize the continent so that the benefits of Africa's labor and resources can serve her own people, rather than serve the interests of multi-national capitalism. To Malcolm, the capitalistic system is like a vulture, sucking the lifeblood of the weak and helpless:

> Colonialism or imperialism, as the slave system of the West is called, is not something that is just confined to England or France or the United States. The interests in this country are in cahoots with the interests in France and the interests in Britain. It's one huge complex…This international power structure is used to suppress the masses of dark skinned people all over the world and exploit them of their natural resources.[123]

Therefore, the need for a united African people becomes paramount in the face of European and American imperialism.

Even as early as the 1940s, the Council on African Affairs, led by such noted Afro-Americans as Paul Robeson, W.E.B. Du Bois, and William Aphaseus Hunton, was also addressing itself to this same issue. In the February 1952, Council newsletter, *Spotlight on Africa,* Hunton speaks of the Middle East and Africa as the target of the United States and her Atlantic Pact Allies. In discussing the council's job, he further explains:

> The Council's job—more urgent and important than ever before—is to help make the opposition of Americans to such policy organized, vocal and effective…We must launch mass campaigns around the specific immediate issues affecting the subject peoples of Africa, the Caribbean and other areas. We must publish and disseminate more information in order to shatter the iron curtain of silence and hypocritical lies intended to conceal the drive for super profits and war preparations in Africa and other enslaved lands.[124]

It was during the latter half of the twentieth century that the world witnessed the revolutionary fervor of oppressed, colored peoples against the forces of colonialism, imperialism, and racism. The success of the Chinese Revolution, Cuban Revolution, Algerian Revolution, Vietnamese Revolution, Mozambique Liberation, and countless other struggles still being waged in Africa, Latin America, and Asia represent important transformations in international affairs.

Malcolm X taught Black people to see themselves in the context of this worldwide struggle against racism and capitalism. On numerous occasions, he alluded to the Bandung Conference of 1955: there the nonwhite peoples of the world came together to discuss their common oppression and exploitation by the white powers. He asserted his hope that as these newly emerging peoples broke free from the chains of colonialism, they would establish governments in which the masses of the people would be served and not the elitist oligarchy—governments in which the means of production would be for the use of all and not for the profit of the privileged few. Malcolm explained the significance of the fact that in many of these countries, capitalism is being replaced by socialism.

Socialism is essential for planned social development that would distribute social welfare to all strata of society and reduce social contradictions. It provides a method for bringing the masses of the population into a politics of participation, and organizes society against developing capitalist relations and neo-colonialist, social-economy policy that distorts development through over-dependence on international markets before the development of internal markets.

Malcolm X saw America as the bulwark of racism and capitalism. Like Garvey before him, Malcolm realized that the African in America could not depend on an alliance with the white working class. As in no other country, the issue of racism itself is a formidable obstacle to the unity of the proletariat. Malcolm studied the historical relationship between working-class whites and Blacks in this country. He saw the failure of the Communist Party and other such groups in America. As far as Malcolm X was concerned, because of the socio-economic bases of racial conflict between Black and white workers, and collaboration between labor and American capitalists, no white man could grow up in America free from some vestige of racial chauvinism. He understood why and how the "working class whites have been just as much against not only working Negroes, but all Negroes period.[125] Therefore, Malcolm stresses as a priority before workers' solidarity that there must first and foremost be Black solidarity. His concept of Black solidarity was Pan-African, extending itself to the other 100 million Back people in Latin America and the Caribbean islands, and inseparable from the struggle of the 300 million Africans on the continent itself.

Finally, his theory of struggle was revolutionary—uncompromising and protracted. He insisted that African Americans should study revolutionary movements. While traveling throughout the African continent, Malcolm had the experience of meeting with African liberation fighters. One of the most rewarding experiences was his stay on the boat *Isis*, which was set aside for all "the liberation movements that exist on the African continent." With revolutionaries from Angola, Mozambique, Zimbabwe, and South Africa, Malcolm got "a feeling of the pulse of a true revolutionary…and an opportunity to listen to them tell of the real brutal atmosphere in which they live in these colonized areas."[126] In the course of talking to these freedom fighters, Malcolm also learned "what is going to be necessary to bring an end to the brutality and the suffering that we undergo every day."[127]

The significance of Malcolm's work represents a new relationship between African people in America and Africans on the continent. In all of the prior periods of the back-to-Africa movement, the African American had always been himself in the leading role to free Africa and all her people. From Cuffee to Garvey, the Africans in the West were considered the helmsmen in the redemption of Africa. But as Africa becomes an important area in international events, the

African Americans now look to progressive African leaders for ideological direction and inspiration in the struggle against racism and capitalist exploitation in an age of imperialism. Consequently, the pull of Africa has reemerged in the formations of Pan-Africanism throughout the Black diaspora.

Notes

1. H. N. Sherwood, "Paul Cuffee," *The Journal of Negro History,* Vol. 7, No. 2, April 1923, 159 [The Association for the Study of Negro Life and History, Washington, D.C.].
2. Ibid., 160.
3. Ibid.
4. P. J. Staudenraus, *The African Colonization Movement, 1816–1865* (New York: Columbia University Press, 1961), 9.
5. Ibid., 10.
6. Ibid.
7. Ibid.
8. Richard Moore, "Africa-Conscious Harlem," *Freedomways,* Vol. 3, No. 3, Summer 1963, 80.
9. Staudenraus, 56.
10. Ibid., 57.
11. Ibid., 65.
12. Herbert Aptheker, *A Documentary History of the Negro People in the United States,* Vol. 1, 71.
13. Ibid., 109.
14. Ibid., 71.
15. Ray Allen Billington (ed.), *The Journal of Charlotte Forte: A Free Negro in the Slave Era* (New York, 1953), 8.
16. Staudenraus, 191.
17. Ibid.
18. Aptheker, 72.
19. Staudenraus, 190.
20. Ibid.
21. Aptheker, 70.
22. August Meier and Elliott Rudwick, *From Plantation to Ghetto* (New York: Hill and Wang, 1968), 71.
23. Hollis Lynch, *Edward Wilmot Blyden* (London: Oxford Press, 1967), 25.
24. Ibid., 6.
25. Ibid., 20.
26. W.E.B. Du Bois, *The Souls of Black Folk* (New York: Fawcett, 1961), 163.
27. Howard Bell, "The Negro Emigration Movement, 1849–1854," *Phylox,* Vol. 20, No. 2, 1953, 133.
28. Ibid.
29. Ibid.
30. Ibid.
31. Ibid.
32. Lynch, 23–24.
33. Bell, 136.
34. Ibid., 138.
35. Ibid.
35. Ibid., 139.
36. Ibid.
37. Lynch, 23.
38. Ibid., 25.
39. Ibid., 35.
40. Ibid.
41. Martin D. Delany, *The Condition, Elevation, Emigration and Destiny of the Colored People of the United States, Politically Considered* (New York: Arno, 1968), Appendix.

42. Ibid.
43. Lynch, 18.
44. Ibid., 62.
45. Ibid., 61.
46. Ibid., 62.
47. Ibid., 66.
48. Ibid., 46.
49. Ibid.
50. Meier and Rudwick, 157.
51. Ibid., 165.
52. Marcus Garvey, *Philosophy and Opinions of Marcus Garvey,* 2 Vols., Amy Jacques-Garvey (ed.) (New York: Atheneum, 1968), preface by Hollis Lynch.
53. George Shepperson, "Notes on Negro American Influences on the Emergence of African Nationalism," *Journal of African History,* Vol. 1, No. 2, 1960, 300.
54. Ibid., 311.
55. George Tindall, *South Carolina Negroes, 1877–1900* (Columbia: University of South Carolina, 1952), 155.
56. Ibid.
57. Ibid., 160.
58. Ibid., 161.
59. David Llorens, "Separatism in Perspective," *Ebony,* September 1908, 88 [Chicago: Johnson Publication].
60. Meier and Rudwick, 201–202.
61. Ibid., 202.
62. Ibid.
63. Williams Bittle, *The Longest Way Home* (Detroit: Wayne State University, 1964), 19.
64. Ibid., 69.
65. Ibid., 99.
66. Ibid.
67. Lynch, 111–112.
68. Gilbert Osofsky, *Harlem: The Making of a Ghetto* (Evanston: Harper, 1968), 22.
69. Ibid.
70. Garvey, preface by Hollis Lynch.
71. W.E.B. Du Bois, *The World and Africa* (New York: Viking Press, 1947), 7.
72. Shepperson, 306.
73. Garvey, preface.
74. Meier, 190.
75. Ibid.
76. John Hope Franklin, *From Slavery to Freedom* (New York: Knopf, 1947), 465.
77. Ibid., 471.
78. Ibid., 467.
79. Meier, 194.
80. Edward Cronon, *Black Moses* (Madison: University of Wisconsin, 1968), 113.
81. Garvey, preface.
82. Lerone Bennett, *Confrontation Black and White* (Chicago: Johnson, 1965).
83. E. U. Essien-Udon, *Black Nationalism* (Chicago: University of Chicago Press, 1967), 39.
84. Garvey, preface.
85. Ibid.
86. Ibid.
87. Ibid.
88. Cronon, 60.
89. Ibid.
90. Garvey, preface.
91. Ibid., Vol. II, 72.
92. Ibid.
93. Cronon, 61.

94. Garvey, Vol. II, 69.
95. Cronon, 177–178.
96. Garvey, Vol. II, 39.
97. Ibid., Vol. I, 16.
98. Ibid., Vol. II, 96.
99. Ibid.
100. Ibid., Vol. II, 82.
101. Ibid., Vol. I.
102. Ibid., Vol. II, 19.
103. *Report of the National Advisory Commission on Civil Disorders* (New York: Bantam Books, 1968), 10.
104. Ibid., 203.
105. Ibid., 203–204.
106. W.E.B. Du Bois, *Dusk of Dawn* (New York: Schocken, 1968), 195.
107. George Breitman (ed.), *Malcolm X Speaks* (New York: Grove Press, 1965), 20.
108. Ibid.
109. Ibid., 74.
110. Ibid., 72.
111. E. U. Essien-Udom and Ruby M. Essien-Udom, "Malcolm X: On International Man," in *Malcolm X: The Man and His Times,* John H. Clarke (ed.) (New York: Macmillan, 1969), 260.
112. Breitman, *Malcolm X Speaks,* 85.
113. Clarke, 319.
114. Ibid.
115. George Breitman (ed.), *The Last Year of Malcolm X: The Evolution of a Revolutionary* (New York: Merit, 1967), 115.
116. Breitman, *Malcolm X Speaks,* 63.
117. Breitman *The Last Year of Malcolm X,* 117.
118. Ibid.
119. Breitman, *Malcolm X Speaks,* 124–125.
120. John H. Clarke, "The New Afro-American Nationalism," *Freedomways,* Vol. 1, No. 3, Fall 1961.
121. Kwame Nkrumah, *Neo-Colonialism: The Last Stage of Imperialism* (London: Thomas Nelson and Sons, 1965), xv.
122. Breitman, *Malcolm X Speaks,* 127.
123. Ibid., 160.
124. William Alphaeus Hunton, *Spotlight on Africa,* Vol. 11, No. 1, February 1, 1952.
125. Breitman, *The Last Year of Malcolm X,* 46.
126. Breitman, *Malcolm X Speaks,* 82.
127. Ibid.

3

Toward the Evolution of a Unitary Discipline: Maximizing the Interdisciplinary Concept in African/Afro-American Studies

Karla J. Spurlock

Karla J. Spurlock has served for the past two years as Assistant Professor and Director of Undergraduate Studies in the Department of African and Afro-American Studies at the State University of New York at Albany. She is presently Director of Minority Affairs and a lecturer in history at Haverford College in Pennsylvania. She is completing her doctoral dissertation in American Studies at Emory University, Atlanta, Georgia.—The Western Journal of Black Studies, September 1977, Vol. 1, No. 3

The programs in Afro-American Studies which emerged in the late 1960s, though differing in administrative structure, ideology, course content, and degree of community involvement, seemed to have shared at least one feature in common. Almost without exception, each was avowedly committed to exploring the experience of peoples of African descent through the kaleidoscopic lens of an *interdisciplinary* course of study.

Black Studies came in a number of different administrative packages. At one end of the spectrum were programs whose sole offerings consisted of two courses given in sequence, joined together by a title such as "Survey of the Black Experience." At the other end of the continuum were Black Studies programs organized in whole college units, either within a larger university framework like Oakes College (College 7) at the University of California, Santa Cruz, or as physically separate units such as at Medgar Evers Community College in Bedford Stuyvesant, Brooklyn. In between these two poles one could find the overwhelming majority of programs being established as: (a) special programs, which loosely coordinated a series of closely related courses offered in different conventional departments; (b) independent institutes with power of faculty and curriculum selection, though generally funded experimentally through private sources or through temporary institutional channels; or (c) regular departments with conventional powers over faculty, course selection, and curriculum design, and with funding through conventional university channels.[1]

While it is true that, for the majority, the last option seemed by far the most realistic and viable alternative for fulfilling and sustaining the goals of the newly devised curricula, either the "department model" or the "program model" seemed infinitely preferable to a structure allowing traditional disciplines to establish Black-related courses (to fit) within the conservative bastions of conventional academic departments.

Mike Thelwell, chairman of Black Studies at the University of Massachusetts during the critical gestation period of the late 1960s, wrote: "(The approach of) leaving the responsibility to individual departments to proceed at their own pace and in their own unique styles will merely institutionalize and perpetuate the fragmented, incoherent approach to the subject which has been the only approach in the past." He continues that the concept of Black Studies requires "an autonomous interdisciplinary entity, capable of coordinating its curriculum in traditional disciplines to ensure an historical, substantive progression and organic coherence in its offerings."[2]

The benefits of the interdisciplinary approach—whether through coordination of traditional departmental offerings or through courses devised in independent Black Studies units—even at the very inception of the Black Studies movement, held an unstated appeal. What *were* and *are* the benefits of interdisciplinarity?

First, the world forces with which Black people must grapple in order to survive operate on us as an interconnected whole—not as a fragmented series of arbitrary sets of experience that neatly correspond to the established academic disciplines. Traditional, compartmentalized, academic fields are too often inadequate to deal with the holistic nature of human experience. When confronted with the challenge, such departments are immediately exposed as incapable of providing insight, either descriptively or analytically.

The Yale Afro-American Studies curriculum, devised in the late 1960s, speaks as eloquently as any other to the particular strengths of Black interdisciplinary studies:

> Afro-American Studies introduces students to a great variety of approaches to human problems. Students whose interests are broader than the usual major within a specific department can learn about some of the key issues in the humanities and the social sciences and discover ways to adapt their specific knowledge to some of the most vital needs of society in Afro-American Studies...Afro-American Studies prepares students for graduate study in a variety of careers by developing special competence through systematic training in methods, materials, tools, and interpretations of several disciplines as they relate to the Black experience in the United States, Latin America, Africa, and Europe. Afro-American Studies trains students to view contemporary

issues from the perspective of several disciplines in relationship to many cultures.[3]

One of the most vital benefits of the interdisciplinary mode is the stimulus it offers to creative thinking. The student/scholar, exposed to a variety of research tools and logical systems of ordering relevant data, feels no compulsion to follow accepted, calcified versions of reality defined by any single traditional approach. With options for ordering data, the student or scholar can more readily offer an objective critique on one or another approach to research questions. Ideally, Black Studies offers an arena for disciplinary *encounter*.[4] The interdisciplinary mode places the student/scholar in a virtual intellectual crossfire. As ideas arising out of different and potentially conflicting disciplinary methods bang against one another, the opportunity for creative synthesis—of new understandings and shared levels of meaning within African and Afro-American Studies—emerges.

Clearly, then, the ideal of Afro-American Studies as an interdisciplinary experience is pregnant with potentialities for growth in the individual and in the academy. Unfortunately, however, one of the preeminent problems facing Black Studies programs today is their failure to maximize fully the possibilities of a truly interdisciplinary structure. Many programs have never realized the meaning of *interdisciplinarity*, strictly defined. According to very useful definitions coming out of an international seminar on interdisciplinarity in universities, sponsored by the Center for Educational Research and Innovation of the Organization for Economic Cooperation, "discipline" refers to a specific body of teachable knowledge with its own background of education, training, procedures, methods, and content areas. The Center then defines "multidisciplinary" as an adjective to describe the juxtaposition of various disciplines assumed to be more or less related. We might usefully contrast this definition of "multidisciplinary" with that of "interdisciplinary," which is described as an adjective suggesting *interaction* among two or more disciplines. Interaction may range from simple communication of ideas to the mutual integration of organizing concepts, methodology, procedures, terminology, data, and organization of research and education in a fairly large field. Interdisciplinary groups, then, consist of persons trained in different fields of knowledge with different concepts, methods, data, and terms, organized into a common effort on a common problem with continuous intercommunication among the participants from the different disciplines.[5]

Figure 1.

Multidisciplinary → Interdisciplinary → Unidisciplinary

The schema presented in Figure 1 clearly suggests the logical potential for Black Studies to become an effective interdisciplinary unit and, ultimately, a unified disciplinary unit. But the necessity of fostering interaction among constituent disciplines is absolutely a prerequisite of progressive movement toward consolidation. It becomes obvious that the benefits of interdisciplinary exchange do not necessarily follow the declaration that several courses with "Black" in their titles are linked together in an academically discrete unit. Even the creation of an entire curriculum of Black-related courses drawn from traditional disciplinary programs does not imply a working interdisciplinary process unless meaningful interaction among these courses is encouraged.

In the absence of countervailing efforts, the tradition in Afro-American Studies of separate treatments by separate academic enclaves serves to impair communication and the development of independent, unifying core concepts—concepts which might act as a centrifugal force in the interdisciplinary orbit. Another problem arises from the fact that, of necessity, most faculty are recruited from traditional fields. Though often specialists in their areas, such faculty are often ill-equipped or unwilling to grapple with the activities of colleagues of different training. Sometimes it is difficult to generate enthusiasm among faculty for any program different from the model established by their own prior training. Specialized graduate work frequently locks faculty into fixed molds, despite their subsequent employment in avowed interdisciplinary programs.

The common problem of stimulating exchange among specialists within a common traditional discipline is multiplied tenfold in the effort to bring historians, sociologists, economists, political scientists, anthropologists, and humanists into a common network of discussion. But it is not out of such discussion *alone* that an organizing framework can be realized, within which different approaches may be systematically evaluated and taught to achieve a holistic vision, fused from multiple disciplinary perspectives. This coalescence of approach is the *sine qua non* of survival and autonomy for Afro-American Studies in the coming decade.

How might Black Studies move toward a practical realization of its interdisciplinary and, ultimately, its unidisciplinary potential? First, there are a number of curricula remedies to the problem. One obvious solution is to maximize the interdisciplinary mix in the structuring and teaching of individual courses. In the Department of African and Afro-American Studies at the State University of New York at Albany, for example, such courses as "Dynamics of Racism," "Problems in the Black Community," "Black Women in America," and "Seminar on Community Development" offer a natural opportunity for the interfertilization of traditional disciplinary concepts and methods. But even courses that indicate a tie to a specific traditional discipline—for instance, "The History of the Black Man in Latin America and the Caribbean"—can be infused with the interdisciplinary spirit.

James Banks, in his important article, "Teaching Black Studies for Social Change," details how courses such as history can be made truly interdisciplinary. Though Western history has largely been the history of formal political events, history has always claimed to concern itself with the totality of man's past. History so conceived neatly fits into an interdisciplinary framework and, as such, is potentially capable of reflecting the unique conceptual frameworks carved out by separate disciplines to view human behavior. Funneling analytical concepts from each discipline into a historical vessel, Banks devises a schema for realizing an interdisciplinary perspective. In his example, history would ask more of the past than which great generals led which battles. Rather, stimulated by a concern for values and norms (borrowed from sociology), power (borrowed from political science), culture (from anthropology), personality (from psychology), regional and spatial relations (from geography), and goods, services, and production (from economics),[6] new and more meaningful questions would arise to demand an interdisciplinary reply.

The second logical solution to the problem of maximizing interdisciplinary is through a planned, coordinated curriculum with structural inducements to interdisciplinary exchange. The State University of New York at Albany has moved toward an answer by revising the curriculum to address more adequately the challenge of interdisciplinary coordination.

Twelve major disciplines were isolated that were considered minimally essential to the task of equipping students with the knowledge and skills necessary to understand and grapple with the interplay of the myriad forces (economic, socio-cultural, political, psychological, and historical) that affect the lives of peoples of African descent. Areas of study and the courses devised under each include—Anthropology: "Peoples of Africa South of the Sahara," and "African Peoples in the Americas"; Economics: "Economic Structure of the Black Community," and "Economics of Developing Black Nations"; Education: "Education and the Black Child," "Education and the Black Community," and "Teaching through the Black Experience: Methods and Materials"; Environmental Studies: "Environment and the Peoples of the Black Diaspora"; History: "Introduction to African and African-American History, A and B," "History of Black Protest in the Americas," "Black Women in America," "Black Urban History," "History of Africa South of the Sahara, A and B," "History of the Black Man in Latin America and the Caribbean," and "Selected Topics in African and African-American History"; Language: "Elementary Swahili," and "Intermediate Swahili"; Literature: "Literature of the Black Pluriverse," "The Black Novel," "The Black Essay," "The Black Short Story," "Black Theatre," "Black Writer's Workshop," and "Studies in Black Literature"; Music and Art: "The Black Musical Tradition, A and B," "African and African-American Dance," and "African and African-American Art, A and B"; Philosophy: "Third World Philosophies," and "Seminar in Third World Thought"; Political Science: "Contemporary World African Politics,"

"Nationalism and Pan Africanism in the Black Diaspora, A and B," "Blacks and the American Political System," "Black Political Thought in the Americas," and "Contemporary African-American Politics"; Psychology: "Dynamics of Racism," and "Psychology of the African and African-American Experience"; Sociology: "Social Dynamics of the Black Community," "Law and the Black Community," "African and African-American Family," "Seminar on Community Development," "The Urban Dimension," "Mass Media and the Black Community," "The African-American Church," and "African Religion"; Independent Work: "Independent Study in African and African-American Studies."

To circumvent the multidisciplinary fate predicted earlier, tremendous emphasis is placed on two courses committed to forging a truly interdisciplinary mastery of the curriculum:

1. "Colloquium in African and African-American Studies," a two-and-one-half hour per week interdisciplinary course. The requirement of participation by the entire faculty is important. The course, an exploration of key issues, is team-taught, and it serves as an interdisciplinary introduction to key issues in African and African-American Studies; and

2. "Research Tools for African and African-American Studies," an introductory exposure to the various modes of gathering and ordering data that aims toward the integration, or at least the coordination, of techniques.

These seminars are intended to have a highly integrative impact. It is hoped that students and professors brought together in this way may achieve new insights, perceive previously unnoted relationships, and arrive at different and more coherent organizations of the common store of knowledge. The integrative seminar is designed to encourage both independence and interdependence and to promote breadth, depth, and synthesis.

But there are other, extracurricular, strategies for maximizing interdisciplinarity in Black Studies. For instance, departments might encourage team teaching on a wide scale. Or they might establish a regular speaker's forum that would consider topics of general concern. The department or program should support interdisciplinary journals and conferences both locally and nationally. This support, of course, would help consolidate a separate identity and concretize a common language of scholarly interchange. Very important also is the need to define and name ourselves as a separate entity. Perhaps we might call ourselves "Africologists" or "Pan-Africologists"—the label itself being, of course, less important than the assertion of ourselves as conceptually separate from our constituent disciplinary identities. But perhaps most important of all, we should push Black Studies down the academic scale to the elementary and secondary schools and up the scale to the Ph.D., our own terminal degree. This expansion would serve to legitimize the field as a unitary discipline, providing both separate, unitary professional training and a guaranteed market for the skills of our trained scholars and educators.

There are, in sum, innumerable strategies, both curricular and noncurricular, which we may employ to maximize interaction and interdisciplinary cooperation within Black Studies. As we move toward interdisciplinarity, we assuredly move along a continuum toward the end-point of a unified perspective, toward trans- or unidisciplinarity. Enhanced interdisciplinary functioning eventually must lead to a close mesh and a blending of disciplines into a new discipline. Disciplines are, after all, nothing more than categories for ordering data. There is nothing fixed or pre-ordained about them. Traditional disciplines such as political science, economics, and sociology broke away and established themselves as distinct categories for ordering relevant information in just that way at the beginning of the twentieth century. The criteria for the emergence of new disciplines vary with time and circumstances. At one time, "method" may determine the distinction; at another time, the field of observable phenomenon; and, at another, a unique theoretical framework.

At this juncture in its history, Black Studies may very well rest its future on an aggressive claim to autonomous status, grounded in the capacity to articulate a coherent theme or set of principles unifying the tributary disciplines. There are, of course, dangers in moving toward a unitary discipline. While attaining the permanence, security, and autonomy enjoyed by established disciplines, we must take care to incorporate the positive aspects of the interdisciplinary mode—the innovation, the eclecticism, the creative spark. Nevertheless, the gains of becoming unidisciplinary far outweigh the possible risks of slipping back into more multidisciplinary coexistence.

Notes

1. Nick Aaron Ford, *Black Studies: Threat or Challenge* (Port Washington, N.Y.: National University Publications, Kennikat Press, 1973), Ch. 6. See also John Blassingame, "The Black Presence in American Higher Education," in *What Black Educators are Saying,* Nathan Wright, Jr. (ed.) (New York: Hawthorn Books, 1970), 146–149.
2. Mike Thelwell, "Black Studies: A Political Perspective," *Massachusetts Review,* Vol. 10, Autumn 1969, 710.
3. Ford, *Black Studies,* 129.
4. See Karla J. Spurlock, "The Value of a Major in African/Afro-American Studies," *Habari Newsletter of the Department of African/Afro-American Studies, State University of New York/Albany,* Vol. 3, No. 2, January 27, 1977.
5. *Center for Educational Research and Innovation, Interdisciplinarity: Problems of Teaching and Research in Universities* (Paris: OECD Publications, 1972), 25.
6. James Banks, "Teaching Black Studies for Social Change," in *Black Scholars in Higher Education in the 1970s,* Roosevelt Johnson (ed.) (Columbus, Ohio: ECCA Publications, 1974).

4

An Ideology for Liberation: A Response to Amiri Baraka and other "Marxists"

BETTY J. COLLIER AND LOUIS N. WILLIAMS

Betty J. Collier is presently an Assistant Professor at the University of the District of Columbia, Mount Vernon Campus, in the Department of Economics. She received the Ph.D. in Economics from American University. Dr. Collier has done research and published a number of articles in the areas of economics, racism, and oppression.

Louis N. Williams has published articles in the areas of Black psychology and physiological psychology. He is a Professor at the University of the District of Columbia, Mount Vernon Campus. He received the Ph.D. from the University of Washington.—The Western Journal of Black Studies, *December 1977, Vol. 1, No. 4*

Introduction*

We are an oppressed people. Such a statement has become a cliché within the level of political consciousness that characterizes the present age. As with most clichés, however, the implications of such a statement are not always understood. To say that we, as well as two-thirds of the world, are oppressed is to say that the contemporary American social and political structure embodies power of extreme magnitude. If this is so, it would follow that such power actually extends itself into the realm of liberation movements.

Direct control, i.e., criminal charges, wiretapping, spying, etc., constitutes the most apparent use of power in order to control attempts toward liberation. By its very nature, direct control requires that a large reservoir of manpower be employed in intelligence operations and similar external techniques of control. Accordingly, no system of suppression can be maintained by direct force alone. Rather, indirect patterns of control are built into the very fabric of the day-to-day

---

* The writers are responding to a position paper by Amiri Baraka that appeared in the January-February 1975 issue of *The Black Scholar*.

life experiences of the oppressors and the oppressed. The oppressors, in order to continue in their dominant role, embrace oppression-maintaining patterns of behavior. The oppressed, unknowingly and unwittingly, are socialized into oppression-maintaining patterns of action. *These oppression-maintaining patterns of behavior are so pervasive that they extend themselves into the very ideologies that the oppressed embrace in their active search for analyses leading to social change!*

The purpose of this paper is: (1) to illustrate that Amiri Baraka's (and other Marxists') current ideology and solutions lead to behavior supportive of the system of oppression from which it seeks liberation, and (2) to suggest alternative paradigms and solutions. Specific reference will be made to Baraka's position paper that appeared in the January-February 1975 *Black Scholar.*

A Summary of Baraka's Position Paper

All ideologies consist of three basic parts—a definition of a problem or problems, an analysis of the causes of a problem, and a set of solutions that follows from the analysis. Amiri Baraka is concerned with the problem of Black Liberation, which he carefully defines. Little argument can be made with Baraka's definition of the problem. Rather, it is in Mr. Baraka's analysis of causes that assumptions are made that reinforce anti-liberation behavior patterns amongst African people.

According to Mr. Baraka, "the main obstruction to our complete liberation is the system of monopoly capitalism and imperialism"[1] After defining capitalism as "the system of private ownership of the means of producing wealth in a society,"[2] he continues with a description of the distribution of income and wealth in the United States. He implies that income and wealth are unequally distributed because "surplus value goes to the capitalist"[3] who "uses that wealth to rip off even more of the world's resources and build capitalism stronger to keep this social system that allows them to live better than any old-time kings."[4] Such statements evoke the question, "How are capitalists able to carry out the described charges?" The answer to such a query is also provided by Baraka: "the initial wealth is produced by the labor of workers, yet it is stolen by capitalists, enforcing this theft with armies called police who are paid out of your jive salary with another rip-off called taxes!" It is at this point that Baraka offers a first solution to the problem of Black Liberation: "if we are going to create a movement to destroy capitalism we cannot do it alone, but only by uniting all those people oppressed by it."[5] Such a statement indicates that the new ideology of the Congress of Afrikan People views the problem of Black enslavement as a mere subset of the universe of capitalist oppression.

Amiri Baraka continues his outline of the Congress of Afrikan People's new position by providing information about the history of capitalism. In doing so, he recites verbatim the Marxist interpretation of history, offering no fresh insights and concluding without challenging that "all the ideas, inventions, philosophies, customs, religions, laws, come from the material base of a society, that is, its economic foundations."[6] In light of this historical analysis, Mr. Baraka voices the opinion that the solution to our enslavement is "to force a revolution in this society, and contribute to revolutions all over the world, that will eliminate the capitalist systems and replace it with a socialist system."[7]

A question that must be answered by an ideology such as Baraka's is: "What forces caused the shift from European feudalism to capitalism?" Baraka answers the question by saying that "Europe itself had oppressive internal conditions that drove its people to seek new systems, to press out of its weather and disease-locked perimeters to search for wealth and resources and ideas."[8] Baraka suggests that the transition to capitalism initially had a positive thrust. "European society was driven to the point that with the emergence of the bourgeoisie who challenged the divine right of kings, capitalism at first even had a progressive air since it opposed the myths and rituals, the metaphysics and mysticism, and raised to a popular level the philosophy of realism and materialism. Until of course, it found a way to utilize mysticism, metaphysics and even the old royalty to serve its ever practical ends."[9]

Finally, Mr. Baraka offers an explanation of the causative relationship between the enslavement of African people in America and capitalism:

> The growing, expanding capitalism needed laborers to build the new world into an economic gold mine, and it was this force that created the slave trade.[10]

Then:

> It is out of the slave trade that racism developed. The institutionalizing of enforced submission and hence inferiority. The development of pseudoscience, history, sociology and religion to justify the humiliation of an entire race of people, and from the beginning of the slave trade the super exploitation of Afrikan people became something that was indelibly linked to the economic advancement of EuroAmerican society, and racism an indelible aspect of Euro-American culture.[11]

Although Mr. Baraka's position paper contains other comments, these are illustrations and/or explanations of the major themes discussed. They are also comments generally illustrative of the Marxist position as applied to the oppression of African people.

An Alternative Framework

Before looking in detail at the ideology of the Congress of Afrikan People, it must be stated that the upcoming remarks transcend the current debate amongst African people on the relative merits of Cultural Nationalism and Marxism-Leninism as ideological frameworks for liberation. The comments to be made are equally applicable to both positions. Secondly, the assumption is made that an ideology in itself is insignificant. Rather, it is the forms of behavior that are induced by an ideology that determine whether or not liberation takes place. As with religion, alternative paradigms may produce identical patterns of behavior, and ultimately it is behavior, particularly overt behavior, that directly determines an individual's or a nation's state in life. We are therefore specifically concerned with how Baraka's ideology (as well as other current ideologies of change) affects overt and covert behavior. We may begin by looking at the nature of society.

Individuals form societies in order to increase their chances of survival. An integral part of the structure of social organizations are those rules and regulations governing behavior, which we call sociocultural norms. The norms for any society grow out of the consensus, or agreement, of the members thereof. Accordingly, societies, and the parts thereof, represent a co-partnership. It is this element of copartnership that Mr. Baraka's ideology (Cultural Nationalism and orthodox Marxism) overlooks.

To say that human relationships occur with the consensus and cooperation of the individuals involved is not to imply that such relationships are equal or near equal. A brief look at statistics on American society makes obvious these inequalities. Economic inequalities exist:

Table 1.

Family Groups	Income Range	Percent of total national income received by each group
Lowest tenth	0 - 2,700	2
Second tenth	2,700 - 4,000	3
Third tenth	4,000 - 5,500	5
Fourth tenth	5,500 - 7,000	6
Fifth tenth	7,000 - 8,600	7
Sixth tenth	8,600 - 10,045	9
Seventh tenth	10,045 - 12,010	11
Eighth tenth	12,010 - 15,000	13
Ninth tenth	15,000 - 20,000	17
Highest tenth	20,000 - and over	27

Compiled from data in U.S. Department of Commerce, *Statistical Abstract of the United States, 1972* (Washington, D.C.: GPO, 1972), 324.

Social inequalities also exist. These social inequalities transcend class and comprise caste relationships! Caste relationships reflect covert internalized psychological parameters that reflect themselves in external behavior. In America, European and African Americans form two distinct castes. These caste relationships are reflected by economic data:

Table 2.

Poverty	33 percent of all American-African families	9 percent of American-European families
Median Income	$6,860	$11,550
Income over $25,000	0.4	2.8
Unemployment	10.0	4.0

Compiled from data in U.S. Department of Commerce, *Statistical Abstract of the United States, 1973*, and *Manpower Report of the President, 1973*.

Caste inequalities in American society transcend the economic to affect every aspect of life. Again sample data illustrate this point (see Table 3). Additionally, other levels of inequalities may exist.

Table 3.

Areas of life	American Africans	American Europeans
Status & Role	450 Architects 11 Radio Stations 3,000 Lawyers 22 Federal Judges 178 City and State Judges	23,650 Architects 6,327 Radio Stations 297,000 Lawyers 437 Federal Judges 11,822 City and State Judges
Health	65.1 per 100,000 cases of tuberculosis 8.4 per 100,000 deaths from tuberculosis 37.5 per 100,000 maternal death rate 64.6 life expectancy	15.3 per 100,000 cases of tuberculosis 2.8 per 100,000 deaths from tuberculosis 19.7 per 100,000 maternal death rate 71.3 life expectancy
Education	58 percent finish eighth grade 40 percent finish high school	73 percent finish eighth grade 62 percent finish high school

Compiled from data in U.S. Department of Health, Education, and Welfare, U.S. Department of Labor, *Manpower Report of the President, 1972*.

Inequalities are of two kinds. They are inherent and they are institutional. Inherent inequalities may be assumed to be distributed equally between human groups. Institutional inequalities are built into the structure of a social organization and reinforced by the mores and folkways of the society. *Institutional inequalities such as those illustrated by the data define what are commonly called systems of oppression.* American society has several different systems of oppression built into the mechanisms through which it operates. The arrangement of economic status and roles constitutes a system of oppression favoring the top 1 percent of the population. The system of social stratification is composed of two separate systems of oppression. One of these, a class system, is based upon objective factors such as income, occupation, education, birth, etc. The other form of stratification, the caste system, oppresses groups of individuals upon the basis of physical differences. This form of oppression is commonly called racism. Simultaneously, status and roles are assigned by sex, by age, and so forth. Thus, oppression exists in many forms (parents oppress their children). Individuals interested in opposing oppression may work *extensively* and attempt to fight institutional inequality at all levels, or they may work *intensively* and concentrate on that area of oppression towards which their experiences and/or interests guide them. Thus, Amiri Baraka emphasizes economic oppression. Haki Madhabut's experiences have led him to emphasize racism. Shirley Chisholm's interests have led her to work against sexism, etc. It is interesting that, whatever the particular perspective from which oppression is viewed, the *problem is causally defined in precisely identical ways.* Marxism-Leninism views economic exploitation as "caused" by capitalists. Nationalism is concerned with the victimization of African people by Europeans and American Europeans. Feminism views the male as the oppressor and the female as the oppressed. The newly emerging Children's Civil Rights Movement views adults as the cause of the oppression of children. *Each movement of change thereby becomes automatically self-defeating by inappropriately analyzing oppression in a fatalistic, deterministic framework.* This point will be discussed later.

All human relationships exist through the consent, either overt or covert, of the individuals involved. This element of consent or co-partnership occurs through the mechanism of socio-cultural norms that direct human behavior. These norms are supportive of the relationships of inequalities previously delineated. They define the behavior of the oppressor and the oppressed. Through the mechanisms of sanctions, the oppressor and oppressed are rewarded for behavior supportive of oppression, and punished for behavior non-supportive of oppression. Thus, oppression is causally related to both the oppressor and oppressed: the oppressed is trained and conditioned to behave in such a manner as to maintain his oppression, the oppressor via positive and negative reinforcement is trained to perpetuate his role model's oppressive behavior.

Baraka and other Marxists have embraced an ideology that indicates precisely the opposite. *The proletariat is a victim, having nothing to do with his own enslavement.* Such an ideology has negative behavioral consequences. The victim, by virtue of his victimization, has no behavioral control over the villain. Simultaneously, Marxism and other current ideologies leave the victim without behavioral control over himself, while simultaneously telling him to revolt. The victim's unconscious mind registers the conflict. The logical extensions of such a position make several statements to the oppressed.

Base statement:

You are a poor victim, tossed like a leaf in the wind by the Omnipotent System (Marxists-Leninists) and the Omnipotent Man (Cultural-Nationalists), or Omnipotent Male (Feminists).

Supporting statements:

1. You have no choice in the matter.
2. You would behave differently but the oppressor will not "let" you.
3. The oppressor is omniscient and is always aware of any attempts toward liberation.
4. The oppressor is innately evil while the oppressed are "good."

Logical conclusion:

There is nothing that I can do to change my position in the present social organization.

For Marxists and other victim-oriented ideologies, behavior is also prescribed by their formula:

1. "Consciousness raising" in others, sometimes called "political education," or, in the language of laymen, "talk."
2. Continuation in personal life forms of behavior supportive of oppression.

   Examples: (a) The Marxist-Leninist remains totally dependent upon the market for food, clothing, and shelter, etc. (b) Females continue to seek males who are "achievement-oriented" while protesting male/female stereotypes, etc.

The failure of the ideology to lead to change is then rationalized:

1. Oppressed people will not listen.
2. Oppressed people will not unite.
3. Oppressed people fight amongst themselves.

Since Baraka and other Black Marxists analyze capitalist oppression as it relates to racial oppression, we will begin to use our partnership-in-oppression framework to look at these issues. Because statistics indicate that racism exists aside from capitalist exploitation, we will begin by examining racism.

Partners in Oppression

As social scientists, we recognize that all societies consist of several basic structures that are labeled pivotal institutions. Each of these pivotal institutions, as mentioned earlier, serves as a mechanism for satisfying some survival-related need. When a society is characterized by oppression, the oppressed perform oppression-maintaining behavior within the framework of each pivotal institution. For the purpose of analysis, we will designate oppression-maintaining behavior of the oppressed as behavior set Y, and oppression-maintaining behavior of the oppressor as behavior set X. Behavior set Y is endogenous to the victim of a system of oppression and therefore controllable by him. Behavior set X is exogenous to the victim. But, as in any coordinated system, both sets of behavior must take place in order for oppression to continue. We may now proceed to view racism within the framework of our paradigm and from the vantage point of each pivotal institution.

A. Racism and the Economic Institution

Statistics were presented earlier that indicated that even when other relevant variables are equal, American Africans command less in the market than American Europeans. Such statistics attest that factors exogenous to the "victim" are at play. They exemplify direct institutional racism. Indirect institutional control, however, trains and/or acculturates and/or conditions American Africans and American Europeans into patterns of behavior that will reinforce and sustain the status quo. Some of these economic norms determining behavior of both groups are isolated below.

I.   **Societal norms for economic success**
    These in themselves are nondiscriminatory by race, as Black Marxists attempt to point out:
    a.   ownership, use, and sale of factors of production other than labor;
    b.   "ownership" and sale of a form of labor which is in scarce supply (i.e., athletes and/or entertainers);
    c.   origination of a new process or method of production (Ford's assembly line), a new invention (the hula-hoop) and/or the vision and foresight to recognize an opportunity for economic gain (Afro products during the sixties);
    d.   large expenditures of mental energy and effort in income-producing directions;
    e.   the use of income as a base for the accumulation of income-producing objects (a tractor vs. an automobile, chinchillas vs. a chinchilla coat, etc.).

II. **Exogenous variables leading to relative greater economic success of American Europeans**
    a.   earlier acquisition of non-labor factors of production via slavery, early industrialization, etc.;
    b.   preference in the market for European labor when all other factors are equal (this would hold true if economic decisions were made by a European Central Planning Board because of the psychological base of racism);

c. exposure of European-American young to "success" models, wider experiences in the economic world, and formal training and education designed for economic survival in American society;

d. parental and social pressure to achieve;

e. a rate of time preference favorable to delayed consumption.

"Victim" analysis models of oppression emphasize the above exogenous variables. Conservative models of oppression emphasize factors such as those listed below. It is crucial to point out that the effort herein is to pull the two sets of behavior pattern together in such a way that corrective behavior can be presented.

III. Endogenous variables leading to lesser economic success of American Africans, or behavior of American Africans cooperative with oppression

a. large expenditures of physical and mental energy in non-income producing activities (i.e., African teenagers' relative allotment of time to dancing as opposed to academics, the high rate of homicides amongst American Africans (the 5th cause of death), etc.;

b. "subcultural" values that emphasize maximum output with minimum input (small neighborhood businesses with periodic opening and closing time, etc.). This norm is a carryover from slavery wherein it was a survival function for a slave to give minimum input;

c. an emphasis upon the purchase of "conspicuous" consumer's goods in opposition to the purchase of investment goods (a pimp's Mercedes as opposed to the purchase of land, etc.);

d. creative energy channeled towards the fine arts rather than economic innovations.

It can be argued by Nationalists and Marxists that there exist sound historical reasons for behavior that cooperates with oppression. It is readily admitted that these reasons exist, but it is also asserted that individuals and groups can break free of historical circumstance! If this were not so, history would exist as a static portrait. It is further asserted that no ideology for liberation can succeed which fails in recognizing and analyzing the dual nature of oppression.

B. Racism and Social Institutions with Specific Reference to Marriage and the Family

Whereas the role of the economic institution is apparent, that of marriage and the family is less obvious in contemporary Western and Western-emulated societies. Marriage and the family play several roles. At the most basic level, they are institutions for the propagation of the human species. In order to fulfill this function, the family becomes an institution for the socialization of the young. Additionally, marriage and the family provide a stable source of warm, human companionship. For the individual interested in social change, marriage and the family are crucial institutions, since it is within these frameworks that the child learns behavior supportive of oppression. Although "the family is the smallest unit of a nation," in the five years from 1968 to 1973, the number of American African families headed by both parents declined from 68 percent to 61 percent. Below are listed sample forms of social behavior supportive of marriage and the family.

Forms of social behavior non-supportive of oppression

A. Marriage
    a. the establishment of an intense and continuous commitment between the involved individuals;
    b. mutual support of involved individuals in day-to-day activity;
    c. common interests, goals, and values.

B. The Family
    a. early academic training of children so that they may obtain easy mastery of Western knowledge (particularly Western science);
    b. emphasis by parents upon games that train the child towards creative approaches;
    c. acute consciousness amongst parents of their roles as living models;
    d. the instilling in the child through nonverbal behavior pride in self as (1) individual, (2) family member, (3) African descendant, (4) homo sapien;
    e. instilling in the child personal self-definition and individual responsibility.

The illustrations discussed thus far are merely illustrations of the kind of analysis which our alternative paradigm elicits. They also indicate that the described framework can be used to examine other forms of oppression. The suggested framework of analysis is not so naive, however, as to suggest that all one must do is to cease cooperating with oppression in order that liberation take place. Accordingly, other comments are in order.

Once the individual ceases cooperating with oppression in each of the basic institutions, he corrects the endogenous variables creating oppression. But the exogenous variables still remain. Baraka and other Marxists tell African people that revolution is the cure. Yet, no precise outline is offered as to how this revolution is to take place. Revolution can only occur through grasping power. Power, or control, flows from two sources in modern society—the possession of superior artifacts of war and highly efficient artifacts of production. These tools of power originate from two sources so simple as to defy exposure—namely, the intermixture of knowledge and creativity. If a revolution between oppressor and oppressed occurs, the oppressor will surely win if the oppressed fights with tools of war conceived, designed, and engineered by the oppressor, for surely the master is more expert at his own creations than the slave. The slave must therefore learn all of the master's knowledge and use it as ingredients towards the creation of new artifacts of war and new artifacts of survival. Finally, the slave must cease chasing the notion that he must unite with the masses of other slaves before he can act. The slave must forego the myth of democracy. The lesson of history is that social change takes place through the uniting of individual men of power in small groups that then strategically engineer the masses towards the desired goal.

With all respect to Brother Baraka and other Marxists, Nationalists, and all groups and individuals who are concerned about oppression, let it be stated that this alternative paradigm is presented in humility as one of a number of possible approaches to the liberation of African people. For those individuals and groups involved in the war against oppression, may the words below provide comfort when our spirits near defeat:

> *I am only one*
> *But still I am One*
> *I cannot do everything,*
> *But I can do something*
> *And because I cannot do everything*
> *I must not refuse to do*
> *The something that I can do.*—Ernett E. Hale

Notes

1. "The Congress of Afrikan People: A Position Paper," *The Black Scholar,* January-February 1975, 2.
2. Ibid., 3.
3. Ibid.
4. Ibid.
5. Ibid., 4.
6. Ibid., 5.
7. Ibid.
8. Ibid.
9. Ibid.
10. Ibid., 6.
11. Ibid.

5

Historical Consciousness and Politics in Africa*

LANSINÉ KABA

Lansiné Kaba *is from Guinea and is an Associate Professor of History at the University of Minnesota in Minneapolis. He is a graduate of the Sorbonne in Paris and Northwestern University in Evanston, Illinois. His works include many scholarly articles in English and French, and the book,* The Wahhabiyya: Islamic Reform and Politics in West Africa. *In 1975, he received the Herskovits Award for outstanding contribution to African Studies.*—The Western Journal of Black Studies, *Spring 1979, Vol. 3, No. 1*

Despite the impressive accomplishments by Africanist scholars during the last three decades, most Westerners continue to perceive Africa with prejudice and narrow-mindedness. Some recent examples of such views include the reactions against *Roots* and the coverage of the uprisings in Zaire and Zimbabwe. Lewis H. Lapham of *Harper's* magazine, in an editorial blitz against Andrew Young for supporting majority rule in Southern Africa and Alex Haley for suggesting the existence of an African civilization, wrote:

> During the early years of African independence…as a newspaper correspon-
> dent assigned to the [U.N.] General Assembly, I was obliged to write down
> whatever I was told. The newly arrived [African] delegates spoke about the
> evils of colonialism (evils that I also could name and condemn), but then
> they went on to conjure forth the phantom civilization of Prester John and
> the Queen of Sheba. Their eloquence forced me to go to libraries in search of
> proofs…Although I could find little evidence for civilizations of any kind, I
> could read extensively about the slave trade, cannibalism, tribal wars, wood
> carving, raffia weaving, and the steady state of Stone Age cultures that had
> survived for possibly as long as 250,000 years.[1]

---

*An earlier version of this paper was presented in the Minnesota Forum Public Lectures Series at the University of Minnesota, May 24, 1978.

The diatribe accused Africans of enslaving their own friends, wives, and children. Not surprisingly, Lapham has tried to ease the consciences of his white readers by stating that "the Western European nations sickened of slavery in a far briefer period than did the Greeks, the Romans, the Arabs, or the Africans." Lapham had probably done some research, but it is clear that he looked in the wrong places and with preconceived ideas. Consequently, he noted only those works that could substantiate his preconceptions. Undoubtedly, Lapham must return to libraries and consult more serious works in order to accomplish something of greater significance in his editorials.

Larry Heinzerling of the Associated Press, and most United States daily papers, which published his "analysis" of the invasion of Zaire in May 1978, exhibited other kinds of misrepresentations and biases. According to them, "Whites were hunted," and "Africa is deeply troubled by political instability, by poverty and by tribal divisions."[2] The continent "suffers from the effects of the vacuum left when the European colonial powers withdrew…The key element in all this remains tribalism." His "analysis" overlooks the dominant economic and political conditions and the disruptive consequences of neocolonial exploitation.

The preceding examples show that the old myths about Africa and Africans as being "primitive" and "savage" have not vanished. They have retained, in Basil Davidson's words, a kind of underground existence, have settled like a layer of dust and ashes on the minds of large numbers of otherwise thoughtful people, and are constantly being swirled about.[3] Therefore, the question of whether Africans ever reached the stage of historical consciousness is a crucial issue. A positive answer to this question will enhance our understanding of racism and exploitation, and our commitment to African liberation. The central problem is one of emancipation from political and economic domination, and hence of control over one's history and future. Such understanding has a definite ideological implication.

This paper will define historical consciousness in general and discuss the reasons why and how its existence in Africa was first denied, and then acknowledged. As a historiographical exercise, it will illuminate some African writers' contributions to the field of African history and hence the connection between scholarship and politics. Hopefully, this groundwork may lead to a better understanding of the predicaments of contemporary Africa.

Consciousness as Knowledge and Social Reality

The consciousness of proceeding toward the future is one of the main characteristics of human life. We as living beings are aware of a specific quality of time, and tend to use it for our purposes. To be is to be conscious of time and space, with all the implications of this awareness. Given the gregarious nature of human beings, it follows that societies are also affected by the same dynamic drive to achieve their goals in a progressive manner. All great societies and civilizations attempt to deal with this challenge and hence are necessarily concerned with consciousness in a historical perspective.

It seems, however, that the degree of historical consciousness cannot be the same for all groups or individuals. Its forms depend on broad societal and inter-societal relationships. The political domination of a country or of one group by another, the presence of uneven exchange relationships between two economic zones, and the existence of an unequal distribution of wealth within a society greatly affect the nature of historical consciousness. Implicitly, one is not born with any particular form of consciousness. Rather it results from a combination of factors, material as well as social.

As living units, individuals and societies obey the general laws of motion, causality, and necessity. Consciousness is an element of their relations to themselves, others, and the outside world. It is, in part, what some philosophers have called "immanence," "inwardness," or "interiority," that is, the quality of remaining and operating within oneself.[4] This quality is one of the starting points of most human experiences and activities, including thoughts, feelings, and creativity. At this level, consciousness refers to an acute awareness of both one's existence in the universe and separation from it. Clearly, this process cannot be limited to "interiorization," because to exist implies a necessary coexistence with others. It contrasts a conscious subject with an external reality that is the object of the awareness. Consciousness is a way of dealing with others and the world, and thus is a source of knowledge, which requires reasoning capacity.

The preceding remarks assume little dichotomy between reason and consciousness. Although reason appears to be the primary tool of the objective study of the external world and consciousness is the "gate to the knowledge of oneself," their goals nevertheless remain almost analogous—they aim at comprehending oneself and the universe. The two processes are complementary. In a broad sense, consciousness can be viewed as a process of thought which may relate itself to its own self, to another, or to the outside, thereby indicating one's existence in the world in general and in a society in particular.

Within this context, historical consciousness represents the highest level of consciousness because of the historical essence of human beings as both the product and authors of history—for all human actions occur in a historical process, and societies evolve historically. Social systems are never completely still. They are in a constant process of change either forward or backward. This view implies that history consists of dynamic periods rather than undifferentiated and static units. Every society must be analyzed in its own historical context.

Therefore, to understand any society dynamically requires an effort to analyze its foundations, the causes of its growth, and the internal contradictions that may lead to its decline. Thus, historical consciousness is at the root of a methodology based on the idea that change is necessary in historical analysis. It is above all a consciousness of motion.

Historical consciousness deals with a sense of historicity rather than an encyclopedic knowledge of facts. It asserts the historical nature of every society, regardless of its material conditions; establishes causation between two stages of development; and helps to formulate objective approaches to problems confronting societies. Therefore, its political implications are manifest.

The differences existing within a society make it necessary for each of its groups to develop a particular historical consciousness reflecting its conditions and needs. For example, the consciousness of a ruling class mainly deals with how to reinforce and perpetuate its domination and legitimize its position, while disadvantaged groups want to eliminate inequality and promote a just system. Likewise, the historical consciousness of the colonized or oppressed opposes that of the colonizers and oppressors. Nkrumah, Fanon, Cabral, Biko, and Malcolm X could not have the same historical consciousness as Churchill, DeGaulle, Salazar, Vorster, and Lyndon Baines Johnson. In other words, people having antagonistic interests cannot be expected to develop identical views of history. Therefore, historical consciousness tends to have a class character, each group having its own needs and ideology. As new conditions emerge, they call for new visions and consciousness. Any significant change in the socioeconomic context affects other aspects of social life, including thoughts and world views.

Scholarship is, by definition, engaged in the propagation of a particular form of consciousness. This situation is especially true of African studies, a multi-disciplinary field dominated by non-African scholars and derived in part from two opposite sources, namely the colonial administrations' political needs and the emergence of African nationalism. These factors should enable one to view historical consciousness as the active force at work in a positive affirmation of people's identity, worth, and contribution to world civilization. Consciousness as a source of knowledge and an ideology implies an affinity between the subject and object of history. The notion of affinity raises the question of whether and under which conditions a scholar can objectively study a foreign society and can write a dispassionate account of its history. A balance can be found between objectivity and subjectivity. The task is not impossible, but it is difficult because of the strong tendency to exhibit ethnocentrism despite good intentions.

African Historical Consciousness and European Expansion

Despite the thought that humans are *par essence* historically minded, Western scholarship once questioned the historicity of African societies. The question was whether those who, in Césaire's words, "neither invented gunpowder and compass nor tamed steam and electricity,"[5] could reach historical consciousness. Hegel, an eminent scholar examining the philosophical history of the world, opined that Africa, is a land of childhood, removed from the light of self-conscious history and wrapped in the dark mantle of night...In Africa, history is in fact out of question. Life there consists of a succession of contingent happenings and surprises. No aim or state exists whose development can be followed...The characteristic feature of the Negroes is that their consciousness has not yet reached an awareness of any substantial objectivity—for example, of God or the law—in which the will of man could participate and in which he could become aware of his own being.[6]

Hegel cannot be considered a racist or a bigot. Unlike some other European scholars, he related "Africans' backwardness" to geographical factors rather than to biological deficiencies, such as the small size of the brain, or deficiencies associated with the frontal lobes, the cortex, or the genes. Hegel had one of the most encyclopedic minds of his generation, and is one of the greatest philosophers of all times for the long-lasting influences his logic and thought had on the evolution of philosophy. He firmly believed in universal motion, and contradiction as an essential part of thought. Hegel's *Philosophy of History* is a major piece of scholarship designed to prove that thought is essential to humanity. The work further states that "the only thought which philosophy brings with it to the contemplation of History is the conception of Reason."[7] Describing reason as the "Sovereign of the world," Hegel viewed history as a necessarily rational process characteristic of humankind. Africa, however, was not included in his notion of humanity. Hegel denied rationality, intelligibility, and history to African peoples. This denial is a serious contradiction in a system that claimed to be universal and logical.

Hegel was undoubtedly ignorant of African history because the Black scholars of Timbuktu indeed dealt with all aspects of knowledge, including theology and history.[8] However, no one would hold a grudge against Hegel for his lack of information. After all, from the point of view of the Europeans of the 1820s there was no major history worth studying beyond those of the West and the Mediterranean. The main problem lies in the tendency of most European writers to make eloquent self-serving generalizations and to express unsubstantiated opinions with the appearance of rigorous scientific truth. This dogmatic ethnocentrism, to be satisfactorily understood, must be related to the class interests of the bourgeoisie extending its hold over the world economy. Philosophers and other scholars tended to legitimize this process of global domination by ignoring or minimizing other people's achievements and cultures.

Since Hegel's time, generations of Western intellectuals have further elaborated on the absence of history and civilization in Africa. Frenchmen, such as Jules Romain and J. Gourou, and British writers, such as F. B. Jevons, J. C. Carothers, and H. Trevor-Roper, to name only a few, have, according to their fields, suggested reasons for the backwardness of African societies. In a strong spirit of self-glorification, they have also related historical awakening in Africa to contact with "superior" European civilization. African history was then viewed as an extension of the Western historical experience, a product of Europe's benevolent expansion and enlightenment. Implicitly, Hegel's authority was lent to such views.

Despite Lévi-Strauss's analysis that history is not superior to myth,[9] Black Africa has been disparaged as the land of mythical thought inferior to historical consciousness, a world consisting of an amorphous mass of uncivilized societies known as "tribes," and hence not worthy of serious historical attention.

To refute methodically such biases calls for some historical recollection. Europe and Africa had no direct contacts before the Atlantic navigation of the 15th century. Prior to this time there could not have been any cultural arrogance on the part of the Europeans. For example, references to Blacks in a letter from the French theologian Abélard to his beloved Héloise in the 1130s contained no derogatory remarks about Africa despite his belief in the superiority of Catholicism. Even after the first years of direct contact between Europe and Africa, images changed very little. To paraphrase the scholar Césaire, Eanes de Azurara, Valentim Fernandes, or Ca de Mosto, and other chroniclers of the navigation on the Guinea Coast did not "claim to be the harbingers of a superior order."[10] The Portuguese respected the kings of Mali, Benin, and Congo to the point that they envisioned diplomatic exchange with them.

Therefore, the hypocrisy, in Césaire's words, is of recent origin. It goes back to the discovery of America and the need to exploit its vast resources after the decimation of the Indians. The subsequent rise of the slave trade as the single most important pattern of relations between Africa and Europe during three full centuries drastically altered the nature of the contact and attitudes of the Europeans. Obviously, the growing bourgeoisie could not condone slavery and at the same time accept Africans as being intelligent and equal. Montesquieu made some pertinent comments about this issue in his *Lettre sur l'esclavage des Noirs*. It is well known that any system of exploitation and oppression must promote an ideology legitimizing its practices.

As a result, the derogatory image associated with African peoples originated in the need to legitimize morally an obnoxious trade system created by and for the European expanding economy. This fact explains why there was no significant gain of knowledge about African civilization in the 17th and 18th centuries despite the scientific atmosphere of the Enlightenment era. The myth about Africa's stagnation led to a systematic indifference to her positive achievements. The work of Arab scholars and Christian writers who mentioned the strength and splendor of African states and institutions were abandoned to oblivion.

Consequently, the myth of Africa's darkness reflected the Westerners' ignorance of the African past rather than Africa's lack of historical consciousness. Although the trans-Atlantic slave trade had declined by the 1820s when Hegel was writing his *Philosophy of History*, this myth had reached even larger proportions; newer self-serving ideas were emerging. Subsequently, slavery became an obstacle against the establishment of "legitimate" trade and the penetration of European influence to civilize Africans and had to be abolished. However, it was for the benefit of those who promoted it in the first instance.

Accordingly, the scholarship is neither totally objective nor neutral despite the repeated claims of impartiality made by many writers. The orientation of the historiography, whether implicit or explicit, reflects economic and other interests and personal predispositions. This condition applies to the writings of Hegel and other Western scholars who followed him, and whose names have been associated with the myth of African societies' lack of historical consciousness. Their works contributed to justify commercial, political, and missionary activities in Africa, and also led to the colonial powers' self-glorifying claims, such as the theories of their "civilizing mission" and the "white man's burden."

With the establishment of colonial rule in the late 1890s and early 1900s, the political implications and role of the social sciences became even bolder and served then as part of the broad methodical plan of domination and acculturation. African history was reduced to the history of conquest and colonization. Not surprisingly, ethnology, which later became anthropology, dominated the field of African studies. This discipline, unlike history or sociology, originated in the need of the colonizers to understand and control the colonized rather than in the broad philosophical questions about society. Thus, anthropology was essentially the academic discipline that facilitated European expansion.

On the other hand, no one can ignore all the ramifications of anthropology. At the time when most Europeans considered African values as savage or at best as exotic curiosities, anthropologists attempted to study and appreciate their functions and rationale. They tried to explain scientifically the political institutions and religious, social, and aesthetic values. Such efforts were then positive and significant. However, for too long anthropologists held a timeless view of African societies. They ignored history, and generally rejected a historical interpretation of the traditions and institutions under study. Africa was depicted as being unaffected by the law of dynamic progression. Hence, change was seen in terms of the impact of the superior Western civilization upon blurred masses.[11] Such synchronic observations suited well the self-serving ideology of colonialism. The collusion between this sort of scholarship and colonial doctrine culminated in the rise of the "tribal" image of African societies among Westerners and was the origin of the conservative aspect of anthropology.

Despite the vagueness of the concept of "tribe" in its present usage, the tribal concept generally refers to a type of society and to a stage of social evolution very different from, and inferior to, Western ones. "Tribalism," according to the Western concept, clearly denotes primitiveness and backwardness. Such views were most consistent with the colonial doctrine. Elliot Skinner's view that "many of the so-called 'tribal' groups were creations of the colonial period"[12] is very pertinent in that it provides a special insight into pre-colonial and colonial politics.

It is possible to argue that there were no "tribes" before colonization, and that African states transcended "tribalism." Ethnic groups spoke different languages and practiced different religions yet some kind of cooperation and value-congruency bound them together. For example, ancient Ghana and Mali, Muenemutapa and Ashanti, only to name a few, included various ethnic and linguistic groups, despite their particular local origins. The process of historical development overcame narrow regionalism and horizons, and thereby reinforced unity. In other words, "tribal" ideology is *par essence* foreign to Africa. Hence, African scholars who speak of African societies in terms of "tribalism" may not be fully aware of the implications of this terminology.

Whatever the case may be, the words "tribe" and "tribalism" are derogatory when they exclusively apply to non-Western groups and values. Most writers who view Africa from a "tribal" perspective will not use the same terms in a Western context analogous to the African one. For instance, "tribalism" has yet to be applied to the Irish crisis or the Basque and Brittany questions or the problem of national integration in Belgium. Obviously, the concepts of "tribe" and "tribalism" lack cross-cultural applicability. Hence, they are questionable, if not derogatory and improper.

Historical Consciousness and Political Change

The rise of African history as a full-fledged field of study has been associated with the historical foundations of African unity and the worth of Africa's past achievement. Such pan-African consciousness dismisses "tribal" ideology. As "a reflection of Africa's recovery and reawakening,"[13] it involves strong philosophical and political commitment to the struggle for true independence and development instead of neocolonial dependence. At the core of this positive consciousness lie four main principles reclaiming Black cultural and historical values and having direct political implications.

First, African societies are historical groups obeying the general laws of progression and following rational processes. As such, they are dynamic and can respond to internal or external challenge, and control it. As a corollary, they can absorb new values and adapt to new conditions in an orderly fashion. They can engage in meaningful forms of contact and exchange with other societies without losing their sense of identity and pride. This dynamic process requires the right and the freedom to determine the path of one's historical progression. These attributes were incompatible with colonial rule. Consequently, this consciousness calls for strong anti-colonialist thought and action.

Second, such thoughts must transcend the individualistic interpretation of history. African historical consciousness asserts that the people as groups committed to particular goals make history, and that individuals succeed only when their actions become part of a collective effort, such as in the cases of Sundiata of ancient Mali, Samori of Guinea, Chaka of South Africa, and Cabral of contemporary Guinea-Bissau, who led their societies to great achievements and symbolized political values of the highest order.

Third, this consciousness categorically rejects the myth widely spread by racists and colonialists that Africa is a backward continent that contributed nothing to universal civilization. To refute this belief it must be noted that Africans tamed the continent from which, according to available scholarly information, humankind originated;[14] that, despite the predispositions of most Western historians and art historians, Pharaonic Egypt—one of the earliest turning, and high, points in world history—was neither Semitic nor Caucasian, but African, and hence African civilization affected the growth of science and philosophy in the Mediterranean world;[15] that the civilizations of Timbuktu and the Swahili city-states in the 15th and 16th centuries achieved a brilliant level in the humanities and philosophy; and finally, that African music and African arts have made the greatest contributions to the cultural heritage of humanity in this century because of their liberating and refreshing effects on Western traditions.[16] The awareness of this achievement is a major weapon against acculturation and inferiority complexes. Césaire wrote:

> I have always thought that the Black man was searching for his identity. And it has seemed to me that if we want to establish this identity, then we must have a concrete consciousness of what we are—that is, of the first fact of our lives: that we are Black; that we…have a history, a history that contains certain cultural elements of great value; and that *Negroes** were not born yesterday, because there have been beautiful and important Black civilizations. At the time we began to write, people could write a history of world civilization without devoting a single chapter to Africa, as if Africa had made no contributions to the world. Therefore, we affirmed that we were *Negroes* and that we were proud of it, and that we thought that Africa was not some sort of blank page in the history of humanity; in sum, we asserted that our *Negro* heritage was worthy of respect, and that this heritage was not relegated to the past, that its values…could still make an important contribution to the world.[17] [*I italicize this word to show that the word "nègre" in French is as derogatory as its English counterpart "nigger." Césaire used it as a defiant mechanism.]

This positive consciousness is based in part on the notion that no society is inherently superior or inferior, despite the differences in technological and economic levels. It rejects European cultural arrogance and the racist interpretation of world culture and history. The matrix of history does not reside in biological or psychological factors, but rather in peoples' capacities to respond to both external and internal challenges, resist exploitation and oppression, and control their destinies. At this level, historical consciousness turns into a potent ideology at the service of the peoples' struggle. This situation is what has occurred among Africans.

Since 1945, African peoples have seriously asserted their culture and have expanded their nationalist movements, actions which imply a positive Black consciousness and pride, a belief in the historical unity of all people of African descent, and a commitment to African peoples' struggle against colonialism and racism. To a large extent, whether it remained positive or became exploitative,[18] a strong relationship existed between this emerging nationalism and the need for rigorous African studies. In fact, one activist anti-colonialist African scholarship devoted to a positive interpretation of Africa's past emerged under the leadership of several writers who later on assumed major political responsibilities. The scholarship of Aimé Césaire of the Antilles, Cheikh Anta Diop of Senegal, Boubou Hama of Niger, Fodéba Keita of Guinea, Kwame Nkrumah of Ghana, Dike and Ajayi of Nigeria, and Jomo Kenyatta of Kenya, only to name a few, shows no contradiction with their anti-colonialist positions in the 1950s. Their political engagement made their writing pertinent, while their erudition heightened their political actions. This example of symbiosis between theory and praxis has contributed to decolonization and liberation.

The first generation of Africanist historians encouraged archaeological research and a methodic use of oral traditions. These efforts have resulted in a greater understanding of the history of many societies. A substantial effort has also been made to reinterpret the writing of ancient historians about Egypt, the Muslim travel accounts about the kingdoms of the Sudan,[19] and the memoirs of the 15th century Christian navigators about the coastal states. Africans are reclaiming their history. In the process, the Black African origin of the Pharaonic civilization and of the impressive Muenemutapa ruins has been established. The prosperity and the high level of political organization in Ghana, Mali, and Songhay have been asserted. The scholarship of the Sudanese scholars and the humanism of Timbuktu in the 15th and 16th centuries have eloquently refuted the myth that "African consciousness has not reached an awareness of...God, the State or the law." The leaders of the African resistance against colonialism are no longer viewed as "bloodthirsty tyrants," but rather the heroes of nationalism. African art has been recognized as a heritage of humanity. To deny African history or to overlook Africa's contribution to world civilization would be a testimony to ignorance and bigotry.

Conclusion: A Different Emphasis

As this writer has suggested, history can be both a methodical scholarly endeavor and an ideological force. It is the joint action of these two dimensions of historical consciousness that has led to the establishment of African studies centers and the acceptance of African history as a legitimate branch of history.

However, in the exercise of reconstructing the history of Africa, the tendency has been for nationalist-conscious African historians to present the cultures of pre-colonial African states as harmonious and classless for the sake of national cohesion. Thus, present stratifications in African societies are accounted for as remnants of the colonial legacy. But since the first years of independence, it has become evident that the history of African peoples cannot be presented as conflict-free, however grandiose their achievements might have been. For example, most African societies experienced "domestic slavery" and other forms of oppression and exploitation, although their intensity should not be exaggerated. It is necessary, therefore, to analyze the full range of African social organizations and the processes of their internal differentiation. The role of the commoners, for example, cannot be ignored for the sake of national cohesion. Thus, class analysis with its emphasis on the material bases of history and the social formations corresponding to these material conditions may help to get a more complex understanding of Africa's past.

Furthermore, this approach is more consistent with the analysis of the constraints that external relations have placed on African states in both pre-colonial and post-independent eras. Since the 1960s, most writers have noticed a growing dependence of the Third World on the industrialized world, and a worsening underdevelopment in Africa in particular. Neo-colonialism, a more subtle and pervasive form of domination, has replaced the old colonial system in Africa. Therefore, the continent is confronted with the prospect of growth without economic development and political independence without economic freedom and national security. Within this context of neo-colonialism, a new historical consciousness, which is critical of both the control of African economy by the capitalist world and the African political elite's connivance with this process, has emerged.[20] This consciousness operates on two main premises: (1) that underdevelopment must be studied historically because a society's capacity to shape its destiny is partly determined by its past and real conditions; and (2) that an analytical critique of Africa's uneven relations with the outside world may heighten African peoples' consciousness and subsequently lead to a radical social change that will ensure true liberation and development. Class analysis and revolutionary consciousness have come to dominate historical thought in African historiography.

Notes

1. Lewis H. Lapham, "The Black Man's Burden," *Harper's*, June 1977, 16.
2. Larry Heinzerling, "Attack on Zaire Reflects Poverty and Tribal Divisions in Africa," *Minneapolis Tribune* (AP), May 21, 1978.
3. Basil Davidson, *African Genius* (Boston: Little-Brown, 1969), 25.
4. For instance, see Jean-Paul Sartre, Søren Kierkegaard, or Henri Bergson—Sartre, *Existentialism* (New York: 1947); Kierkegaard, *Philosophical Fragments* (Princeton University Press); Bergson, *Les deux sources de la morale et de la religion* (Paris: P. U. F., 1969 edition).
5. Aimé Césaire, *Return to My Native Land* (Paris: Presence Africaine, 1968), 1.

6. Georg Wilhelm Friedrich Hegel, *Lectures on the Philosophy of History*, H. B. Niblet (trans.) (London: Cambridge University Press, 1975), 174–176.

7. Ibid., 9.

8. See Sekene-Mody Cissoko: *Tombouctou et l'empire Songhay* (Dakar, Senegal: N. E. A., 1975).

9. Claude Lévi-Strauss, *La pensée sauvage* (Paris: Plon, 1962), 5–27.

10. Aimé Césaire, *Discourse on Colonialism*, Joan Pinkham (trans.) (New York: Monthly Review Press, 1972), 11.

11. See, Bronislaw Malinowski, *The Dynamics of Culture Change: An Inquiry into Race Relations in Africa* (New Haven: Yale University Press, 1945).

12. Elliot P. Skinner, "Group Dynamics in the Politics of Changing Societies: The Problem of Tribal Politics in Africa," in June Helm (ed.), *Essays on the Problem of Tribe* (American Ethnological Society, 1968).

13. Kwame Nkrumah, "Address to the Opening of the First International Congress of Africanists," in L. Brown and M. Crowder (eds.), *The Proceedings of the First International Congress of Africanists* (Evanston: NUP, 1960), 10.

14. See, L. S. B. Leakey, "Man's African Origin," *Annals of the New York Academy of Sciences*, 96 (1962), 495–503.

15. See, Cheikh Anta Diop, *Antériorité des civilisations nègres: Mythe ou vérité historique* (Paris: Presence Africaine, 1967).

16. See, W. Fagg and E. Elisofon, *The Sculpture of Africa* (New York: Praeger, 1958); or Frank Willet, *African Art* (New York: Praeger, 1971).

17. Aimé Césaire, "An Interview with Aimé Césaire," *Discourse*, op. cit., 76.

18. There is no doubt that many people have profited from African studies. Some of them have abandoned it because of political and other reasons.

19. Sudan refers to the "Land of the Blacks" in general. In the context of this discussion, I am speaking of the Western Sudan, which extends roughly from Chad Lake to the Atlantic.

20. Examples of this literature include: Frantz Fanon, *The Wretched of the Earth* (New York: Grove Press, 1963); E. A. Brett, *Underdevelopment and Colonialism in East Africa* (New York: NOK, 1977); Samir Amin, "Underdevelopment and Dependence," *The Journal of Modern African Studies*, Vol. 10, No. 4, 1972; Walter Rodney, *How Europe Underdeveloped Africa* (Washington: Howard University Press, 1977); I. Wallerstein and P. Gutkind, eds., *The Political Economy of Contemporary Africa* (New York: Monthly Review, 1976); Basil Davidson, *Can Africa Survive* (Boston: Little, Brown, n.d.), and many more.

6

The Intellectual Foundations of Racism

CHUKWUEMEKA ONWUBU

*Chukwuemeka Onwubu is an Assistant Professor of Sociology in the Depart-
ment of Pan-African Studies at Temple University. He received the Ph.D. degree
from Michigan State University.*—The Western Journal of Black Studies, *Fall
1979, Vol. 3, No. 3*

At the turn of the century, the man who has been hailed[1] as one of America's most catholic thinkers had prophetically concluded: "The problem of
the Twentieth Century is the problem of the colorline."[2] In his prophetic
vision, W.E.B. Du Bois years later also noted, with particular reference to American Black-white relations: "What was true in 1910 was still true in 1940 and will
be true in 1970."[3] The inauguration of the First Universal Races Congress[4] in
London (1911), in which Du Bois himself played a major role, would seem to
have lent support to the genuine concern he had expressed that the "color problem" has ever remained with us and, perhaps, will continue to haunt mankind for
some foreseeable time.

The issue of race and racism is one that has engaged a great deal of attention
and has preoccupied a good many scholars. It has inspired a stupendous amount
of literary work, both scholarly and popular. It has also instigated a good deal of
pretentious trash.

It is not the intention here to add to the complexity. Rather, to the extent that
the idea of "races" has any basis in fact, the central argument in the present under-
taking is that the intellectual has played a leading role in cultivating the social soil
upon which the epiphenomenal evil of racism has thrived. More specifically, the
intellectual, historically, has aided and abetted the cause of racism. This situation
has been effected either in a most blatant way, in some cases, or, in most other
cases, in a rather insidious and most dangerous fashion.

Thus, if the intellectual did not create the monster of racism, he has mediated the process of its ravages in society. If he did not originally kindle the flame
of racism, he has wittingly or unwittingly provided the fuel that sustains the
conflagration. If the intellectual is not himself an avowed racist, he has, at least,

put his service and expertise at the disposal of the racist proper. It is in light of these considerations that this writer attempts to argue the case for the intellectual basis of racism. It would seem logical to proceed with the consideration of the fundamental definitive issues of the intellectual and race, racism, and racialism. One might then ask: Who is the intellectual?

The Intellectual

As conceived by one of the high priests of American sociology, Robert K. Merton,[5] the intellectual is distinguished as such by virtue of his social role, rather than in terms of some innate attributes that constitute his total personality. More specifically:

> We shall consider persons as intellectuals *insofar as* they devote themselves to cultivating and formulating knowledge. They have access to and advance a cultural fund of knowledge which does not derive solely from their direct personal experience. Their activities may be vocational or avocational; this is not decisive…"the intellectual" refers to a social role and not to a total person… Thus, we normally include teachers and professors among the intellectuals…but it does not follow that every teacher or professor is an intellectual… He may or may not be, depending on the actual nature of his activities.[6]

In a sense, an intellectual can be conceived as one who, through formal education or training or otherwise, has been opportuned to develop his intellect, thereby cultivating and accumulating special knowledge. In dealing with and formulating solutions to issues and problems, the intellectual is properly situated—potentially or in actuality—to apply the knowledge predicated on the logic of the intellect, rather than on the whims of emotion. Thus, the intellectual could be located in all walks of life, including the roles of the teacher and the college professor, as Merton has already intimated. He could also be identified in the lawyer, although it is by no means the case that every lawyer should be considered an intellectual. He may as well be the practicing politician, albeit it would be rather naive to imagine that more than a handful of politicians could really pass as intellectuals. But the intellectual could also be discovered in the professional in different fields of endeavor; nevertheless, most professionals would, if anything, be better characterized as "contra-intellectuals."

Merton is perhaps correct in noting, in this respect, that "the teacher is no more an intellectual than a radio announcer who merely reads a script prepared for him by others," who simply transmits the text of a book without the benefit of insightful interpretation and application.[7]

Thus, while it may be said of every intellectual that he is educated, it does not necessarily follow that every "educated" person could assume the role of the intellectual. It could then be argued that the critical mark of the intellectual consists, not so much in the "special" knowledge *per se* accumulated by him, as it inheres in the logic of its formulation and application. With this in mind, consideration must be given to the idea of "race" as well as the epiphenomenal notions of racism and racialism.[8]

"Race," Racism, and Racialism

The question of race is one that has engaged the consciousness of man in contemporary societies—and for good historical reasons. The term "race" is believed to have appeared in the English language for the first time as early as the 16th century; however, Montagu suggests that it was not until the mid-18th century that it was incorporated in the scientific vocabulary.[9]

The rather capricious nature of the grouping of human populations into so-called "races" had been recognized by the eminent scholar and thinker W.E.B. Du Bois, when, before the turn of the century, he asked, "What is the real meaning of race…?"[10] The conclusion he reached was that there could be no definite conclusion regarding the *true* meaning of "race." To him, therefore, what generally passes as a "race" is but "a vast family of human beings, generally of common blood and language, always of common history, traditions and impulses, who are both voluntarily and involuntarily striving together for the accomplishment of certain more or less vividly conceived ideals of life."[11]

The arbitrariness, or ambiguity, inherent in the conception of "race" is evidenced not only in the works of individual scholars, but also in those of social technologists of the established order.[12] Fairbanks and Smith, basing their argument partially on Coon's authority, suggest "two major facets to race": (1) the biological and the cultural; and emphasize, in contradistinction to Coon's genetic determinism[13] (2) the preponderance of genetic similarities across groups over the dissimilarities amongst them.[14] Proceeding from the assumption of "racial" groupings, racism, as such, has been conceived as a form of defense and adjustment mechanism. White racism in America, as such, is then viewed as an aspect of the historical imperatives of the specific American situation.[15] Armed with this form of logic, many analysts have argued the case for the sexual basis of racism.[16]

In any case, the problem of "race," as well as the attendant racism and racialism, still persists. In point of fact, Du Bois' prophetic pronouncement cannot be taken very lightly when it is realized that the definitive problem of "race" has engaged the efforts of bodies of scholars the world over.[17] But while the traditional taken-for-granted attitude about so-called human races still prevails among many scholars, it seems encouraging to realize that others have made some systematic attempts to resolve the issue decisively and conclusively.[18]

Thus, conceiving "race" as a "cultural displacement," Bohannan and Curtin maintain that only by fiat can the idea be invoked as a criterion for natural distinction among human groups.[19] While race has been confused with language and general culture, the concept of "race" is nothing more than the genetic nomenclature for interbreeding populations.[20]

According to Montagu, the idea of "race," which he sees as man's most dangerous myth and, as such, a fallacy, was a special creation of anthropologists.[21] "Race," as such, is a socially created reality within a given social setting. Besides, it is but an institutionalized mode of behavior and a special form of social class distinction.[22] A race problem, then, is essentially a social problem, and racism, a socially defined behavior.[23]

Within the British sociological tradition, Banton views racism "as the doctrine that a man's behavior is determined by stable inherited characters deriving from separate racial stocks having distinctive attributes and usually considered to stand to one another in relations of superiority and inferiority."[24] Considering it as both a concept and an epithet, Banton locates the origin of racism in "the morphological approach to human biology" evidenced in comparative anatomy.[25] But Banton, interestingly enough, is categorical in his affirmation that there can be no race consciousness, or "racism," in a situation lacking the presence and concept of "race."[26] This view, as will be evidenced, is in contradistinction to the view taken by van den Berghe.

Perhaps the British scholarship on race relations is best represented by John Rex, who conceives prejudice as a colonial phenomenon.[27] Rex makes a fundamental distinction between "racism" on the one hand, and "racialism" on the other. Whereas the former alludes to the doctrine of "racial differences between man," the latter concept describes the practices that derive from this doctrine.[28] But, whereas the problem of "racist theory and ideas" can best be formulated in terms of the basic relationships between ideas and social structure,[29] there are specific and limited social-structural situations that can lead to genuine race relations problems.[30]

In view of the fact that social categories such as "race" owe their existence to subjective definitions, one of the primary tasks of a genuine student of race relations, then, is to unmask the pseudo-scientific myths that give sustenance to the doctrine of racism to show the real nature of the differences which distinguish groups of mankind.[31]

Pierre van den Berghe has dealt quite elaborately and rather extensively with the subject of race and racism.[32] Like Montagu, he regards the idea of "race" as but a subjective, social phenomenon, devoid of any intrinsic meaning except that assigned to it by "racists."[33] However, he differs from Banton in his insistence that it is the existence of races in a given society that presupposes the incidence of racism, "for without racism physical characteristics are devoid of social significance."[34]

Whereas "race" connotes different meanings to different people in various walks of life, "racial" distinction or classification is viewed from the sociological perspective as nothing other than a special case of structural or social pluralism—as distinct from ethnic division, which is conceived in terms of "cultural pluralism."[35] Racism, as such, is a doctrine consisting in the belief or assumption that causal links exist between socially relevant abilities or intellectual qualities, on the one hand, and physical traits or differences (real or imagined) among human populations, on the other.[36] Racial prejudice is "the totality of reciprocal relations of stereotyping, discrimination, and segregation existing between human groupings that consider themselves and each other as races."[37]

Where Rex[38] has identified racial prejudice and racial distinctions with colonialism, van den Berghe[39] maintains that, "Whenever phenotypical differences have existed between groups of people, racial differences have arisen." Although van den Berghe is not persuaded that there are any compelling reasons that would warrant the developing of a special theory of race outside the general cultural and institutional context of a given society,[40] Rex is committed and subscribes to the proposition that the analysis of race relations demands, and calls for, the development of a special theoretical framework.[41] Both writers seem to concur on the proposition that a realistic approach to the problem of race relations calls for a special kind of intellectual orientation.[42]

From the foregoing, then, it would seem fair to conclude that so-called "races" are but an invidious mode of distinction among human populations, the overriding objective of which is to effect the imposition of one human group upon another. Insofar as this is granted, racism is nothing more than a social doctrine that sanctions—and as such legitimates—the exploitation of one group by another. Bunche is therefore justified in his denunciation of racialism as "a myth…a dangerous camouflage for brutal economic exploitation."[43] Any significance that is attached to the ideas of "race" and "races" in their current usage in effect implies that skin color has become a popular criterion for the grouping of human populations. With this in mind consideration must be given to the contributions that the intellectual has made towards the creation, propagation, and promotion of this myth.

The Intellectual Basis of Racism

It seems rather interesting, in light of the conceptual framework here, that the "first racist" had been identified in the character of an intellectual and in the person of Robert Knox, an Edinburgh anatomist, who, according to Banton, "suffered public obloquy, probably unfairly, because of his association with Burke and Hare." This stemmed primarily from his so-called "theory of transcendental anatomy."[44] In the same British tradition, another famous (or perhaps notorious) intellectual, David Hume, has been credited with one of the first formulations of the doctrine of Black inferiority vis-à-vis whites, as early as the mid-18th century, on the assumption that the former had never developed any major civilization.[45]

In a sense, Hume had pre-empted the racial trappings of Gobineau, the acclaimed French "inventor of twentieth-century racism."[46]

However, this pseudo-scientific tradition has continued to the present century, perhaps reaching its high-water marks in the works of Seligman, Linnaeus, and such eminent scholars as Spengler and Toynbee.[47] In fact, it was no other than a Regius Professor of History, Thomas Arnold, at one of England's oldest and most venerable universities, who in 1841 had propounded the doctrine of racial determinism of history.[48] It was no mere coincidence that, a little more than a century later, another Regius Professor of History at the same institution saw the need to make the declaration, "Perhaps in the future there will be some African history to teach. But at present there is none; there is only the history of Europeans in Africa. The rest is darkness…and darkness is not a subject of history."[49]

Interestingly enough, this statement was an echo of a voice from a former era. Hegel, one of Europe's greatest thinkers, had dismissed Africa and African history in what would appear to be most deprecating language:

> Africa proper, as far as History goes back, has remained—for all purposes of connection with the rest of the world—shut up; it is the Gold-land compressed within itself—conscious history, is enveloped in the dark mantle of night. Its isolated character originates, not merely in its tropical nature, but essentially in its geographical condition…The peculiarly African character is difficult to comprehend, for the very reason that in reference to it, we must quite give up the principle which naturally accompanies our ideas—the category of Universality. *In Negro Life the characteristic point is the fact that consciousness has not yet attained to the realization of any substantial objective existence*…in which the interest of man's volition is involved and in which he realizes his own being… *The Negro*, as already observed, *exhibits the natural man in his completely wild and untamed state*. We must lay aside all thought of reverence and morality—all that we call feeling—if we would rightly comprehend him; there is nothing harmonious with humanity to be found in this type of character. *The copious and circumstantial accounts of Missionaries completely confirm this*, and *Mahommetanism* [sic] appears to be the only thing which in any way brings the Negroes within the range of culture… *want of self-control distinguishes the character of the Negroes. This condition is capable of no development or culture*…The only essential connection between the Negroes and the Europeans is that of slavery…The gradual abolition of slavery is therefore wiser and more equitable than its sudden removal…At this point we leave *Africa*, not to mention it again. For it is *no historical part of the World*; it has no movement or development to exhibit.
>
> *Historical movements in it—that is in its northern part—belong to the Asiatic or European World…Egypt…does not belong to the African spirit*. What we properly understand by Africa is the unhistorical, undeveloped spirit, still involved in the conditions of mere nature.[50] [emphasis added]

The above calls for no further elaboration.

In the United States, the special historical situation of slavery has given a unique twist to the role of the intellectual *qua* legitimator of social practice.[51] Thus, in pre-Civil War America, it was, as Montagu points out, not the rabid, naive racists, but rather influential anthropologists who had formulated the doctrine of the natural inequality of man.[52] But this was—and has remained—true of post-Civil War America, as Du Bois has very carefully documented.[53] In point of fact, racial chauvinism was championed by eminent scholars at the nation's most venerable institutions. As Du Bois has noted more specifically, it was Professor John Burgess of Columbia University who, reflecting on the emancipation of slaves as well as the subsequent Reconstruction program, had declared:

> There is no question, now, that Congress did a monstrous thing, and committed a great political error, if not a sin, in the creation of this new electorate. It was a great wrong to civilization to put the white race of the South under the domination of the Negro race. The claim that there is nothing in the color of the skin from the point of view of political ethics is a great sophism. *A black skin means membership in a race of men which has never of itself succeeded in subjecting passion to reason, has never, therefore, created any civilization of any kind.*[54] [emphasis added]

John W. Burgess, professor of political science at Columbia University, it should be noted, came from Tennessee, the birthplace of the Ku Klux Klan.[55]

Du Bois remarks at length on the special role that the intellectual has played in promoting the cause of racism in America. Thus, the Southern planter's "pseudo-scientists gather and supplemented all available doctrines of race inferiority; his scattered schools and pedantic periodicals repeated these legends until for the average planter born after 1840 it was impossible not to believe that all valid laws of psychology, economics, and politics stopped with the Negro race…Thus a basis in reason, philanthropy and science was built up for Negro slavery. Judges on the bench declared that Negro servitude was to last"[56] And while noting some exceptions, he affirms "that there is scarcely a bishop in Christendom, a priest in the church, a president, governor, mayor, or legislator in the United States, *a college professor or public school teacher*…who does not in the end stand by War or Ignorance as the main method for the settlement of our pressing human problems. And this despite the fact that they may deny it with their mouths everyday." [57] [emphasis added]

These concerns were later to be corroborated by Myrdal in his classic work in the context of what he calls "intellectual defeatism" and the "convenience of ignorance" evinced by the American intellectual.[58] More specifically, "white people had for their defense a consistent and respectable theory, endorsed by the church and by all sciences, printed in learned books and periodicals, and expounded by the…greatest statesmen in the Capital at Washington. The

Negro's subordinate status was a principle integrated into a whole philosophy of society and of human life."[59]

The issues being addressed here need not be viewed as isolated incidents punctuating the otherwise progressive and smooth pace of contemporary civilization. The intellectual can be regarded as the harbinger or torch-bearer of Western civilization whose role has been primarily one of providing and sustaining the ideological roots of racism. This traditional role of the intellectual *qua* legitimator of the social policies and practices goes back to Aristotle's dictum: "Some men are born to serve and some to rule."[60] There then dawned the age of chauvinistic social Darwinism, whose foremost representative was Herbert Spencer,[61] with William Graham Sumner following on his heels.[62] Regarding the social Darwinism of the latter, Myrdal has succinctly remarked: "The unification of the two streams in Sumner's thinking gives us an example of the fallacious attempt to draw practical conclusions from purely factual premises."[63] Sumner, it must be noted, was not just a crank. He was a respectable professor at one of America's most prestigious institutions, Yale, where, in the words of Myrdal, "he continued to indoctrinate generations of Yale undergraduates with the economic doctrines of Manchester-liberalism."[64]

The enormous disservice that the intellectual renders to society at large, with regard to the perpetration, propagation, and perpetuation of racism and racialism, has been underlined by Ryan in his intimation that these ideological monstrosities are not the work of naive, rascally, racist monsters. On the contrary, the ideological basis of racism derives "directly from the lectures and books of leading intellectual figures of the time, occupants of professorial chairs at Harvard and Yale. Such is the power of an ideology that so neatly fits the needs of the dominant interests of society."[65] In this context, it should be recalled that the immigration quota legislation adopted by the U.S. government early in the present century was based on the blatant bigotry and dubious formulations of the intellectual *qua* knowledgeable social scientist. The intellectual breed addressed by Myrdal and other observers has not completely disappeared from academe even today.

Racism and the Modern Intellectual

In the past the intellectual race-monger had practiced his craft rather blatantly and with unabashed audacity, protected and secure in the insulation of his academic sanctuary, yet waxing strong in the respectability attendant upon his connection with the university. Today he continues to be as committed as ever to his racist philosophy. With unabated diligence, although in a more subtle and rather insidious fashion, he continues to pontificate from his professorial chair in the major colleges, universities, and other institutions of higher learning. His insidious trappings continue to guide official policies in the guise of "objective science" and "value-free" scholarship. Thus, his racist doctrines, cloaked in ponderous and confounding formulations and couched in insidious language, continue to be disseminated in lectures forced down the intellectual throat of the student, and set the tone for the academic community at large, through publications and in learned journals; and his intellectually introverted views and dicta continue to be foisted on the general public *qua* "expert opinions." His intellectual pretensions continue to inspire awe among the naive and respectability among those unacquainted with his crafty art of dissimulation.

The modern intellectual race-monger comes fully garbed in the cloak of academic respectability in the Jensens and Eysencks, parodying the social-experimental crudities of the pseudo-science of a by-gone era.[66] He may even wear the badge of a Nobel-laureate-physicist-turned-racial-crusader, as in the Shockleys. In whatever guise he comes, this intellectual breed is a real "true-believer" in his "scientific proof" of the differences in "intelligence" as the "natural" cause of racial inequality, frequently vaunting his challenge for "experimental evidence" against his "scientific proof" of inherent inferiority of the Black "race." But germane to this issue of "scientific" validation or refutation is the argument advanced by Rex, who reasons thus:

> Fortunately, neither he [the intellectual race-monger, that is] nor his opponents are able to undertake such experiments. Since, however, the crucial variable is the difference between white and negro history and the fact that negro history involves the fact of slavery, experiment would mean subjecting the group of negroes to white experience over several hundred years or subjecting a group of whites to negro experience. The empirical study which holds constant size of income, type of neighborhood and length of schooling in the United States of the present day, therefore, should in theory be supplemented by an experiment in which the peoples of Africa conquer, capture and enslave some millions of Europeans and American whites under conditions in which a very large proportion of the white population dies, in which the white culture is systematically destroyed, and in which, finally, a group of emancipated whites living in "good neighbourhoods" are then compared to their negro masters.[67]

While this view requires no further elaboration, it must be pointed out that the intellectual posture taken by Rex underscores van den Berghe's insistence that race-relations studies be undertaken historically, holistically, comparatively, and with little or not pretensions to "scientific objectivity."[68]

But the trappings of a modern intellectual racemonger can also assume a more subtle and insidious—and therefore more dangerous—character, often difficult to detect by the audience untrained in, and unacquainted with, the technique of his craft. This is the type that has prompted the castigation of American social science by the British sociologist Stanislav Andreski.[69] Although the writer has remarked elsewhere[70] on a particular aspect of this issue, it calls for further elaboration.

It is in his approach to the issue of interracial marriage and interracial sexuality that the modern intellectual *qua* social scientist perhaps betrays his role as a purveyor of insidious racism. The argument that follows is based on a critical examination of a sample of the intellectual trappings of one of the doyens of American sociology, Robert K. Merton.

In an article originally published in *Psychiatry* in 1941, Merton had advanced a "structural" thesis to account for the incidence of Black-white intermarriage and sexuality, generally. In a preamble, it states that every marriage is, literally speaking, intermarriage, because it involves individuals "deriving from different social groups of one sort or another." More specifically, it is conceived as "marriage of persons deriving from those different in-groups and out-groups other than the families which are culturally conceived as relevant to the choice of a spouse."[71] Proceeding on the premise of the metaphysical transformation of Black and white populations into lower and upper "castes," Merton argues: "we may entertain the hypothesis that *hypogamy is understandable in terms of the social structure.*" And what is hypogamy? "We may introduce the term hypogamy to denote the pattern wherein the female marries into a lower social stratum." And, as an example of "hypogamy" Merton suggests: "*marriage between white females and Negro males.*"[72] [emphasis added] He goes on to explain that: "most illicit miscegenation involves negro women and white men...Intercaste sex relations largely involves upper-caste males and lower-caste females." More germane to the issue is the further elaboration that:

> Marriage between an upper-class white female and an upper-class Negro male, when it occurs, will not involve mutual compensation with respect to socio-economic position...[and] the relation is asymmetrical in as much as *the Negro male does not compensate for the upper-caste status of his wife...*[But] we should expect the pairing of a lower-class white woman and an upper-class Negro man to occur most frequently, for it involves a reciprocal compensatory situation in which the Negro male *"exchanges" his higher economic position for the white female's higher caste status.*[73] [emphasis added]

Divested of all its "structural" scaffoldings and rendered in a very simple and ordinary language, all this intellectual rigmarole amounts to saying that, since whites are *ipso facto racial superiors* of Blacks, marriage between both parties occurs only when the party from the inferior caste—the Black partner, that is—has something to offer to the equivalence of, or in exchange for, the *racial superiority* of the former.

But how does one account for the seeming reluctance of white males, relatively speaking, to marry Black females, notwithstanding the fact that "most intercaste sex relations—not marriages—are between white men and Negro women"? Again, the answer is "structure." Thus, Merton elaborates:

Once again, *sex roles and caste-and-class structure would appear to account for the facts.* Given the dominance of the white male with his relative immunity from active retaliation by *the lower-caste male*, there is no pressure to legitimate his liaison by marriage. *Concubinage and transient sex relations are less damaging to his status*, since these may be more easily kept secret and, even if discovered, *are less subject to violent condemnation by fellow caste members*, since they do not imply equality of the sex partners.[74] [emphasis added]

But it must be pointed out that underneath this structural-intellectual mystification lurks an implicit—if not explicit—racist doctrine because it assumes Black "racial inferiority" and white "racial superiority." For otherwise, what is the point of these metaphysical perambulations regarding the "Negro's lower-caste," and the "white female's upper-caste class" exchanges? In point of fact, this intellectual metaphysics is not far removed from the less sophisticated—if naive, but more blunt—crudities of the rabid racist on the street, who would assert that only "poor white-trash" women would intimately mingle with "niggers," much less marry them.

Needless to say, since this thesis was pontificated by Merton, it has been accepted almost as an article of faith by a host of intellectual disciples and myrmidons; succeeding generations of sociologists have taken it as a given.[75]

It must be emphasized that Merton's theory of reciprocal caste-class exchange was not based on any empirical facts. For, if one proceeds within the framework of Weber's method of *verstehen* and comprehends social action from the standpoint of the meaning which the actor assigns to his action, and insofar as he attributes meaning to his action, the crucial variable here, it would seem, is the reason which the spouse gives for marrying his/her interracial partner. Thus, contrary to the implications of the Mertonian "structural" metaphysics, if it is asked why a white woman marries a Black man, the obvious answer, must be for the same reason that she would marry a white man. *Mutatis mutandis*, the same goes for the Black man opting for a white female spouse.

Why does the white man indulge in the sexual exploits of the Black woman, but shy away from accepting the latter as his conjugal partner? Since the realm of speculative intellection is not the exclusive preserve of any one person, the writer would venture the suggestion that the white man is still seriously burdened with ethnocentrism while his female counterpart, the white woman, is not.

Contemporary Social Issues and the Intellectual

In the rather checkered history of the protracted struggle for civil rights by the various minorities of American society, notably Blacks, one often wonders what contributions the intellectual—the white intellectual, that is—has made towards the promotion of that cause. Any true lover of liberty must, of course, pay proper tribute to the genuine and honest commitment of intellectual statesmanship best typified by the indomitable Charles Sumner, whose pronouncement Du Bois has very appropriately characterized as "a *Magna Charta* of democracy in America."[76] But it is also the case that the intellectual of a different description has traditionally impeded the progress of interracial harmony and promoted the cause of racism and racialism.

It was in the dictum of the intellectual that the "inherent racial inferiority" of the Black man was proclaimed, and his humanity denied, when the nation's highest jurors ruled in the notorious *Dred Scott* case, as well as in the nullification of the 1875 Civil Rights Bill.[77] It was also the intellectual who led the hue and cry almost a century later against the 1954 Supreme Court School desegregation ruling, when the jurors reversed the opinion of their 19th century predecessor. More specifically, it was a Yale-educated circuit judge who had denounced the opinion of his senior colleagues in the Supreme Court in a most crude and base language. Thus, declared Tom Brady in his *Black Monday*:

> The decision which you handed down on Black Monday has arrested and retarded the economic and political and, yes, the social status of the Negro in the South for at least one hundred years…When a law transgresses the moral and ethical sanctions and standards of the mores, invariably strife, bloodshed and revolution follow in the wake of its attempted enforcement.[78]

Incidentally, it is on the issue of race relations in public schools, specifically school desegregation, that the insidious disservice of the modern intellectual becomes very evident. Outright intolerance for, and revulsion against, the mixing of Black and white school children has been variously expressed and articulated in bland euphemisms of "quality education," "neighborhood schools," and "community school control."

Thus, proceeding from the "sociological insight" through a rather dubious "spirit of scientific neutrality," Professor Milton M. Gordon defines the government's role to effect desegregation;[79] but, paradoxically, the same government is denied both the responsibility and the prerogative of either "imposing" integration or "racial criteria positively in order to (enforce) desegregation upon public facilities in an institutional area where such segregation is not a function of racial discrimination directly but results from discrimination operating in another institutional area, or from other causes." These metaphysical distinctions of different "institutional areas," on the one hand, and of "integration" and "desegregation," on the other, call to mind such similar trappings and metaphysics of "structure," "caste," and "class" as have already been considered under intermarriage.

In any case, Gordon proceeds with his intellectual acrobatics. Thus, in an apparent "spirit of scientific neutrality," no doubt, he concludes:

> The attempt by well-meaning "race liberals" in a number of northern communities to desegregate public schools by overturning *the principle of* neighborhood *assignment*—that is, to positively promote Negro-white intermix-

ture by means of racial assignment across neighborhood lines—is, in my opinion, misguided. *It is misguided because it does exactly what is in principle wrong, regardless* of how laudable the goal. It puts the government in the business of using race as a criterion for operating one of its facilities.[80] [emphasis added]

Proceeding on the same "spirit of scientific neutrality," he sees a fundamental inequity in the government's stipulation of quotas in the hiring and promotion guidelines and regulations. More specifically:

> It goes without saying that job hiring and promotion at all levels should be made on the basis of individual merit, not racial quotas, however benignly the latter may be motivated. Present wrongs do not solve the problems created by past injustices and only assure that the underlying social evil will further plague the future. We do not want "see-saw discrimination" in American life; we want the dismantling of the discrimination apparatus.[81]

A Touch of Irony

One senses a certain touch of irony in the typing and apparent denunciation of "race liberals" by an "objective," "detached" intellectual committed to the principle of "scientific neutrality," on the one hand, and defending with the fervor of a true believer, "the principle of neighborhood assignment," on the other. Professor Gordon considers himself a "race realist." Consequently, one must ask: Has it ever occurred to your intellectual realist to question the "scientifically neutral" criterion or criteria upon which the institution of those "neighborhood lines" were based in the first place? Have the Professor Gordons *qua* intellectuals and "racial realists" ever wondered about the inconsistency in permitting the flow of Black and white dollars across "neighborhood lines," on the one hand, and upholding "the principle of neighborhood assignment" of Black and white children to their respective racially exclusive and segregated school facilities, on the other? Where were the Gordons—the "race realists," the self-styled guardians of "the spirit of scientific neutrality"—when the much-talked-about "forced-busing" was officially sanctioned in order to keep Black school children out of segregated white schools, and to effect complete solidification and consolidation of segregated neighborhoods?

Professor Gordon claims that it is not the responsibility of the government to "impose integration." Granted. But the "race realist" conveniently forgets that it was the same and very government that conveniently connived at, if not actively encouraged and imposed, segregation and discrimination, which, Professor Gordon must admit, "created past injustices."

Professor Gordon also decries the principle of "quota" assignment in the government's employment guidelines as fundamentally "wrong," maintaining that hiring and promotion should be based on the consideration of "individual merit." However, could Professor Gordon, on the basis of his "scientific neutrality," determine that the hiring and promotion practices, which have systematically and traditionally excluded and victimized the racial minorities, have been based solely on the consideration of the "individual merit" of the whites who have constituted the primary beneficiaries from these practices?

It is simply naive and rather simplistic to pontificate that present wrongs do not right past injustices. The crucial question is, Professor Gordon should be reminded, how does one compensate for these past injustices; how does one correct for the imbalance that has already been created from past wrongs. The problem does not find resolution in the simple assurance of "equal opportunity" for all; rather the crucial question should be how to mitigate the inequality that already exists between the "races." The Gordons, the "race realists," would like to see "the dismantling of the discrimination apparatus," but they do not tell us how, specifically, they will proceed to accomplish this task without the necessity of "imposing integration." They do not want "see-saw discrimination in American life"; yet they offer no program for dealing with the existing inequity and discrimination, and for equilibrating the current tilt of racial inequality.

What one is witnessing here is a case of a racist doctrine presented with a rather colorful facade of academic respectability. Thus, when one completely divests it of the elaborate trappings, intellectual scaffoldings, and structural metaphysics, what stands out is insidious racism. It is in this respect that the modern intellectual *qua* a "neutral," "objective," and "detached" "scientist," or "expert," renders a great disservice to society. Consequently, one must impute to the intellectual the fundamental responsibility for cultivating, nurturing, fostering, and perpetuating the evil of racism in human society.

Notes

1. Gunnar Myrdal, *An American Dilemma: The Negro Problem and Modern Democracy* (New York and London: Harper and Brothers, 1944), 807.
2. W.E.B. Du Bois, *The Souls of Black Folk* (Greenwich, Connecticut: Fawcett, 1961), 41.
3. Quoted in Gunnar Myrdal, op. cit., 797.
4. See, G. Spiller (ed.), *Inter-Racial Problems: The Complete Papers of the First Universal Races Congress, London, 1911* (New York: Citadel Press, 1970).
5. Robert K. Merton, *Social Theory and Social Structure* (New York: Free Press, 1908), 261–278.
6. Ibid., 263.
7. Ibid., 263–264.
8. Ralph J. Bunche, *A World View of Race* (Washington and New York: Kennikat Press, 1968), 4.
9. Ashley Montagu, *Man's Most Dangerous Myth: The Fallacy of Race* (New York and London: Oxford University Press, 1974), 33, 54.
10. Quoted in Philip S. Foner (ed.), *W.E.B. Du Bois Speaks*, Vol. I (New York: Pathfinder Press, 1970), 74.
11. Ibid., 75–76.
12. George K. Hesslink, *Black Neighbors: Negroes in a Northern Rural Community* (Indianapolis: Bobbs-Merrill, 1974), 214n.
13. Ashley Montagu, op. cit., 68, 74–83.
14. Charles H. Fairbanks, and Hale A. Smith, "Anthropology and the Segregation Problem," in James Preu (ed.), *The Negro in American Society* (Tampa, Florida: Florida Grower Press, 1958), 1–3.

15. James P. Comer, "White Racism: Its Roots, Form and Function," in Charles W. Thomas (ed.), *Boys No More* (Beverly Hills, California: Glencoe Press, 1971), 9, et seq.
16. See, for instance: (1) Lerone Bennett, *Before the Mayflower: A History of the Negro in America, 1619–1964* (Baltimore, Maryland: Penguin Books, 1966), 221, 242, et seq.; (2) Charles H. Fairbanks and Hale A. Smith, op. cit., 13, et seq.; (3) George K. Hesslink, op. cit., 127, et seq.; (4) Winthrop D. Jordan, *The White Man's Burden: Historical Origins of Racism in the United States* (New York: Oxford University Press, 1974), 202, et seq.; (5) Gunnar Myrdal, op. cit., passim; (6) Chukwuemeka Onwuba, "Sexuality in American Race Relations," in *Umoja: Southwestern Afro-American Journal*, Vol. 1, No. 1, Spring 1973, 17–24; (7) Robert Staples (ed.), *The Black Family: Essays on Studies* (Belmont, California: Wadsworth, 1971), 119–122, 149–159; (8) Robert Staples, *The Black Woman in America* (Chicago: Nelson-Hall, 1973), 172, et seq.; (9) Joseph R. Washington, Jr., *Marriage in Black and White* (Boston: Beacon Press, 1970).
17. See, for instance: (1) John Rex, "The Concept of Race in Sociological Theory," in Sami Zubaida (ed.), *Race and Racialism* (London: Travistock, 1970), 35–36; (2) John Rex, *Race Relations in Sociological Theory* (London: Weidenfeld and Nicolson, 1970), 2–5.
18. See, for instance: (1) Paul Bohannan, and Philip Curtin, *Africa and Africans* (Garden City, New York: Natural History Press, 1971), 35–55; (2) Ashley Montagu, op. cit.; (3) John Rex (1970), op. cit.; (4) John Rex, *Race, Colonialism and the City* (London and Boston: Routledge and Kegan Paul, 1973); (5) Pierre L. van den Berghe, *Race and Racism, A Comparative Perspective* (New York, London, and Sydney: John Wiley and Sons, 1967); (6) Pierre L. van den Berghe, *Race and Ethnicity: Essays in Comparative Sociology* (New York and London: Basic Books, 1970).
19. Paul Bohannan and Philip Curtin, op. cit., 35, et seq.
20. Ibid., 9, et seq.
21. Ashley Montagu, op. cit., 53.
22. Ibid., 136, 402.
23. Ibid., 115–116, 119–120, 177.
24. Michael Banton, "The Concept of Racism," in Sami Zubaida (ed.), op. cit., 8.
25. Ibid., 19.
26. Ibid., 18.
27. John Rex (1973), op. cit., 75.
28. Ibid., 191.
29. Ibid., 221.
30. John Rex (1970), op. cit., 39–40; ibid., 203, et seq.
31. Ibid., 191–192.
32. Pierre L. van den Berghe (1965, 1967, 1970), op. cit.
33. Pierre L. van den Berghe (1967), op. cit., 21, 148.
34. Ibid., 11.
35. bid., 9, 132; (1970), 10.
36. Ibid., 11, 38n.
37. Ibid., (1970), op. cit., 75.
38. John Rex (1973*)*, op. cit., 75.
39. Pierre L. van den Berghe (1970), op. cit., 73.
40. Pierre L. van den Berghe (1967), op. cit., 6.
41. John Rex (1973), op. cit., 177.
42. Ibid., 21, et seq.; van den Berghe (1967), op. cit., 148–149; van den Berghe (1970), op. cit., 11–13, 167–169.
43. Ralph J. Bunche, op. cit., 25.
44. Michael Banton, op. cit., 25.
45. Ibid., 22.
46. Michael D. Biddis, "Gobineau and the Origins of European Racism," *Race*, Vol. 8, No. 3, January 1966, 255–270.
47. Paul Bohannan, and Philip Curtin, op. cit., 40, et seq., 47, et seq., 51.
48. Ibid., 52.
49. Ali A. Mazrui, "The Patriot as an Artist," in G. D. Killam (ed.), *African Writers on African Writing* (Evanston, Illinois: Northwestern University Press, 1973), 74.
50. G. W. F. Hegel, *The Philosophy of History* (New York: Wiley, 1944), 91, 93, 99.

51. Ashley Montagu, op. cit., 13, et seq., passim.
52. Ibid., 39.
53. W.E.B. Du Bois, *Black Reconstruction* (New York: Harcourt, Brace, 1935), passim.
54. Ibid., 381.
55. Susan Lawrence Davis, *Authentic History: Ku Klux Klan, 1865–1877* (New York: American Library Service, 1924).
56. W.E.B. Du Bois (1935), op. cit., 39.
57. Ibid., 678.
58. Gunnar Myrdal, op. cit., 19, et seq., 40, et seq.
59. Ibid., 1002.
60. Ralph J. Bunche, op. cit., 2.
61. Ibid., 5.
62. William Ryan, *Blaming the Victim* (New York: Random House/Vintage, 1971), 20, et seq.
63. Gunnar Myrdal, op. cit., 1048.
64. Ibid.
65. William Ryan, op. cit., 21.
66. John Rex (1973), op. cit., 321, et seq.
67. Ibid., 233.
68. Pierre L. van den Berghe (1967), op. cit., 48–49; (1970), op. cit., 11–13.
69. Stanislaw Andreski, *Social Science as Sorcery* (London: Andre Deutsch, 1972).
70. Chukwuemeka Onwubu, op. cit. See also, my review of Lucile Duberman's "Marriage and Its Alternatives," in the *Journal of Marriage and the Family*, Vol. 37, No. 3, August 1975, 692–695.
71. Robert K. Merton, "Intermarriage and the Social Structure: Fact and Theory," in William J. Goode (ed.), *Readings on the Family and Society* (Englewood Cliffs, New Jersey: Prentice-Hall, 1964), 57 [originally published in *Psychiatry*, August 1941, 361–54, 370–72].
72. Ibid., 59.
73. Ibid., 60, 61.
74. Ibid., 63.
75. See, for instance: (1) Jessie Bernard, "Note on Educational Homogamy in Negro-White Marriage, 1960," *Journal of Marriage and the Family*, Vol. 28, No. 3, August 1966, 274–276; (2) Lucile Duberman, *Marriage and Its Alternatives* (New York and Washington: Praeger, 1974), 86; (3) David M. Heer, "The Prevalence of Black-White Marriage in the United States, 1960," *Journal of Marriage and the Family*, Vol. 36, No. 2, May 1974, 246–258; (4) Pierre L. van den Berghe (1970), op. cit., 54, et seq.
76. W.E.B. Du Bois (1935), op. cit., 193, et seq.
77. Lerone Bennett, Jr., op. cit., 125–126, 158.
78. Ibid., 312.
79. Milton M. Gordon, *Assimilation in American Life* (New York: Oxford University Press, 1964), 246, et seq.
80. Ibid., 249–250.
81. Ibid., 251.

7

The Ideology of European Dominance

Dona Richards

Dona Richards *is a former Field Organizer for the Student Non-Violent Coordinating Committee (SNCC), Director of the Tougaloo Work-Study Project, and a worker in the Freedom Registration Campaign in Mississippi during the 1960s. Currently, she is Assistant Professor in the Department of Black and Puerto Rican Studies at Hunter College of the City University of New York. She holds the Ph.D. in Anthropology from the New School for Social Research.*—The Western Journal of Black Studies, *Winter 1979, Vol. 3, No. 4*

Introduction

This article is intended as an admonishment against the uncritical use of social scientific theory as it is presented in academic training. The writer will look critically at Western European social thought in terms of the values and judgments which are implied therein, especially as it relates to Africans and their heritage. This writer argues, as others have done, that because of the intimate connection between the Western European world view and Western European social theory, it is either irrelevant or, as in most instances, dangerous to people of African descent. It is obvious that science is not pristine and that scientists do not exist in a vacuum. Black social theorists presumably have no use for the myth of objectivity, a myth that has served the interest of Western European political objectives. Contrary to the propaganda of academia, white social theory does not represent a universally valid and "objective" body of thought, nor a neutral tool to be used for the purpose of understanding human experience. It might be argued, instead, that it represents a particular view of the world as seen from the perspective of supposed Western European superiority, and that an image of the inferiority of African civilization is inherent in the terms, definitions, and theoretical models on which white social theory is based.

This paper will present certain key aspects of the intellectual and emotional roots of Western European social thought generally, and the genesis of anthropological theory in particular. Anthropology will emerge, not as a "science of man," but as a particular manifestation of Western European culture. The fact that these particular culturally based, theoretical models have been presented and imposed as universals is a fact of serious political consequence.

Ideology and World View

It is possible to isolate certain seminal ideas that have served as organizing principles in Western scientific thought. These ideas emerge as a series of interrelated themes, sometimes hidden, at other periods more visible. Though an attempt will be made to single them out, they are not usually distinguishable as separate and distinct ideas, but together they help to determine the contours of the Western European world view.

These themes are intimately related to the Western European attitude towards other peoples and imply a particular relationship to them, which will subsequently be referred to as "ethos." This term is used to indicate the emotional tone of a culture, the uniqueness of its people. It refers to their collective ego, which enables them to behave as they do and, indeed, explains that behavior. The Western European ethos appears to thrive on the perception that those who are culturally and radically different are inferior. It relates to other cultures as superior or inferior, as powerful or weak, as "civilized" or "primitive." The European world view reflects these relationships.

This analysis can begin with the "Great Chain of Being" idea. Some scholars trace its origins all the way to Plato, as most Western intellectual constructs are variations of the themes stated in Platonic theory. Although the idea has been expressed in many different ways, from Classical Greece to the present, it can be characterized as being consistently monolithic without sacrificing accuracy. It is a conception of the universe, which holds that all beings relate as part of a hierarchy, their value increasing as they reach the top. Differences of kind imply differences of value. For Aristotle the hierarchy was based on the "powers of the soul," and each Being or organism possessed its own power in addition to those "beneath" it. For the Scholastics the most natural organisms were in the bottom ranks of the hierarchy, God and the angels held the top positions, respectively, while man had a key position being both "nature" and "spirit." Two essential ingredients presupposed in this idea were that there was an ultimate reason or rational explanation for everything that existed in the world, and that everything, every phenomenon had a place in which it existed in sequential relationship to all others.[1] The lineal relationships developing here form a very crucial aspect of Western thought and help to put things in a perspective necessary for the satisfaction of the Western self-image.

The writer is concerned with the ideological and cultural implications of these philosophical conceptions. First of all, "man" becomes number one in this chain since, practically speaking, God and the angels are not really in the picture.

The "power" of man's soul endows him with rational abilities and this gives him control and superiority over the "lesser" beings. One does not have to speculate as to what occurs when the factors of race and culture of mankind are added to this picture. In the Western European ethos, the ranks do not skip from "higher" animals to man, instead finer gradations are discernible, with white men at the top and Black men almost always coming barely above the higher animals. (According to some theorists they did not make it that high.) The Great Chain of Being concept has had a tremendous influence on the theoretical models of Western European scientific thought. What is implied about the African heritage in this conception? How can it be used other than to distort and denigrate African civilization? But, then, its purpose is to express the Western European ethos—not the African ethos. It presents the white man with a view of the world in which he is ranked highest in a hierarchy of beings with other peoples perceived as inferiors to him.

Two other seminal ideas are even more closely related; that of unilinear, or universal, evolution and the "Idea of Progress." During what Europeans have called their Renaissance, the Chain of Being idea was expressed in a new form. With God and the angels apparently diminished in significance, "man," *white European man*, is placed solidly in a dominant position. Subsequently, the idea of progress came to the fore. From Biblical eschatology came the idea of a meaningful historical process, but the Western European ethos could not express itself comfortably within a religious conceptualization. It needed the "freedom" of a secularized view of history, one which said that there were no holds barred and openly stated the ascendancy of man. In a rapidly expanding industrial society, for a culture whose imperial drive was meeting with success after success, this concept fitted perfectly. It said that man, "white men," were advancing in the right, the *only* direction. What allowed European whites to do this above all was their ability to rationalize the universe, to apply the principles of "science." Since this progressive movement was a good in itself, as Francis Bacon had helped them to see, science was indeed above moral scrutiny. Progress was a new morality. It encompassed a mood of arrogance, superiority, power, and, most certainly, expansion. The idea of progress is essentially expansionistic, incorporating all that has past, gathering it up and carrying it towards an infinite and undefined future. "Progress" will never end, it will continue indefinitely, and what continues indefinitely means the growth of empire and the mechanization of society. The idea was embraced at the same time the Protestant Reformation was making way for the triumph of capitalism in the West. In terms of the Western European ethos, it was the perfect ideological mode for the acquisitive instinct, expansionism, the white man's burden, and the exploitative imperial quest: the conquering mentality.[2]

For the philosophers of the "Enlightenment," *progress* was the blessed unfolding and unleashing of man's capacities for reason and goodness. The Encyclopedists of the 18th century struggled to formulate "inevitable" laws of a "universal history" into which all human experience could be fit, thereby making it intelligible. It was out of this effort that the peculiarly Western European concept of culture was born: universalistic, elitist, and chauvinistic. Given their political relationship to the rest of the world, these Europeans were precisely the wrong people to formulate the so-called universal laws of human nature or to construct a universal science of man. The concept of a "common humanity" became a tool that was used to impose Western European ideology on the world rather than a vehicle for the recognition of and therefore validity of other cultural experiences.

And so the stage was set for the dominant evolutionary theories of the 19th century. Spencer and Comte state that if one accepts the fact that progressive historical movement is that which propels humans through time, then it becomes logical that society must have progressed through stages which relate to each other in a lineal sequence of the less to the more progressive. Society can be understood as having progressed through certain evolutionary stages, representing increasing stages of enlightenment, rationality, propriety, mechanization, and so forth. The point of reference was always European society, which represented the most evolutionarily advanced stage at any given point. The next predictable addition to this picture is that *again*—at any given point—the other cultures and societies of the world are fitted within the evolutionary scale to relate lineally to the most evolved society. In this way evolution becomes universal and unilinear. Humanity is moving through the same stages *in the same sequence*. Human beings are all therefore judged by the same ideology, since this is after all an ideological and not merely a theoretical construct. The result is a more up-dated version of the Great Chain of Being.

Taken together these ideas present a view of the world in which Western European man becomes the "most progressive" and therefore "superior." He relates, then, to others who represent varying degrees of inferiority. Quite properly he "teaches," "controls," "orders," and "exploits" them. Since the European white man knows best, his blessings he confers through slavery, colonialism, expansionistic imperialism, and neocolonialism. Thus, Africa becomes a victim of exploitation. Africans are made to believe that their victimization is *just*, since the African heritage is "backward," "primitive," and "underdeveloped." Africans become victims of an imposed world view.

These theories are not really totally distinct models or concepts, but threads of one ideological construct. They have in common the fact that they all help to create a spectrum, or scale, that judges or rates races and cultures—the Western European always being that model which is most valued according to the logic of these schemes, and those cultures which are most different from white Western Europe being lowest in value.

Africanists are obligated to make it clear to social theorists that all of these ideas mentioned above are but theoretical models, not "proven" truths, but tacitly accepted presuppositions, which form the white Western European frame of reference. These are their givens, not argued for, but assumed. There is no reason for African peoples to assume a view of the world that places them hopelessly in a position of inferiority and justifies their powerlessness. Yet as Africans have inherited these forms of thought from the European, they have tended to accept them as givens, not realizing their inherent implications.

The Uses of Anthropology

It is now necessary to turn to the subject of anthropology to see how it relates specifically to the foregoing discussion. The writer will consider anthropology only in its history as an academic discipline, but it must be understood that this endeavor reaches back to the beginnings of the Western consciousness. Anthropology might indeed be born out of the Western European consciousness, and it is always projected when European people study "the strange," "the exotic," or that which is different from and therefore considered less than Western culture.

As a recognized theoretical endeavor, anthropology grows out of the Spencerian-Comtian milieu. This mental environment was itself a manifestation of the Western European ethos, which reached its heightened and matured expression in the 19th century, and it must be understood as part of a continuum traceable from Classical Greece to contemporary American society. The Western European ethos and consciousness seeks expression in the theory of white racial and cultural superiority and is manifested in the political control and economic exploitation of peoples who are not of this race or culture. The discipline and activity of anthropology has, therefore, a particular relationship to the projected image and behavior toward and treatment of civilizations, cultures, and people who are not white and who are not Western European.

It was the Western European ethos that created "the savage," then explained his existence by giving the Chain of Being a historical dimension, so that in terms of world view African peoples were placed spatially and temporally in relationship to whites in a scheme which explained *their* superiority. The task of anthropological theory was to explain cultures as part of a series of sequence of evolutionary events, in genetic relationship, in a hierarchical structure. The fact that social phenomena are all thought to be explainable in terms of these principles of order is a legacy from Plato via Scholasticism and Neo-Platonism.[3]

It is this realm which Lewis Henry Morgan and Edward Wilmot Tylor entered in the late 1800s. The way had been paved for them through the combined efforts of a tradition of undeclared physical anthropology and social evolutionism. The outlines of subsequent anthropological theory had already been drawn. Writing in 1803, Saint-Simon, architect of a nascent sociology and socio-technical order, said that "the Negro, because of his basic physical structure, is not susceptible of rising to the intellectual level of Europeans."[4] In his efforts to unify Europe he argued that:

The surest means of maintaining peace in the confederation will be to keep it constantly occupied beyond its own borders, and engaged without pause in great internal enterprise. To colonize the world with the European race, superior to every other human race; to make the world accessible and habitable like Europe, such is the sort of enterprise by which the European parliament should continually keep Europe active and healthy.[5]

For all European social theorists of the 18th and 19th centuries, "civilization" was the reserve of whites, and the "problem of race" simply meant to them the theoretical problem of how different races came to be and how they were evolutionarily related to one another. The monogenists with their heavy Biblical loyalties said that white Adam and Eve were the parents of all people, and that other races represented degeneration from the original stock. The polygenists argued that God created other "species" of man besides Adam. This view hinted at as early as the 17th century continually gained ground and flourished in the mid-19th century. The proponents of polygenism said that differences could not be accounted for by environment, and that, indeed, the differences were so great that races constituted separate species. Polygenism was the prevailing opinion of physical anthropologists in the mid-19th century, and, in the late 19th century, racial craniology was the order of the day. The structure of the crania was said to determine racial achievement, and there was much measuring of brain size to predict mental capacity. The French anthropologist Gratiolet in 1856 said that Black inferiority was due to the fact that cranial sutures of Africans closed earlier than whites.[6] These ideas dominated the American School of Physical Anthropology of the 19th century.

Herbert Spencer mapped out the stages through which society evolved; again it had to be the white man who happily was the agent of its evolution, and *all* men did not reach the top of the evolutionary scale, since mental capacities were determined by race and the "savage" peoples lacked abstract ideas. It was all right that certain groups (the Tasmanians, for instance) had become extinct since this was a law of evolution.[7]

It is easy to piece together the threads and trends of white racialist thought that was to become sociology and anthropology. Civilization was progressing. It was moving not only through time, but it was advancing rationally. It was getting "better." It was the culture of the whites of Western Europe that always advanced it. Why? Because they were physically constructed so that they could *think* better. Brain differences accounted for cultural differences. Culture must be analyzed in conjunction with anatomical and physiological differences. All of this would help the European to determine the universal laws of progress in human civilization. It is not incidental that such reasoning resulted in a scientific hierarchy of "superior" and "inferior" races. It is the Western ethos that turns human diversity into "raciology."

What one often fails to understand is that the "racial" and the "cultural" are not really two isolated aspects of human experience in the white man's mind; they are not two separate methods of explaining and comparing human differences. To the contrary, race is *both* physical and cultural, and when raciology ceased to be heavily physical in nature, if it ever really did, it did not cease to *be*. The sociocultural component of the ideology went hand-in-hand with its physical aspect.

By the time Edward Tylor, the "Founder" of anthropology, began to write, it was easy to speak of "lower" and "higher" races in scientific discourse. His dichotomy is between "savage man" and "cultured man." Differences in cultures are due, not to different tastes, values, or commitments, but to different evolutionary stages. There are no "cultures"; therefore, there are only *stages* of culture (in the singular). This implication and this image of non- European cultures did not die with the 19th century, but persists now. There is still a tendency to compare peoples at "stages" of development, in spite of the fact that these "stages" are manufactured and exist only in the mind.

For Tyler, the "lower races" were "the same from Dahomey to Hawaii."[8] They were at the same evolutionary stage of culture. The value of studying them was to show European man what his prehistoric ancestors must have been like. Such analogy or comparison is unfounded, but again it supports the Western ethos. This is, in fact, recounting the construction of a culturalist and racialist mythology, with each aspect supporting and reinforcing the other, so as to build a systematic scheme expressing the tenets of white, Western European ideology. This objective is that which gave birth to Western anthropology—to lay the strongest scientific basis possible to the mythological system—to provide the theories ("and facts") that demonstrated white, Western European physical and cultural superiority. In this tradition, "science" itself becomes "myth."

Symptomatic of the disciplines of Western social science is the penchant for erecting schemes that other cultures can be "fit" into. This, of course, helps to satisfy the urge to power and the need to control. The unilineal evolutionary scale did—intellectually, academically, in scientific terms—what Europe was doing politically in the 19th century—expanding borders of control and seeking new methods of exerting ever-greater power over conquered peoples.

As a Victorian evolutionist, Tylor's mission was ostensibly to discover the successive stages of the human intellect. Primitive culture represented man at a crude intellectual level, with an underdeveloped brain. Civilized man could think better and use his brain more efficiently. The superior intellect of the progressive races had raised nations to heights of culture. It is partly a misunderstanding, partly an over-simplification, to say that Charles Darwin influenced the social sciences, or, as the apologia usually goes: "They took his theories and misapplied them—in ways that he did not intend." The relationship is reciprocal, circular, and very close between the biologist, the physicist, and the social theorist of this time. They all influenced and used each other, for, after all, they were of one mind;

their goal was the same. Darwin used not only the Great Chain of Being concept to support his theories, but he also used the racial theories that were being offered by the anthropology of his day. It was believed that men like Tylor, John McLennan, and Sir John Lubbock had demonstrated that man had progressed from a lowly condition to the highest civilized state. Darwin said that the gaps in the forms represented by various evolutionary stages in the physical development of man were explained by extinction. In the future, he said, they could expect Africans to become extinct, then the evolutionary gap between civilized man and animals would be much wider, instead of as it was then—between the "Negro" and the gorilla.[9] If it could be shown that human history had progressed in terms of a single evolutionary development, from savagery or barbarism to civilization, and if white people could accept the idea of being descended from barbarians or savages, argued Darwin, then they should be able to accept the idea of being descended from the baboon. It was anthropology which had developed racialist thought most successfully and could therefore help Darwin's theorists gain acceptance.

If a physical scientist is to be singled out as being most influential in terms of anthropological racialist theory, it is the work of Chevalier de Lamarck that must be chosen. The doctrine of the inheritance of acquired characteristics coming one-half century before Darwin's theory of evolution was perfect. It was just what was needed to seal the "marriage" of race and culture.

Lewis Henry Morgan, the most prominent American anthropologist of the 19th century, said that as men created new institutions, made inventions, and discoveries, the cerebral portion of their brains enlarged. This improvement was, of course, passed on. His work, *Ancient Society*, explicated his evolutionary theory of human society in an elaborate scheme. The amazing thing about Western social theorists is that as long as their theories suited the purposes of Western European ideology, there were few holds barred, and imaginations were free to run rampant. Morgan's scheme was a very imaginative creation indeed. In it, stages of culture were neatly lined up in order of evolutionary advancement, not only technologically, but economically, morally, religiously, socially, and politically. Even the terms by which people addressed their relatives and even languages were either savage, barbarian, or civilized. For the Western European it all worked out very well and was self-fulfilling. Monogamous marriage systems were more civilized than others, and that made sense because Morgan was writing for an audience whose society he used as the model of what it meant to be civilized. (It is significant that Engels found his scheme very useful in explaining the origin of the family, private property, and the state.)

Though many of Morgan's conclusions are now out of vogue, his evolutionary theory of society, along with that of Comte and Spencer, formed the basis of the assumptions and presuppositions with which socio-cultural and racial phenomena are approached. Conservative, liberal, and leftist alike, Western

Europeans generally assume an evolutionary hierarchy in which certain forms are superior and have evolved from other, inferior forms. It should be obvious that such a view of social history does not allow for a pluralistic conception, nor admit of the validity of cultural diversity. It explains away diversity—uses it to create, sustain, and reinforce the white self-image.

Victorian evolutionism encouraged by Morgan, Tylor, and, above all, Spencer, made itself felt in Western social theory avowedly until the 1920s, and tacitly it still remains. The reason is clear if one looks at the content of this theory. Only white-skinned, large-brained races had reached the top of the evolutionary scale and because they had created and participated in this higher culture their brains developed further. Darwin's descent of man succeeded in placing Africans, like other living "savages," as he called them, in a chain. A racial hierarchy of universal evolution that went from ape to European. All of this was to give a new rationale to the theory of white superiority. During the period 1890 to 1910, evolutionary social theory was being incorporated into the establishment of the social sciences as part of official academia, with all that that honor implies in Western society.

Politically, with the end of chattel slavery, new methods were needed by which to assure control. Relinquishing the slave clearly did not imply surrendering the white self-image or the image of the Black man on which it depended. That self-image and its dialectical opposite had to depend on a new mode of control. This is where Western social science came into play. In the earlier stages the burden fell most heavily on anthropology, later on sociology and psychology. Intellectual, ideological control was the order of the day. The objective was to prove racial inferiority to the Africans, not with a whip, but with a textbook.

Conclusion

The writer has offered these arguments out of a specific concern for the Black anthropologist, who is especially concerned with anthropology in relation to Africa and to the needs of African peoples' self-determination.

The contemporary white anthropologist has allowed himself to become irrelevant by typically focusing attention on small, powerless cultures, which he theoretically and superficially abstracts from the political context surrounding them. The culture concept, depoliticized, Europeanized, is then used to make "objects" of African peoples, while placing white people above ethnological scrutiny. It was this misuse and limitation of the concept of culture that made the cultural and intellectual imperialism of Western social science possible, while at the same time it helped to sell the image of the "uncommitted scholar." An intimate relationship exists between the conventional stance of white Western anthropology and the political fact of Western imperialism, and as European domination is successfully challenged, as white men lose their political subjects, the white anthropologists loses his "objects" of study. It is Pan-Africanism and other self-deterministic ideologies which tend to expose Eurocentrism in anthropological conception. Either anthropology will be redefined or it will become obsolete.

If Black anthropologists are to be legitimate contributors to the redemption of Africa then it would seem that they must create a "new" anthropology, one which severs the ties between social theory and white supremacist ideology; one that no longer serves the interests of Western European imperialism in *any* of its forms. Africans must emphasize the political significance of the culture concept, focusing on the relationship between ideology and group commitment, value, and the mobilization of human energies. The Black anthropologist must be a politically committed one, who uses his or her sense of culture to change what needs to be changed in the interest of African self-determination.

The writer ends by reiterating the caution made by a colleague, Professor George Bond, in 1971.[10] It is not enough to repudiate the negative images of the African heritage that whites have produced, assimilated, and exported. Rather, African social scientists must look more critically at the theoretical assumptions and presuppositions on which these disciplines are founded. It would appear to be the mission of all African social scientists, at home and in the diaspora, to devote their energies to the radical reconstruction of the disciplines in which they have been trained. Without such an approach, African peoples run the risk of incorporating the theoretical, mythological, and ideological models of white social science into their own methodologies, thereby unknowingly internalizing the values of Western European society, including the negative image of Africa that white racialism and culturalism has created.

Notes

1. Arthur O. Lovejoy, *The Great Chain of Being* (Cambridge: Harvard University Press, 1966), 58–59. This work constitutes an excellent critique of a dominant theme in the European philosophical tradition.
2. For a rare and perceptive discussion of this concept see: Henryk Skolimowski, "The Scientific World View and the Illusions of Progress," *Social Research,* Vol. 41, No. 1, Spring 1974, 52–82.
3. Margaret T. Hodgen, *Early Anthropology in the Sixteenth and Seventeenth Centuries* (Philadelphia: University of Pennsylvania Press, 1964), 389. Hodgen presents a good in-depth discussion of the intellectual and emotional origins of anthropology.
4. Quoted in George W. Stocking, *Race, Culture, and Evolution: Essays in the History of Anthropology* (New York: Free Press, 1968), 38.
5. Henri de Saint-Simon, *Social Organization: The Science of Man and other Writings* (New York: Harper Torchbooks, 1964), 49.
6. Stocking, op. cit., 55.
7. Ibid., 119.
8. Edward Tylor, *Primitive Culture* (London, 1871), 6.
9. Stocking, op. cit., 113.
10. George C. Bond, "A Caution to Black Africanists," *Phylon,* Spring 1971.

8

Black Studies and Sensibility: Identity, the Foundation for a Pedagogy

Johnnella E. Butler

Johnnella E. Butler *is Chairperson of Afro-American Studies at Smith College and former Chairperson of the Five College Black Studies Executive Committee. She has lectured widely on topics relating to literature, poetry, and Black ideology.*—The Western Journal of Black Studies, *Winter 1979, Vol. 3, No. 4*

In discussions and efforts toward curriculum revision of Black Studies departments and programs, one is ultimately faced with the questions: What holds Black Studies courses together? What makes them truly different from traditional courses in the liberal arts curriculum that attempt treatment of Blacks? Inevitably, such questions lead to considerations of what holds Blacks as a people together? Then, too often comes the realization that inclusion of courses of Black subject matter into a curriculum, in order to correct omission or even to permit analysis of Black reality, fails to buttress sufficiently the argument for maintenance of such courses in the liberal arts curriculum, just as recognition of a common race and a common condition have failed to support a political analysis and base strong enough to provide unified political action.

History has demonstrated that even the assertion of a common consciousness based on the common condition of oppression is not viable. However, Blacks as African peoples have survived, mediated the world, and created. This essay, in explaining the foundation of the discipline of Black Studies, proposes that a common sensibility, an African sensibility, forms the organizing principle for a pedagogy. Pedagogy in this essay refers to curriculum and methodology; the what and the how. The link between the classroom and the Black community has been perceived and acted on to greater or lesser degrees in the structure and the function of Black Studies programs. However, from the inception of Black Studies courses, programs, and departments varying views are held as to the relationship between the Black Studies curricula and the Black community. Understanding terms such as culture and sensibility as they relate to the Black experience might help in the description of a pedagogy. Cultural identity and the dynamics of that identity provide the organizing principles of that pedagogy.

Certain scholars of Black Studies, particularly George Kent, James Cone, Paul Carter Harrison, and Lawrence Levine, share a perspective in their works that is consistent with Paulo Freire's analysis of oppression and education within the Western world and the relationship between identity and oppression, and also with Du Bois' discussion of sensibility in *The Souls of Black Folk* and Charles Frye's work on philosophy and Black Studies.[1] In each perspective, the Black person's experience is shaped basically by two forces constantly interacting with one another and never operating separately: (1) the encounter of his/her world view with the world, both physically and spiritually; and (2) the mode of oppression. For George Kent, this becomes the adventure between Blackness and Western culture. His literary analyses flow from the sensibility of the work itself as it relates to the world and these forces.[2] James Cone, in the *Spiritual and the Blues,* essentially sees the Spiritual and the Blues as artistic manifestations of the fingering of the jagged grain, and argues the encounter of the African, then with the passage of time African/ American sensibility, with the historical reality. Black folk transform reality and are able to give strength by transforming that reality or commanding their world *as if* they had control in areas where control is impossible—in song, tales, dance, actions to covert protest, wearing the mask, etc.[3] This is not escapist, it is not transcending reality, instead it is transforming reality, utilizing that reality for not simply survival, but for sustenance, that which allows the race to continue to be, to mediate the world, to continue to struggle.

In the *Drama of Nommo,* Paul Carter Harrison understands theatre to be a reflection of life and examines the expressions of the African continuum in Afro-American life. As the continuum encounters Western culture, it generally adapts and integrates (as opposed to assimilates), that is, it transforms the reality and creates a new reality (i.e., Afro-American culture). Depending upon the strength of oppression in the encounter, the move toward transformation can result in either a positive action or a turning of one's own human potentiality against oneself.

Lawrence Levine argues for the existence of and demonstrates that Black culture and consciousness persist through folk expression in much the same fashion as Kent does through literature and Harrision through theatre. However, he makes clear that much interpretation depends upon the concept and definition of culture. He asserts that culture is not a static entity and states that culture is,

> not a fixed condition but a process: the product of interaction between the past and present. Its toughness and resiliency are determined not by a culture's ability to withstand change, which indeed may be a sign of stagnation not life, but by its ability to react creatively and responsively to the realities of a new situation. The question, as VeVe Clark recently put, is not one of survivals but of transformations. We must be sensitive to the ways in which the African world view interacted with that of the Euro-American world into

which it was carried and the extent to which an Afro-American perspective was created.[4]

He further presents Robert Redfield's argument that "style of life" may be a better description of culture, implying that people with very different specific contents of culture may have very similar views of the good life. A people who have different religions, customs, and institutions may share "certain general ways of looking upon the world, or the emphasis on certain virtues and ideals...But 'style of life', like 'culture' does imply some continuity through time, the generations looking backward to their own lives in the past and again to their own lives in the future."[5]

Levine's definition of culture is consistent with the traditional West African world view and with the view of humankind held by Kent, Cone, Harrison, Du Bois, Freire, and Frye. To understand culture, it is paramount to perceive its manifestations in political, economic, and social systems and to examine its effect in these systems. However, in seeking to offer a unifying rationale for Blacks in the diaspora and in the search for an organizing principle among Black Studies courses, there is a need for a terminology that recognizes the variations and diversity among African people. There is also a need for a terminology that acknowledges the sensibilities of the African and the American—two sensibilities that are at various levels of co-existence, agreement, and opposition.

Redfield's "style of life" appears to be the best term. However, when describing "style of life," considering its transforming encounters with another "style of life," perhaps sensibility is a more accurate term. In regard to African peoples, no matter what their oppressive or dominating cultural manifestations—American, British, French—the African consciousness may not be immediately perceived in the physical world since initially its manifestation seems to route itself through the spiritual, creative, and sensual (see Cone, Kent, Levine, Harrison). Consequently, sensibility more aptly describes the realm of African consciousness that characterizes the cultures within the Black diaspora.

Charles Frye, in *Towards a Philosophy of Black Studies,* defines Black (Eastern) and White (Western European) cultural patterns:

> Black cultural patterns are characterized by a feeling-intuitive-subjective-internal-figurative-wholistic communal-archaic-Eastern approach to life and living. White cultural patterns, on the other hand, are characterized by a sensing-thinking-objective-external-analytical-literal-individualistic-modern-Western approach to life and living.[6]

This writer contends that what he refers to as cultural patterns are sensibilities. Culture then becomes the product of sensibility mediating the world, a process of interaction between past and present. Ethnic groups may then be seen as variations within a given culture, which is characterized by a given sensibility. The African sensibility then becomes the organizing principle for Black Studies.

W.E.B. Du Bois's oft-quoted yet seldom analyzed concept of two warring ideals, the African and the American, is consistent with Kent's perception of these ideals within the same context in Afro-American literature, Harrison's speculations in African-American theatrical expression both on stage and in life, Cone's understanding of the slave expression as it grew in its awareness and its interaction with the dominant oppressive sensibility, and Lawrence Levine's explication of Black culture and consciousness in the slave community. It may be demonstrated further that Paulo Freire's duality of self and the *other,* observed in Brazilian peasants, is consistent with the "two-warring ideals" model on the basis of humankind's reaction to oppression and the struggle of sensibilities under oppression.

Clearly, Freire's method brings the peasants to a political realization; but with further analysis, it may be argued that this political realization is based on their cultural identity, their world view, their sensibility. The crux of Freire's pedagogy is the freeing of that cultural identity from the shackles of an imposed sensibility in order for humankind to mediate the world, put in motion the cultural process, and thereby transforming reality and creating history. Oppression is then defeated and liberation occurs. Freire argues that any revolution that does not accomplish this form of liberation, which this author more precisely describes as a liberation of sensibility, is pseudo.[7]

The liberation is twofold. One part of the oppression of the cultural identity involves physical, political oppression; and the other oppression is of sensibility. Freire's analysis attests to the inextricability of these two oppressions. Freire's model becomes more and more acceptable when one perceives the Black sensibility (the Black cultural patterns) permeating the substance and perspective of Freire's analyses, whether dealing with the peasants in Brazil, Chile, or Guinea-Bisseau. He specifically relates his "sense of being at home on African soil" through expression of his feelings as he first stepped on African soil in Tanzania:

I make this reference to underline how important it was for me to step for the first time on African soil, and to feel myself to be one who was returning and not one who was arriving. In truth, five years ago, as I left the airport of Dar es Salaam, going toward the university campus, the city opened before me as something I was seeing again and in which I reencountered myself. From that moment on, even the smallest things, like old acquaintances, began to speak to me of myself. The color of the skies; the blue-green of the sea; the coconut, the mango and the cashew trees; the perfume of flowers; the smell of the earth; the bananas and, among them, my very favorite, the apple-banana; the fish cooked in coconut oil; the locusts hopping in the dry grass; the sinuous body movements of the people as they walked in the streets, their smiles so ready for life; the drums sounding in the depths of night; bodies dancing and, as they did so, "designing the world"; the presence among the people of expressions of their culture that the colonialists, no matter how hard they tried, could not stamp out—all of this took possession of me and made me realize that I was more African than I had thought.

Naturally, it was not only these aspects, considered by some people merely sentimental, that affected me. There was something else in that encounter: a reencounter with myself.

There is so much I could say of the impressions that continue and of the learning I have done on successive visits to Tanzania only to emphasize the importance for me of stepping on African soil and feeling as though I were returning somewhere, rather than arriving.[8]

Identity, the foundation of a pedagogy of Black Studies, is rooted in a recognition of the sensibility of the two warring ideals, the adventure of Blackness and of Western culture, or, specifically, the modes created by the various interactions between Black and white sensibilities. Furthermore, Black Studies revolves around an African foundation. Subjects in the realm of celebration—literature, art, music, and dance[9]—reveal most keenly the African sensibility and contribute toward Black self-knowledge relative to the traditional disciplines of political science, history, sociology, and philosophy. Thus, the pedagogy must develop according to the interdisciplinary nature of Black Studies and organize itself around the explication of Black sensibility within each discipline and within the field as a whole.

Notes

1. Charles A. Frye, *Towards a Philosophy of Black Studies* (San Francisco: R and E Research Associates, 1978); W.E.B. Du Bois, *The Souls of Black Folk* (New York: Signet, 1969 [1903]).
2. George Kent, *Blackness and the Adventure of Western Culture* (Chicago: Third World Press, 1972).
3. Ibid. "Langston Hughes and the Afro-American Folk and Cultural Tradition," 53–75.
4. Lawrence Levine, *Black Culture and Black Consciousness* (New York: Oxford University Press, 1977), 5.
5. Robert Redfield, *The Primitive World and Its Transformations* (New York: Cornell University Press, 1953), 51–53. Also cited by Levine.
6. Frye, op. cit., 37.
7. Paulo Freire, *Pedagogy of the Oppressed* (New York: Seabury, 1970), 75–118.
8. Freire, *Pedagogy in Process* (New York: Seabury, 1978), 5–6.
9. Charles A. Frye, "Black Studies: Definition and Administrative Model," *The Western Journal of Black Studies*, Vol. 1, No. 2, June 1977, 93–97.

9

Notes on an Africentric Theory
of Black Personality

JOSEPH A. BALDWIN

*Joseph A. Baldwin is an Associate Professor of Psychology and the Director of
the Community Psychology Graduate Program in the Psychology Department at
Florida A&M University. He received the Ph.D. in Psychology from the University of Colorado, and his professional interests are in the general area of African
psychology.*—The Western Journal of Black Studies, *Fall 1981, Vol. 5, No. 3*

Introduction

The notion of the interrelatedness of personality and race has an extensive
history in Western psychology. In fact, most of the concepts relating
to the psychological qualities and behavioral characteristics of human
beings throughout the history of Western social science and psychology have
always been placed within a racial context (Baldwin, 1976, 1979; Coon, 1962;
Gossett, 1970; Dreger and Miller, 1960, 1968; Thomas and Sillen, 1972). Thus,
the idea of "racial personality" is certainly not new to social science in Western
society. While as a scientific endeavor, in and of itself, this tradition would seem
to be defensible, it is now firmly established that the basic motif undergirding and
directing the racial personality thrust is purely racist. That is, white social scientists merely set out to bring so-called "scientific credibility" to existing stereotypes
and fantasies of European racial supremacy. Needless to say, no credible data
(scientific or otherwise) have ever been generated to support the racist fallacies
and fantasies inherent in Western psychology and social science.

The present theory of the Black or African personality, while operating from this premise of the interrelatedness of personality and race, departs from the conceptual and philosophical framework of the Western psychological tradition in all other respects. Conceptually, this theory is forged within the framework of African psychology. By this the writer means that African psychology takes as its conceptual framework the African reality structure (history, philosophy, culture, and so forth), or what is generally referred to as the "African cosmology."

Race, Cosmology, and Social Definition

In explicating this "Africentric" theory of Black personality, several basic assumptions must first be articulated. The first premise undergirding this theory concerns the nature of the universe itself. It is assumed that the basic nature of the human phenomenal universe is "social." Thus, humans live and exist in a social universe from which derives all meaning and significance for the individual. One's experiential reality is therefore social in its basic nature (Baldwin, 1980; Nobles, 1976a). This basic premise provides the framework for the other assumptions to follow. For example, within this framework, it is assumed that race—one's collective "bio-genetic" definition—constitutes the individual's fundamental social definition; it is "original," concrete, and consistent or enduring from birth to death. Theoretically then, the individual's very *first social definition* is of race (biogenetic commonality) from which derives all other social meanings and significance in the social universe. Another basic assumption of this theory is that the individual's cosmology or world-view (that is, collective reality) evolves directly from his/her primary social definition, as does his/her culture. These attendant processes, cosmology and culture, represent the *collective survival thrust* of the racial group to which they are indigenous. As race varies, then so does cosmology, culture, and survival thrust. Hence, race is conceptualized as the basis of cosmology, and cosmology reflects and facilitates the survival thrust of the racial-cultural group to which it is naturally identified. In other words, one's biogenetic definition forms the basis of one's reality structure, which is reflected in all other basic social commonalities, institutionalized processes, physical artifacts and products, and so forth, that define one's approach to survival. These are interdependent, interchangeable processes as defined by the natural order. Thus, to speak of race under normal-natural conditions is to speak of cosmology, culture, and the survival thrust inherent in and projected by these basic social processes (Baldwin, 1980).

Following the above discussion, one can propose the existence of such phenomena as "African" cosmology and "European" cosmology, as well as African culture and European culture. Each defines and reflects the respective "survival thrusts." This theory not only assumes the existence of fundamental differences between African and European cosmologies, but also attributes an "opposite-incompatible" nature to these differences. This means in effect that the survival thrust inherent in European cosmology is incompatible with the survival thrust inherent in African cosmology (Baldwin, 1980; X (Clark), et al., 1975; Dixon, 1976; Nichols, 1974; Nobles, 1976a, 1976b). This is a natural relationship between African and European cosmologies (see Figure 1).

Figure 1. Race, Cosmology, and Culture: The African and European survival thrusts.

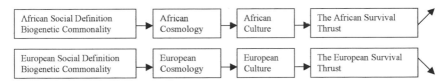

What then constitutes the basic natures of these fundamentally different cosmologies? As has been noted previously (X (Clark), et al., 1975; Dixon, 1976; Nobles, 1976a, 1980), in African cosmology, the human-nature relationship is inseparable, interdependent, and total. One could say that a basic emphasis in the African reality structure is toward "inclusiveness." In short, African cosmology is said to be characterized by the basic theme of "Man-Nature Harmony" or Unity, oneness of being. In European cosmology, on the other hand, so-called human-nature relations are separate, compartmentalized, and independent. One could say that a basic emphasis in the European reality structure is toward "exclusiveness." The basic theme characterizing European cosmology is that of "man versus nature," of conflict and antagonism, with the emphasis being on man's mastery and control over nature through domination, oppression, suppression, and unnatural alteration. Numerous differences in modes of thought and behavior between Africans and Europeans have been delineated from the framework of these oppositional cosmologies (see Dixon, 1976). Suffice it to say that for the present purpose this type of perspective on approaches to reality, existence, or "being" provides the framework for conceptualizing the intricate interdependence of race and psychological phenomena.

Race and Personality

Given this framework for Black personality theory, one is now in a position to make several basic assumptions about the relationship between race and psychological experience. It is assumed first that biological and psychological phenomena are interrelated and interdependent as defined by the natural order, such that psychological experience derives from a biological basis. Second, it is assumed that the biogenetic (heredity)-environmental interaction is intricate and inseparable in nature. A third assumption is that biogenetic phenomena are dominant over environmental phenomena in the nature-nurture interaction. Finally, it is assumed that personality forms or develops according to natural law.

From these basic assumptions about personality in relation to biological and psychological phenomena, it is proposed that personality is primarily a biogenetically determined phenomenon, which in many respects defies social-environmental forces, but in many other respects interacts with these forces in such intricate ways that it becomes utterly meaningless to attempt to separate or isolate their relative contributions. Notwithstanding the intricate biogenetic environmental interaction, heredity is always assumed to represent the dominant force where the basic nature and direction of personality is concerned. Thus, the basic nature and direction of personality are normally consistent. Only the "conscious-expressive medium" (conscious behavior) is conceivably open to modification by social-environmental forces. It is also proposed here that personality is primarily an "internal-intrapsychic" phenomenon (psychological experience) composed of an external medium of expression as well, and it cannot be meaningfully separated from the totality of its components. In other words, personality cannot be analyzed into parts separate and isolated from the context of the whole. In addition, personality is conceptualized as being essentially a social, collective, or modal phenomenon, and can only be meaningfully understood and explained in such terms. In a social universe, it should be understood that personalized-individualized distinctions are not functionally meaningful because they do not provide any significant information about the person-in-context.

Finally, and based on all of the foregoing, it is proposed that as one's biogenetic make-up varies to extremes, reflecting one or the other major racial classifications, one's personality can be expected to vary in similar fashion. In other words, different biogenetic (racial) types define different natures of personality, each having its own distinct set of psychological and behavioral traits or dispositions and can be so characterized on this basis (that is, racial personality types-traits, and so forth).

When these basic principles about personality are applied specifically to the concept of Black personality, three fundamental propositions are deducible: (a) that Black personality is definitively African (racially-culturally) in its basic nature; (b) that exposure to European culture and the psychological forces of racial-cultural oppression has affected only the conscious-expressive medium of Black personality and not its basic African nature as well; and (c) that "Africanity"[2] or Africanism dominates the personality pattern of racially mixed individuals if the biogenetic presence is minimally evident in the physical characteristics of the person; for example, where they cannot "pass" for a pure type of their non-African ancestry. It is assumed here, in other words, that the biogenetic principle of "dominance/recessiveness" in genetic interaction is as psychological as it is biological (see X (Clark), et al., 1975; Welsing, 1970).[3]

The Nature of Black Personality: Its Basic Core

Within the framework of African cosmology, the "African Self-Extension Orientation" has been proposed as the basic core or fundamental organizing principle in Black personality (Baldwin, 1976). It gives coherence, continuity, and, most importantly, *Africanity* to the basic behaviors and psychological functioning of Black people. The African Self-Extension Orientation is a deep-seated, innate, and unconscious process (that is, it is a biogenetically defined psychological phenomenon). It has been defined, in part at least, as "felt experience" at the deepest level of psychical experience, as a "total involvement" in experience, and as a "spiritualistic transcendence" in experience. This *spirituality* is believed to represent the key ingredient which allows for "self-extension" to occur in African psychological experience (Akbar, 1979a; Dixon, 1976; Toldson and Pastuer, 1976; Mayers, 1976). Operationally, this process involves (again, in part at least) the "urge for mergence" into the totality of phenomenal experience. Thus, the fundamental content of the African Self-Extension Orientation is this spirituality. It comprises the basic energy source inherent in this process (see Akbar, 1976, 1979b; X (Clark), et al., 1975; Nobles, 1980). The African Self-Extension Orientation then represents a biogenetically defined (inherent-permanent) psychological disposition (a propensity) that all Black people share, and it can be inferred in all of the basic behaviors characteristic of African people.

African Self-Consciousness, a second basic component of Black personality which derives from the African Self-Extension Orientation, is conceptualized as *the conscious level process of communal phenomenology*. It operates synonymously with the African Self-Extension Orientation under "normal-natural" conditions. However, because it is a conscious level process, it is subject to social-environmental forces and influences. Beyond these defining criteria, perhaps the most important aspect of African Self-Consciousness is that it represents the conscious embodiment and operationalization of Africanity, or the African survival thrust (the conscious expression of Africanity in Black people). Under normal conditions, this includes: (a) the recognition of oneself as "African" (biologically, psychologically, culturally, and so forth) and of what being African means as defined by African cosmology; (b) the recognition of African survival and proactive development as one's first priority value; (c) respect for and active perpetuation of all things African, including African life and African institutions; (d) a standard of conduct toward all things "non-African" and toward those things, peoples, and so forth, that are "anti-African" (that is, active opposition against all things that are anti-African). African Self-Consciousness thus defines, reflects, and facilitates the conscious level of the survival thrust of African people.[4] It represents the natural "conscious collective survival thrust" of African people (including conscious-purposive Africanisms in Black people's psychological functioning and behavior). It should also be recognized that in defining the nature and direction of the African survival thrust, African Self-Consciousness functionally gives conscious meaning and purpose to the operation of the innate-unconscious African Self-Extension Orientation. This intricate relationship between the African Self-Extension Orientation and African Self-Consciousness is illustrated in Figure 2.

Figure 2. The African Self-Extension Orientation and African Self-Consciousness as the basic core of the Black personality.

Some Basic Characteristics: oneness-harmony with nature, communal phenomenology, self-knowledge, "we," group/spiritualistic transcendence, collective survival thrust, self-reinforcing-enhancing beliefs, attitudes, values, and behaviors.

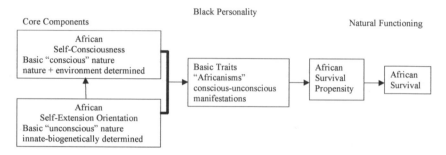

Figure 2 illustrates the manner in which African Self-Consciousness and the African Self-Extension Orientation operate harmoniously (or as unity) to facilitate and reinforce the African survival thrust in Black people. In other words, African Self-Consciousness represents the conscious level extension of the deep seated and unconscious African Self-Extension Orientation. The "all-pervasive" African Self-Extension Orientation is thus the foundation of African Self-Consciousness, and under normal-natural conditions they exist as one unified undifferentiated process.[5]

This theory therefore proposes that the basic core of Black people's psychological existence (thoughts, feelings, actions) flows into the other, forming one rhythmic unity as defined by the African Self-Extension Orientation. Every dimension of Black personality can be plausibly inferred in practically every dimension of the psychological functioning and behavior of African people. Hence, the centrality of the dynamic operation of the psychological functioning and behavior of Black people is inescapable from a meaningful and functionally relevant model of the Black personality. Again, almost every basic feature of African people's psychological functioning and behavior can be argued to flow through and is defined by this vital process of communal phenomenology. Black psychology can only be meaningfully understood in terms of this uniquely African framework, irrespective of where Black people might be located in space and time (see Figure 3).[6]

Figure 3. Spatial illustration of the Black personality structure.

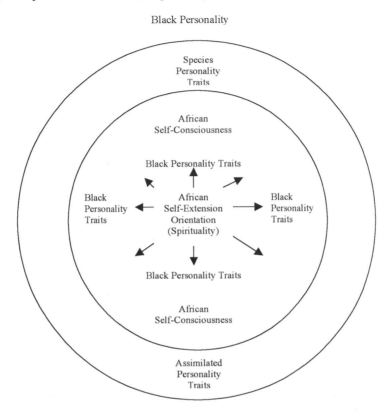

Black Personality

Some Basic Traits of Black Personality

Within the framework of this basic core or structure of the Black personality, a number of theorists have consistently suggested a number of basic traits that are appropriate to this "Africentric" model. Among the most frequently articulated basic traits of Black personality, seven have received widespread recognition and have been reasonably well developed in the relevant literature. These seven basic traits consist of the following: Affect-Symbolic Imagery Synthesis, Multidimensional-Polysense Perceptual Orientedness, Ebonics, Rhythmic-Fluid Physiomotor Responsiveness, Stylistic Expressiveness Orientation, Affiliative-Socializing Orientation, and Religious Orientation. Some defining aspects of these traits are presented in Table 1.[7]

Table 1.
Black personality traits and their defining criteria.

Black Personality Traits	Some Defining Characteristics
Affect-Symbolic Imagery Synthesis	Emphasis on holistic synthesis thinking, diunital logic. Emphasis on perceiving and processing information (phenomenal experience) as a holistic synthesis. Emphasis on the whole over parts in perceptual experience. Synthesizing words and objects with affect to convey meaning.
Multidimensional-Polysense Perceptual Orientedness	Emphasis on equivalent-interacting and interrelated multiple modes of sensory acuity, involving not only the visual, auditory, olfactory, tactile and taste sensory modes but also many other, e.g., psycho-kinesis, precognition, vibes, proprioceptive processes, etc.
Ebonics	Emphasis on holism and expressiveness in communication, e.g., verbal inflection-in-context, abstract and fluid content of language, and bodily movement and rhythmic communication generally, call and response tendency, etc.
Rhythmic-Fluid Physiomotor Responsiveness	Emphasis on the expressive nature of gross motor movements/behaviors; e.g., the spontaneous, flexibility, fluidity, and overall rhythmic features of body movements— "Kinesiology"
Stylistic Expressiveness Orientation	Emphasis on expressiveness, improvisation, flair, etc., in all manners of expressing the Self; e.g., language, movement, instrumentation, etc.—especially noted in aesthetics.
Affiliative-Socializing Orientation	Emphasis on social-communal expression; e.g., group activities, aggregation, interpersonal affiliations, etc., all involving an emphasis on "shared participation," i.e., communal phenomenology.
Religious Orientation	Emphasis on a belief in a Supreme Being, a spiritual force behind life-existence, natural order, etc. Emphasis on a sense of morality, ethics, fairness, and justice in interpersonal relations and experience in general.

It is important to remember that these basic traits or Africanisms all reflect the operation of the African Self-Extension Orientation from which they derive. The basic structure or organization of Black personality thus occurs in terms of the core process (the African Self-Extension Orientation) and the Black personality traits.

Based on this model of the Black personality, the African Self-Extension Orientation defines the nature and coherence of the Black personality traits. These traits are therefore interrelated and interdependent as a result of this core process. They are assumed to overlap and interact in such intricate ways that even when obscured somewhat through artificial isolation for the purpose of analysis (as has been the case here), it seems impossible to misconstrue the intricate interrelatedness among them. This observation thus indicates the fundamental centrality of the African Self-Extension Orientation in Black personality. In sum, then, these basic traits of Black personality all reflect the spiritualistic transcendence phenomenon which operationally (in the dynamic sense essentially) defines the African Self-Extension Orientation.

To clarify some other important implications of this theory, it is obviously true that all African people may not actively exhibit these basic traits of Black personality to the same degree. Where such variability among individual Blacks in the active manifestation of these basic traits is concerned, this theory argues that the extent of individual variability depends upon the degree to which one's early experience (early socialization) and institutional support systems actively nurture and reinforce the innate potential of the African Self-Extension Orientation. For example, one would expect that in a racially mixed context (either biogenetically or socially integrated; the former presumes the active role of a non-African parent in socialization), or in a high socially mobile context, socialization processes which nurture and reinforce the active exhibition of this natural African disposition are likely to be lessened and distorted by these mitigating factors. On the other hand, in a highly homogeneous context of greater psychological and social distance from centers of European cosmology, and so forth, socialization processes which nurture and reinforce the active manifestation of the African Self-Extension Orientation should be more pervasive and viable. Whatever the case may be for individual Blacks, one must understand that *this theory assumes that all Black people possess this natural-innate disposition*. It is simply more suppressed or inhibited in some individuals than in others as a result of differential emphasis—reinforcement during early socialization experiences and a variety of other psychologically distorting circumstances that are usually institutional or systemic in nature (Baldwin, 1980, 1982). The potential for the active manifestation of these basic traits of Black personality is ever-present in African people, and only its actual conscious expression (as in conscious behaviors) is subject to modification in its occurrence.

Conclusion

In conclusion, this theory attempts to present a basic model of the Black or African personality which takes into consideration its biogenetic foundation, its fundamental African nature, its basic structure and dynamics, and the ideological and institutional bases necessary for its maintenance and perpetuation. Notwithstanding these important aspects of the theory, it does not purport to represent a complete view of Black personality. What it represents is one basic model for further research and expansion or modification where necessary until it fully conforms to the African reality as it is known. This theory, then, basically represents a *conceptual framework* for the Black personality which will hopefully have meaningful heuristic value for Black psychology where this vital issue is concerned.

Notes

1. This article is based upon a book entitled *Afrikan (Black) Personality: From an Africentric Framework* (Chicago: Third World Press, 1981).
2. The concept "Africanity" has been used in many ways by contemporary Black theorists. Here it refers more or less to that ingredient (synthesis of all levels of energy, e.g., physical and psychological energy) which identifies a phenomenon as African. It is the very essence of the African nature: that unique, unmistakable African quality in all African phenomena. In short, this concept is best epitomized by the notion of "Spirituality"—that dynamic psychological quality which serves as the connecting link between African people and phenomenal experience generally. This concept will naturally be elaborated on throughout this paper.
3. This last premise specifically addresses the predicament of the African-American situation where the so-called phenomenon of "miscegenation" has been a dominant practice over the past three to four centuries. Any model of racial personality must address the complex issue of racial mixing if it is to be reality-based and useful for our people. While we still know far less about this phenomenon than we should, it is assumed, based on everyday observations, that where racially mixed individuals cannot "pass" for a pure type of their non-African ancestry, then Africanism should characterize the personality pattern of such individuals (regarding the biogenetic "dominance" of African traits see X (Clark), et al., 1975; McGee, 1976; Welsing, 1970).
4. Many of these important aspects of African Self-Consciousness are represented in M. Ron Karenga's "Nguzo Saba" principles (San Diego: Kawaida, 1965). This would also apply to Molefi Asante's principles of "Afrocentricity" (Buffalo: Amulefi, 1980).
5. Although the issue of "disorder in Black personality" is beyond the scope of this paper, it may be noted nonetheless that "disharmony," incongruence and/or differentiation between these core processes represents the condition of disorder in Black personality (see Baldwin, 1982).
6. Note that all subsequent references to the African Self-Extension Orientation are automatically inclusive of the phenomenon of African Self-Consciousness unless specified otherwise. The reader should recall that these phenomena represent one "undifferentiated" process under normal and natural conditions.
7. Of course, this listing of basic traits of Black personality is not exhaustive. A number of other potential traits have been identified in the relevant literature (see Akbar, 1976; Baldwin, 1976; Nobles, 1980; Phillips, 1976; Toldson and Pastuer, 1976). However, more extensive research seems to be required in order that such additional traits may be fully articulated.

Bibliography

Akbar, N. 1976. "Rhythmic Patterns in African Personality," in *African Philosophy: Assumptions and Paradigms for Research on Black Persons*, L. M. King, et al. (eds.). Los Angeles: Fanon Center.

_____. 1979a. "African Roots on Black Personality," in *Reflections on Black Psychology*, W. D. Smith, et al. (eds.). Washington, D.C.: University Press of America.

_____. 1979b. "Mental Disorder among African-Americans," paper presented at the Thirteenth Annual Convention of the Association of Black Psychologists, Atlanta, Georgia (August).

Baldwin, J. A. 1976. "Black Psychology and Black Personality," *Black Books Bulletin*, Vol. 4, No. 3, 6–11, 65.

_____. 1979. "Theory and Research Concerning the Notion of Black Self-Hatred: A Review and Reinterpretation," *Journal of Black Psychology*, Vol. 5, No. 2, 51–77.

_____. 1980. "The Psychology of Oppression," in *Contemporary Black Thought*, M. Asante and A. Vandi (eds.). Beverly Hills: Sage.

_____. 1982. "African Self-Consciousness and the Mental Health of African-Americans," unpublished manuscript.

X (Clark), C., D. McGee, W. Nobles, and L. (Weems). 1975. "Voodoo or IQ: An Introduction to African Psychology," *Journal of Black Psychology*, Vol. 1, No. 2, 9–29.

Coon, C. 1962. *The Origins of Races*. New York: Knopf.

Dixon, V. J. 1976. "World Views and Research Methodology," in *African Philosophy: Assumptions and Paradigms for Research on Black Persons*, op. cit.

Dreger, R. M., and K. S. Miller. 1960. "Comparative Psychological Studies of Negroes and Whites in the United States," *Psychological Bulletin*, Vol. 57, 361–402.

_____, and _____. 1968. "Comparative Psychological Studies of Negroes and Whites in the United States: 1959–1965," *Psychological Bulletin Monograph Supplement*, Vol. 70, No. 3 (Part 2).

Gossett, T. R. 1970. *Race: The History of an Idea in America*. New York: Schocken.

McGee, D. P. 1976. "An Introduction to African Psychology: Melanin, the Physiological Basis for Psychological Oneness," in *African Philosophy: Assumptions and Paradigms for Research on Black Persons*, op. cit.

Mayers, S. D. "Intuitive Synthesis in Ebonics: Implications for a Developing African Science," in *African Philosophy: Assumptions and Paradigms for Research on Black Persons*, op. cit.

Nichols, E. 1974. "Culture Affects Thought Processes," *Guidepost*, February 22.

Nobles, W. W. 1976a. "African Science: The Consciousness of Self," in *African Philosophy: Assumptions and Paradigms for Research on Black Persons*, op. cit.

_____. 1976b. "Black People in White Insanity: An Issue for Black Community Mental Health," *Journal of Afro-American Issues*, Vol. 4, 21–27.

_____. 1980. "African Philosophy: Foundations for Black Psychology," in *Black Psychology*, 2nd ed., R. L. Jones (ed.). New York: Harper and Row.

Phillips, C. B. 1976. "Rethinking the Study of Black Behavior," in *Collective Monologues: Toward a Black Perspective in Education*, M. Valley and C. B. Phillips (eds.). Pasadena, California: Stage VII.

Thomas, I., and S. Sillen. 1972. *Racism and Psychiatry*. Secaucus, New Jersey: Citadel.

Toldson, I., and A. Pastuer. 1976. "Therapeutic Dimensions of the Black Aesthetic," *Journal of Non-White Concerns*, Vol. 4, No. 3, 105–117.

Welsing, F. 1970. *The Cress Theory of Color Confrontation and Racism*. Washington, D.C.: private publishing.

10

Toward a Theory of Popular Health Practices in the Black Community*

CLOVIS E. SEMMES

Clovis E. Semmes (Jabulani K. Makalani) is an Assistant Professor of Black Studies at the University of Illinois, Chicago Circle. His primary areas of interest are health care (especially nonmedical beliefs and practices) in the Black community; the sociology of the Black family; the sociology of Black art; Afro-centric theory and method; and cultural change and adaptation in the Black community. He received the Ph.D. in Sociology from Northwestern University.—The Western Journal of Black History, *Winter 1983, Vol. 7, No. 4*

P opular health practices are essential components of culture. They reflect and preserve the identity and supporting worldview of a given group. They also form an infrastructure of beliefs, habits, and traditions that directly affect health status. Medical institutions touch only a small part of this infrastructure of health; it is what people do in their everyday lives that is most important. Afro-American popular health practices are more than curiosities or impediments to the imposition of Western or modern medicine. They are efforts to make life orderly and knowable, and they explicitly or implicitly address the problem of how to live. They are dynamic elements of cultural adaptation and change.

The definition of popular health practices used in this paper roughly corresponds with that of Spicer (1977). Terminologically, "folk medicine" is often associated with present-day medical traditions that are out of touch with Western medicine. So, too, "folk medicine" may connote a tradition that is waning. Finally, the label "folk" may have a connotation that is either good or bad. "Popular medicine" is a more neutral term and is defined by Spicer (1977) in the following way: "The view to be emphasized is that these traditions are maintained

---

* Earlier versions of this paper were read at the 9th Annual Third World Conference, Chicago, 1983; the 6th Annual Black Studies Conference, Olive-Harvey College, Chicago, 1983; and the Annual Convention of the Popular Culture Association, Wichita, Kansas, 1983.

by ethnic and class segments in any society, rather than by the specialists engaged in scientific and Western medicine…, these traditions are of the people rather than of the scientists."

In addition, the writer prefers to use "health practices" as opposed to "medical practices." Connotatively, medicine is too closely associated with a particular curative approach, which involves drugs, surgery, and radiation. Popular health practices have a broader connotation that includes a wide range of beliefs, habits, and traditions that directly affect health, and involve curative and preventive approaches extending beyond the limits of drugs, surgery, or radiation.

This paper will survey various popular health practices of Afro-Americans from the period of West African enslavement to the present post-urban period. The writer's purpose will be to provide conceptual and theoretical understanding of the significance of popular health practices for cultural development and group identity formation.

E. Franklin Frazier (1957) provided significant empirical and conceptual insight into the impact that European contact with Africa had on Africa's ecological relationships and institutional structures. Relationships to the land were destroyed, and certain biological processes were disturbed. For example, the introduction of new physical objects, changes in plant and animal life, and changing patterns of consumption transformed African health. Tobacco, cotton, sugar, etc. as cash crops contributed to the development of the plantation system and the demand for slave labor.

However, in a more devastating sense, the introduction of venereal diseases, tuberculosis, smallpox, measles, strong alcoholic beverages, and firearms severely ravaged African culture. The destruction of diversified agricultural subsistence economies destroyed dietary practices through the concomitant effect on the food supply, and subsequently weakened the resistance of Africans against the onslaught of European diseases. Furthermore, the fragmentation of family and religious life disturbed the institutional context through which health practices were maintained. In short, European contact set the stage for Afro-American popular health practices, which were the result of African retentions, the context of European enslavement and cultural practices, and new flora and fauna. Thus, traditional West African culture became in the New World slave culture.

Blassingame (1979) indicated that African foods and food preparation techniques were practiced in the New World. He stated: "Since the early slaves found it difficult to eat European dishes without adding African spices, they also used them to prepare savory stews and rice dishes for their owners quite unlike the lightly seasoned English dishes they had known." The availability of corn contributed to Afro-American innovation. "The bondsmen took Indian maize and turned it into hoe cakes, mush, and dumplings akin to African Fufu and Kenkey. Spoon bread, a soft pudding-like dish made from corn meal, grew out of this mélange and appeared on the master's table" (Blassingame, 1979).

Despite African influences, the slave diet was largely characterized by the New World diet of fat pork and corn meal (Kiple and Kiple, 1977). This diet, in conjunction with distinctive biological traits, probably resulted in chronic and often severe deficiencies in calcium, magnesium, iron, vitamin C, protein, and the B-complex vitamins. Most Africans had a lactose intolerance and thus were unable to break-down and assimilate milk sugars from bovine milk. Their skin pigmentation mitigated production of vitamin D—a nutrient needed for the utilization of calcium. Hemoglobin abnormalities such as sickle cell trait and anemia were probably higher among incoming Africans.

The above characteristics, plus environmental and work conditions, affected Black nutritional requirements in unique ways. Nevertheless, Black people were coerced by the demands of chattel slavery and plantation life to develop food tastes largely centered around pork and corn. The consumption of vegetables was sometimes discouraged by the slave owner or were of limited availability and diversity. Thus the slave diet as a cultural adaptation was important in health terms, but it was also important in symbolic terms. The substance of this diet later became known as "soul food" and developed as a distinguishing feature of Black culture and identity. Consequently, this diet achieved all of the attendant, symbolic power of cultural traits that reify a group's self-image (Fauthauer, 1969).

Several studies illustrate Afro-American dietary practices subsequent to chattel slavery. Grant and Groom (1959) identified a Southern rural diet that relied heavily on cereal grains and their products—e.g., rice, grits, corn meal, and wheat flour, with more or less regular use of legumes, sweet potatoes, greens, watermelon, fat meat, fish, and chicken. Rice and black-eyed peas or "Hoppin' John" were traditional, as were soups and stews, which included "pot licker." Urban areas were usually characterized by the use of more commercially prepared foods—e.g., bread, cold cuts, and soft drinks. However, fat meat, starchy foods, chicken, and various greens were relatively constant across the Southern, rural, and urban milieu. Jerome (1969) similarly reported that the core of the Southern diet consisted of pork, pork products, chicken, fish, wild meats, collard, turnip, mustard greens, poke salad, kale, dried beans, dried peas, corn grits, syrup, molasses, butter, and buttermilk.

A study by Mayer (1965) indicated that in the rural South, shopping was done once a week, and women were involved in producing food for self consumption. Children collected wild greens and berries. Men and boys fished for catfish and other river fish. On the seaboard they collected crabs, shrimp, clams, and crayfish. Breakfast included eggs on rare occasions, brains, canned mackerel, salt herring, sausage, or fried chicken. Servings of protein foods were generally small. Fruits, fruit juice, and milk were seldom consumed. Yellow cheese was a Sunday treat.

Jerome (1969) also observed that the traditional Southern breakfast consisted of fried meats, rice, grits, biscuits, gravy, fried sweet or white potatoes, coffee, and milk. Thus breakfast was a heavy meal. Lunch consisted of leftovers from breakfast. Dinner was eaten between one and three in the afternoon and was a heavy, boiled dinner as compared with the fried breakfast meal. Dinner consisted of boiled vegetables or dry legumes seasoned with a variety of meat products, accompanied by corn bread, sweet or white potatoes, a sweet beverage or milk, and an occasional dessert or fruit. Portions of this meal were saved for supper.

Mayer's study (1965) noted that noon and evening meals tended to be similar. Protein foods were served at one of these meals two to three times a week and consisted of lard, fat, fish, or eggs. There were cooked vegetables—usually cabbage or potatoes. Corn bread and greens were almost always in combination and made up the rest of the meal. Biscuits made for breakfast were available throughout the day. In season, there were sweet potatoes, tomatoes, cucumbers, and melons from the summer garden.

Urbanization in the South and the North transformed traditional eating patterns. Because of the changing organization of work, the large mid-day meal was eaten in the evening. Breakfast became a lighter meal. Boiled meals were replaced by fried meals. The heavy breakfast and large mid-day boiled dinner became a weekend phenomenon. Protective foods (e.g., fresh meats, fruits, and vegetables) consumed in the rural South were often less available in urban centers. Commercially processed foods became more used. However, Southern rural food selection persisted in the cities and the traditional focus on fat meats, most notably pork products, starchy foods, and varieties of cooked greens remained. Consumption of other vegetables remained constricted and limited (see Grant and Groom, 1959; Meyer, 1965; Jerome, 1969).

The post-urban period has seen the above pattern proliferate with increased frying days. Food preparation has in many cases passed into the hands of fast-food chains and the manufacturers of commercial convenience foods. Such foods usually have less nutritional density and are laden with additives, salt and/or sugar (Bowering, et al., 1978; Karp, et al., 1980; Bradfield and Coltrin, 1970). Nevertheless, the basic Southern diet with its roots in the slave experience has persisted, albeit modified, into the post-urban era. However, concomitant with periods of heightened social consciousness in the Black community, one finds an ideological tendency that rejects traditional Southern dietary patterns. Thus, as shall be revealed, dietary change became in the urban and post-urban context significantly linked to nationalistic and revitalization propensities.

In addition to adaptive dietary patterns, Afro-Americans developed a wide range of curative practices. Conjure, voodoo, hoodoo, and root doctoring combined herbal and magical approaches to healing and maintained strong elements of an African cosmology (Blassingame, 1979; Webb, 1971; Wintrob, 1973; Snow, 1974 and 1978; Hurston, 1931; Puckett, 1926). Enslaved Africans brought with them knowledge of performing caesarean sections and many women were skilled midwives. One slave invented a method for smallpox inoculation, and others provided cures for syphilis and rattlesnake bites. Many slaves achieved notoriety as healers and cured both Blacks and whites (Morais, 1967; Savitt, 1978).

In the present era one continues to find a persistent and profound spiritual and magical dimension to health and healing practices among Afro-Americans. Man is a spiritual being living in a spiritual universe; thus, health and disease are often viewed in that context. Living itself is understood to be a quest for harmony with a Divine order (Snow, 1974; Stewart, 1971; Jackson, 1976). Unlike the Southern diet, the spiritual and magical dimension embodies a consistent underlying African cosmology (Edgerton, 1971; Odejide, et al., 1978). Conjure, voodoo, hoodoo, or root doctoring all have to do with the belief that the behavior of others can be controlled through ritual and manipulation of natural objects. They attend to the belief that some illnesses are natural, and some are unnatural. Natural illnesses are those caused by imbalances between the way one lives and the way God intended one to live. Extremes of cold or dampness, wrong eating habits, unchecked emotions, and so forth can cause illness. Sin can bring about Divine punishment in the form of illness. Unnatural illnesses are those caused by someone with magical powers and may be the result of some interpersonal conflict—e.g., jealousy. Health and illness can also be a function of direct intervention by good or evil spirits. Special people who can contact the spirit world are needed in this situation (Ruiz and Langrod, 1977).

Treatments for natural and unnatural illnesses are varied, but the unifying concept is that everything in nature is connected. The goal is to understand these relationships or find the appropriate practitioner who does. Everything in creation is natural, whether they are spirits or so-called material phenomena. Thus, there is no "supernatural," since nothing is beyond or greater than nature. In both the seen and unseen world there is the continuing clash between good and evil or the forces of integration and disintegration. Furthermore, the movement and position of the sun, moon, and planets are often believed to affect health since they are part of natural phenomena. Health is based on the maintenance of harmony between dialectical forces existing in nature. Thus one must be aware of the natural laws that govern life. "What goes around comes around," "You reap what you sow," and "Everything is everything" are common expressions that embody the above African worldview.

Symbolically, maleness, femaleness, and age may be factors in explaining disease. Extreme fear, worry, and sorrow are also etiologically significant. Sometimes there is a concern for the purity and viscosity of the blood and for elimination. For example, for some, purifying the blood through herbal laxatives, enemas, colonics, or fasting is believed to be an important preventive health practice. Sometimes purifying the blood is believed to be more important at the change of the seasons—especially winter to spring. For others, blood retains significant symbolism with regard to states of health. One may have high blood or too much blood, low blood, or not enough blood, or thin blood. For some, unexplained illness may be the work of voodoo, hoodoo, conjure, or the spirit world (Snow, 1977a and 1977b; Wintrob, 1973; Jackson, 1976; Brandon, 1976; Webb, 1971; Hautman, 1979; Lauer, 1973).

A significant feature of the spiritual dimension involves the belief in the power of the word—i.e., words as the expression of thought have the capacity to become things. Thoughts are things. Invoking incantations in the name of God or lesser divine beings implies that one is able to draw upon a Divine relationship between the word and things created. Similarly, God created all things through the power of the word. Objects can be endowed with special power to protect and heal after being affected by the word (thoughts). The power of belief is the force behind the word and belief is the key to affecting one's existential world. Not all Black Americans express this cosmology in the same way; however, few deny the significance and capacity of the spiritual realm. This spiritual thread extends unbroken from the African context to the present Afro-American context. Usually it is observed in so-called Black religious expression, but it is also strongly and consistently expressed in popular health practices.

The church, of course, has been the traditional institution where faith healing is practiced. The Wednesday night prayer meeting was specifically a time for invoking and receiving the "Holy Spirit." Testifying, spirit possession, and prayer in the context of polyrhythmic breathing, vocalizing, music, and dance are forms of collective healing. At times social scientists have viewed these practices as reactions to poverty, racism or, oppression; they are instead the continuation of an ancient approach to healing. They are traditional techniques for making the individual and the community whole. Through ritual, the disintegrating forces of life are reversed. The belief is that invoking the spiritual powers of God will make one whole. Collective affirmation through ceremony, fasting, anointing with oil, and other ritual actions heighten the central force of belief (or faith) mentioned earlier. Folks must believe "right," and they must believe "strong." The African and Afro-American healer recognizes this and knows that at least part of his or her job is to affect belief (see Snow 1973, 1977a and b; Griffith, et al., 1980; Hall and Bourne, 1973).

The present post-urban period has seen the prominent expression of popular health practices that are more self-conscious and ideologically developed. The seeds of these practices were planted during the early period of Black migration to the urban North. The flowering of these practices occurred during the Black consciousness renaissance of the late 1960s, and found their strongest expression in such religious and cultural nationalist organizations as the Black Hebrew Israelites and the Nation of Islam. Numerous other cultural nationalist expressions espoused specific dietary and health practices. As a result there has been a slow but sustained diffusion of health beliefs and practices, which run counter to dietary patterns that perpetuate the rural Southern and slave diet. Various forms of vegetarianism and a growing preference for "natural" foods are a part of this expression. Concomitantly, the practice of herbalism, which has sustained itself throughout the Afro-American experience, remains strong. Many Afro-Americans are also turning to the nonmedical healing arts, which do not use drugs, surgery, or radiation to treat disease (Semmes, 1982). This popular post-urban health practice includes a conscious preference for or return to "natural" curative approaches. However, the spiritual and magical dimension remains central to popular post-urban practices. In some instances, dietary patterns have become self-consciously intertwined with spiritual development.

One of the earliest Black American Islamic Sects, Moorish Science, was founded by Timothy Drew in 1913. This group rejected meat and eggs in favor of fish and vegetables. Early Black Hebrew sects founded in the 1930s also rejected pork (Fauset, 1970). However, it was not until the prominence of the late Honorable Elijah Muhammad and the Hebrew Israelites of the 1960s that dietary laws began to take on such prominence in the Black urban community. Symbolically, diet became a requisite for spiritual development, rejection of slave culture and white oppression, self determination, and self (collective) development.

In his book *Eat to Live* (1972), Mr. Muhammad set forth dietary laws for his followers. He espoused the virtues of a vegetarian diet. Meat eating was believed to be against life, but eaten once a day, every other day, or twice a week it was not so bad. This pattern, he preached, would lengthen lives. Eating pork, however, was against Divine Law and was forced upon Black Americans by Caucasians for the purpose of enslavement. Fresh fruits and vegetables were advocated, as well as whole-wheat bread, disease-free milk, and pure butter. Not all vegetables were considered edible and Mr. Muhammad opposed such foods as black-eye peas, yellow peas, red peas, lima beans, collard greens, cabbage sprouts, and soybeans. He counseled against nuts, peanut butter, popcorn, and hominy grits—presumably because they were considered difficult to digest. Corn bread, half done bread (bread should be baked at least twice), fried breads or pancakes, and sweet potatoes shortened one's life. White potatoes produced too much starch.

According to Mr. Muhammad, one should eat fish weighing a half pound to ten pounds. Larger fish were discouraged. Scavenger fish should not be eaten. Fish that suck their food or fish that look like animals, with heads like animals or forefronts like animals, should not be eaten. Eels or "water snakes," oysters, lobster, crab, shrimp, and snails were discouraged as food. Wild game with the exception of squab should not be eaten. Navy beans, however, were considered by Mr. Muhammad to be a great food and were the main ingredient in the famous Muslim bean pie.

The great stress of Mr. Muhammad's dietary techniques was to eat one meal of the right food every 24 hours. One should eat only when fully hungry. Mr. Muhammad argued for simple, fresh food. Artificial flavoring and coloring were thought to be slow death. He saw proper food as central to self sufficiency, nation building, and spiritual development. Eating correctly is following Divine Law.

Mr. Muhammad advocated breast-feeding, discouraged drugs during pregnancy, and opposed all intoxicants. He expressed that if people live right, they would not need drugs, and would live a very long life.

Mr. Muhammad's dietary teachings had significant influence on non-Muslim Black Americans. Since Mr. Muhammad's philosophy was reflected at Muslim food stores and restaurants, these structures served as a kind of outreach to the broader Black community. As a result, many non-Muslim, Black Americans began to reject pork, became vegetarians, ate one meal a day, fasted, consumed "natural" foods, breast-fed their babies, and generally re-evaluated their lifestyles. Thus, Black cultural awareness demanded an assessment of diet and lifestyle. Consequently, Mr. Muhammad's teachings severely challenged dietary patterns that had evolved out of the slave experience (Lincoln, 1961). Thus for many Black Americans, "soul food" became a symbol of Black enslavement.

Hebrew Israelites or "Black Jews" have had a similar impact on the Black community. Many people during the Black cultural awareness renaissance of the 1960s were attracted to this philosophy and way of life. Hebrew Israelites were not as prominent as the Nation of Islam in the 1960s, but nevertheless contributed to an increased dietary and health consciousness among Black Americans. Even though many of their members immigrated to Israel and parts of Africa during the 1960s and early 1970s with hopes of establishing a homeland, they continued to make an impact on the Black community and often advocated very strict forms of vegetarianism. In Chicago, for example, there are a number of Hebrew groups whose lifestyles vary, but for whom dietary laws are central. The basic beliefs of Hebrew Israelites are illustrated in a publication of one of the most prominent Hebrew groups, *The Kingdom of God*:

> The Bible was written by Black men who because of their disobedience and violations of the Laws (instructions) lost favor with God. Consequently, they yielded the rule of dominion of the world to the Euro-gentiles for an appointed period of time. During the gentile reign, the African Hebrews (children of Israel) underwent a chastisement (slavery) that caused them to descend to the lowest ebb of existence among the people of the world...with the truthful interpretation of the Holy Scriptures and its prophecies, the season of salvation is set in motion. (Ammi, 1982)

The idea that Black people, as the original Hebrews mentioned in the Bible, had fallen from God's favor is central to the lifestyle and dietary approach of Hebrew Israelite philosophy. Black people must again seek to live by Divine Law:

> As we continue to examine "culture" as the measure of our position in the quest for God, we see great danger for man. Even the way he eats has become ungodly. Let us view food preparation and consumption at the highest level of mankind's development. For certainly we cannot overlook such an

important area of cultural expression as this. I must remind you that your blood, tissues and all your organs are made of what you eat. (Ammi, 1982)

Hebrew Israelites advocate "natural" foods and vegetarianism sometimes to the exclusion of all dairy products. Pork consumption is also considered a symbol of enslavement and an abomination in Divine Law. Garments made of natural substances—for example, cotton or wool—are encouraged. They advocate natural childbirth and breast-feeding, and are opposed to abortion. Tobacco and drugs are generally discouraged. Hebrews counsel against excessive television which they say destroys body and mind. Healthy thoughts are important since, for example, "A large part of the mental and social ailments of children have been caused by the state of mind of the mother during conception" (Ammi, 1982). Since self sufficiency is a value, health problems are often addressed within the group, utilizing herbal remedies.

Hebrew Israelite philosophy promotes establishing harmony with nature in accord with Divine Law. They teach:

> Maintaining the ecological balance of nature compliments the righteous worship of God. Keeping in harmony and attuned to the natural cycles of God insures one's existence and confirms his oneness with the Creator. This fact is confirmed on every level, as demonstrated by the fact that when one chews his food, works his mouth, and grinds his teeth, the more masticated the food, the easier it is digested. The easier the digestion the less wear and tear on the inner organs, greatly reducing the chances of becoming ill. For good health means a healthy body and a healthy body presents a strong foundation or temple, in which God may dwell. It is very important to know that the worship of God is so much more than just a mere word, such as religion or religious. The worship of God is life-living-existence-breathing-acting. (Ammi, 1982)

Similar to the past practices of the Nation of Islam, Hebrew Israelites have influenced numerous Black people who were not members of their group to reflect upon and even change various aspects of their diet and lifestyle. Although there is substantial variation among Hebrew groups with respect to their actual dietary and health practices, their philosophy has reinforced dietary and health practices counter to the slave and rural tradition. Hebrew Israelites have helped strengthen values that reflect African spirituality and an orientation toward living in accord with nature. Their restaurants and businesses also helped expose the broader Black community to different ways of eating and living.

Other groups and movements also emerged during the late 1960s and early 70s that affected the dietary and health practices of numerous Afro-Americans. In Chicago, the Affro-Arts Theater (Semmes, forthcoming), which became a nationally recognized Mecca for Black culture, provided health classes to the Black community and was a strong advocate for vegetarianism. The Affro-Arts' approach to health also reinforced the concept that proper diet was necessary for spiritual and cultural development. They also promoted the view that there are natural laws which define how one should live.

Subsequent to the Affro-Arts Theater, the Institute for Positive Education in Chicago, a nationally recognized Black independent educational institution, also advocated vegetarianism (Kunjufu, 1975). However, their approach was more severe and secular in orientation. In 1973 the director of the Institute wrote, "The superior diet is a frugitarian diet—that of fruits. Yet in this country, it is almost impossible to be a strict frugitarian…all the nourishment that the body needs to function at its highest capacity is found in abundance in fruits and vegetables" (Lee, 1973). During this period, Black political activist Dick Gregory gave additional credence to strict vegetarian and fruit diets. He also reinforced the practice of fasting as a way to remove "disease-producing waste" from the body (Gregory, 1973).

Dietary change, however, has presented some new health problems and two studies (Bachrach, et al., 1979; Zmora, et al., 1979) have documented nutritional deficiencies by Blacks who had changed their diets, but who had not achieved proper nutritional balance. The writer's ongoing research in this area (Semmes, 1981) has uncovered numerous Afro-Americans who expressed serious difficulties as a result of severely restricting their diets. Sometimes these individuals had removed all dairy products from their diets as well as flesh foods. Excessive fasting, improper nutritional balance, and insufficient food intake were problems.

A contributory belief was that flesh food and dairy products produced mucus, which was believed to be the cause of disease. Thus signs of mucus being excreted from the body could stimulate greater restriction of food intake. Fasting, for some, became couched in the belief that since waste from food caused disease, then less food or perhaps no food would be better. The mucus-as-the-cause-of disease theory can be found in popular literature sold in health food stores (Ehret, 1953). Nevertheless, the Black consciousness movement of the 1960s contributed to substantial dietary experimentation and change among Afro-Americans and was linked with a self-conscious effort toward cultural development.

Many Afro-Americans in the post-urban context have sustained and extended the link between identity, lifestyle, and spiritual development by a unique incorporation of Eastern, ancient, and occult health practices. Vegetarianism, meditation, and health arts such as yoga and tai chi are incorporated in an effort to produce a lifestyle geared toward spiritual and cultural development. Variations of these approaches are espoused by individuals who sometimes develop study groups, closed communities, and lecture circuits to disseminate and develop their views. These practices have symbolic significance because they are believed to have originated from a common ancient source, African culture.

One approach is that spiritual development is linked to cultivation of the life force. The life force can be enhanced through diet, meditation, specific health arts, and living in harmony with the cyclical constructive and destructive forces of nature. This approach is concomitant with the view that Black people had fallen from a correct mode of life that had previously insured them good health and a higher level of spiritual development, which included facility with psychic and magical powers (Straughn, 1976). However, the inclination to look to the ancient past is not new in the Black community; it has played a pivotal role in many nationalistic and revitalization tendencies. Nevertheless, popular health practices in the Black community have distinctive historical roots and are integrally intertwined in processes of cultural innovation, change, and development. Such processes have profound implications for the ultimate health status of the Black community as well as its evolving cultural identity.

References

Ammi, Ben. 1982. *God, the Black Man, and Truth*. Chicago: Communicators Press.

Bachrach, Steven, et al. 1979. "An Outbreak of Vitamin D Deficiency Rickets in a Susceptible Population," *Pediatrics*, Vol. 64, 871–877.

Blassingame, John W. 1979. *The Slave Community*. New York: Oxford University Press.

Bowering, Jean, et al. 1978. "Infant Feeding Practices in East Harlem," *Journal of the American Dietetic Association*, Vol. 72, 148–155.

Bradfield, Robert B., and Dorothy Coltrin. 1970. "Some Characteristics of the Health and Nutritional Status of California Negroes," *The American Journal of Clinical Nutrition* Vol. 23, 420–426.

Brandon, Elizabeth. 1976. "Folk Medicine in French Louisiana," in *American Folk Medicine: A Symposium*, Wayland D. Hand (ed.). Berkeley: University of California Press [pp. 215–234].

Edgerton, Robert B. 1971. "Traditional African Psychiatrist," *Southwestern Journal of Anthropology*, Vol. 27, 259–278.

Ehret, Arnold. 1953. *Professor Arnold Ehret's Mucusless Diet Healing System*. Cody, Wyoming: Ehret.

Fauset, Arthur H. 1970. *Black Gods of the Metropolis*. New York: Octagon.

Fauthauer, George H. 1969. "Food Habits—an Anthropologist's View," in *The Cross Cultural Approach to Health Behavior*, L. Riddick Lynch (ed.). Rutherford, New Jersey: Farleigh Dickenson University Press [pp. 59–69].

Frazier, E. Franklin. 1957. *Race and Culture Contacts in the Modern World*. Boston: Beacon Press.

Grant, Faye W., and Dale Groom. 1959. "A Dietary Study among a Group of Southern Negroes," *Journal of the American Dietetic Association*, Vol. 35, 910–918.

Gregory, Dick. 1973. *Dick Gregory's Natural Diet for Folks Who Eat*. New York: Harper and Row.

Griffith, Ezra E. H., et al. 1980. "Possession, Prayer, and Testimony: Therapeutic Aspects of the Wednesday Night Meeting in a Black Church," *Psychiatry*, Vol. 43, 120–128.

Hall, Arthur, and Peter G. Bourne. 1973. "Indigenous Therapists in a Southern Black Urban Community," *Archives of General Psychiatry*, Vol. 28, 137–142.

Hautman, Mary Ann. 1979. "Folk Health and Illness Beliefs," *Nurse Practitioners*, July-August, 23–34.

Hurston, Zora N. 1931. "Hoodoo in America," *The Journal of American Folk-Lore*, Vol. 44, 317–417.

Jackson, Bruce. 1976. "The other Kind of Doctor: Conjure and Magic in Black American Folk Medicine," in *American Folk Medicine: A Symposium*, Wayland D. Hand (ed.). Berkeley: University of California Press [pp. 259–272].

Jerome, N. W. 1969. "Northern Urbanization and Food Consumption Patterns of Southern-born Negroes," *The American Journal of Clinical Nutrition*, Vol. 22, 1667–1669.

Karp, Robert J., et al. 1980. "Increased Utilization of Salty Food with Age among Pre-teenage Black Girls," *Journal of the National Medical Association*, Vol. 72, 197–200.

Kiple, Kenneth F., and Virginia H. Kiple. 1977. "Slave Child Mortality: Some Nutritional Answers to a Perennial Puzzle," *Journal of Social History*, Vol. 10, 284–297.

Kunjufu, Johari M. 1975. *Commonsense Approach to Eating*. Chicago: Institute of Positive Education.

Lauer, Roger M. 1973. "Urban Shamans: The Influence of Folk Healers on Medical Care in Our Cities," *The New Physician*, August, 486–489.

Lee, Don L. 1973. *From Plan to Planet*. Chicago: Institution of Positive Education.

Lincoln, C. Eric. 1961. *The Black Muslims in America*. Boston: Beacon Press.

Mayer, Jean. 1965. "Food Habits and Nutritional Status of American Negroes," *Post Graduate Medicine*, January, A-110–115.

Morais, Herbert M. 1967. *The History of the Negro in Medicine*. Washington: Publishers Company.

Muhammad, Elijah. 1972. *How to Eat to Live (Book #2)*, Chicago: Muhammad's Temple of Islam No. 2.

Odejide, A. O., et al. 1978. "Traditional Healers and Mental Illness in the City of Ibadan," *Journal of Black Studies*, Vol. 9, 195–205.

Puckett, Newbell Niles. 1926. *Folk Beliefs of the Southern Negro*. Chapel Hill: University of North Carolina Press.

Ruiz, Pedro, and John Langrod. 1977. "The Ancient Art of Folk Healing: African Influence in a New York City Community Mental Health Center," in *Traditional Healing*, Philip Singer (ed.). New York: Conch Magazine Limited [pp. 80–95].

Savitt, Todd L. 1978. *Medicine and Slavery*. Chicago: University of Illinois Press.

Semmes, Clovis E. 1981. "Lifestyle Change among African Americans," unpublished paper presented at the 7th Annual Third World Conference of Governors, State University, Chicago, Illinois.

_____. 1982. "African Americans Seeking Nonmedical Health Care," *The Western Journal of Black Studies*, Vol. 5, 254–263.

_____. (forthcoming.) "Music and the Resurgence of Black Culture in Chicago: Phil Cohran and the Afro-Arts Theatre," in *Aesthetics and Philosophy of Afro-American Art*. Athens: Ohio University Center for Afro-American studies.

Snow, Loudell F. 1973. "I Was Born Just Exactly with the Gift: An Interview with a Voodoo Practitioner," *Journal of American Folklore*, Vol. 86, 272–281.

_____. 1974. "Folk Medical Beliefs and Their Implications for Care of Patients: A Review Based on Studies among Black Americans," *Annals of Internal Medicine*, Vol. 81, 82–96.

_____. 1977a. "The Religious Component in Southern Folk Medicine," in *Traditional Healing*, Philip Singer (ed.) [pp. 26–51].

_____. 1977b. "Popular Medicine in a Black Neighborhood," in *Ethnic Medicine in the Southwest*, Edward H. Spicer (ed.).

_____.1978. "Sorcerers, Saints, and Charlatans: Black Folk Healers in Urban America," *Culture, Medicine and Psychiatry*, Vol. 2, 69–106.

Spicer, Edward H. (ed.). 1977. *Ethnic Medicine in the Southwest*. Tucson: University of Arizona Press.

Stewart, Horace. 1971. "Kindling of Hope in the Disadvantaged: A Study of the Afro-American Healer," *Mental Hygiene*, Vol. 55, 96–100.

Straughn, R. A. 1976. *Meditation Techniques of the Kabalists, Vedantins and Taoists*. New York: MAAT.

Webb, Julie Y. 1971. "Louisiana Voodoo and Superstitions Related to Health," *HSMHA Health Reports*, Vol. 86, 291–301.

Wintrob, Ronald M. 1973. "The Influence of Others: Witchcraft and Rootwork as Explanations of Behavior Disturbances," *Journal of Nervous and Mental Diseases*, Vol. 156, 318–326.

Zmora, Ehud, et al. 1979. "Multiple Nutritional Deficiencies in Infants from a Strict Vegetarian Community," *American Journal of Diseases of Children*, Vol. 133, 141–144.

11

Theories of Black Culture

Amuzie Chimezie

Amuzie Chimezie has a Ph.D. degree from Indiana University. He is an Associate Professor in the Department of Afro-American Studies, University of Cincinnati, Ohio. His research focus is on Black culture, language, education, and child development.—The Western Journal of Black Studies, *Winter 1983, Vol. 7, No. 4*

Introduction

The idea of Black culture has generated divergent views. Some theorists have flatly denied the existence of a distinctive Black culture. Others have affirmed its existence and explained it in terms of retention of African traditions. Still others, while conceding the existence of a distinctive Black culture, have explained that distinctiveness in terms of Blacks' New World experience. This paper will present, analyze, and attempt to explain the various points of view and explanatory models that have surfaced in the literature on Black culture.

The heart of the issue is whether or not Blacks are in any way culturally different from white Anglo-Saxon Americans whose culture dominates the mainstream. The theoretical positions that affirm the existence of a distinctive Black culture will be presented first, followed by those views that deny or negate the existence of such a culture. In this discussion, affirmative theories refer to those explanatory views which subscribe to the position that there is a distinctive Black culture regardless of the variables displayed as responsible for the distinctiveness. In other words, the common bond among affirmative theories is that they affirm Black cultural distinctiveness even though they may diverge on the question of the crucial variables involved in the distinctiveness. They include the African-heritage theory, the affirmative New World-experience theory, and the eclectic theory.

African-Heritage Theory

This theory posits that Black American culture is distinct from white Anglo-Saxon American culture and that most of this distinctiveness is explainable in terms of some of those elements of African culture that the enslaved Africans carried over to America. It maintains that, although some of those cultural carry-overs have been modified beyond easy recognition, a careful scientific investigation involving close comparison with African culture would reveal that these elements are modified from African culture.

The African-heritage theory is based on three main facts. First, many of the distinctive cultural elements involved are generally not characteristic of white American Euro-centric culture (e.g., the extended family and Brer Rabbit stories). Second, they are found among virtually all Afro-centric communities in the New World, especially in the Caribbean. Third, those elements still characterize African culture today, especially West Africa, from where most of the Africans were captured for enslavement. The widespread presence of these distinctive cultural elements in the Afro-centric world (in Africa and the diaspora) is one of the most persuasive arguments used by the proponents of the African-heritage theory of Black culture (e.g., Herskovits, 1958). There are several conspicuous cultural elements that have been used as examples of carry-overs from Africa which have survived in Black culture. One is the Black dialect, including the Gullah dialect. Some features of these dialects have been attributed to interference from the African languages spoken by the Africans enslaved in America. Another example is Black folklore. It has been pointed out by the proponents of the African-heritage theory (Herskovits, 1958) that some of the stories in Black folklore (e.g., the Tar Baby story and other animal stories) were carried over from Africa. A third example is Black adult-child relationships in which respect and obedience are expected of the child. A fourth is Black music, some aspects of which have been shown to share many features with African music. There are many more micro and macro examples that have been used to support the African-heritage theory, but the above will suffice to show that certain elements in Black culture have actually been identified and pointed to as carry-overs from Africa.

The African-heritage theory is usually associated with Melville Herskovits, Carter G. Woodson, Lorenzo Turner, Wade Nobles, and others. In *The Myth of the Negro Past*, Herskovits connected many macro and micro elements in Black culture with their theorized origins or prototypes in African culture. He discussed such dimensions as childrearing, music, religion, language, folklore, and family structure, and he identified the Africanisms in them. Carter G. Woodson, in *The African Background Outlined* (1968), discussed Black generosity or hospitality, respect for the law, keen sense of justice, and the work ethic as part of Blacks' African heritage. Lorenzo Turner studied the Gullah (Blacks in the coastal areas of South Carolina and Georgia) and identified the Africanisms in their dialect. Turner's work *Africanisms in the Gullah Dialect*, was the first serious effort to explain the Gullah dialect in terms of the speakers' African heritage. In a 1974 article, "Africanity: Its Role in Black Families," Nobles saw the strong kinship bond, the role flexibility, and the informal adoption that characterize Black culture as continuations of African values.

It appears there are three hurdles that this persuasive theory has to clear. One of the hurdles is created by the similarity between certain aspects of African culture and some of the experiences of Blacks during slavery. For example, the original enslaved Blacks were familiar with physical punishment as a disciplinary measure used on children in Africa. They (Blacks) were also whipped when they got out of line as slaves. Is the Black use of whipping to discipline children a function of African tradition or the slavery experience? Because of this kind of theoretical problem, African-heritage explanations of some aspects of Black culture are sometimes questioned. On a second look, this kind of a hurdle is not as problematic as it appears because the African-heritage explanation is more parsimonious and in such a case should be preferred. The second hurdle arises from the similarity between some aspects of Black culture and lower-class white culture. An example is dialect, which tempts some theorists to explain Black culture as poverty-induced rather than as an African carry-over. The third hurdle is the tendency on the part of some theorists and laymen to reject the African-heritage theory because Africa is perceived as a "badge of shame." Herskovits (1958) mentioned this problem in his work. He observed that: "Because of the emotional 'loading' of attitudes toward the problem under discussion, the attempt to trace Africanisms is too frequently met with the counter-assertion that the Negroes of the United States are not Africans, regardless of the fact that no implication of this kind is involved." If social scientists are committed to truth, then they should not permit "emotional loading," a sense of embarrassment, or sociopolitical considerations to suppress any truths about the sources of Black culture that implicate Africa.

Affirmative New World-Experience Theory

This model affirms or recognizes the existence of a distinctive Black culture, but unlike the African-heritage theory, explains that distinctiveness in terms of the experience of Blacks in the New World (America). Such experiences mostly involve contact with Euro-Americans and its consequences. In other words, instead of explaining Black cultural distinctiveness in terms of African traditions, it searches for explanatory variables in Black experiences in America. A New World-experience theorist of Black culture might, for example, explain Blacks' high positive valuation of fertility and tendency toward large families as a function of the slavery (New World) experience, since Black women were encouraged to produce many children for the enslaver (Franklin, 1974). Such a theorist might argue that Blacks developed positive valuation of fertility and large families during slavery, even though such a value was part of Blacks' African heritage and therefore predated their New World slavery experience (Herskovits, 1958). Such theorists might also explain Black use of physical punishment in disciplining their children (Staples, 1976) as a result of the slavery (New World) experience of being physically whipped by the enslaver (Blassingame, 1972; Genovese, 1976) even though the enslaved Africans had already used that method of discipline in Africa before their American experience (Herskovits, 1958). Roger D. Abrahams, who clearly recognized the distinctiveness of Black culture (1970), explained the "dozens" not as a carry-over from Africa, but as a function of New World experience-induced mother rejection (Abrahams, 1962). Hortense Powdermaker, in *After Freedom* (1939), described a clearly distinctive culture among the Blacks of a rural Mississippi community fictitiously called Cottonville; however, she explained the use of physical punishment on children among these Blacks in terms of the New World slavery experience. Here is her theory:

> The grandparents of the present young colored parents were themselves whipped by their white masters…The Slaves adopted whipping as the approved way of correcting and punishing faults. Moreover, they had no means of retaliating for their own beatings, unless on their children…
>
> Although whipping was a pattern taken over from the masters, and still survives among the descendants, today the failure of Negro parents to whip their children may be criticized as "aping the Whites."

It is true that Blacks were physically whipped during slavery; but to say that Blacks' use of physical punishment as a method of disciplining children *originated* from slavery is to totally ignore Blacks' previous experience in Africa. It would be closer to the truth to say that the slavery experience possibly *reinforced* this practice among Blacks. Powdermaker's theorizing on this issue represents a case of too much psychologizing at the expense of anthropology.

Biculturation Theory

This mode views Black culture as composed of Black and white elements. According to this model, Blacks are bicultural both collectively and individually. According to Charles A. Valentine (1971):

> The collective behavior and social life of the Black community is bicultural in the sense that each Afro-American ethnic segment draws upon both a distinctive repertoire of standardized Afro-American group behavior and, simultaneously, patterns derived from the mainstream cultural system of Euro-American derivation. Socialization into both systems begins at an early age, continues throughout life, and is generally of equal importance in most individual lives.

It is true that Blacks participate in Euro-American culture; however, most of the participation is effected through coercion and the use of punishment if one fails to participate. Also, it is doubtful whether a majority of Blacks relate to the white part of the cultural dualism in their community with the same feeling as they do to the Black part. In fact, Robert Staples (1976) suggests that some of the values of the Euro-American culture that Blacks are forced to accept are antithetical to their own values. He elaborates:

> The commitment to Euro-American values that Valentine speaks of is not necessarily positive. Many of the Euro-American values required for successful achievements—e.g., formality, materialism, individualism—may be seen as values lacking in intrinsic merit. While Afro-Americans may engage in such cultural practices, this should not be taken as a strong commitment to those values requiring such behavior.

It is therefore doubtful whether both parts of the cultural duality are "of equal importance" to Blacks as Valentine suggests.

In his article, "Deficit, Difference, and Bicultural Models of Afro-American Behavior," Valentine rejected the difference and deficit theories of Black culture. He conceded that Black culture has distinctive elements; a "repertoire of standardized Afro-American group behavior"; but he rejected any notion that Blacks are so culturally distinct that they are untouched by Euro-American culture. Hence, this biculturation theory is, among other things, an attempt to remind the "difference theorists" that the Euro-American elements in Black culture should not be ignored. In the sense that it recognizes at least two major sources of Black cultural distinctiveness, the biculturation model could be seen as eclectic.

The Eclectic View

This view of Black culture attempts to identify the salient factors that have influenced or affected the development of a distinctive Black culture and to associate them with the relevant elements in Black culture for which they are theorized to be responsible. It definitely recognizes the distinctiveness of Black culture, but it does not take an adamant position that no aspect of Black culture is a carry-over from Africa or that Blacks have not been culturally influenced in any way by their experience in the New World. It realizes that many various factors have influenced and affected Black ways of life and accordingly recognizes those factors. Some of the factors in Black culture recognized in this view include but are not limited to Africa, Christianity, white supremacy and oppression, relative poverty, lower-class status, and contact with other groups in the American society. From the above list of factors, it is obvious that the eclectic view comprehends virtually all the current theories without an exclusive commitment to any single one of them. That, of course, is the essence of eclecticism.

Among the eclectic theorists of Black culture are Robert Staples (1976), Robert Blauner (1970), Andrew Billingsley (1968), and Johnnetta Cole (1970). Staples (1976) discusses African survivals, oppression, and slavery as "sources of Black culture." Blauner (1970) elaborates on "the many sources of Negro American culture, including Africa, white racism, the South, emancipation, Northern migration, poverty, and lower-class status." Billingsley (1968) includes Africa, slavery, and "systematic exclusion from participation and influence in the major institutions of this society" among the factors that made Blacks "an ethnic sub-society with a distinct history." To Cole (1970), Black culture has Black, white, lower-class, and oppressed-people components.

"Negative" theories of Black culture are those models which argue that a valid, distinctive Black culture does not exist. They deny or negate the existence of a Black culture that is appreciably different from the dominant white Anglo-Saxon American culture. They include those models which categorically deny the existence of cultural differences between Blacks and whites, or attribute disparaging characteristics to Blacks or to any obvious differences as a way of invalidating the culture. Thus, they argue that Black culture is no different from white culture, is pathological, lower-class, induced by poverty, or is a product of white cultural influence (cultural imitation) and therefore cannot be regarded as a valid, distinctive culture. Theories that posit Black-white cultural identity tend to explain those differences they concede in terms of oppression, poverty, social class status, or other variables that draw attention away from Blacks' African heritage, innovativeness, and cultural integrity. The writer will now discuss some of these theories and their characteristic observations on Black culture.

Negative New World-Experience Theory

This theory denies Black cultural distinctiveness and attributes any observable Black-white cultural differences to Black experience in the New World (particularly the white effects), or Black inability to master white culture. Unlike the affirmative New World-experience theory, it uses the New World experience to *explain away* Black cultural distinctiveness, thus negating the concept of Black culture.

Two factors seem to underlie some of the affirmative and negative New World-experience theories of Black culture—white ethnocentrism and Black rejection of Africa. How did white ethnocentrism influence or at least reinforce the New World-experience theory of Black culture? Around the time that Europeans and Euro-Americans were imperialistically destroying the cultures of other societies in the world, a notion emerged in the white world that "inferior" or non-literate cultures cannot survive when brought into contact with "superior" (white) cultures (Herskovits, 1958). George P. Krapp (1924) reflected this notion of cultural deference when he wrote: "The native African dialects have been completely lost."

Since Euro-Americans regarded African and other non-white cultures (e.g., American Indian cultures) as inferior, they were resistant to any suggestion that African culture, as borne by Blacks, survived the onslaught of their "superior" Euro-centric culture. To Euro-Americans, that was impossible, given their ethnocentric "axiom" that "inferior" cultures yield or defer to "superior" cultures on contact. Hence, many of the attempts made by whites to explain Black culture at the beginning of the 20th century were New World-experience theories, which in essence both asserted and implied that most of the cultural characteristics associated with Blacks were unsuccessful attempts to master Euro-American culture rather than a demonstration of the resiliency of African traditions under attack.

Another factor that underlies the New World theory of Black culture is Black rejection of, or non-identification with, Africa. This non-identification was a function of the disparagement of Africa in both popular culture and "scholarly" writings. For example, Africans were characterized as follows: savage (uncivilized), heathenish (non-Christian), "real" black, "oversexed," bestial, related to apes, polygamous, lustful, and immoral (Jordan, 1974). These characteristics were all perceived as negative by Europeans and Euro-Americans, and also by Blacks who had been made to feel ashamed of their distant cousins in Africa. John H. Van Evrie, "a northern physician," wrote as follows in 1861:

> The Negro on the contrary is at this moment just where the race was four thousand years ago, when sculptored on Egyptian monuments. Portions of it in contact with the superior race have been temporarily advanced, but invariably, without exception, they have returned to the African standard as soon as this contact has ceased, or as soon as the results of amalgamation between them have disappeared.[1]

Contemporary negative portrayals of Africa include the Tarzan movies, the various television programs on poverty, malnutrition, and disease, and the fact that Africa is rarely featured on television except when there is something negative to show. Add to these the horror stories and the pathetic pictures that missionaries to Africa paint of Africa—perhaps, to make their congregation thankful that they are Americans and better than "these miserable people."

It was the internalization of the images of Africa that made Phyllis Wheatley write the following poem titled, "On Being Brought from Africa to America":

> 'Twas mercy brought me from my pagan land,
> Taught my benighted soul to understand
> That there is a God, that there is a *Saviour* too:
> Once I redemption neither sought nor knew.
> Some view our sable race with scornful eye,
> "Their colour is a diabolic die."
> Remember, *Christians, Negroes*, black as *Cain*
> May be refin'd and join th' angelic train.[2]

Like most slaves, Wheatley was probably taught that being sold into slavery and brought out of Africa was an act of mercy (see the first line of the poem) for which she should be thankful. There is no question that Wheatley had been taught that Africa was heathenish or pagan, in darkness, practicing the "wrong" religion that did not include the worship of Jesus of Nazareth (the Saviour), evil as Cain, and in need of refinement to qualify to join the train of white angels (as opposed to "black Cain"). It would not be wrong to assume that most Blacks of her time internalized the same indoctrination that disparaged Africa.

Consequently, Africa was rejected. It was perceived as a culture not to be associated with. Not only that, as Woodson noted, Blacks began to "accept as a compliment the theory of a complete break with Africa, for above all things they do not care to be known as resembling in any way these 'terrible Africans.'"[3] To a Black scholar who has this kind of attitude toward Africa, a New World-experience theory would be more acceptable than an African-heritage theory. Also, some of the white liberal social scientists whose intention is to shield Blacks against white vituperation (Davidson, 1969) would be inclined to divest them of the "badge of shame" by adopting the New World-experience theory in explaining Black culture. Thus the rejection of Africa could rightly be seen as underlying some of the New World theories of Black culture.

White ethnocentrism (with its attendant notion of cultural deference), white need to disparage Blacks, and the ignoring of Africa as a factor in the equation for Black culture have led to half-baked and downright untenable negative New World-experience theoretical statements about Black culture. For example, Krapp (1924), in keeping with the cultural deference "axiom" that "inferior" cultures cannot withstand the onslaught of "superior" cultures, completely ruled out African influence on the Black dialect and denied that Blacks contributed "anything of importance" to American language. Having asserted that practically nothing about the Black dialect is African and that virtually every characteristic of the dialect is traceable to "ancient English or other European sources," he went on (1924) to explain why it should be so:

> That this should have happened is not surprising, for it is a linguistic axiom that when two groups of people with different languages come into contact, the one on a relatively high, the other on a relatively low cultural level, the latter adapts itself freely to the speech of the former, whereas the group on the higher cultural plane borrows little or nothing from that on the lower.

Subsequently, Herskovits (1958) and Turner (1969) proved many of Krapp's assertions about the Black dialect to be false and misleading, and pointed out many African-influenced characteristics of the dialect. There is no doubt that Blacks were linguistically influenced by the type of English spoken by those whites who were in close interaction with them, but it is also true that pre-existing linguistic habits established in Africa contributed to the structures of the dialect.

Continuing the negative New World-experience view of Black culture, Myrdal (1944) Euro-Americanized Black culture to a point where almost every aspect of it is a copy and retention of old or present white American culture. He asserted:

> Negro institutions are, nevertheless, similar to those of the white man. They show little similarity to African institutions. In his cultural traits, the Negro is akin to other Americans. Some peculiarities even to be characterized as

"exaggerations" of American traits…Even the "exaggeration" or intensifica-
tion of general American traits in American Negro culture is explainable by
specific caste pressures. In his allegiances the Negro is characteristically an
American. He believes in the American Creed and in other ideals held by most
Americans, such as getting ahead in the world, individualism, the importance
of education and wealth. He imitates the dominant culture as he sees it and
insofar as he can adopt it under his conditions of life. For the most part he is
not proud of those things in which he differs from the White American…

In practically all its divergencies, American Negro culture is not something independent of general American culture. It is a distorted development, or a pathological condition, of the general American culture.

A major flaw in Myrdal's theory is that it presents Black culture as Euro-
American, a result of "caste pressures" or a pathological exaggeration of the Euro-
American culture. There is no place in this theory for African and certain unique
Black values as factors in Black culture. For this reason alone, the theory is seriously deficient as a conceptual framework for fully and accurately understanding
Black culture. Another flaw is that it has the typical weakness of most models that
fail to concede that Black culture, in many respects, is not a duplication of, nor
a function of inability to successfully and exactly copy white culture: it explains
the differences that the senses cannot but perceive as pathological, induced by
poverty, lower-class status, or some other "negative" factor, but never by genuine
Black values and traditions.

Charles Johnson, in a report of his study (1966) of a rural Black community
in Alabama (first published in 1934), continued the point of view of the negative
New World-experience theorists. He described most of the cultural characteristics
of the Blacks he studied as borrowed from European or Euro-American culture.
The following was his assertion:

> In a sense the southern rural Negro population has tended to represent the
> surviving traditions of an earlier period. They have been the repositories
> of certain folk ways which, in the changing pattern of American life, are
> being discarded…Their dialect is in part a survival of the English of the
> colonies, their superstitions most often are borrowed from whites, their reli-
> gious beliefs are in large part the same as those held by isolated whites, their
> folklore is scarcely distinguishable from that brought over from Europe by
> the early colonists, their religious emotionalism is similar to that commonly
> demonstrated in white Methodist camp meetings until very recently.

Perhaps it is appropriate to mention the novelist Ralph Ellison in this section.
It is clear that he saw the Black way of life as a product of the New World. In
Shadow and Act (1953) he presented this rhapsody about Black Culture:

> The American Negro people is North American in origin and has evolved
> under specifically American conditions: nutritional, historical, political and

social. It takes its character from the experience of American slavery and the struggle for, and the achievement of emancipation; from the dynamics of American race and caste discrimination, and from living in a highly industrialized and highly mobile society possessing a relatively high standard of living and explicitly stated equalitarian concept of freedom. Its spiritual outlook is basically Protestant, its system of kinship is Western, its time and historical sense are American (United States), and its secular values are those professed, ideally at least, by all of the people of the United States.

It appears that Ellison's rejection of Africa as a factor in Black culture was so thorough that he had no qualms in extravagantly claiming that Blacks originated in North America. Culturally or biologically, this claim is *irresponsibly* rhapsodic. It was because of his position that the Black way of life is a product of the New World (specifically, the Euro-American influence in North America) that Ellison has been mentioned in this section. In another sense, however, he could be seen as not ignoring all the unique cultural characteristics of Blacks, although he was definitely uncomfortable with any notion that Blacks are culturally different from Euro-Americans. First, he could not deny the evidence of the senses; so he conceded that Black ways of life constitute "one of the subcultures...of the United States." Then he went on (1953) to mention some of the areas of distinctiveness of the Black "subculture":

This "American Negro culture" is expressed in a body of folklore, in the musical forms of the spirituals, the blues and jazz; an idiomatic version of American speech (especially in the Southern United States); a cuisine; a body of dance forms and even a dramaturgy which is generally unrecognized as such because still tied to the more folkish Negro churches. Some Negro preachers are great showmen.

But, uncomfortable with the idea of Black cultural distinctiveness, he saw the use of the terms "black culture" and "white culture" as racist. (Note that he put quotation marks around "American Negro culture" in the excerpt just quoted.)

Clearly, Ellison took a New World-experience view of Black culture. However, he was definitely ill at ease with the idea that Blacks are culturally different from whites even though he could not deny the imposing distinctiveness of some dimensions of Black culture. His, therefore, was the problem of a middle-class Black man, who desired to see Blacks identified with this "highly industrialized and highly mobile society" that has "a relatively high standard of living and an explicitly stated equalitarian concept of freedom," but who was confronted with the reality that Blacks are only tangentially a part of this "high civilization." In his rhapsodic ecstasy, Ellison failed to consider the fact that scholars, who have studied the Black family, have found that Blacks have extended, augmented, and other family structures that are different from white family structures (Staples, 1976; Billingsley, 1968). Moreover, researchers have found axiological or value differences between Blacks and whites (Staples, 1976).

Having looked at one category of negative New World-experience theories of Black culture, a second category will now be discussed. Perhaps the difference between the two categories is not significant. However, for greater cognitive clarity, it is felt that the slight difference should be pointed out. This category of New World-experience theories comprises those that categorically state that Blacks have no culture. Since every human group has a culture (by 20th century definition of culture as the totality of a people's way of life), it is valid to assume that these theories mean that Blacks have so completely copied white culture in America that they cannot be said to have a distinctive culture. If this is what these theorists mean, their view, though a negative New World-experience position, is a little different from that of the theorists already discussed in this section. Krapp, Myrdal, Johnson, and Ellison alluded to or mentioned cultural differences, but were unwilling to accord them the status of a valid, distinctive culture, but Frazier, Stampp, and Glazer and Moynihan, the theorists that are going to be discussed next, flatly state that Blacks have "no" special culture.

Stampp, and Glazer and Moynihan, have made concise and candid statements. Stampp (1956) claimed that Blacks are "white men with Black skins,"[4] meaning that they are completely culturally white. Nathan Glazer and Daniel Patrick Moynihan, in *Beyond the Melting Pot* (1963), assert that "the Negro is only an American, and nothing else. He has no values and culture to guard and protect." The belief-attitude complex underlying this statement was partially revealed a few lines later when the authors said that Blacks are "the product of America" and alluded to Blacks finding "nothing positive" in the Black group. It is clear from those statements that Stampp, and Glazer and Moynihan, saw nothing Black in the Black way of life for, according to Glazer and Moynihan, Blacks are "made in U.S.A."

The fourth theorist in this category is E. Franklin Frazier. In *The Negro in the United States* (1957), he had this to say about Black culture:

> Although the Negro is distinguished from other minorities by his physical characteristics unlike other racial or cultural minorities the Negro is not distinguished by culture from the dominant group. Having completely lost his ancestral culture, he speaks the same language, practices the same religion, and accepts the same values and political ideas as the dominant group. Consequently, when one speaks of Negro culture in the United States, one can only refer to the folk culture of the rural Southern Negro or the traditional forms of behavior and values which have grown out of the Negro's social and mental isolation.

In the above quote, Frazier implied that the cultural identity, which he observed between Blacks and whites, was a result of Blacks imbibing white culture. But in an earlier article (1934) he put it differently by saying that Blacks had no culture:

The traditions and culture of the American Negro have grown out of his experiences in America and have derived their meaning and significance from the same source…To be sure, when one undertakes the study of the Negro he discovers a great poverty of traditions and patterns of behavior that exercise any real influence on the formation of the Negro's personality and conduct. If, as Keyserling remarks, the most striking thing about the Chinese is their deep culture, the most conspicuous thing about the Negro is his lack of a culture.

One would have wondered what he meant by Blacks' "lack of a culture" had it not been for the opening sentence of the quote, which established some kind of a culture. What Frazier seemed to be saying here is that the culture that Blacks have is not Black but white. This was made clearer in his 1957 work, quoted above. To understand Frazier's statements on Black culture, it is necessary to be aware of three things. First, he presumably identified with white culture, including a white sense of sexual morality and a white concept or definition of social familial pathology and disorganization. Second, he implied that there is virtually nothing positive in Black culture; hence, to him, acculturation or the adoption of white cultural norms was the only way for Blacks to go since he apparently believed they (Blacks) had culturally nothing worthy of preservation. Third, he began his writings about Blacks in the 1930s, when it was necessary to refute the racist theory that Black cultural difference from whites was a sign of Black inferiority and that the inferiority was a function of race and genes (Johnson, 1978).

Frazier may have accepted the white ethnocentric claim that white culture was superior to Black culture—hence, he recommended acculturation into white ways of life for Blacks—but rejected racial-genetic determinism as a theoretical framework for understanding the "inferiority" of Black culture. Instead, he posited social determinism. From then on, his test was to show that Black cultural "inferiority" was a function, not of race and genes, but of socio-environmental factors—a position that is commonly referred to as environmentalism.

One of the ways Frazier attempted to prove that Black cultural "inferiority" was not genetic was to show that Blacks had lost their "inferior" African culture and picked up white culture as a result of contact or change in environment. Hence, he insisted that Blacks had no culture, meaning "no Black culture," asserting, inter alia, that they speak "the same language…as the dominant group." One might realize that he could not be serious when he ignored the fact that about 80 percent of Black American children speak a dialect of American English that is sufficiently distinctive to cause a cultural clash in the classroom (Dillard, 1972). The following statement (also quoted above in this article) could also be seen as an attempt by Frazier (1957) to show that only isolated Blacks, that is Blacks in the "wrong" environment, exhibited cultural divergence from whites:

Consequently, when one speaks of Negro culture in the United States, one can only refer to the folk culture of the rural Southern Negro or the traditional forms of behavior and values which have grown out of the Negro's social and mental isolation.

In this and other statements, Frazier was being consistent with his purpose of demonstrating not the validity of Black culture, but how its "inferiority" is a function, not of genes, but of environment. He erred when he failed to question white ethnocentric claims to cultural superiority, when he let his cultural preference seriously tamper with his scientific enquiry, and when he investigated the Black community, not to understand and analyze it in its own right, but to judge it using white culture, which he preferred, as a yardstick.

The Lower-Class Theory

This model posits that Blacks are not really culturally different from Caucasians and that what is regarded as Black culture is nothing but lower-class culture often induced by poverty. Attempts are often made to support this theory by reference to the similarities between some aspects of Black culture and lower-class white culture.

There seems to be an assumption in this theory that middle-class Black culture (which is closer to, but not really identical with, white culture) is, or should be perceived as, the Black culture. (Note that if it is so perceived, then Black culture as such would not really exist because of the similarities between white and Black middle-class cultures.) Even some middle-class Blacks take it as a point of duty to ensure that appropriate distinction is made when Black culture is discussed because "we are not all alike." Some complain (Frazier, 1948) that "the white people draw the line at the wrong point and put all of us in the same class." What is not realized by the theoreticians and Blacks who take this position is that among whites, the middle-class is the majority subgroup, but among Blacks, the lower-class is in the majority (Staples, 1976). Therefore, while the assumption that middle-class white culture is the white culture may be valid (based on numbers), a similar assumption for Black culture would not be valid because it would lack quantitative support.

Among the theorists who perceive Black culture as lower-class, non-ethnic, culture are Frazier, John H. Scanzoni, Oscar Lewis, and Bennett M. Berger. Frazier (1957) ruled out "the folk culture of the rural Southern [lower-class] Negro" as legitimate Black culture. To him, such folk (lower-class) culture was not acceptable as Black culture. Scanzoni (1971) asserted:

> The underlying point to remember is that whatever differences emerge between black and white family structures are largely the result of discrimination and differential access to opportunity. They are not due to any racial or biological proclivities.

In other words, Scanzoni saw no basic value differences between Blacks and whites that would explain the observable cultural divergences. To him, Blacks are merely being prevented by poverty—induced by what Scanzoni called "differential access to opportunity"—from manifesting culturally their axiological identity with whites. Scanzoni would be unwilling to accept any suggestion that Blacks have a distinctive, valid, "ethnic" culture that is not a function of poverty. In *La Vida* (1965), Oscar Lewis suggested that the distinctiveness of several dimensions of Black culture, which other theorists had tried to explain in terms of slavery and other factors, were "traits of the culture of poverty" because he observed similar traits among other relatively poor groups in other parts of the world—e.g., Puerto Rico.

Criticizing Charles Keil (1966), who took the position that Blacks do have a distinctive culture, Bennett M. Berger claimed that what Keil called Black culture is nothing but a Black version of American lower-class culture. He warned (1967, 57):

> For stripped of its mystique, black culture is basically an American Negro version of *lower class culture*, and, race prejudice aside, it can expect *on this ground alone* to meet strong resistance from the overwhelming majority of the American population which will see in the attempt to legitimate it an attempt to strike at the heart of the ethic of success and mobility, which is as close as this country comes to having any really sacred values. No lower class culture has ever been fully legitimated in the United States.

A few comments on Berger's assumptions and perceptions as revealed in the foregoing quote are necessary at this juncture. First, Berger assumed that Black culture is exclusive of what he calls "the ethic of success and mobility." However, in actuality Blacks indeed do value success and mobility, but not the Caucasian, social Darwinistic, individualistic, law-of-the-jungle, the strong-devour-the-weak variety; rather Black values may tend to be more collectivistic and humane. Second, if Berger's assumption is that "the ethic of success and mobility" is absent from lower class white culture and that this absence is a function of negative valuation of "success and mobility," he cannot rightly make the same assumption about Blacks. Whites have had a lot of opportunities and preferential treatment in this society; therefore, any lack of success among any subgroup of them has to be explained somewhat differently from the poverty present in the Black community. Most of the poverty in the Black community is a function of white oppression rather than negative valuation of "success and mobility." Therefore, the implication in Berger's assertion, that the recognition of Black cultural distinctiveness is a celebration of an anti-success ethic, is untenable. Third, Black culture is not the way of life of a group of poor people who happen to be black as implied in Berger's statement; rather, it is the way of life of an ethno-racial group, many of whose members just happen to be relatively poor. Fourth, Berger's statement is an example of how mislabeling leads to mischaracterization. Having labeled it lower class, Berger went on to characterize Black culture as lacking "the ethic of success and mobility" and to predict that it will suffer the same fate as lower-class culture in this society: rejection, suppression, and punishment. Thus, mislabeling and mischaracterization could be fatal to Black culture.

Like E. Franklin Frazier and others, Berger was unwilling to accept the Black way of life as a valid "ethnic" culture. Apparently, his main reason for rejecting this culture was that he did not see anything in it to be affirmed. Berger persisted in calling on the affirmative theorists to specify what is to be affirmed in Black culture (1967), thus implying that he did not see anything in it to be affirmed. Berger obviously did not have an affinity for Black culture. But the existence of any culture is independent of the theorists' values, preferences, and biases.

There are various reasons why the lower-class theory would appeal to certain groups of people. To those Blacks who want to be perceived as "non-niggers," this theory would be appealing because it says their culture is really not different from that of whites (only the lower-class Black culture is), which is what they want to hear. To those who are arduously working to prove that Blacks can be white, this theory is acceptable because it says that only lower-class Blacks are different, that Blacks have the capacity to become white ("civilized"), and that those Blacks who have had the opportunity to become middle-class have become white, and that, given the same opportunity, the rest would be acculturated. This theory would also appeal to those who like to think that the Black-white tension in society is a function of social class differences rather than racial oppression regardless of social class. Once Black cultural distinctiveness is reduced to and labeled as an interclass cultural difference, then it would become easy to eliminate Blacks culturally (an overwhelming majority of who belong to the so-called lower class) without anyone protesting ethnic or racial-cultural genocide. The contemporary consciousness seems to tolerate interclass oppression better than it does interracial or interethnic oppression. To those whites who see no need for Black Studies, nor adjustments in society to accommodate Black cultural differences, this theory would be welcome, since the dominant group would then not have to make adjustments for Blacks, any more than they have for poor lower-class whites.

Some critical commentary on this theory is in order at this juncture. To say that *some* characteristics of Black culture *look similar* to lower-class white cultural characteristics is valid. But this does not necessarily mean that all those "shared" characteristics originated from poverty or from the same philosophical axiological base. Also, to say that Black culture as such does not exist because what does exist is not middle-class (in other words, white) is to make a value-laden statement. If one is committed to science and sociology rather than racial values and ethnocentrism, one has to recognize the validity of a culture practiced by a majority of Black Americans, irrespective of its sources or the socioeconomic status of the people who practice it. In the final analysis, the ultimate question is whether or not a majority of Blacks accept, identify with, and practice a culture;

not whether or not the culture came from a "positive" source. It is possible for aspects of a culture to come from a "negative" source; and, yet, in time become a well-accepted, permanent part of a people's way of life. Moreover, Black culture is different from lower-class white culture in many ways.

One of the results of the invalidation of Black culture because it is perceived as lower-class is the labeling of Black children as culturally deprived. This implies that they have not been raised in the "right" (white-type) cultural context. Therefore, they are perceived as deprived of culture. This negative label was, of course, rejected by Blacks, including Black children. Under pressure from the Black community, it is gradually disappearing from current literature and being replaced by a more objective phrase—"culturally different."

The Pathology Theory

This theory views Black culture as sick or diseased. It also perceives the culture as deficient and deviant. When a pathology theorist looks at Black culture, all he sees and wants to see is alcoholism, promiscuity, disorganization, etc. The literature of this theory is liberally spattered with such terms as "disorganized," "fatalistic," "immoral," "role confusion," "illiterate," "promiscuous," and so on. Reacting to Lewis's characterization of the "culture of poverty," Charles Valentine (1968) commented: "If one could truly find a human mode of existence characterized only by these traits, it might be something like the chronic patient population in the back ward of a state mental hospital." That is the image the Black community assumes—"the chronic patient population in the back ward of a state mental hospital"—in the hands of a pathology theorist regarding Black culture.

Though not the first to view Black culture as diseased or pathological, Daniel Moynihan (1965) is a good example of a theorist who perceives Black culture in terms of deviance and pathologies. Among the "deviant" and "pathological" characteristics he saw in Black culture were matriarchy, illegitimacy, marital break-ups, academic failure, crime, and the emasculation of males. Most of these were blamed on the structure of the Black family, particularly what he called matriarchy, which itself was seen as a pathology. Moynihan theorized:

> Nonetheless, at the center of the tangle of pathology is the weakness of the family structure. Once or twice removed, it will be found to be the principal source of most of the aberrant, inadequate or anti-social behavior that did not establish, but now serves to perpetuate the cycle of poverty and deprivation.[5]

Reflecting the pathology view, Myrdal (1944) asserted that Black culture "is a distorted development, or a pathological condition, of the general American culture." Other theories of Black culture that look at it as pathological include Joan Aldous (1969), Jessie Bernard (1966), Lee Rainwater (1970),[6] E. Franklin Frazier (1948), and Elliott Liebow (1967). The pathology theory has been fostered by the negative attitude of many social scientists, most of whom are white and middle-class, toward cultures that are different from their own. It is therefore a reflection of the social scientists' apparent inability to keep their middle-class and/or racial ethnocentrism in check when studying cultures that are different from theirs, especially Black culture. Most of them do not seem to be able to describe Black culture scientifically without, directly or indirectly, making moral and value judgments or using such negative and phenomonological terms as "role confusion," "broken homes," and "illegitimate" to describe practices that often are realistic cultural adaptations. It also appears that it is hard for some social scientists to see order, organization, or system in a culture that does not have a middle-class, white-American brand of order and organization. To them, a family that is not made up of just a husband, a wife, "two and a half" children, and a dog is deficient, incomplete, promiscuous, broken, confused, or disorganized. A family in which the members creatively and adaptively interchange certain roles or take care of their family needs without the kind of inflexible role division found in middle-class white culture is, in their eyes, suffering from role-confusion pathology. To perceive a people's system of discharging roles as role-confusion, a theorist must have either failed to understand these people, or must be measuring their culture with a foreign yardstick.

One other aspect of the pathology theory is that it implies, and sometimes explicitly states, that Blacks are sick white people—a strange definition. It shows what could happen when a theorist insists in seeking black as white and still has to account for the unavoidable differences. Myrdal (1944) insisted that Blacks are white in every sense of the word, but, confronted with the highly observable differences, he had to make them sick whites in order to continue to maintain his position that they are white. Hence, he explained Black culture as "a distorted development, or a pathological condition, of the general American culture." Liebow (1967) saw the cultural characteristics of the Black people he studied as pathological attempts to camouflage their failure to achieve the larger society's goals, values, and expectations, rather than as possibly a function of allegiance to a distinctive system of goals and values. Liebow's problem appears to be that of a sociologist who pushed himself into a tight corner by denying the cultural distinctiveness of his subjects, and consequently had to wriggle out through the pathological chimney.

This focus on pathology, distortion, failure, etc. in describing Black culture is a function of four possible factors: the unwillingness to admit that Blacks are not whites—physically, psychologically, or culturally; the theorists' inability to break loose from the clutches of their own values; the white myth that Blacks are characterologically deficient (Newby, 1968); and socio-political motivation. With regard to the socio-political motivation factor, some scholars see political motives in certain attempts to portray Black culture as pathological. For example, Moynihan's assertion that the Black family is responsible for the "pathologies" on which he blamed Black poverty has been perceived as motivated by a need to blame the victim. Robert Staples (1978) observed that the Moynihan report (1965) put the blame on Blacks. Staples elaborated on its political dimensions and implications:

> Moynihan and his followers...initiated the study of Black families as a patho-logical form of social organization at precisely the time when Blacks were beginning to indict institutional racism as the cause of their oppression. The Civil Rights Movement was moving into a militant phase when the govern-ment-subsidized Moynihan study made public the assertion that it was weak-nesses in the Black family, for example, illegitimacy, female-headed households, and welfare dependency, that were responsible for poverty, educational failures and lack of employment in the Black population. His efforts put Blacks on the defensive and diverted their energy into responding to his charges.

It would be naive to deny Staple's observation categorically, because it has documented that race-relation research is often influenced by a contemporary political atmosphere and popular moods, attitudes, and opinions.[7]

In conclusion, it is clear, from the definitions and descriptions presented throughout this essay, that most of the "negative" theories view Blacks as having no culture, other than what Blacks have emulated, or tried to copy, or have been made to adopt from whites. In sharp contrast, the "affirmative" theories recognize the validity and distinctiveness of Black culture.

Notes

1. Taken from John H. Van Evrie, *Negroes and Negro Slavery: The First an Inferior Race; The Latter, Its Nor-mal Condition* (New York: Van Evrie, Horton, 1861), quoted in Carlene Young (ed), *Black Experience: Analysis and Synthesis* (San Rafael, California: Leswing Press, 1972), 94.
2. See Arthur P. Davis and Saunders Redding (eds.), *Cavalcade: Negro American Writing from 1/60 to the Present* (Boston: Houghton Mifflin, 1971), 11.
3. From Carter G. Woodson, "Life in a Haitian Valley" [book review], *Journal of Negro History*, Vol. 22, 366–369, quoted in Melville J. Herskovits, *The Myth of the Negro Past* (Boston: Beacon Press, 1958), 31.
4. See Robert Blauner, "Black Culture: Myth or Reality?" in *Afro-American Anthropology: Contemporary Perspectives*, Norman E. Whitten and John F. Szwed (eds.) (New York: Free Press, 1970), 348.
5. See Daniel P. Moynihan, "The Tangle of Pathology," in *The Black Family: Essays and Studies*, Robert Staples (ed.) (Belmont: Wadsworth, 1978), 5.
6. Staples, "The Black Family Revisited," Ibid., 14.
7. See Thomas F. Pettigrew, "Trends in Research on Racial Discrimination," *Racial Discrimination in the United States* (New York: Harper and Row, 1975), 11–34.

References

Abrahams, Roger D. 1962. "Playing the Dozens," *Journal of American Folklore*, Vol. 75, 209–220.
          , 1970 *Positively Black*. Englewood Cliffs, New Jersey: Prentice-Hall.
Aldous, Joan. 1969. "Wives' Employment Status and Lower Class Men as Husband-fathers: Support for the Moynihan Thesis," *Journal of Marriage and the Family*, Vol. 31, 469–476.
Berger, Bennett M. 1967. "Soul Searching: Review of *Urban Blues* by Charles Keil," *Transaction*, Vol. 4, 54–57.
Bernard, Jessie. 1966 *Marriage and Family among Negroes*. Englewood Cliffs, New Jersey: Prentice-Hall.

Blassingame, John W. 1972. *The Slave Community*. New York: Oxford University Press.

Blauner, Robert. 1970. "Black Culture: Myth or Reality?" in *Afro-American Anthropology: Contemporary Perspectives*, Norman E. Whitten and John F. Szwed (eds.). New York: Free Press [pp. 347–366].

Cole, Johnnetta B. 1970. "Culture: Negro, Black, and Nigger," *The Black Scholar*, Vol. 1, 41.

Davidson, Douglas. 1969. "Black Culture and Liberal Sociology," *Berkeley Journal of Sociology*, Vol. 14, 164–175.

Dillard, J. L. 1972. *Black English: Its History and Usage in the United States*. New York: Vintage.

Ellison, Ralph. 1953. *Shadow and Act*. New York: Random House.

Franklin, John Hope. 1974. *From Slavery to Freedom: A History of Negro Americans*. New York: Alfred A. Knopf.

Frazier, E. Franklin. 1934. "Traditions and Patterns of Negro Family Life in the United States," in *Race and Culture Contacts*, E. B. Reuter (ed.). New York: McGraw-Hill [pp. 191–207].

_____. 1948. *The Negro Family in the United States*. Chicago: University of Chicago Press.

_____. 1957. *The Negro in the United States*. New York: Macmillan.

Genovese, Eugene D. 1976. *Roll, Jordan, Roll: The World the Slaves Made*. New York: Vintage.

Glazer, Nathan, and Daniel Patrick Moynihan. 1963. *Beyond the Melting Pot*. Cambridge, Massachusetts: M.I.T. Press.

Herskovits, Melville J. 1958. *The Myth of the Negro Past*. Boston: Beacon Press.

Johnson, Charles. 1966. *Shadow of the Plantation*. Chicago: University of Chicago Press.

Johnson, Leanor B. 1978. "The Search for Values in Black Family Research," in *The Black Family*, Robert Staples (ed.) [pp. 28–34].

Jordan, Winthrop D. 1974. *The White Man's Burden: Historical Origins of Racism in the United States*. New York: Oxford University Press.

Keil, Charles. 1966. *Urban Blues*. Chicago: University of Chicago Press.

Krapp, George P. 1924. "The English of the Negro," *American Mercury*, Vol. 2, 190–195.

Liebow, Elliott. 1967. *Tally's Corner: A Study of Negro Street Corner Men*. Boston: Little, Brown.

Lewis, Oscar. 1965. *La Vida: A Puerto Rican Family in the Culture of Poverty—San Juan and New York*. New York: Random House.

Moynihan, Daniel P. 1965. *The Negro Family: The Case for National Action*. Washington, D.C.: U.S. Department of Labor.

Myrdal, Gunnar. 1944. *An American Dilemma: The Negro Problem and Modern Democracy*, Vol. II. New York: Harper and Brothers.

Newby, I. A. 1968. *Jim Crow's Defense: Anti-Negro Thought in America, 1900–1930*. Baton Rouge: Louisiana State University Press.

Nobles, Wade. 1974. "Africanity: It's Role in Black Families," *The Black Scholar*, Vol. 5, 10–17.

Powdermaker, Hortense. 1939. *After Freedom: A Cultural Study in the Deep South*. New York: Viking Press.

Rainwater, Lee. 1970. *Behind Ghetto Walls: Black Families in a Federal Slum*. Chicago: Aldine.

Scanzoni, John H. 1971. *The Black Family in Modern Society*. Boston: Allyn and Bacon.

Stampp, Kenneth. 1956. *The Peculiar Institution*. New York: Random House.

Staples, Robert. 1976. *Introduction to Black Sociology*. New York: McGraw-Hill.

_____ (ed.). 1978. *The Black Family: Essays and Studies*. Belmont, California: Wadsworth.

Turner, Lorenzo D. 1969. *Africanisms in the Gullah Dialect*. New York: Arno Press.

Valentine, Charles. 1968. *Culture and Poverty: Critique and Counter-Proposals*. Chicago: University of Chicago Press.

_____. 1971. "Deficit, Difference, and Bicultural Models of Afro-American Behavior," *Harvard Educational Review*, Vol. 41, 137–157.

Woodson, Carter G. 1968. *The African Background Outlined: Or Handbook for the Study of the Negro*. New York: Negro Universities Press.

12

Toward an Understanding of Black Male/Female Relationships

Delores P. Aldridge

Delores P. Aldridge *is a Director of African-American and African Studies at Emory University and also is Chairperson of the National Council for Black Studies. She received her training as a sociologist at Purdue University.*—The Western Journal of Black Studies, *Winter 1984, Vol. 8, No. 4*

There has been growth, albeit recent, in the literature of psychology and sociology concerning the Black male and Black female. The direction of the literature has been such that there are two streams of writing, one devoted to the Black female and another to the Black male. Representative of the first are such writers as Ladner (1972), Staples (1973), Lerner (1973), and Rodgers-Rose (1980). Wilkinson and Taylor (1977), Liebow (1967), and Gary (1981), among others, have written concerning the Black male.

What is curious, however, is a relative lack of social psychological works dealing with both Black males and females within the same endeavor. A case can be made, of course, for monadic rather than dyadic focus. The individual organism, stripped from its social ecosystem, is presented for critical analysis. One's vision is not beclouded by the intervening variable of the opposite gender. There remains, of course, the question of the ways in which the opposite gender has affected the overall characteristics of the monad under study. Man is born of woman and so is woman born of woman. Thus it would seem that viewing Black males and females within a social context or, better yet, a social psychological frame of reference enables one to generate a set of questions and insights differing from those drawn from Black monadic studies.

When one begins to draw a border around the global concept of Black males and females, it would appear important to concentrate upon communications that go toward defining Black male/female relationships. A delimitation in terms of Black male/female relationships suggests a series of questions that form topics for the subject:

Why are male/female relationships important?
Why is it significant to isolate as well as focus upon Black male/female relations?
What is a useful schematic and structural framework for examining male/female relationships?
What are the manifestations of the schematic and structural framework?
What are the implications of and recommendations for maintaining sound relationships and improving non-existent or weak relationships?

The Importance of Male/Female Relationships

Karenga (1981) notes that male/female relationships are of fundamental and enduring concern and importance for several reasons: First, because of their indispensability to the maintenance and development of the species. Second, they are a barometer, i.e., measurement of our distance from the animal world—in other words, our humanity. Third, they are an indicator of the quality of social life; the treatment of women in relationships and, by extension, in society becomes as Toure (1959, 72) notes, "a mirror that reflects the economic and social conditions, the levels of political, cultural and moral development of a given country." Fourth, they are a measurement and mirror of personal development and identity—a revelation of who persons really are. Fifth, they are a measurement of a people's capacity for struggle and social construction—as a fundamental unit of the nation, their strengths and weaknesses determine a nation's capacity to define, defend, and develop its interest.

Importance of Black Male/Female Relationships

The issue of indispensability to the maintenance and development of the species within the context of Black male and female relationships may be viewed both in terms of the nuclear family as well as the single parent family. There is a need for an increased amount of sensitive research focused upon the maintenance and development characteristics and outcomes of Black female-headed families. Within a social system frame of reference, one might ask whether the maintenance and development characteristics of Black female-headed families might not represent a type of response by Black people to the overall messages they receive from white America? What is being suggested here is that Black males, as a "subspecies," may need to be socialized by mothers rather than fathers, insofar as their role behavior for future functioning in American society is concerned. Note, this is not an issue posed by the differential demography of Black males compared to Black females. Instead, it is a question that arises from demographic givens, and becomes proper within the context of a social psychological frame of reference.

The Black female-headed family, differing as it does from the mass media vision of the nuclear family, operates in the eyes of many critics as a deficit model, one whose deviation from the official norm dooms it to internal dysfunctions and external mal-adaptations to the environment. Such a view is, of course, limited by the analytical focus of those who denigrate the Black female-headed family. From a general systems point of view (Berrien, 1968), it can be seen that the Black female-headed family is, once again, an innovative Black adaption to the social-economic and cultural pressures of the dominant society, an adaptation based in and growing from the scarcity of Black males.

It is important to note that the maintenance and development of the species is carried on within the Black female-headed family. But it is also important to note the need for, as noted above, sensible and sensitive research into the structure, dynamics, and outcomes of role socialization in the Black female-headed family. One suspects that there are strengths that have not yet entered the official vocabulary of the research literature.

Given the pressures upon Black people in America, the continued maintenance and development of Black children brought about through the love of Black men and women for each other is, indeed, a critical measurement of the strength of Black people. Yet, when one reviews the statement by Toure, cited above, that male/female relationships are important—and especially the treatment of women in relationships—one needs to ask what the treatment of Black women reflects in the national political, cultural, and moral mirror of American society. One is forced to return, once again, to the image of the Black woman as reflected in the mass media—and even in the latest telecommunications format, musical video.

The standard of beauty that is communicated by television and only partly contradicted by such publications as *Essence* has, one suspects, much to do with setting the criteria of beauty for many Black women and Black men. When it is considered that there are strict limitations on what is acceptable in Black politics, culture, and morality on the part of the dominant society, one might be moved to wonderment as to the survival of any Black male/female relationship.

Significance of Black Male/Female Relationships

Social scientists, psychologists, novelists, political scientists, and psychiatrists have all discussed and examined the significance of Black male/female relationships. The reader may want to examine the sociological writing (Staples, 1978; Jackson, 1978; Karenga, 1982; Scott, 1976; Hare, 1979), the psychological literature (Akbar, 1976; Tucker, 1979; Nobles, 1978), the writings of political scientists (Wilcox, 1979; Gary, 1981), the psychiatric literature (Welsing, 1974; Poussaint, 1979; Grier and Cobbs, 1968), and works of fiction (Wallace, 1979; Jordan, 1977). The gamut of perspectives has ranged from an Afrocentric mode (Asante, 1980; Akbar, 1976; Karenga, 1982), to a popularist model (Wallace, 1979).

What unites all the writings cited above is the theme of Black male/female relationships developing and surviving in the face of tremendous odds. At the same time, the presence of quite substantive historical problems, whose characteristics have become more acute in the last several decades, is also acknowledged.

The lack of relationships due to the scarcity of Black males (Jackson, 1971) and the mutually degrading games one plays in order to begin and sustain relationships (Staples, 1978) are but two of the present problems that threaten Black male/female relationships. Even the quality and future of existing Black male/female relationships remain open to continuing questions and challenges, given the social stress and strain of living in American society.

Despite what has been said about the problems of Black male/female concerns, the writer is in agreement with Karenga (1982) that the following relevant facts need to form a background for future studies and research:

1. Black male/female relationships are probably no more problem ridden than other male/female relationships.
2. Life, itself, requires problems and the effort to solve those problems.
3. Many Black male/female relationships are healthy; however, enough are in trouble to require a sustained critical view.
4. There are enough Black males and Black females without relationships so that discussion focusing upon this fact needs furthering.
5. Any criticism of Black male/female relationships is, at the same time and in equal measure, a criticism of American society—the society that has shaped them to fit and "properly" function in it.

These five facts serve as a point of departure for any serious analysis of Black men, Black women, and their relationships. To further underscore the point of view that argues that Black people are products of their social conditions is to use the same argument for the connection between Black relationships and social conditions. In order to properly understand Black men and Black women within the context of their relationships, one must understand the historical characteristics that have shaped them. Superimposed upon these variables is the complexity of mental, emotional, and physical factors that have also shaped the behavior of Black men and women.

A Structural Framework for Examining Black Male/Female Relationships

American society is defined by and derived from four major structure and value systems: capitalism, racism, sexism, and Judeo-Christianity. Capitalism may be defined as a socio-economic system in which private ownership is the primary means for satisfying human needs. Another characteristic of capitalism is a strong and continuous pursuit of profit. The emphasis upon private ownership of things tends to often shape the view of human relationships, i.e., the conceptual conversion of human beings into things to be owned or similarly the profit motive in which people may subconsciously be viewed as objects for purchase and resale.

Racism may be defined as a system of denial and deformation of a people's history and humanity based primarily on the specious concept of race and hierarchies of races. Racism in America was born from European feelings of racial superiority and bred within the moral contradiction between Christian concepts and economic beliefs. Slavery represented an attempt at dehumanization of both the proponents as well as those who were enslaved, given the idea of Christianity. On the other hand, slavery represented the extension of private ownership and profit theories into the realm of human relationships. In the contemporary world, neo-colonialism links capitalism and racism, resulting in nations that dominate, and nations that are owned by the dominators. In this context it is important to understand that capitalism and racism extend their influence from the intrapersonal system to the world system of human organization.

Sexism is the social system and resultant practice of using gender or sex as an ascriptive and primary determinant in the establishment, maintenance, and explanation, i.e., justification, of relationships and exchanges. As a system, sexism is composed of assumptions and acts, theories, and practices, which imply and impose unequal, oppressive, and exploitive relationships based upon gender. When capitalism and racism are reviewed for their effects upon human relationships, it may be seen that sexism converts the dominated to a subordinate feminine stereotype, open and waiting to be used.

The Judeo-Christian tradition is a religious system that has its roots in Judaism and Christianity and which draw heavily upon the cultural and social experiences of Jews, whites, and males. The tradition encourages identification with males as leaders and heroes, but more importantly it emphasizes the leader-hero tradition as being one with white males and their socio-economic experiences. A racist, sexist, and Judeo-Christian macrosystem forms the basic framework for understanding Black male/female relationships. From this understanding can be generated a set of questions germane to the topic of this paper:

> *What are the manifestations of the conceptual framework?*
> *What are the values implied by the conceptual framework?*
> *What are the concrete factors influencing male/female relations emerging out of a racist, sexist, capitalist, and Judeo-Christian society?*

In the following discussions, the writer will attempt to respond to these questions.

Factors Influencing the Quality of Interaction between Black Males and Black Females

Four factors shape the interactive nature of communication between Black males and Black females; the scarcity of Black men, differential socialization of males and females, sexism and women's liberation, and the modes of connecting. Jackson (1971) focuses attention on the shortage of Black males through a novel paradigm that Black males have a higher rate of infant mortality, a shorter life expectancy, a high rate of accidents and homicide, form a disproportionate segment of the prison population, and are a significant segment of the drug addict population. Staples (1978) reports that there is only one acceptable Black male for every five Black females, excluding married, imprisoned and homosexual Black males. Data from the 1977 U.S. census indicates that there were 732,000 more Black females than Black males in the 22–24 year old range in 1977. More recent census data shows that no closure of the gap has occurred.

These statistics serve to underline certain grave consequences for Black male/female relationships. The insufficient supply of eligible Black males pit Black women against each other in competition for the attention of this scarce resource. Secondly, many Black men are aware of the imbalance and play a power game with Black women, requiring them to accept the Black male upon his terms. If Black women fail to buy into the power game, interracial courtship is an option increasingly available to those who are so inclined. It comes as no surprise, of course, that the Black woman sees interracial heterosexual relations as a personal rejection of her own desirability.

Differential Socialization of Males and Females

Jourard (1971) explored the deadening aspects of the male role, advancing the notion that the socially-defined male role requires men to appear tough, objective, striving, achieving, unsentimental, and emotionally unexpressive. If behind this social persona a man feels tender, if he cries, he will be viewed as unmanly by others. The contradiction between the ways in which Black men are expected to present themselves in small and large group situations and their real emotional feelings is a key to understanding the nature of being a Black male in America. The learned tendency of males to mask their true feelings makes it difficult for Black men to achieve insight into and empathy with Black women.

To the extent that women require expressions of intimate and personal emotions in exchange for their availability as social or sexual partners, the non-expressive or limited-in-expressiveness male may find himself in a difficult situation, observed Braithewaite. If he is to execute properly his role as a Black man by associating with women who demonstrate their attraction to him, he must be fairly successful at something for which he has received contradictory signals—that is, to express emotions of gentleness, tenderness, and verbal affection toward women while at the same time being strong, unexpressive, and cool.

According to Braithewaite (1981), the high degree of verbal facility among Black males makes it easier for them to create an initial impression of genuine feelings and, thus, they readily enter into relationships with women. As the relationship continues and the woman becomes more familiar with the male's ways, it becomes increasingly difficult for the Black male to camouflage his absence of genuine feelings for his partner. The male must constantly "fake it" and express sentiments he really does not feel. Perhaps this is part of the reason for seemingly unexpected physical attacks upon one's partner followed by loving apologies. Given that the male continuously runs the risk of "blowing his cover" with the outcome of a terminated relationship, the cardinal issue becomes plain. The issue is not one of entering relationships with women. The issue is one of *sustaining* relationships with women.

Tucker (1978) indicates that success with women is important to many men because they are engaged in covert competition with other men. The belief is that success will enable them to avoid ridicule and to be perceived as "hip." Given this process, women become targets and the communication structure by which they become targets assumes the status of an end in itself rather than a means to an end. The process is in many ways dysfunctional to Black men. There is feeling that expression of emotions must not leave the man vulnerable. This rapidly passes over into the self-rejection of those emotions, the display of which might leave one vulnerable.

The pattern of initial contact and verbal gaming that is summarized above represents a well-patterned response to the teachings of capitalism and sexism. The woman becomes an object; one gains in profit as one "scores" on an increasing number of women. And, of course, the expression of, as well as the possession of, emotions that might reveal oneself, as well as the women as feeling individual beings, is contraproductive to the capitalist mentality. At this point, one is tempted to wonder whether the "new morality" is not, in itself, a logical out-growth of capitalism and sexism—e.g., the body becomes the object of buying and selling—the inner person is reduced to a dancing (either in public or in the bedroom) object available for the man's pleasure.

Tucker suggests that women can help men by letting the latter know that they measure manhood not in terms of "cool," but in terms of responsiveness, support, care, and honesty. Black women can further help by encouraging Black men to struggle and deal with their emotions rather than to conceal them. Black women need to share with Black men an assurance that a man is found to be more attractive when he shares his feeling with them. And while it is true that Black men may complain about women who force them to deal with issues, ultimately they respect such women far more than they do meek, compliant women who make no demands (Tucker, 1979).

Given what has been said, one may conclude that self-disclosure is a major factor influencing the quality of interaction between Black men and Black women.

Sexism and Women's Liberation

Many scholars admit that sexism is present among Black males and has the effect of inhibiting and corrupting meaningful relationships. In recent years, the criticism of sexism among Black people has become an issue. It is an issue, however, that also threatens the broader Black community through assault upon the Black male. Staples (1979) argues that female equality involves not only personal relationships, but also political and economic relationships. A substantial number of the inequalities perceived in male and female relationships need to be remedied through re-education of men and women toward changes in their sex-role socialization.

For Black women, involvement in a feminist movement entails a tripartite battle against sexism, racism, and capitalism. Racism and capitalism are forces that have subjected Black women to political and economic subordination. Staples (1979) is among those who see feminism as a divisive force in an oppressed community such as Black America. There are other points of view. Lorde (1979) supports feminism, arguing that since Black women bear the brunt of sexism, it is in their interest to abolish it. He continues by suggesting that it is the responsibility of Black women to decide whether or not sexism in the Black community is pathological. According to Lorde: "Creative relationships of which Staples speaks are to the benefit of Black males, considering the sex ratio of males and females." Salaam (1979) contends that the struggle against sexism is not a threat to Black masculinity; the forces that attack Black women individually, institutionally, and ideologically also assault Black men.

On the other side of the question, many Black men and women have spoken out against feminism (Larue, 1970; Duberman, 1975). The arguments they advance are:

> *Black people as a race need to be liberated from racism.*
> *Feminism creates negative competition between the Black male and the Black female for economic security.*
> *White women hoard the benefit of the struggle from Black women.*
> *Feminism facilitates increased tension in the already strained interpersonal atmosphere in which Black men and Black women interact.*

One might argue, in the light of the many views presented above, that women's liberation—as it is presently defined and implemented—impacts negatively on the Black liberation movement and on Black male and female relationships. The essence of the writer's disagreement with women's liberation is the basically conservative mode of its beliefs and functions. Women's liberation operates within the capitalist tradition and accepts the end goals of sexist white males; simply stated, women's liberation strives to place women on an equal par with men without considering whether the male position—the white male position—is basically a humanizing position.

Black women are victims of capitalism and sexism. How, then, will relations between Black males and females be bettered through feminine adherence to a male-defined path? Black liberation involves males and females openly and courageously seeking mutual liberation; Black liberation cannot have the luxury of a liberation movement operating inside the capitalist tradition and seeking goals defined by perpetuators of the sexist tradition. It will be seen, then, that Black liberation, especially within Black male and Black Female relations, has a far more complex task than women's liberation. Black liberation seeks the establishment of a lovingly, free movement within and between Black males and Black females that re-creates both parties and establishes a tradition that is non-capitalist, non-sexist, and draws from the cultural experiences of free Black people.

Modes of Connecting

Black men and women often engage in relationships that are not in their mutual best interest. Karenga (1982) describes four modes through which Black males and Black females come together: (1) the Cash Connection, (2) the Flesh Connection, (3) the Force Connection, and (4) the Dependency Connection. Karenga (1979) defines these connections as "a short-term or tentative association which is utilitarian and alienated and designed primarily for the mutual misuse of each other's body. On the other hand, a quality relationship is a stable association defined by its positive sharing, its mutual investment in each other's psychological well being and development."

The "Cash Connection" is based upon a point of view epitomized by such statements as "everything and everybody has a price," "anything you can't buy ain't worth having," "what you invest assets into, is yours," and "money is the measure of and solution to everything." The primary motivation in the dyadic relation controlled by the cash connection is the presence of financial resources by at least one of the dyad's members. Women spar with other women over available men with money; men spar with each other over available women with money. In essence, men and women are looking at each other as potential "marks" in a petty confidence game.

The "Flesh Connection" is rooted in the new morality that characterizes much of contemporary society and is based predominantly on the pursuit of sex. This particular linkage focuses on the body and all the things one can do with all selected parts of it. It is not at all extreme to suggest that the flesh connection is basically a perverse connection, a corruptive reduction of the members of the dyad to definitions of self and other, primarily, in terms of the physical. A rejection of the body is not at all intended here; instead, what is being said is that Black males and females cannot afford to reduce themselves to an intrapersonal and interpersonal image that define them as slaves. For the slave is seen as a body capable of work, impregnation, and reproduction. What one must remember is that the final stage of colonization results in the colonized taking over the attitudes of the colonizers, and proceeding to maintain a colonial society based upon the colonizer's mentality. The flesh connection is, perhaps, the most damaging of connections for Black males and Black females, since it is entirely contradictory to the basic canons of a healthy Black liberation.

The "Force Connection" is predicated on the violent nature of society, part of the species' inheritance from its earlier ancestors. The force connection is fueled by the "macho" mentality of men, who take what they are compelled to take as a result of their illusions of ownership. Lurking behind the macho mentality is a particular self-view that is, once again, delimiting and, ultimately, insecure. It is delimiting in that viewing women as objects to be owned calls for the diminution of any self-view that suggests feeling and thoughts beyond those which enable one to own others. It is insecure, since the very idea of a balanced self cannot abide within a self that is limited in its own definition, as well as in those whom it seeks to own.

The "Dependency Connection" results from entering into a relationship based upon any of the three preceding connections. The dependency connection is a different level, psychologically and sociologically speaking, since it flows from negative connections rather than summarizes an initiating connection. It would be a mistake to call all dependency a negative form of interaction. A Positive Dependency can be the hallmark of what Karenga (1982) terms a stable association. Positive dependency flows from the growing strength of each member of the Black dyad as they grow within themselves. If love is a process, rather than a "falling in," then it requires the presence of the other within each other as a rewarding stimulus for the individual "I" and the collective "we."

Implications

From the above discussion, one can proceed to recommendations for improving weak relationships, growing out of non-relationship states of being, and maintaining sound relationships. Most of the social scientists referenced in this work have advanced theories for improving and maintaining relationships. Their consensus is that it is important that,

Social scientists develop and explore researchable questions examining the nature of the context in which Black male/female relationships are embedded;

Demographers focus attention on the scarcity of Black males as a national phenomenon having potentially grave consequences for the race and having deleterious effects on Black women;

Black men and women address unsatisfactory interpersonal relationships by participating in personal growth and human relations group sessions;

Universities develop and include a course on male and female relationships as a part of their general education curriculum;

Black national organizations place on their program agenda the issue of strategies for strengthening relationships between Black men and Black women.

If these theoretical constructs are pursued, one suspects that the socially-generated illnesses that define too many Black male and Black female relationships may begin, finally, to diminish and disappear.

The issues explored here should direct one's attention not only to Black male and Black female relationships, but to the foundation of American society.

Although this essay deals with the interpersonal and the intrapersonal, the implications are rooted within the too easily accepted and not too often examined Euro-American roots of this nation. As a nation, America practices upon weaker Third World countries precisely what men and women practice upon each other. Thus, although this paper is intended as a thesis in social psychology, the directional flow of its development is toward philosophy and, in particular, axiology—the study and criticism of values. Values are what shape one's perception of self and other, as well as one's internal and external communication, not to mention the definition of social goals.

References

Akbar, N. "Rhythmic Patterns in African Personality," in *African Philosophy and Paradigms for Research on Black Persons*, L. King, et al. (eds.). Los Angeles: Fanon Center, 1976.

Asante, M. *Afrocentricity: The Theory of Social Change*. Buffalo, New York: Amulefi, 1980.

Berrien, F. K. *General and Social Systems*. New Brunswick, New Jersey: Rutgers University Press, 1968.

Braithewaite, R. L. "Interpersonal Relations between Black Males and Black Females," in *Black Men*, L. E. Gary (ed.). Beverly Hills, California: Sage, 1981.

Duberman, L. *Gender and Sex in Society*. New York: Praeger, 1975.

Gary, L. E. (ed.). *Black Men*. Beverly Hills, California: Sage, 1981.

Grier, W., and P. Cobbs. *Black Rage*. New York: Basic Books, 1968.

Hare, J. "Black Male-Female Relationships," *Sepia*, November 1979.

Jackson, J. "But Where Are the Black Men?" *The Black Scholar*, Vol. 4, 1971, 34–41.

Jordan, J. *Things That I Do in the Dark*. New York: Random House, 1977.

Jourard, S. *The Transparent Self*. New York: Jan Nostrand, 1971.

Karenga, M. *Introduction to Black Studies*. Inglewood, California: Kawaida, 1982.

Ladner, J. *Tomorrow's Tomorrow: The Black Woman*. New York: Doubleday, 1972.

LaRue, L. "Black Liberation and Women's Lib," *Transaction*, Vol. 8, No.1, 1970, 59–63.

Lerner, G. *Black Women in White America*. New York: Vintage, 1973.

Liebow, E. *Talley's Corner*. Boston: Little, Brown, 1967.

Lorde, A. "Feminism and Black Liberation," *The Black Scholar*, Vol. 10, Nos. 8 and 9, 1979, 17–20.

Noble, J. *Beautiful, Also, Are the Souls of My Black Sisters: A History of Black Women in America*. Englewood Cliffs, New Jersey: Prentice-Hall, 1978.

Poussant, A. "White Manipulation and Black," *The Black Scholar*, Vol. 10, Nos. 8 and 9, 1979, 52–55.

Rodgers-Rose, L. *The Black Woman*. Beverly Hills, California, 1980.

Salaam, K. "Revolutionary Struggle/Revolutionary Love," *The Black Scholar*, Vol. 10, Nos. 8 and 9, 1979, 20–24.

Scott, J. "Polygamy: A Futuristic Family Arrangement for African-Americans," *Black Books Bulletin*, 1976, 13–19.

Staples, R. *The Black Woman in America*. Chicago: Nelson-Hall, 1973.

_____. "Masculinity and Race: The Dual Dilemma of Black Men," *Journal of Social Issues*, Vol. 34, No. 1, 1978, 169–183.

_____. "A Rejoiner: Black Feminism and the Cult of Masculinity: The Danger Within," *The Black Scholar*, Vol. 10, Nos. 8 and 9, 1979.

Toure, S. *Toward Full Reafricanization*. Paris: Presence Africiane, 1959.

Tucker, R. *Why Do Black Men Hide Their Feelings?* New York: Dial Press, 1979.

Wallace, M. *Black Macho and the Myth of the Superwoman*. New York: Dial Press, 1979.

Welsing, F. "The Cress Theory of Color Confrontation and Racism," *The Black Scholar*, Vol. 5, 1974, 32–40.

Wilcox, P. "Is There Life for Black Leaders after ERA?" *Black Male/Female Relationships*, Vol. 2, No. 1, 1979, 53–55.

Wilkinson, D., and Taylor, R. L. (eds.). *The Black Male in America*. Chicago: Nelson-Hall, 1977.

13

Conceptual and Logical Issues in Theory and Research Related to Black Masculinity[1]

CLYDE W. FRANKLIN II

Clyde W. Franklin is an Associate Professor of Sociology at The Ohio State University. He received the M.A. degree from Atlanta University and the Ph.D. from the University of Washington.—The Western Journal of Black Studies, Winter 1986, Vol. 10, No. 4

In surveying the literature in gender, men's studies, Black female-Black male relationships, and the Black family, an alarming fact becomes apparent. There is a dearth of literature related to the Black male experience. Relatively few research studies, articles, books, etc. focus on Black men's socialization, Black men's perceptions, Black men's social interaction patterns, and like topics. This is not to say that there are no reports on Black men's behaviors. It is to say, however, that such reports are inadequate since one only receives piecemeal accounts of Black masculinity; and even these accounts frequently are contained in literature related to crime, deviance, and other pathologies. In addition, reports that link Black men to crime, deviance, and the like seldom offer explanations for the race-behavior link.

Interestingly, in 1981 Joseph Pleck observed "the male role is the most neglected topic in gender research" (p. 1). Since then, much more research has been devoted to the male role, but it has focused, in large part, on the white masculine role.[2]

Going beyond the initial emphases in men's studies, it should become more apparent that the white masculine role is but one of several models in American society. Moreover, the white masculine role, as well as other masculine roles, *may* or *may not* be race-specific in terms of role assumption. In other words, a major point of departure for the discussion here is the premise that socioeconomic factors, social contact factors, and other experiential factors all are significant influences in male role assumption. This means, for example, that while it remains true that those most likely to assume a white masculine role are white males; and, those most likely to assume a Black masculine role are Black males, race no longer can be thought of as the sole factor influencing male role assumptions.

Based in part on the above premises, several conceptual issues in theory and research on the Black male role loom as important because of their relationships to the continued racial oppression of Black men in America and the dreaded and debilitating consequences of such racism. Before discussing these conceptual issues it is necessary to define precisely what is meant by the "white masculine role" and the "Black masculine role."

Conceptual Issues in Black Masculinity

The White Masculine Role

While the white masculine role has undergone some change in the last fifteen years, it still remains largely locked within what Pleck calls the "Male Sex Role Identity Paradigm" (Pleck, 1981). According to Pleck, the MSRI paradigm is "a set of ideas about sex roles, especially the male role, that has dominated the academic social sciences since the 1930s and, more generally, has shaped societal culture's view of the male role" (Pleck, 1981, 1). These ideas assume that psychological maturity as a male *or* female requires accurate cognitive awareness of one's sex and manifested sex-appropriate traits, attitudes, and interests by the individual involved.

Important for males from the MSRI perspective is the fact that numerous factors often interact to "thwart the attainment of healthy sex role identity, particularly for males (e.g., the actual or relative absence of male role models, the believing of traditional role distinctions, women's changing roles)" (Pleck, 1981, 2). What is a healthy sex-role identity? David and Brannon (1976) have delineated and defined several dimensions of masculinity that are congruent with the MSRI paradigm. They are: "the big wheel" (success, status); "the sturdy oak" (toughness, confidence, independence); "give 'em hell" (aggressiveness, violence); and "no sissy stuff" (sufficient disdain for and avoidance of femininity in male behavior). A healthy sex role identity for any male, then, from a MSRI paradigm perspective, is the psychological internalization of these dimensions as appropriate for himself, and behavioral manifestations of such dimensions by him in appropriate social situations.

In discussing the white masculine role, however, it is critical to point out that its direct congruence with the MSRI paradigm perspective is being challenged by many contemporary theorists and researchers (e.g., Doyle, 1983). The new paradigm that has emerged under the watchful eye of Joseph Pleck, one of the foremost authorities on the male sex role, is the "sex role strain" paradigm. Contending that "it is difficult to live up to the norms and stereotypes defining traditional roles because frequently they are highly idealized and internally contradictory," Pleck suggests a sex role strain analysis as appropriate for studying the male sex role (Pleck, 1981). Such a perspective by contrast implies that many dimensions of the traditional male role such as competitiveness, violence, aggression, inexpressiveness, decisiveness, independence, etc. can be characterized as dysfunctional in numerous social environments and/or situations.

Summarily, the white masculine role today is some continuation of traditional male behavioral and dispositional expectations and modern day recognition of contradictions and inconsistencies within the male sex role, both of which render most white males "anomic."[3]

The Black Masculine Role

While the white masculine role is undergoing modification and leaning toward a sex role strain interpretation, the Black masculine role appears to be in its early stage of development within a sex role strain paradigm (due to societal constraints based on racial group affiliation). The concept "marginal man" seems extremely applicable to the Black masculine role in the United States.[4] In part, this is due to the fact that Black men have been recognized as "men" by most of society only since the modern day civil rights movement, and, as a result, socialization into the traditional masculine role for many Black men remains a difficult, if not impossible, task due to structural (societal) and social psychological (interpersonal) constraints.

The "marginality" of the Black male's role is seen further if one considers the role requirements Black men must fulfill in order to be considered "successful" by the larger society and by the smaller subculture (the Black community). Black men must conform to three different, although somewhat related, sets of role expectations. They are expected to assume a "societal male sex role" that may include competitiveness, aggressiveness, the work ethic, decisiveness, independence, protectiveness, providing, etc. Also critical for many Black men is the meeting of a second set of role requirements that revolves around the fact that they are "Black" in America. This set of role requirements mandates that the Black male assume what Nobles (1978) and others call an Afrocentric perspective, which involves cooperation, promotion of the group, survival of the group, etc. This perspective on masculinity is in direct opposition to the aforementioned societal perspective. In fact, Black men as "men" in American society can only "step" partially into this "Black" role if they are to achieve any measure of societal success. Finally, as an adaptive response to an often hostile environment, many Black men can be characterized as holding membership in an amorphous Black men's group that has its own set of Black male role expectations. These role expectations often are permeated with sexism, irresponsibility, violence, intraracism, and other individually dysfunctional and societally disorganizing elements. It is not an overstatement to say that most Black men in America today are surrounded by these three "worlds" and, as confusing as it may seem, are socialized by them.

Factors Constraining Black Male Societal Role Assumption

It is relatively easy to recognize the structural constraints that keep Black men from assuming a "masculine role" in American society, but it is, perhaps, more difficult to understand the more subtle psychological factors mitigating Black males' internalizations of a societally sanctioned male sex role.

Quite simply, most informed persons recognize that such things as race differences in national unemployment rates (whites, 7.3 percent, and Blacks, 14 percent; June 1985, Bureau of Labor Statistics), median incomes (white men, $23,114, and Black men, $16,410[5]; 1983, Population Reports), and occupational segregation all are indications of continued structural constraints Black men face in American society. More complex, however, and harder to discover are those mixed messages Black men receive from their peers and others within the Black community and the larger society, which basically say to them that they are doomed to fail in American society; that their efforts to be successful are futile; and, that, generally, the future for Black men in America is bleak. Unfortunately, in addition to these messages, national statistics on Black male suicide, Black male homicide, Black male incarceration, Black male commitments to mental hospitals, etc. seem to support the dire prediction for Black America, generally, and Black men in particular.

Also important to point out is the fact that many Black men are locked psychologically within a largely Black male environment that imparts defeatist attitudes, messages of irresponsibility, intrarace aggression, and dysfunctional submissiveness. Indeed, it is possible to say that for most Black men there is no clear agenda or blueprint for becoming a functioning member of American society. In the immediate past, this has been debilitating for Black men, resulting in what some call the "institutional decimation" of Black men (Stewart and Scott, 1978).

Critical Factors in Examining the Black Male Role

 Two factors seem critical to point out, then, when examining the Black masculine role: (1) the concept "man" is a relatively "new" ingredient of the Black male role; and (2), structural and societal constraints in conjunction with dysfunctional socialization messages from society and the Black community produce ambiguous conceptions of the masculine role for many Black males. At best, the Black masculine role today can be characterized as "an emphasis on physical strength, an expectation of both submissiveness and strength in women, angry and impulsive behavior, functional (and often violent) relationships between men and between men and women, and strong male bonding" (Franklin, 1984, 60–61).

This definition of Black masculinity or similar ones that characterize the sex role script played out by numerous Black men undoubtedly present serious problems for many. The problems arise from two sources: (1) the inherent conflict between the sets of sex role expectations for Black men; and (2), the relatively new status ("man") assigned to adult Black males with which many are unfamiliar and/or confused. As a result of this conceptual ambiguity, not only are Black males themselves affected, but also affected are theory and research related to Black males. The writer shall now turn to some other issues affecting the study of Black males—logical ones.

Logical Issues in Black Masculinity Theory and Research

The Social Construction of Black Masculinity

Undoubtedly, Michele Wallace struck a nerve in 1979 when she published *Black Macho and the Myth of the Superwoman*. Black publications, Black conversations, Black television and radio commentaries, and occasionally even the white media have devoted a modicum of attention to the "social construction" of Black masculinity. While Wallace's work was critical of Black males' social constructions of Black masculinity, she did direct attention to the process and ensuing results. Expectedly, *Black Macho and the Myth of the Superwoman* has been interpreted in a variety of ways. Some have acclaimed her work as quite insightful and creative (Lorde, 1979); others, however, suggest that Wallace is responding from personal hurt and in actuality has committed an unpardonable sin by attacking the defenseless and guiltless Black man. Consider the following statement by Robert Staples (1979, 30):

> Ms. Wallace is, oh, so correct when she says that the last 50 years has seen a growing distrust, even hatred, between black men and women. She acknowledges that it was perpetuated by White racism but claims that black ignorance of the sexual politics of their experience in the country played its part…What I question and why I am troubled by her book, is how she comes to the conclusion that the addicted, imprisoned and unemployed black male is the main culprit in this scenario.

In another defensive stance, Ron Karenga (1979) took Wallace to task and indicated that Wallace's analysis of Black men was biased and based on her own personal experiences. Karenga stated:

> Wallace's romanticized version of black man-woman relations is marked by two main features: (1) its reductiveness, and (2) its political character…She appropriates Carmichael for her own; he is for her not so much a political leader as a sex symbol. But she is angry with Black men, perhaps most definitely, the rough street men she dated to break from the stifling sterility and fantasy of black middle class life. Somewhere, someone has hurt her and she urges black women to never forget 'the black man let us down.' In essence, however, this is a personal agony, evaluation and solution which Wallace masks as a collective experience and position. (1979, 36)

Despite the biting criticism directed at her, Wallace made several important contributions, including, firstly, the recognition that Black masculinity is socially constructed; secondly, that many Black men in the United States construct even more pathological versions of masculinity than the typical white male conventional construction; and thirdly, that such social constructions are inimical to Black female-Black male relationships, in fact, the Black community.

While many of Wallace's critics have spent much time lambasting her feminist perspective, most failed to point to a key logical flaw in her position that centers around "the social construction of masculinity." The logical problem lay in Wallace's failure to recognize and emphasize those dysfunctional aspects of traditional masculinity as well as the inappropriateness of drawing analogies between white masculinity and Black masculinity. Moreover, the latter problem with Wallace's analysis is a problem that characterizes the work and observations of many others. In fact, it is related to a crucial omission in theory and research on Black masculinity—the lack of an articulate Black male definition of Black masculinity. Lorde (1979) called for such a definition in her response to Staples' criticism of Wallace. Yet, to my knowledge, there has been no such definition forthcoming. Part of the reason for this oversight may lie in the flux and change that has characterized conceptions of generic "masculinity" in the last fifteen years; and in the aforementioned point that adult Black males have only been recognized as "men" in the United States within the past twenty years. Thus, the idea of a "Black man" is relatively new and it should not be surprising to find that no model exists. This lacuna in gender research is, perhaps, one of the major conceptual and logical issues related to theory and research on Black masculinity. Just as Pleck (1981) feels that the MSRI paradigm is no longer viable as a conceptual framework for understanding the male role and its problems, and instead, new lines of research dictate an emerging new paradigm that emphasizes traditional sex roles as problems themselves (sex role strain paradigm), this writer believes that it is important to emphasize that sex role strain for Black men is such a major part of the Black male's experience until it renders traditional male role expectations completely unworkable for most Black men. Unfortunately, this is hardly recognized in the meager contemporary theory and research on Black masculinity.

In contrast to the conservative bias, which characterizes a static definition of Black masculinity not taking the unique historical position of the Black male into account, there are other more liberal biases that can threaten the logical adequacy of Black masculinity theory and research. These liberal biases are (1) the persistent uses of tautological and teleological explanations and (2) the existence of an "anti-self criticism" ideology among many Black scholars theorizing about and/or doing research on the Black experience.

The Inadequacy of Tautological Explanations

One of the most frequent variable linkages, when interpreting the meager findings and conclusions on Black men, relates white racism to some negative Black male consequence or consequences. For example, it is not unusual to find an author explaining an observed relationship between race and Black victimization as "the *result* of white racism." The explanation can be illustrated as follows:

> White racism causes Black men to do a lot of things—one of which is to victimize other Black people. How do you know? Because when Black men face White racism they victimize other Black people. When Black men do not victimize other Blacks, it is because they do not face White racism.

Obviously, such an explanation is circular and overly simplistic. Nevertheless, this explanation follows the same pattern of logic that forms the theoretical underpinnings of numerous explanations of Black male behavior. An obvious flaw in such explanatory systems is the circularity of the proposition. The proposition is not falsifiable—Black victimization is a function of white racism and since there is always white racism, there is always Black victimization. While such an explanatory system may be an effective political tool to use in mobilizing persons to fight for a cause, it does not provide logically adequate explanatory systems that can be subjected to empirical test.

A closely related, although different, logical issue in Black male role research and theory is related to teleological explanations, which are discussed below.

The Inadequacy of Teleological Explanations

Teleological explanations in Black male role theory and research use a consequence to explain a cause. Consider the following question and answer: Why do some Black men rape Black women? Is it because these Black men want psychiatric help about their feelings toward Black women in a racist society? If the answer to these questions is yes, they likely rape Black women because this increases the likelihood that they will be caught and have to undergo psychiatric treatment. Again, the simplicity of the above example should not detract from the seriousness of such logical problems in findings and conclusions related to research and theory on Black masculinity. Staples (1979), for example, has suggested that the Black males' "condition" in society is what bothers Black males and causes much of the Black male pathological behavior. This is tantamount to saying that the reason why increasing numbers of Black males may be becoming an "endangered species" is because large numbers of Black men have experienced "institutional decimation," precisely the type of explanation that *must be avoided in Black masculinity theory and research.*

Interestingly, both tautological and teleological reasoning in Black male theory and research may be related to a final conceptual and logical issue that threatens the legitimacy of work on Black males—the anti-self criticism ideology, which underlies much work by many Black men and other "well-meaning" scholars. Audre Lorde (1979) implied this observation following the attacks on Wallace by Karenga and Staples. A similar observation became apparent after the publication of William Julius Wilson's *The Declining Significance of Race* (1978) resulted in numerous misinterpretations. The basic fact of the matter is that few operationally and empirically valid studies *or* logically and pragmatically adequate theoretical formulations about Black masculinity can be developed as long as an anti self-criticism ideology prevails among some researchers and theorists.

While it is recognized that the scientific process is not completely value-free, it is also recognized that effort should be made to produce unbiased results, interpretations, and conclusions. This is as essential in work on Black masculinity as it is in other theory and research endeavors—indeed, it may be more essential. When captions on the covers of magazines or on news articles in newspapers read some version of "Is the Black Male an Endangered Species?" (*Ebony*, 1983), or "Group's Study Says Future Bleak for Today's Black Children" (*Columbus Dispatch*, June 4, 1985), the pragmatic adequacy of theory and research on Black males, indeed the Black community, becomes imperative. The writer is convinced that only when scientifically-oriented theorists and researchers discard their anti-self criticism stances will positive intervention into the social ills that plague Black America in the middle 1980s become a reality. The "protection" given to Black males by assuming biased anti-self criticism in theory and research efforts is needless and can only facilitate perpetuation of the decimation of Black men and the eventual destruction of all Black people in the United States.

Notes

1. Please do not cite or quote from this article without permission from the author.
2. There are notable exceptions.
3. See Franklin's discussion of the "anomic" male in *The Changing Definition of Masculinity* (1984).
4. It can be said that Black men are condemned to live in two societies and one subculture that are not merely different, but often are antagonistic. The result, according to the concept, is restlessness, instability, and all sorts of deviation from a harmonious and well-balanced personality type. Originally developed for Jews and other white immigrants to America and applied indiscriminately to mulattos immediately after slavery, the concept presently may be especially applicable to Black men in present-day America who receive socialization messages that place them in two still separate and unequal societies and one contradictory subculture.
5. These figures are based on the entire year in 1983. The source is U.S. Bureau of the Census, *Current Population Reports*, Series P-20, No. 146, Money Income of Households, Families and Persons in the United States: 1983 (U.S. Government Printing Office: Washington, D.C., 1985), 155–157, Table 46.

References

Columbus Dispatch, "Group's Study Says Future Bleak for Today's Black Children," June 4, 1985, 2A.

David, D. S., and R. Brannon (eds.). *The Forty-Nine Percent Majority: The Male Sex Role*. Reading, Mass.: Addison-Wesley, 1976.

Doyle, J. A. *The Male Experience*. Dubuque, Iowa: William C. Brown, 1983.

Franklin, C. W. *The Changing Definition of Masculinity*. New York: Plenum Press, 1984.

Karenga, M. R. "On Wallace's Myth: Wading through Troubled Waters," *The Black Scholar*, May/June 1979, 36–39.

Leavy, W. "Is the Black Male an Endangered Species?" *Ebony* 41, August 1983, 46.

Lorde, A. "The Great American Disease," *The Black Scholar*, May/June 1979, 17–20.

Nobles, W. "Toward an Empirical and Theoretical Framework for Defining Black Families," *Journal of Marriage and the Family*, Vol. 40, 1978, 679–690.

Pleck, J. H. *The Myth of Masculinity*. Cambridge, Mass.: M.I.T. Press, 1981.

Staples, R. "The Myth of Black Macho: A Response to Angry Black Feminists," *The Black Scholar*, March/April 1979, 24–32.

Stewart, J. B., and J. W. Scott, "The Institutional Decimation of Black American Males," *The Western Journal of Black Studies*, Vol. 2, No. 2, 1978, 82–91.

Wallace, M. *Black Macho and the Myth of the Superwoman*. New York: Dial, 1979.

Wilson, W. J. *The Declining Significance of Race*. Chicago: University of Chicago Press, 1980.

14

Race and Raceness: A Theoretical Perspective of the Black American Experience

Jacqueline E. Wade

Jacqueline E. Wade is the Director of the Afro-American Studies Program at the University of Pennsylvania where she earned a Masters of Social Work degree and a Ph.D. in Education.—The Western Journal of Black Studies, *Spring 1987, Vol. 11, No. 1*

Concepts of race and raceness have been prevailing themes of life in America, from its early beginnings as a country promising economic, religious, and personal fulfillment, to its current stance as a nation of vast economic, political, and cultural power. Consequently, the matter of one's racial identity always has been a mark of social standing and category, which requires that all people identify themselves as members of a particular racial group at some time or another during the course of their lives. This racial identity becomes the "symbol" of one's individual and collective power needed to negotiate all manner of social arrangements.

This paper gives a theoretical perspective of the multi-dimensional nature of Black-race/white-race consciousness which, more than any other social consciousness, undergirds the whole spectrum of the American social order. Its basic premise is that American perceptions of race and raceness are distinct and persistent socio-cultural forces that are detectable in behaviors, attitudes, feelings, beliefs, life styles, expressive patterns, and socialization processes of all people who live in this society. On the one hand, as used in this paper, race refers, socio-culturally, to a human group that either defines itself, or is defined by others, as belonging to a specific "race" by virtue of innate and immutable physical characteristics such as skin color, hair texture, facial features, body build, and ancestry, as well as cultural proclivities.

Raceness, on the other hand, crystallizes this concept of race, thereby, moving it to a particular historical context that reinterprets and relegates both physical and cultural forces in terms of racial superiority, racial inferiority, and cultural "differentness." Viewed specifically within the American scheme of life and with particular focus on Black America, raceness is determined by the historic patterns of colonialism, slavery, and the resultant relationships between Black and white people.

Race and raceness, in the final analysis, ground psychological perspectives, procure sociological reference points, inculcate visions of the world, and provide people with ways of interpreting reality, relating to others, and accepting a general design for living. Configurations of white-race centeredness, Black-race stigma, and the evolutionary process of Black-race affirmativeness in the face of an ever pervading Euro-American cultural ethos are interlocking motifs in this discussion.

White-Race Centeredness

Historically, formulations of social standards, mores, cultural patterns, life styles, behaviors, human interactional routines, and social values of Western European culture instilled the ideology of white-race dominance and the proposition that "whiteness" was the norm by which all other races would be measured. Consequently, white-race centeredness became the very fabric from which American culture was formed. The salience of this white-race centeredness to the early colonists was noted by Schwartz and Disch (1970) who proposed that: "By the time the first English Colonist had arrived in the new world, they had already inherited a host of associations tied to the word 'black' which became important as men put language to use in first defining and later justifying the status they desired of non-whites" (p. 6).

As noted by Franklin (1956), the powerful stake of white-race centeredness in all levels of American life began to be well exhibited throughout the country's history. Franklin stated that:

> While uniting the various economically divergent groups of whites, the concept of race also strengthened the ardor of most Southerners to fight for the preservation of slavery. All slaves belonged to a degraded, "inferior" race, and by the same token, all whites, however wretched some of them might be, were superior. In a race-conscious society, whites at the lowest rung could identify themselves with the most privileged and efficient of the community. (p. 85)

Blumer (1958) broadened this perspective by asserting the inevitable consequences:

> In race prejudice there is a self assured feeling on the part of the dominant racial group of being naturally superior or better. This is commonly shown in a disparagement of the qualities of the subordinate race as an alien and fundamentally different stock…Thus, vis-à-vis the subordinate racial group, the unlettered individual with low status in the dominant racial group has a

sense of group position common to that of the elite of his group. By virtue
of sharing this sense of position such an individual, despite his low status,
feels that members of the subordinate group, is inferior, alien, and properly
restricted...He forms his conception as a representative of the dominant
group; he treats individual members of the subordinate group as representatives of that group. (pp. 4–5)

Given this perspective, the image of the Black African as a person apart, an
outsider, a barbarian, and a pagan propelled the establishment of mechanisms—
from slavery, peonage, and Jim Crowism, to institutionalized racism—for sustaining the multifarious dimensions of Black-race subjugation. Historically, then,
Black Americans have carried an indelible "scar" of unacceptability with a clarity
that elsewhere could never have been so profound (Elkins, 1959). As Tannenbaum (1946) posed:

> The Negro became identified with the slave, and the slave with the eternal
> pariah for whom there could be no escape. The slave could not ordinarily
> become a free man, and if chance and good fortune conspired to endow him
> with freedom, he still remained a Negro, according to the prevailing belief,
> he carried all of the imputation of slave inside him. (pp. 100–102)

Although other immutable factors of the human experience related to oppression (such as gender and age), as well as factors of socially designated inequities
(such as economic class, national origin, sexual orientation, and religious preference), are definite aspects of America's evolution, the promulgation that white is
good and "normal" and Black is *bad* and "not normal" has been sustained as the
basis of the varied social relationships among all people in this society. Therefore,
notions of white-race superiority and Black-race inferiority became the threads
with which the whole of American culture was woven and by which the stigma
of being Black was transmitted through lineages, thus, perpetually contaminat-
ing *all* people of African ancestry. Even though other racial groups in this society
(e.g., Native Americans and Asians) have encountered racial degradation and
exploitation, the substance of such oppressive encounters were, and remain,
incontrovertibly born out of white-race projections *against* Blackness.

Empirical Evidence of White-Race Centeredness

Research focusing on the essence of racial preference relative to American human
growth and development confirms that white-race centered cultural perspectives
are associated with what's "good" and "normal" (even when some of the research
subjects are Black). For example, Moreland (1963), documenting that racial bias
develops early in an individual's life, found that the majority of three-year-olds
(both Black and white) preferred and identified with whites even before they were
able to make correct racial self-identifications. More specifically, the Renninger

and Williams (1970) study conducted in pre-school settings in North Carolina demonstrated that white children's awareness of color connotations develops between the ages of three and five. White children, they discovered, held a bias against the color black and Black playmates, and favored the color white and playmates of their own race. Williams and Roberson (1967) similarly showed that racial awareness develops concurrently with color meanings and that the latter reinforced the former. The researchers noted that the extent of racial bias that already existed in their white pre-school subjects was highly evident, e.g., over 86 percent of the five-year-olds scored in the racially prejudiced direction 11 or 12 times out of 12 opportunities. This study indicated that there were strong and early pressures in the children's environments, which fostered a rejection of the color black and of Black Americans.

Additionally, the assessment of racial prejudice and racial preferences of white adults have taken a variety of forms and produced significant conceptualizations of white-race centeredness. Campbell and Schuman (1968), who surveyed racial attitudes of whites in fifteen major American northeastern and mid-southern cities, concluded that while whites supported the principles of non-racial discrimination in housing, employment, and education, they were very reluctant to support laws that prevented such discrimination. Over a decade later, the research of Kinder and Sears (1981), focusing on white suburbanites' clear and prevalent resistance to changes in the whole scheme of American white-race dominance, exhibited white-race centered views holding that Blacks, generally, violated such traditional American (i.e., white) values as individualism and self-reliance, the work ethic, obedience, and self-discipline. The researchers proposed that these beliefs were predicated on the whites' adherence of their social proprietary positions relative to their early-learned white-race preferences and Black-race stereotypical viewpoints. Significantly, these white-race centered notions had little to do with any tangible outcomes of Civil Rights laws or Black oriented social change initiatives on the private lives of the research subjects.

Finally, the Gaertner and Dovidio (1981) studies on white Americans who considered themselves "non-racist," "pluralistic," and "liberal" found that, under specific white-race-threatening circumstances, such people held attitudes about and behaved toward Blacks in ways that were not statistically different from that of white research subjects who openly acknowledged their racial antagonisms. More than 80 percent of the respondents used a subtle form of "white-race-interest" ratings to describe beliefs that Blacks, in comparison to whites, were less intelligent, less kind, less good, less reputable, less reliable, and less responsible. Additionally, the researchers found that this pattern of white-race centeredness was most manifested in the attitudes and behaviors of well educated whites who either influenced or administered programs designed to counteract the effect of Black racial oppression and discrimination.

The above data, as well as the aforementioned historical context, indicate that the whole scheme of white-race centeredness in American society exists primarily through whites' strong penchant for white-group power and position rather than merely a set of feelings held by individual whites toward Blacks! Thus, white-race centeredness (and the evidence of its racial biases and discriminations) is a collective process of honing and sustaining white-race dominance and control to succinctly frame white/Black relationships.

The Blumer (1958) perspective of racial prejudice supports this notion and, when reinterpreted, illustrates that whites, as the dominant race, hold four basic types of feelings, attitudes, and/or beliefs that are always present at some level and degree in the whole gestalt of white/Black interactions: An attitude of superiority, a belief that Blacks (the "subordinate race") are substantially different and alien, a feeling of proprietary claim to certain areas of privilege and advantage, and an almost visceral fear and suspicion that Blacks harbor designs on the prerogatives of white-race dominance. Importantly, the feeling of race prerogative is a powerful dimension of white/Black involvements, for it denotes a special sense of entitlement to exclusive and/or apriori rights in most important areas of life ranging from the "ownership" of social systems and institutions (e.g., education, health, religion, communications media, housing, distributive justice, and politics) to the claim of white-race advantage in certain positions of social prestige, including the display of symbols and accouterments of these positions. This deep sense of white-race prerogative, when combined with the other basic features of white-race dominance, maintains a racial status quo that promulgates an exceedingly "in-one's-own-self-interest" rationale that ultimately benefits whites.

Furthermore, these basic perceptions distinctively refer to a unique race status positioning in the white/Black encounter. The attitude of white superiority places Blacks below whites; the belief of Black-alienness places Blacks beyond whites; the feeling of white proprietary claim excludes Blacks from white social prerogatives; and the white fear of Black-race encroachment on white dominance bars Blacks from advancing into the common white group positioning. Consequently, whites are not essentially concerned with Blacks as individuals, but are deeply invested in the white-group position relative to Blacks as a group. This positioning supplies whites with frameworks of perception, standards of judgment, patterns of sensitivity, and emotional affinities. Accordingly, the sense of white-race dominant positioning is a generalized form of racial orientation, and it cannot be merely reduced to individualized feelings such as hatred, hostility, or antipathy. This sense of racial essence stands for what always ought to be—i.e., a sense of where the two racial groups belong. It is a group norm and an imperative, guiding, inciting, cowering, and coercing all spheres of American life—overtly or covertly, consciously or unconsciously—and invariably culminating in white-collective negative images of Black-raceness.

There are a multitude of ways in which this white-collective image of Blacks is expressed at any given time and place. Blumer (1958) amplifies this reality when he noted that:

> Some whites may feel bitter and hostile towards Blacks with strong antipathies, with an exalted sense of superiority and with a lot of spite; others may have charitable and protective feelings, marked by a sense of piety, and tinctured by benevolence; and others may be disposed to politeness and considerations with no feeling of truculence. (p. 4)

Moreover, white Americans, on the average, truly believe that they are unprejudiced about Blacks in terms of their sense of group responsibility for the problems that Blacks face. They often espouse white-race favorable belief-statements—e.g., that whites are doing as well as can be expected regarding the race problem; that all this trouble between the two races is due to "outside agitators"; that when Blacks become more educated as a group things will be better for them; that Blacks who are educated or upwardly mobile are "exceptional" Blacks; that Blacks have the right goals, but the wrong methods for their advancement—and other ideas that refute the realities of deeply inculcated white-race proclivities (Thalberg, 1972). Whites, then, unconsciously (and, often, quite consciously) endorse the presence of institutionalized racism, particularly if it operates as unobtrusively as possible, to basically maintain the prevalence of white advantage and Black disadvantage. Therefore, American society is replete with socio-cultural themes, structures, and human interactions that proclaim and normalize white-race dominance and Black-race submission (often declared as "inherent" white-race superiority and Black-race inferiority).

While there are many aspects of American life that perpetuate the phenomenon of white-race centeredness, the English language is, perhaps, the most poignant example of a medium that fosters the perception of white-raceness as normal and Black-raceness as deviant. For the use of the language is intensely implicated in race-conscious thought and deed since it is a major means by which Blacks and whites know, define, and shape their reality and know themselves and others. The connotations of the language are used, by both Blacks and whites, consciously and unconsciously, to denote white propitiousness, and to generally express a world-view from which the characteristics of Blackness are seen as inferior, and the culture and way of life of whites are seen as superior. Davis (1969) found that standard English dictionaries have a wide range of specifications associated with the words "black" and "white":

> The word whiteness has 145 synonyms; 44 of which are favorable and pleasing to contemplate, i.e. purity, cleanliness, clear, chaste, unblemished, unsullied, innocent, honorable, upright, just, straight forward, fair, genuine, trust-worthy, (a white man's colloquialism). Only ten synonyms for whiteness appear to have negative implications—and these only in the mildest

sense—gloss-over, whitewash, gray, wan, pale ashen, etc...The word blackness has 126 synonyms, 60 of which are distinctly unfavorable and none of
them mildly positive. Among the offending 60 were such words as: blot,
smut, smudge, sully, begrime, soot, becloud, obscure, dingy, murky, low-
toned, threatening, forboding, forbidden, sinister, wicked, malignant, deadly,
unclean, dirty, unwashed, etc...Not to mention 20 synonyms directly related
to race, such as Negro, Negress, Nigger, darky, blackamoor, etc. (p. 74)

In sum, white-race centeredness, one may logically conclude, pervades the
entire scope of American social perspectives and human interactions. It is the genesis of racist attitudes and beliefs and ideological pronouncements of white privilege and dominance. The concept of white-raceness thus becomes the hallmark
of full personal dignity as well as full participation in American society. Black-
raceness, however, is deemed by whites as an inferior social status that relegates
Black people to life processes of discrimination, degradation, and oppression.
This social condition causes Blacks to devise many responses to their situations,
which are described in the remainder of this paper.

Black-Raceness and Patterns of Managing Racial Stigma

In view of the above conceptualization of white-race centeredness, it is quite
apparent that Blacks' social standing and social category in American society,
historically and currently, convey that they are less desirable beings. They are
stigmatized and deemed to be in negative departure from "normalcy." In terms of
white-race dominant ideals, Blacks are effectively reduced from whole and "usual"
persons to people who are discounted from the mainstream of living and being.
Consequently, their "heritage" (so called by whites) as descendants of "primitive
Africans," "children of slaves," and "culturally deprived" people, coupled with
their self-defined progressive activism for social, political, and economic equality
and acceptance, are interlaced with ever increasing attempts to come to terms
with the contradictions of being Black, i.e., a pariah, in white America.

Throughout their history in American society, Blacks have mounted a variety
of practices for responding to and attaining acceptance and racial affirmation in
white society. Insights into the resulting dynamics, and specifically into what
remains problematic, is offered by Erving Goffman's model of "stigma and the
management of a spoiled identity in a world of normals." According to Goffman
(1963), the stigmatized generally subscribes to the same basic concepts of identity
related to normals. Yet, the stigmatized perceives that he or she does not fit the
mode of whatever the "real" normals profess, and readily perceives that the real
normals are not ready to make contact or relate on equal grounds. The standards
that stigmatized persons have incorporated from the wider, normal society equip
them to be intimately alive to what normals see as their failing, inevitably causing
the stigmatized, if only for moments, to agree that they indeed fall short of what

they really ought to be; thereby internalizing this social stigma. In order to confront this condition the stigmatized must embark on a life course that Goffman calls the *management of stigma identity*.

The application of the Goffman model to the whole thrust of Black-life postures in a racially stigmatized predicament can result in the following interpretations: (1) Blacks at some level of life functioning may adopt the solution of supporting the "norm" of white-raceness in American living, but define themselves (in conjunction with whites) as people not fully able to realize the norm and personally put it into practice; (2) Blacks, realizing that they cannot maintain an identity as prescribed by whites, alienate themselves from the white community and openly rebel against any form of generalized white superiority/Black inferiority ideologies; (3) Blacks may "pass" or "cover" (i.e., deflect their Black-raceness) as carbon-copy whites, especially if skin color and/or other physical attributes help hide the fact that they really *are* Black, and they strongly adhere to white value orientations for religion, social customs, behaviors, and convictions, and other aspects of "white-is-better" predilections. At various times and places Blacks may select to interrelate these modes of identity-management techniques to best steer the inevitable Black/white life encounter. In other words, Blacks are ever bound to exercise special applications of identity management in order to exert strategic control over the "Black image in the white mind."

It should be noted, however, that defensive stances against a sense of inherited worthlessness, inadequacy, and social impotence—suggestive of age-old Black stereotypes such as being lazy, incompetent, childish, oversexed, troublesome, and low-class (i.e., "nigger imagery")—compel Blacks to utilize some measure of all three of these modes in order to standardize an ability to cope, survive, and flourish in America. Additionally, Blacks will reorganize or reconstitute the modes in ways that deliberately mislead whites in their conception of the Black behavior. For example, on the one hand, Blacks will "pass" as the stereotype in order to gain an advantage or reach a goal, and, on the other hand, will "cover" and control information about their human frailties in order to deflect whites' tendencies to discredit them. Moreover, Blacks will use information (even openly brag) about their self-defined heritage as a people of valiant strength and capacity to endure and advance—in spite of almost monolithic racial degradation—in buffering against deeply felt anger, cynicism, despair, and/or frustration when goals for equality and freedom go unrealized. Blacks will take offensive and defensive stands, even vacillate between the two vantage points in certain circumstances, to extricate themselves from an imposed sense of devaluation in interactions (both direct and indirect) with whites.

A dilemma emerges from such a "schizophrenic" existence. As has been earlier indicated, the stigmatized person invariably internalizes the dominant societal proscriptions for what is normal, moral, just, honest, mannerable, and other features of a stable, orderly society. Furthermore, standards undergirding basic life supporting patterns for affirmative human growth and development (well institutionalized throughout the customs, traditions, and social systems of the dominant culture) promote the individual's inherent ability to become a person with feelings of worth, esteem, and confidence in one's self and in one's world (Erikson, 1963).

Given this perspective, Blacks invest in established self-affirming imperatives to achieve acceptance (i.e., self-acceptance as well as acceptance from others) and, at some level of social interaction, adhere to the values, norms, and beliefs principally ordained by the wider white society. Yet, the pejoratives of formalized and unofficial rejections of Blacks as "normals" in the main of American functioning cause them to expend tremendous amounts of energy to demonstrate *intrinsic* equality, competence, and humanity. This task takes its greatest toll in the direct relationships between Blacks and whites, causing, as Chestang (1972) posed, a certain superficiality and artificiality in their transactions (no matter what the degree), a basic dishonesty that dilutes the authenticity of the association, and behavior that perpetuates the distrust and suspicion so commonly observed.

Blacks tend to view their interactions with whites as tenuous and fragile at best, and humiliating and demeaning at worst. In the Black/white encounter, the Black person is fundamentally inclined to question whether he or she is given deference, respect, or positive recognition because of a genuine acknowledgment of her equal worth or because he or she is being patronized. While Blacks may adopt white middle-class attitudes and values to alleviate the immediately debilitating effects of their race stigma, they must ever defend against the over-riding reality that at almost every turn in the dominant culture they are subordinate.

The pervasiveness of white cultural dominance and control, which, generally, mobilizes the life practices of most of America and contributes toward the maintenance of institutional racism, has a profound effect on Blacks' abilities to achieve and sustain a true sense of self worth and dignity. Du Bois (1903) conceived that the social status of Blacks in the society caused an almost untenable state in their life functioning when he proposed the following as the ultimate dilemma for Blacks:

> The Negro is sort of the seventh son, born with a veil, and gifted with second sight in this American world—a world which yields him no true self-consciousness, but only lets him see himself through the revelation of the other world. It is a peculiar sensation, this sense of always looking at one's self through the eyes of others, of measuring one's soul by the tape of a world that looks on in amused contempt and pity. One ever feels his twoness—an American, a Negro; two souls, two thoughts, two unreconciled strivings; two warring ideals in one dark body, whose dogged strengths alone keep it from being torn assunder...the history of the American Negro is the history of this strife. (pp. 16–17)

Although this Du Boisian perspective has undergone a variety of changed manifestations—particularly, within the context of current expressions of Black American pride in their African heritage that have produced drives for enculturation instead of acculturation, for liberation rather than integration, and for preservation rather than ethnic assimilation (Baraka, 1969)—Blacks' self concept is still fundamentally related to a color-caste ideology generating a mosaic of biological, psychological, and sociological conditions. Fundamentally, Blacks continue to conform to this social condition in quite distinct ways; for, essentially, a peculiar pact between them and whites was struck early on, exacting a form of tacit cooperation between the two races to sustain the norm (i.e., Blacks in their place, and whites in theirs). Thus, Blacks, individually and as a group, have devised a myriad of approaches to make whites contented with the Black presence in white society, to function in spite of whites' doubts of Black competencies, to display a balance of "Black-rights" concerns with white-status-quo-privileges, and to develop a series of Black-race/white-race relationships on which to actualize a persistency of events manifesting a progression of Black acceptance in the mainstream of American life. Blacks have mapped out an assortment of adaptations to these ends, passing them from generation to generation (consciously and unconsciously), in order to proceed to the ultimate penchant for affirmation of a Black-self in a white dominant social world.

Blacks intuitively know that their openly negative reactions to racial discrimination (especially those acts that are not usually sanctioned by law or formal embodiments, such as sit-ins, boycotts, and "riots") are often deemed by whites as over-reactive, hypersensitive, unreasonable, and even "un-American." Thus, Blacks often couch their complaints that point to overt and covert acts of white supremacy in words that are more or less *acceptable* to whites. Blacks often go to great lengths to avoid any interpretation by whites that their defensive postures to the realities of their race stigma is not a direct expression of their merely being Black (i.e., "acting like a nigger"), and, hence, a justification for the way they *are* being treated. Moreover, Blacks may often over-compensate for their Black raceness in the company of whites. They will engage in almost grueling efforts to master areas of activities that are "normally" felt to be out of reach of what whites perceive as the "average" Black person's abilities. Furthermore, Blacks may often seek to exhibit themselves in ways that expressingly prove that they are indeed different from what most whites expect of the character of their social identity.

Accordingly, recurrent pronouncements of "I want to make something of myself," and "I want to be somebody/I am somebody," herald the succession of each generation of Blacks to shake negative stereotypes of being Black and to employ ever increasing standards of Black-race acceptability among whites. Nadelson (1972) uncovered some of these tendencies when she wrote of Angela Davis' life: "One ambition was to live chastely, thus disproving white charges of animal instincts; another was to speak English correctly, thereby, distinguishing yourself from the masses" (p. 35). Additionally, the histories of the development of predominantly Black populated educational institutions (primarily established for a growing Black bourgeoisie) and efforts to evolve an all encompassing, socially effective Black community are replete with the essence of an overriding ambition to be the "nice Negro" who would fit comfortably into the white world.

Blacks have had to manifest an array of rhetoric, attitudes, and behaviors, which concomitantly account for excuses for ill successes in the white environment. Blacks must be more cautious than whites; must find more discharge outlets; must compensate more for feelings of generalized white-race rejection; and must find an assortment of ways to actualize needs for self-determination in order to assume competence in coping with the realities of their social identities as well as acquiring the impetus for transcending those realities. These efforts eclipse all socio-economic classes of Blacks, because this society primarily delegates Blacks to a single, racially inferior category. The bonds of Black-race stigma are so strong in the lives of many Blacks that no one Black person, regardless of how great the individual prestige, can fully be disassociated from the lesser endowed members of the race.

Blacks, in the company of whites, then, know that they are "on"; that they must be self-conscious and self-calculating about the impressions they are making on whites; and that their life styles (no matter the strengths or weaknesses) are assessed as either signs of remarkability or as scars of racial inferiority. Moreover, the Black person's presence among whites all too often exposes him or her to invasions of self (i.e., race) inclinations: Whites may call upon a Black to speak for or explain the "Black experience" or "Black differentness" to any given situation. In either case the Black person carries a particular anxiety when interacting with whites, and is ever cognizant, in some form or fashion, of the peculiar Black American heritage as belonging to a racial group that has concocted intricate life-supporting systems and mechanisms for "making it" and "hanging in" (affirmative living) in America. As Baron (1969) noted:

> Amidst the ordeals of suppression and resistance the Black community took shape. Adapting to the larger North Atlantic culture into which they had been transported by their white masters and hanging on to what could be saved from their various West African heritages, Black men in America have constructed a unique community. A less hardy people might well have perished, and certainly would not have persisted to become today the most decisive force for social change in American life. (p. 139)

Clearly, the development of the Black community as a cultural setting that distinctively exhibits a Black *ethos* of affirmative life provides a haven for Blacks to gain relief from the demands that are placed on them by whites. However, Blacks cannot escape the necessity of what Chestang (1972) calls "egosyntonic modes" for effective functioning in both the Black and white cultures of American living. Thus, Blacks have a duality of responses (both consciously and unconsciously) to their plights, which becomes a central aspect of their operations in the overall American scene. As Chestang noted:

> The Black man is not a marginal man but a bicultural man. He does not live on the fringes of the larger society; he lives in both the larger society and the Black society. The experience of functioning in two cultures results in…two ways of coping with the tasks, expectations, and behaviors required by his condition. They converge in the adequately functioning Black individual as an integrated whole. (p. 46)

In sum, Blacks stride two parallel paths in managing their Black raceness. Each path is based on adherences to certain values and behaviors. The dilemma of effective social functioning is omnipresent: The one path compels them to loyalty and positive valuation of their race for its forbearance and power to survive and thrive, the other compels them to pragmatically "pass" and "cover" in the white world. One path urges them to an open and life-long rebellion against "nigger imageries" and institutionalized discriminations, the other insists that they assimilate with whites, drop connections with being "typical" (i.e., inferior) Blacks, and at least adapt to, if not adopt, the perspectives and proclivities of the wider society. The duality of the Black American experience has potent implications for the Black achievement, and the failure to actualize a total sense of racial affirmativeness. This duality connotes dreams deferred, and frustrated aspirations; it expresses a kind of "dark joy" in celebrating the triumphs over a social order that promotes Black-race degradation; and it is bathed with cultural distinctions, behavioral practices, and social patterns that were distinctively evolved to cope with the prevalence of a society that consigns Black racial stigmatization.

In the final analysis, what the writer intends to offer in this discussion is a theoretical framework for further examination of the multi-faceted responses that one finds in the question of race and raceness, in America especially, and in the world generally. One may ask, for example, what visible intra-racial perspectives emerge from the Black on Black experience that can be considered relevant to this framework? Similarly, what further interracial perceptions can be, in today's times, detectable between the Black on white encounter (especially encounters with whites who actively live and work against the norms of white-race centeredness, dominance, and control)? Although these questions lie outside the scope of this paper, they, too, must be addressed if the most practical, germane solutions to this issue are to be found.

Bibliography

Baraka, Imamu. "A Black Value System," *The Black Scholar*, November 1969, 54–60.
Baron, Harold. "The Web of Urban Racism," in Louis Knowles and Kenneth Prewitt (eds.), *Institutional Racism in America*. Englewood Cliffs, N. J.: Prentice-Hall, 1969 [pp. 134–176].
Blumer, Herbert. "Race Prejudice as a Sense of Group Position," *The Pacific Sociological Review*, Vol. 1, No.1, Spring 1958, 3–7.

Campbell, A., and H. Schuman. "White Beliefs about Negroes," in Marcel Goldschmid (ed.), *Black Americans and White Racism*. New York: Holt, Rinehart and Winston, 1970.

Chestang, Leon [1972]. "Character Development in a Hostile Environment," in Martin Bloom (comp.), *Life Span Development*. New York: Macmillan, 1980 [pp. 40–50].

Davis, Ossie. "The English Language Is My Enemy," in Neil Postman, Charles Weingartner, and Terence Moran (eds.), *Language in America*. New York: Western, 1969 [pp. 74–86].

Du Bois, W.E.B. [1903]. *The Souls of Black Folk*. New York: Fawcett World Library, 1965.

Elkins, Stanley. *Slavery, a Problem in American Institutional and Intellectual Life*. Chicago: University of Chicago Press, 1959.

Erikson, Eric. *Childhood and Society*, 2nd ed. New York: Norton, 1963.

Franklin, John Hope. *The Militant South, 1800–1861*. Boston: Beacon Press, 1956.

Gaertner, Samuel, and John Dovidio. "Racism among the Well-Intentioned," in J. Bermingham and E. Clausen (eds.), *Racism, Pluralism and Public Policy: A Search for Equality*. New York: G. K. Hall, 1981.

Goffman, Erving. *Stigma, Notes on the Management of Spoiled Identity*. Englewood Cliff, N. J.: Prentice-Hall, 1963.

Kinder, Donald, and David Sears. "Whites' Opposition to Busing: On Conceptualizing and Operationalizing Group Conflict," *Journal of Personality and Social Psychology*, 1985, 1141–1147.

Moreland, J. K. "The Development of Racial Bias in Young Children," in *Theory into Practice*, Vol. 2, 1963, 120–127.

Nadelson, Regina. *Who Is Angela Davis? The Biography of a Revolutionary*. New York: Peter H. Wyler, 1972.

Renninger, Cheryl, and John Williams. "Black-White Color Connotations and Racial Awareness in Preschool Children," in Marcel Goldschmid (ed.), *Black Americans and White Racism*. New York: Holt, Rinehart and Winston, 1970 [pp. 311–320].

Schwartz, Barry, and Robert Disch (eds.). *White Racism: Its History Pathology and Practice*. New York: Dell, 1970.

Tannenbaum, Frank. *Slave and Citizen: The Negro in the Americas*. New York: Vintage, 1946.

Thalberg, Irving. "Viscedral Racism," *The Monist*, Vol. 56, No. 4, October 1972, 43–63.

Williams, James, and K. A. Roberson. "A Method for Assessing Racial Attitudes in Preschool Children," *Educational and Psychological Measurements*, Vol. 27, 1967, 671–689.

15

Consensus and Neo-Conservatism in the Black Community: A Theoretical Analysis of Black Leadership*

Richard A. Davis

Richard A. Davis *is an Associate Professor of Sociology at Winston-Salem State University. He received the Ph.D. degree from UNC-Chapel Hill.*—The Western Journal of Black Studies, *Spring 1988, Vol. 12, No. 1*

Introduction

The controversy surrounding Black leaders has again surfaced, bringing in its wake the specter of Black leadership incredulity. The issues involved here touch upon at least three different concerns. The first involves the very issue of Black leadership itself, by asking directly: Just what is a "black" leader? The second and third involve the related issues of consensus among these leaders, and the amount of agreement shared between them and their constituency.

To tackle the first issue one must decide what a Black leader is. Is it someone who is himself Black, or is it someone who leads a Black constituency? Or is it something else altogether? In other words, do Black leaders have certain characteristics that distinguish them from other leaders? For instance, do they have access to the same public forums as other leaders? Do they hold the same offices? Are their styles any different? Do they have the same qualifications as other leaders?

Obviously it is hard to decide what a Black leader is without first deciding what is really meant by the term "black" itself. As a generic term it is ambiguous. For example, "Is a Black film one that has been directed by a Black man? One

* An earlier version of this paper was presented at the 82nd Annual Meeting of the American Sociological Association, Chicago, Illinois, August 17–21, 1987. This essay benefited from a thoughtful reading by Charlene Macon-Davis.

that features Black actors? For a film to qualify for the label, do at least half of those responsible for its production have to be Black?" It may just be that "When writers and critics refer to 'black' movies, they are really talking less about the movies themselves than about the audience for which these movies have been designed." Thus it could be argued that a Black movie only exists "when Blacks can gain full control over a production, starting with financial backing and continuing all the way through distribution...they would, ideally, be produced and created entirely by Blacks, who would then be able to accept full credit—or blame, as the case might be—for their work" (Mitchell, 1975, 238–241). This approach to defining the term suggests that "black" refers to a transitional period in American history. According to this viewpoint, then, a Black leader is anyone who happens to be publicly defined as such, whether that person leads or seeks to lead a "black" constituency.

If one accepts this definition, one can then turn to three other considerations: (1) tracing-out the phylogenetic basis of disagreement among Black leaders, (2) clarifying the nature of the relationship between these leaders and their supporters, and finally (3) placing all of these issues into a broader theoretical context so that their implications can be better understood.

The Nature of Black Leadership: Consensus and Neo-Conservatism

The National Urban League has concluded that the apparent schism between Black leaders and the Black community is not real, but is instead the result of "an increase in the tempo of assaults on Black leadership." These assaults, the Urban League believes, are bent on discrediting Black leadership and "making it appear that this leadership [does] not represent the thinking of the majority of Blacks" (National Urban League, 1986, viii–ix). The report goes on to say that:

> When the frontal attack failed, a flanking movement was developed under the mask of scholarly research. A public opinion poll was undertaken that measured the views of 105 Black leaders and 600 randomly selected Blacks in a national survey. It concluded that there is a wide opinion gap between Black leaders and their constituents with the former being far out in front of the latter. (National Urban League, 1986, ix)

Thus, the National Urban League's concern centers around the issue of leader-follower consensus. But there is another related issue in this controversy, agreement among the Black leadership itself. This second concern centers around the apparent emergence of a new type of Black leader, the so-called "neo-conservative, Black intellectual." In contrast to so-called traditional Black leaders, these new Black leaders often oppose affirmative action and other government support programs, favor a lower minimum wage, and in general tend to minimize the importance of race in today's society.

The central concern of this paper is to determine whether the above noted divisions are real, and if they are, what their true nature is. The first thing to be noted is that opposing views among Black leaders is not new, but the concern over their disjuncture with the Black community is relatively new. So the real question becomes: How do contemporary Black leaders stack up to Black leaders of the past? Only through this type of analysis can one determine whether this leadership is actually more divided and/or more removed from its constituency.

As with other leaders, Black leaders have always disagreed on certain key issues, even as they agreed on others. For instance, although they were to become the personae for one of the most famous (and in some sense the most important) disputes in Black American history, even W.E.B. Du Bois and Booker T. Washington sometimes agreed (Foner, 1970). In opposing the Federal Election bill, for instance, Du Bois once said:

> We must ever keep before us the fact that the South has some excuse for its present attitude. We must remember that a good many of our people south of Mason and Dixon's line are not fit for the responsibilities of republican government. When you have the right sort of black voters you will need no election laws. The battle of my people in the South must be a moral one, not a legal or physical one. (Foner, 1970, 2–3)

In response, some elements of the Black community accused Du Bois of pandering to white Southerners (Foner, 1970)—a charge he himself would later level at Washington. Yet several years later in stark contrast to this earlier position, and that of Washington, Du Bois came to question this position:

> Is it possible, and probable, that nine millions of men can make effective progress in economic lines if they are deprived of political rights, made a servile caste, and allowed only the most meager chance of developing their exceptional men? If history and reason give any distinct answer to these questions, it is an emphatic no. (Foner, 1970, 129)

But other academicians besides Du Bois did not accept Washington's accommodative approach, even those who understood his motives.[1] There is some evidence that the same kind of schism still exists among Black leaders today, but now it is between traditionalists and neo-conservatives (see Anderson, 1986, and Loury, 1986 for a discussion of this issue). In his characterization of traditional Black leaders, Loury (1986, 169) calls their approach "the Civil Rights Approach"; while Anderson (1986, 153) calls the approach of the neo-conservatives "the new conventional wisdom."

A strong argument could be made that in the past Black leaders were essentially leading citizens in various areas of community life (e.g., religion, education, business, etc.), so the question of leader-follower consensus was largely moot—the leader and the lead were one. But now pundits disagree as to whether there is a split between Black leaders and their constituency. On the right, the consensus seems to be that there is an actual split; on the left, the opposite view is maintained.[2] The left explains this split as an aberration of the methodology employed, while the right sees it as a cohort effect. Sowell, for instance, argues that certain issues have become sacred cows, "and to break with traditional Black leaders and traditional rhetoric on these issues can raise questions of loyalty and dedication," even among individuals who are otherwise indifferent on the issue. He goes on to speculate that since the majority of today's Black population was not even born at the time of the supreme Court decision of 1954, or at the time of the 1964 Civil Rights Act, these individuals often diverge from the views of current Black leaders.

On the other hand, Sowell attributes the growing split among Black leaders to maturing among some, and to stagnation among others. For instance, he argues that Black leaders who came to prominence during the civil rights era tend to disagree with "independent Black scholars" because the latter have, increasingly, come to see the civil rights approach as having already done its work. He argues that:

> Among Blacks today regarded as "conservatives," virtually all were once either liberals or leftists. Harvard professor Glen Loury, who has criticized preferential treatment programs in recent years, was defending such programs earlier in this decade. Walter Williams was such a vocal radical, while serving as a young draftee in the U.S. Army, that he was court-martialed. (Sowell, February 18, 1986)

Thus Sowell hypothesizes that "the case for the political left looks more plausible on the surface but is harder to keep believing in as [one] becomes more experienced." However, it could be that Black leaders now occupy different circumstances. In the past most Black leaders were non-office holders. But now, more than ever, they are being elected to leadership positions. For example, last year, according to the Joint Center for Political Studies, the number of Black elected officials, though still small (1.3 percent of all elected offices in the nation [490,000]), actually increased (*Greensboro News and Record*, July 28, 1986). Yet, they are still more institutionalized than ever before, and as argued below, institutionalization often leads to conservatism.

The Divergence of Political Views in the Black Community

There are good reasons to anticipate certain cleavages in the political views of Black Americans. According to Philip Converse's "black-white" model of social attitudes, there is likely to be a difference between the opinions expressed by most groups and their leaders simply because most members of any group do not hold what could truly be called an attitude on most social issues.[3] According to Converse (1964, but also see Brody, 1986), only the well-informed members of any group (e.g., its leaders) are likely to develop really meaningful attitudes on most social issues. The average person, on the other hand, rarely gathers enough information on most issues to form a meaningful opinion. Thus, Converse argues, because most individuals tend to respond to most issues on the basis of how it affects them, public opinions at any given time are not likely to be very reliable. He contends that this situation applies for all but a very small, well-informed set of individuals in any group. And even though the pattern of who is informed and who is not varies from one topic to the next, the key factor seems to be the availability of information on any given subject. Thus, at any given point in time, only a segment of interested individuals in any group is likely to have clear-cut opinions about a particular subject because the others lack the appropriate information to form a stable attitude on the issue. Thus, it could be argued that substantial portions of the Black community "do not have meaningful beliefs."

It is a matter of saliency. Knowledge becomes salient if it tends to remain topical for an extended period of time. The main point to note, however, is that every issue has its own specific public, or interested, group (Oskamp, 1977). In other words, individuals tend to stack up in different orders depending upon the issue at hand—on one issue some individuals will be well-informed, while on others they may not be (but also see Lane, 1962, for a somewhat different point of view). In general, then, it may be said that:

> In our complex modern world no one can be well-informed in all the areas which touch on his daily life, so a large degree of ignorance is inevitable for everyone. In this situation, it makes sense to concentrate on the knowledge and opinions which are important in one's own job and to largely turn over responsibility for other areas of life to people who are seen as experts in those areas (doctors in health questions, legislators in politics, community leaders in local issues, etc.). It is simply not functional for most people to develop an integrated system of political information and attitudes concerning issues which do not closely affect their everyday lives. (Oskamp, 1977, 116–117)

It is therefore "much less likely (and less necessary) for political beliefs and attitudes to be central and salient in the belief systems of the average citizens than in those of the highly educated, community leaders, and people who are employed in politics or active in political affairs" (Oskamp, 1977, 117).

Either Sowell's or Converse's positions would lead one to anticipate a split between the Black community and its leadership. Neither of those explanations, however, addresses the issue of the re-emergence of such strong disagreement among Black leaders, the likes of which have not occurred since the Du Bois-Washington dispute earlier this century. Thus, one must look elsewhere for a theoretical explanation for the apparent diversity among Black leaders.

The Divergence of Political Views among Black Leaders

According to Max Weber, leadership is based on three forms of authority (but also see Etzioni and Lehman, 1978, and Corwin, 1978 for slightly different perspectives): (1) traditional, (2) charismatic, and (3) legal. Traditional authority is based on a group's belief in the sanctity of tradition (e.g., the belief in the divine rights of kings, respect for religious leaders or the elderly). Charismatic authority is based on a group's respect for certain unique personal qualities or character-istics such as bravery, the use of magic, or spiritualism. Legal authority is based on rational grounds and the impersonal rules that have been legally enacted or contractually established (Weber, 1947).

The civil rights movement, which propelled most Black leaders into promi-nence, gave precedence to charismatic leaders like Dr. Martin Luther King and Rev. Jesse Jackson. But as Weber pointed out, charismatic leadership tends to be unstable, so ultimately it tends to give way to other, more stable forms of author-ity. Charismatic authority, for instance, cannot endure if its possessor has died, if the crisis that called for his or her personal touch has passed, or when the overall operation has become so unwieldly that certain activities have to be "delegated to non-charismatic individuals"; at this point "authority tends to become insti-tutionalized, either in traditional or legal forms" (Corwin, 1978, 69). And when this happens it results in what has been called the "routinization of charisma" (Smelser, 1962, 359; Weber, 1947).[4]

During this phase one of two things tends to happen, the "idealists began to feel that the ideals of the movement could not be realized" and sooner or later they lose "hope for the movement," or "certain committed individuals or groups in the community began to feel that the practical compromises" represent "backsliding and degeneration of the movement" (Smelser, 1962, 361–363). These scrimmages often involve conflicts over legitimacy and, thus, are difficult to resolve short of dissolution. Consequently, a single-minded commitment to agreed-upon goals soon becomes increasingly less likely.

At one point the church formed the main institutional basis of Black leader-ship (Morris, 1984), but now it could be argued that an analysis of Black lead-ership is essentially an analysis of the Black intelligentsia. This intelligentsia, according to August Meier (1977), developed during three major periods, the Classical period (1890–1945), the Period of Consolidation (1945–1965), and the Civil Rights period (1965–present). During the classical period the Black community enjoyed a time of intellectual diversity that was not matched again until the civil rights period. In between these periods conformity was so strictly enforced that diversity was practically stifled. But some have argued that even then a controversy existed over the lack of, or extent of, agreement between Black leaders and their supporters (Larkins, 1959). Even so, it would seem that when the external institutional order is accessible to Blacks, the appearance of unity fades, and the seething diversity of Black intellectuals is set free. More so in the past, racism controlled the growth of power centers in the Black community, so indirectly it allowed for internal censorship within the Black community by certain power brokers.[5]

Thus, during the consolidation period the apparent lack of diversity of opinion in the Black community may have partly reflected the lack of access to the external opportunity structure—without this access Blacks may have appeared far more unified in their views than they actually were.

Conclusions and Discussion

As has been shown, opposing views among Black leaders is hardly new, but the observation that these views no longer find support in the Black community is new. Hopefully, this analysis has shed some light on this second matter. Drawing from the work of Converse and Weber, an attempt was made to bring into clearer focus certain changes that are occurring in the Black community. For one thing, contemporary Black leaders are probably more conservative than their traditional counterparts. This is due in part to a shift in the institutional basis of Black leadership. As a rule, Black intellectuals have been granted greater access to America's major institutions of higher learning. At the same time Black political leaders have shifted to an institutional basis. Many Black political leaders have moved from a power base that was almost exclusively appointive to one that tends more and more to be elective in nature, and correspondingly, less based upon their charismatic abilities and more upon their legal authority.

On the other hand, the perception of a leader-follower split in the Black community, fostered by certain self-serving elements, may have some basis in truth, but self-interest is certainly not the whole story. A more complete, and therefore, more accurate explanation would have to admit that the schism that is developing between the Black leadership and the Black community is real, but it should also point to the role of public knowledge in this process.[6] As Oskamp notes, knowledge becomes salient only if it is widely discussed, rather unique in nature, and tends to remain topical for an extended period of time. If this is the case, then one might expect this gap to remain and to reappear in the Black community every time the issues involved fail to be unique to Blacks, or are not discussed well enough for a broad-based consensus to form between well-informed Black leaders and their less-well-informed followers.

Notes

1. They knew that Washington believed that by telling whites what they wanted to hear about "good" and "industrious" Blacks that he would be able to manipulate the white community and gain concessions in situations where Blacks had little or no power. Academicians like Charles S. Johnson, for instance, were in a better position to express their views since they were cloaked in scholarly garb. In a review of Johnson's book, *Patterns of Segregation*, H. L. Moon notes, "Whatever fury the author, himself a Negro, may have experienced in the preparation of this volume, he has affectively sublimated in his writing. The result is a coldly logical documentation of race relations in America today" (*New Republic*, March 8, 1943; cited in Blackwell and Janowitz, 1974, 83 fn 26).
2. For instance, Thomas Sowell argues that even though the majority of Black leaders favor preferential treatment, oppose the death penalty, favor allowing homosexuals to teach in public schools, and oppose school prayer (October 5, 1985; Marable, 1986), the majority of ordinary Blacks do not share this point

of view. On the other hand, there are those who feel that this view has been exaggerated in public polls. This group argues instead that the apparent split is a statistical aberration. As Eddie Williams, president of the Joint Center for Political Studies in Washington, notes, this whole issue centers around one national telephone poll of Black leaders and supporters conducted by the Center for Media and Public Affairs in which a sharp difference between Black leaders and the Black community on certain key policy issues was reported (*Jet*, October 28, 1986).

3. There are two basic reactions to Converse's "black-white" model, the believers and the doubters. Writers in the first camp argue for the non-existence of political attitudes among the masses. The other camp argues that Converse was wrong to conclude that a different attitudinal dynamic prevails for elites and the mass public (Brody, 1986). In defending his new Black-Gray-White model of attitude stability, Brody points out that Converse himself felt that "as a general rule, questions broad enough for the mass public to understand tend to be too simple for highly sophisticated people to feel comfortable answering without elaborate qualification" (Converse, 1964, 257 fn 21; cited in Brody, 1986, 674). Brody then goes on to point out that "Writing attitude questions for cross sections of the public is indeed difficult. Unless we can strike a delicate balance between the levels of clarity and conceptual difficulty, we must expect that certain subsets of respondents will experience difficulties in answering our questions" (Brody, 1986, 674). Perhaps the apparent split in the opinions reported from the Black community and its leadership rests partly on this point.

4. Morris (1984) argues that charismatic leadership plays an important role in developing effective strategies and tactics, including those typically viewed as part of the collective behavior tradition. But Morris modifies Weber's theory of charisma. The charismatic leader, Morris contends, does not operate in a vacuum—he emerges from and requires an organizational basis—thus, he is probably not the free agent that Weber characterized. With time all social movements begin to routinize or become institutionalized. When this happens there arises certain internal forces that create "disunity" and "instability" within. One of the first occurrences is the appearance of different types of leaders (the formulator, the propagandist, the agitator, the organizer, etc.)—eventually these leaders will clash because their ideals and objectives are so different. Soon, thereafter, a new phase sets in during which the movement has to accommodate the divergent interest of its various factions. This usually occurs "only after it has overcome—or sees the chance of overcoming—a common adversary." At this point controversy often arises over tactics, whether tried-and-true or innovative, resistance always arises from some quarter that feels it is too much or too little.

5. For example, August Meier has argued that Charles S. Johnson, became the "prime mover," "overseer," or "establishment nigger" in academic circles and "the Black for other Blacks to see in matters relating to financial support for, or, in some instances, academic recognition of social science research." This outcome produced "jealousies and feuding" among Black scholars and it tended to force their research "in a direction favored or at least not opposed by [Johnson]" (Meier, 1977, 261–263). "In the end, he established a unique power not only over Black sociologists but over the entire intellectual community." Consequently, Johnson came to be perceived as "the most powerful Negro in America" (Meier, 1977, 261–264). Thus Meier's (1977, 265) observation seems reasonable when he argues that "Johnson's control would not have been possible if race and the Black experience had remained an important concern of mainstream sociology, and if the racism of the academic world had not permitted the creation of a little jim crow fiefdom at Fisk, with power over Black intellectuals."

6. Glen Loury, one of the most outspoken proponents of the neo-conservatives, argues that after a Black has "made it," as many Blacks recently have, a new concern emerges—will he or she be respected for his or her accomplishments, either because "it is presumed that all Blacks, whether directly or indirectly, are indebted to civil rights activity for their achievements" or because what is achieved is not regarded as the result of "unaided accomplishments of individual persons" (Loury, 1986, 171–172). According to Loury, the haves seek respect, while the have-nots seek opportunity, so their strategies, and thus their leaders, will have to be different.

References

Anderson, Bernard E. 1986. "The Case for Social Policy," in National Urban League, *The State of Black America, 1986*. Washington, D.C.: National Urban League [pp. 153–162].

Blackwell, James E., and Morris Janowitz (eds.). 1974. *Black Sociologists: Historical and Contemporary Perspectives*. Chicago: University of Chicago Press.

Brody, Charles J. 1986. "Things Are Rarely Black and White: Admitting Gray into the Converse Model of Attitude Stability," *American Journal of Sociology*, Vol. 92, No. 3, 657–677.

Converse, Philip E. 1964. "The Nature of Belief Systems in Mass Publics," in D. Apter (ed.), *Ideology and Discontent*. New York: Free Press.

Corwin, Ronald G. 1978. "Power," in E. Sagarin (ed.), *Sociology: The Basic Concepts*. New York: Holt, Rinehart and Winston [pp. 65–85].

Cox, Oliver C. 1984. *Caste, Class, and Race*. New York: Doubleday.

Etzioni, Amitai, and Edward W. Lehman. 1978. "Complex Organizations," in Edward Sagarin (ed.), *Sociology: The Basic Concepts*. New York: Holt, Rinehart and Winston [pp. 110–127].

Foner, Philip S. (ed.). 1970. *W.E.B. Du Bois Speaks—Speeches and Addresses, 1890–1919*. New York: Pathfinder.

Greensboro News and Record. 1986. "Number of Blacks in Office Up, but Percentage Still Low," July 28.

Hunter, Floyd. 1953. *Community Power Structure*. Chapel Hill: University of North Carolina Press.

Jet. 1986. "Eddie Williams Raps New Black Public Opinion Poll," October, 28 [p. 8].

Lane, R. E. 1962. *Political Ideology: Why the American Man Believes What He Does*. New York: Free Press.

Larkins, John R. 1959. *Patterns of Leadership among Negroes in North Carolina*. Raleigh, N. C.: Irving Swain Press.

Loury, Glen C. 1986. "Beyond Civil Rights," in National Urban League, *The State of Black America, 1986*. Washington, D.C.: National Urban League [pp. 163–174].

Marable, Manning. 1986. "The So-Called Black Conservatism," *Winston-Salem Chronicle*, June 26.

McGhee, James D. 1983. *Black Solidarity: The Tie that Binds*. Washington, D.C.: National Urban League.

Meier, August. 1977. "Black Sociologist in White America," *Social Forces*, Vol. 56, No. 1, 259–270.

Mitchell, Martin. 1975. "Black Movies and Shades of Gray," in Francis H. and Ludmila A. Voelker (eds.), *Mass Media: Forces in Our Society*. New York: Harcourt Brace Jovanovich [pp. 238–241].

Morris, Aldon. 1984. *The Origins of the Civil Rights Movement*. New York: Free Press, 1984. Reviewed in Jack Bloom, *American Journal of Sociology*, Vol. 91, No. 5, 1270–1272.

National Urban League. 1986. *The State of Black America, 1986*. Washington, D.C.: National Urban League.

Oskamp, Stuart. 1977. *Attitudes and Opinions*. Englewood Cliffs, N. J: Prentice-Hall.

Smelser, Neil J. 1962. *Theory of Collective Behavior*. New York: Free Press.

Sowell, Thomas. 1985. "Surveying the Differing Opinions of Blacks," *Winston-Salem Journal*, October 5.

_____. 1986. "Confronting Reality in the Black Population," *Winston-Salem Journal*, February 18.

_____. 1986. "Watching America's Liberals Grow into Conservatism," *Winston-Salem Journal*, October 2.

Time. 1985. "Redefining the American Dilemma," November 11.

Weber, Max. 1947. *The Theory of Social and Economic Organization*. New York: Oxford University Press.

The Emerging Paradigm in Black Studies

Terry Kershaw

Terry Kershaw is an Assistant Professor of Sociology at the College of Wooster, Ohio. He received the Ph.D. at Washington State University.—The Western Journal of Black Studies, *Spring 1989, Vol. 13, No. 1*

Abstract

The focus of this paper is to reorganize the thinking involved in describing and analyzing the life experiences of African Americans. Traditional sociological literature has treated African Americans as peripheral to the study of "human behavior." Black Studies emphasizes an Afrocentric perspective, which is challenging to "traditional" disciplines. Along with an emphasis on Afrocentrism is the need to develop a corresponding methodology.

The methodology suggested in this paper is a synthesis of positivist and critical methodologies resulting in five basic steps: (1) to identify the problematic relationships by studying the results of past empirical and theoretical work as well as through an historical analysis; (2) to develop measures and methods of collecting data based on historical and empirical interpretations of reality; (3) to compare conditions with understanding; (4) to participate in a program of education; and (5) to alter theory in light of findings.

* * *

Some people would argue that Black Studies is a nonparadigmatic social science. They would make this assumption on the basis that Black Studies cannot differentiate its subject matter from other disciplines (i.e., sociology, psychology, history) and that Black Studies does not have a set of rules for the collection and analysis of data.

A paradigm has been defined in various ways. Friedricks (1970) has defined it as a fundamental image of a science's subject matter. Ritzer (1975) and Masterman (1970) say that paradigms identify what should be studied, how it should be studied, why it should be studied, as well as the rules of method. It distinguishes one discipline from another (Ritzer, 1975) with disciplines focusing on a unique subject matter/a methodology (Gordon, 1981). Thomas Kuhn talks about a community of scholars who accept some basic assumptions about a field of study, which then set the parameters for the field (Kuhn, 1970).

The purpose of this paper is to define a paradigm as a set of assumptions in a discipline that determines a range of phenomena, concepts, theories and methodology. A paradigm of Black studies will determine the proper subject matter as well as the appropriate methodology. The emphasis in this paper will be on identifying the basic assumptions of the Black Studies discipline and showing the inherent relationships between assumptions, range of phenomena, concepts, theories, and methodology. The paper will not focus on the nature of paradigms, but rather on the discipline of Black Studies. It will attempt to answer the questions, "Is Black Studies a discipline?" and, "If it is a discipline, why?"

Basic Assumptions

As suggested earlier, the idea of a discipline of study is directly related to subject matter and methodology. Also, as mentioned earlier the basic assumptions of any paradigm determine the subject matter and the appropriate methodology. The basic assumptions of the field of Black Studies revolve around the concept of Afrocentricity.

Afrocentricity refers to the life experiences of all people of African descent as the center of analysis. It emphasizes an analysis rooted in the historical reality of Black people. It does not negate, nor minimize, the experience of other groups; rather its emphasis is on how those experiences have helped shape Black reality and vice versa. With that in mind the following assumptions are suggested as the basic assumptions of the Black Studies discipline. They are:

1. To assume that Black experiences are worthy of intellectual endeavors.
2. To study, in a scholarly manner, the historical experiences of all people of African descent.
3. To focus on the distinctiveness of Black people from, and their interrelationship with, other peoples.

The first assumption emphasizes the significance of Black experiences. It is worthy of intellectual study because there are millions of people who will attest to that. In the case of the term "Black Experiences" the reference is to the diversity of the total life experiences of Black people. The second assumption is related to methodology by emphasizing the limits of the field (the experiences of all people of African descent), and that any study with Black people as its focus must be done in a scholarly manner. The third assumption centers on the uniqueness of Black people and their relationship with other people. These assumptions emphasize the total life experiences of Black people.

If one accepts these assumptions as valid the range of phenomena becomes self-evident. As mentioned earlier, the second assumption sets the limits of the discipline. The life experiences of Black people include the sociological, political, economic, historical, and artistic (music, art, literature). Therefore, the range of phenomena for Black Studies tends to be tied to all the disciplines (i.e., sociology, history, English, psychology). Any type of behavior with Black people as its focus falls in the domain of Black Studies because the focus of the "traditional" disciplines is on white people. For example, if one takes a look at sociology and focuses on the two dominant theoretical analyses (conflict and functionalism) it will help elucidate the point.

Simply stated, conflict theory emphasizes the importance of looking at interactions between people as being characterized by conflict, coercion and inequality. When one raises the question, "conflict with whom and coerced by whom," the whom tends to be Western industrial society. In particular, for American students, the whom is the United States and the "dominant" majority. Functional theory emphasizes the stability and order found in societies. Functional for whom refers to, for American sociology, American society and the "dominant" group. The dominant group in the United States are white ethnics (i.e., WASP, German-Americans, Irish-Americans); therefore the focus of American sociology tends to be white American relationships. Even when a course is taught that emphasizes race relations, unless the professor is sensitive to a Black Studies perspective, he or she will still teach from a mainstream sociological perspective. Therefore, this researcher claims that the subject matter of Black Studies is its own.

The basic assumptions are also tied to the concepts and theories that characterize the discipline. There are many concepts that help describe the totality of Black life experiences. The list of concepts would encompass many more pages than the writer wishes to spend on this topic. However, there are a number that are more significant than others. Afrocentricity, which was defined earlier, is central to Black Studies. Racism, colonialism, prejudice and discrimination, unfortunately, are part of the life experiences of Black people. There are also concepts emphasizing positive experiences, for example—family, culture, religion and leadership. While this in no way exhausts the list of significant concepts in Black Studies it does provide an example of what we are talking about.

The theories that are presently part of the Black Studies paradigm include Pan Africanism, Colonialism, Historical Materialism and Critical theory. Again, these are not suggested as a complete list, but they serve as an excellent point of departure. Pan Africanism, simply put, refers to a belief that all people of African descent share some similar experiences; one such experience is oppression; consequently, all people of African descent should work towards the liberation and unity of Africa (Berry and Blassingame, 1982). Once Africa is free, Black people throughout the world will be treated with a new sense of respect resulting in an elevated status. Why this would be a theory within the Black Studies paradigm should be self evident.

Colonialism attempts to analyze certain Black-white relations in colonial terms. The Black community is subordinate to the white community economically, politically, militarily and socially. Generally speaking, the community being dominated is inhabited by the indigenous group and the colonizers. However, it is the colonizer who has control of the community. Community, in this sense, refers to a racial group as a minority or majority group within a particular society. For example, African Americans in America and Nigerians in Nigeria have been colonized by white Americans and the British, respectively. Franz Fanon (1963, 1967), among others, has done some work on traditional colonialism while Carmichael and Hamilton (1967) and Blauner (1972) focused on domestic colonialism. All four of these writers emphasized the superordinate and subordinate relations between Black and white people. Also, as with Pan Africanism the emphasis is on Black people and their relations within and without the group.

Historical materialism emphasizes a historical perspective on social relations. Relations between people are confined by historical reality. What may be the basis of relationships today may not have always been the basis. For example, in the antebellum South, Black-white relations were characterized by slavery while race relations in the 1980's are characterized by institutional racism. While these two phenomena are related they are not the same; consequently, the relations are not the same. However, when using historical materialism as a tool for analysis it is important to understand the cumulative effect of historical relations. When one tries to analyze institutional racism one has to analyze slavery and its effect on succeeding historical periods. To analyze race relations during slavery, one needs to understand race relations prior to slavery (i.e., Age of Discovery, Holy Wars).

Historical materialism emphasizes the effect of material conditions on social life. Through this type of emphasis, social change becomes possible as people change matter to suit their purposes. It is dialectical in its emphasis on the interconnection of historical processes (Cornforth, 1971). Humans are constantly shaping matter according to their sense of reality. This process ends when humans end. For the purpose of defining the Black Studies discipline historical analysis is indispensable. Therefore, historical dialectical materialism provides an analysis consistent with the basic assumptions.

Critical theory has as its subject matter humankind and all their potentialities (Horkheimer, 1972). It focuses on ways people are exploited and oppressed. It attempts to identify contradictions between theory and praxis, and once identifying them, unify theory and praxis. The unity between theory and praxis is possible only if praxis occurs before theory construction. Theory construction is dependent on praxis because if theory comes prior to praxis it is like always trying to reach the carrot and realizing that the carrot is always just out of reach.

In an oppressive society this type of thinking reinforces oppression. Critical theory attempts to uncover oppressive relationships by identifying contradictions between relationships and people's understandings of those relations.

As suggested earlier, these theories are examples of the kind one would find in Black Studies. All four of them offer either an Afrocentric perspective or a historical and critical analytical perspective. Both of these perspectives are rooted in the historical struggles of people as they attempt to shape their reality.

Methodology

Praxis must be observed first and then explained as theory if the discipline of Black Studies wishes to maintain its tie to the struggles of Black people. While a discussion of subject matter is crucial to this argument, it is no more important than the method. When discussing a Black Studies methodology, sociology probably contributes more than any other discipline.

In contemporary sociology, there is one main approach to social research (the positive approach); and a lesser used alternative approach emphasizing a critical methodology (Horkheimer, 1972). Positivist methodology consists of seven steps. They are to:

1. Identify a scientific problem by studying the results of past empirical and theoretical work.
2. Develop empirically testable hypotheses that will improve the theory's explanatory and predictive power.
3. Select a proper setting.
4. Develop measures and data collection based on previous research/observations/interviews in the setting/the researcher's common sense/knowledge of social processes.
5. Gather data through experiments, existing documents and texts, surveys, interviews, and observations.
6. Analyze data to test hypotheses.
7. Alter laws and theory in light of findings and restate the next researchable phase of the problem.

Critical methodology also has seven major steps:

1. Identification of social groups or movements whose interests are progressive.
2. Develop a global political understanding of the groups where appropriate.
3. Study the historical development of the groups worldwide.
4. Construct a model of the relations between the groups worldwide and the groups' actions as they attempt to shape their social reality.

5. Compare conditions with understandings, critique the present ideology, discover immanent possibilities for action, and find the fundamental contradictions.
6. Participate in a program of education that gives the group tools to help them see their situation in new ways.
7. Participate in a movement of unifying theory and practice.

The two approaches are contradictory, and the results obtained are, therefore, very different. Positivistic methodology is ahistorical and reinforces the status quo while a critical methodology is historical while emphasizing contradictions between theory and practice. Research using a positivistic methodology can just as easily be done using a critical methodology with the major difference in the conclusions. Moynihan's (1965) research on the Black family will serve as an example to illustrate this point. Moynihan's study was chosen because of its status in mainstream sociological race relations literature.

Moynihan's study, entitled *The Negro Family: The Case for National Action* was done using a positivistic methodology. The problems identified, generally speaking, were the many that Black people encounter in American society—higher unemployment, lower income, poor housing, less education, and other inequalities found in the United States when making comparisons between Black and white Americans. More specifically, the particular "problem" studied was the structure of the Black family and Black opportunities for success.

Moynihan identified the problem above from his understanding of previous empirical and theoretical work. For example, in his discussion of matriarchy he stated "A fundamental fact of Negro American family life is the often reverse roles of husband and wife" (Moynihan, 1965, 30). He based this conclusion on studies previously done on "the" Black family. For example, in 1960, Robert Blood and Donald Wolfe, in a study of Detroit families, found that the majority of white families were egalitarian while the majority of Black families were female dominated (Moynihan, 1965). In 1964 a preliminary report on employment by the President's Committee on Equal Employment Opportunity emphasized that more Black females are in higher prestige occupations, relative to white females, than Black males, relative to white males (Moynihan, 1965). This helped lead Moynihan to his conclusion as stated above.

Moynihan developed empirically testable hypotheses to help advance the development of his theoretical perspective. For example, when discussing the "failure of youth" he looks for a connection between failure of Black youth and Black family structure. From previous studies, Moynihan found that children learn the patterns of work from their fathers (Moynihan, 1965), and that there is a positive correlation between low I.Q. and broken families. He also found that the level of education was a good indicator of potential future success. Therefore, the empirically testable hypotheses he developed were, "Nonwhite boys from families with both parents present are more likely to be going to school than boys with only one parent present, and enrollment rates are even lower when neither parent is present." And, "When the boys from broken homes are in school, they do not do as well as the boys from whole families" (Moynihan, 1965, 83). These hypotheses suggest that Moynihan is expecting to find what he is hypothesizing.

The setting Moynihan chose was a "lower class" Black community, even though he never defined class, rather than a middle class Black community. Considering the "problem" he chose to look at, the unstable Black family, it is understandable that he would study Black lower class families since, as he himself went on to conclude, the children of middle class Black families when given the opportunity, will perform as well, if not better, than their white peers (Moynihan, 1965). Consequently, if a researcher wanted to study why the Black family was unstable, then he would have a tendency to study a lower class community rather than a community where his hypothesis might not be supported.

Moynihan's method of gathering data was to use previous research and his own common sense. Since most of his data and assumptions came from previous research his findings tended to support those previous findings, as evidenced by the fact that, when discussing delinquency and crime in the Black community, Moynihan's analysis led him to assume that the majority of Blacks coming from broken homes would become delinquents and he supported this assumption with previous research.

An example of this earlier research is the work of the Gluecks. Glueck and Glueck identified five factors that, according to their findings, made a difference in whether a child became a delinquent or not: (1) discipline by father; (2) supervision of boy by mother; (3) affection of father for boy; (4) affection of mother for boy; and (5) the cohesiveness of family (Moynihan, 1965). The Glueck sample was used by the New York City Youth Board to test the validity of those five factors. They found that, generally speaking, in homes of delinquents the father was not present. Moynihan used this finding and his previous findings that the Black family is unstable, to lend validity to arrest and prison population statistics, which showed that 37 percent of the population in federal and state prisons were Black, and that 3 out of every 5 persons arrested for crimes against other persons in urban areas were Blacks. Additionally, according to Moynihan, in 44 percent of Black families studied, the wife was the dominant figure (Moynihan, 1965).

After he gathered his data he tested his hypothesis that: (1) the Black family is a matriarchal family type; (2) the failure of Black youth is directly related to the matriarchal family structure; (3) the high crime rate found in the Black community is directly related to a matriarchal family structure; and (4) the problems that Black people face in American society are directly related to an unstable family (suggesting that matriarchy necessitates instability). Again, it must be emphasized that the data and findings generally came from previous research, which did not allow for a significant amount of analysis to be any different from previous analyses and conclusions.

Moynihan did not alter laws regarding the theory on the Black family; rather he emphasized, supported, and reiterated previous research findings. Toward the end of his report he concluded that the tangle of pathology was tightening. He also suggested, indirectly, that the focus of further research should be on the religious movement, or lack of it, in urban areas. Why the religious movement? Along with the family it is the most stable Black institution and a potential social change agent. If Black people are having problems in America and they are responsible for their condition, then it must be the fault of unstable Black institutions.

The following discussion will analyze Moynihan's study using a critical methodology. Are the interests of Black Americans progressive? Yes, because they are an oppressed group in America and their struggle will help identify the contradiction between racism and the "American Creed." The elimination of oppression is the necessary prerequisite to equality—which is the American creed and defines a progressive movement. The civil rights movement of the 1960's was a progressive movement and could be a study of someone using a critical methodology.

Rather than understanding the Black American world view, Moynihan chose to examine the Black family using the white family structure as the criteria. Consequently, he postulated that "the" Black family is matriarchal and directly related to this fact is its unstable structure. If he had developed an interpretive understanding, one based on historical analysis, he would have looked at the function of the Black family relative to the historical social conditions that Black Americans have faced. For example, instead of viewing the Black family as a matriarchy, even though at the time of the study the majority of Black families were not one parent, he would have described a highly adaptable family that is a characteristic of Black family history. The ability of Black women to head the family if necessary is indicative of the synthesis of both roles as well as the egalitarian nature of Black male-female family relations (Staples, 1986).

Even a brief, but critical, look at the historical development of the Black family in America, from an Afrocentric world view, would have revealed an established and adaptive Black family structure ever since the Black man made his appearance in America. For example, even though the Black family was not a legal institution, the rearing of the children was a primary responsibility of the slave family, which they took very seriously (Blassingame, 1974). Historically, the family has always been an integral part of African society. If Moynihan had used a more critical historical approach he would not have assumed that the Black family was destroyed during slavery. After all, if a people refuse to give up their cultural identity can culture be destroyed without genocide? Consequently, he would not have postulated that the "instability" found in the Black family was directly related to the destructive tenets of slavery. He would have found a stable family, relatively speaking, and a highly adaptive family with roots to African family values. The higher proportion of female-headed, one-parent Black families, which resulted historically from their relationships with high rates of unemployment, as well as institutional and individual racism, had led Moynihan to define Black families as unstable. Most of Black America, however, defines the family as the oldest and most respected of all Black institutions.

Much of Black America, as well as Moynihan, perceive education as a viable tool for Black Americans to achieve upward social mobility. However, when one takes a critical look at that relationship one notices a fundamental contradiction. The education of Black Americans tends to, among other things, maintain the unequal distribution of wealth, power, and prestige through culturally biased and value-laden curricula.

Both the family and the school serve as socializing agents designed to produce the "perfect" conforming citizen. Hence, if American capitalist society is ethnically and racially stratified, then socializing agents serving the interests of the status quo reinforce that stratification. Black Americans are presently in unequal political, economic, and social relations with white America. If the education of Black Americans serves the present social structure, then how realistic is the assumption that increased education by Black Americans will in general lead to upward mobility? Also, given the social conditions of racial oppression, the use of the model of white middle class families in order to evaluate Black family structures tends to be oppressive.

If Moynihan had analyzed the higher statistical rate of Black dropouts, as compared to whites, using a critical methodology he would have described the education of Black Americans as a perpetuation of racial inequality. He would have had to identify fundamental contradictions within a society that is racially stratified while emphasizing equality, freedom, and justice for all.

Since Moynihan used a positivistic methodology he described the condition and made generalizations about the subject. As a critical methodologist, however, he would have participated in a program of education with the group under study. He would have had to participate in a dialogical relationship rather than monological relationship, designed to develop, when appropriate, new understandings. The new understandings would come from the group and not the researcher. He would have to work towards a unity of theory and praxis relative to the "American Creed" and racism. Thus one can see, depending on the methodology utilized, different conclusions are reached and the role of the researcher can vary. An appropriate methodology for Black Studies would not be the positivistic nor would it be the critical methodology. It would be a synthesis of the two because both have some features crucial to the assumptions of a Black Studies paradigm.

The first phase in developing a Black Studies methodology is to define the role of the researcher and the purpose of a Black Studies method. The purpose is to identify fundamental contradictions between theory and practice, to help develop tools to help bring a unity between theory and praxis, and to help in the scholarly study of Black life experiences. The oppression of Black people is not a prerequisite of a Black Studies discipline although oppression led to its development.

To accept this as a responsibility of a Black Studies scholar, the researcher has to become involved with the people. The role of the researcher varies depending on the methodology utilized. For example, the role of the researcher using the positivistic methodology is to be objective and distant from the research subjects. A researcher utilizing this approach wants to control his/her bias as much as possible. He/she is doing research without any feelings, assuming an apolitical stance.

In assessing the role of the researcher using the critical methodology one expects the bias of the researcher to determine the selection of problems. The researcher is also expected to participate in a dialogical experience with the subjects. The emphasis is on being political and active in the use of analysis. The Black Studies method emphasizes the latter approach.

The historical and social reality of Black life experiences is what defines the role of the Black Studies scholar. Since most Black people, in general, are victims of oppression then a Black Studies method that does not emphasize ways of alleviating that oppression will be oppressive. Therefore, the Black Studies scholar must be active in "the community" and cannot afford the "luxury" of objectivity. It is a luxury, albeit a false one, because one does not have to confront unpleasant issues and relationships.

With this in mind the following steps comprise the Black Studies method:

1. To identify the problematic relationships, by studying the results of past empirical and theoretical work, and through historical analysis of the relations between the groups involved.
2. To develop measures and methods of collecting data based on historical and empirical interpretations of reality.
3. To compare conditions with understandings, critically evaluate these relationships, and find fundamental contradictions.
4. To participate in a program of education that develops tools that help identify contradictions between conditions and understandings.
5. To alter theory in light of findings and restate the next potential researchable phase in the problem of unifying theory and praxis.

Step 1 emphasizes a synthesis between positivism and critical methodologies. By studying past research with historical analysis, contradictions between intersubjective meanings and objective conditions can be uncovered. If the empirical reality is significantly different from the historical reality, it should serve as an alarm to the researcher that something may be wrong, unless it is common knowledge that social conditions have been significantly changed. This step also emphasizes the relations between groups as the parameters of the problem. Given the basic assumptions, one of the groups, the main group, are people of African descent.

Step 2 is another synthesis between positivistic and critical methodologies. If measures and methods are tied to historical and empirical interpretations of reality there is less of a chance to develop measures that help to reinforce the status quo. This is especially so when the status quo is oppressive; this would also lead to measures developed as a result of the struggles of the people. In terms of methods, when appropriate, both quantitative and qualitative can be used, although one would expect greater emphasis on qualitative than quantitative analysis, because quantitative analysis tends to be ahistorical. However, quantitative analysis could be used along with qualitative to help identify contradictions between intersubjective interpretations and objective conditions.

Step 3 helps to define Black Studies as a discipline that uses a critical analysis to uncover fundamental contradictions between what is and one's understanding of what is. Its focus is on identifying oppressive relations between and within groups of people.

Step 4 defines the role of the researcher as an active participant in a dialogical relationship with the study group. This relationship is not purely dialogical since the development of tools may require more than just dialogue. It may require sustained interaction within the group on both primary and secondary levels.

Step 5 calls for a unity of theory and praxis by altering theories to fit praxis. This step is another synthesis between positivistic and critical methodologies. As one uncovers new interpretations of social conditions one may add or subtract from theories or develop new ones. Praxis defines theory rather than theory defining praxis. This allows the researcher to broaden the subjects' understandings of the totality of historical conditions affecting their intra- and inter-group relations.

These five steps, along with the basic assumptions comprise the Black Studies paradigm. This is an initial attempt at defining the discipline of Black Studies and by no means is this researcher suggesting it is the only paradigm nor should it be the only attempt to do so. As with all new disciplines its development depends on the continual and critical contributions of its scholars—scholars who are trained in a Black Studies method. Black Studies is ready to take its rightful place in the academy as the leader in the development of research and scholarship focusing on Black experiences. Disciplines such as sociology, psychology, history and music cannot provide that leadership in the study of Black people. That authority belongs to the discipline of Black Studies.

References

Berry, Mary F., and John W. Blassingame. 1982. *Long Memory: The Black Experience in America*. New York: Oxford University Press.
Blassingame, John. 1974. *The Slave Community, Plantation Life in the Antebellum South*. New York.
Blauner, Robert. 1972. *Racial Oppression in America*. New York: Harper and Row.

Carmichael, Stokely, and Charles Hamilton. 1967. *Black Power: The Politics of Liberation in America*. New York: Random House.

Cornforth, Maurice. 1977. *Materialism and the Dialectical Method*. International Publishers.

Fanon, Franz. 1963. *The Wretched of the Earth*. New York: Grove Press.

_____. 1967. *Black Skins, White Masks*. New York: Grove Press.

Friedrichs, Robert. 1970. *A Sociology of Sociology*. New York: Free Press.

Gordon, Vivian V. 1981. "The Coming of Age of Black Studies," *The Western Journal of Black Studies*, Vol. 5, No. 3, 231–263.

Horkheimer, Max. 1972. *Critical Theory*. New York: Seabury Press.

Kuhn, Thomas. 1970. *The Structure of Scientific Revolutions*. Chicago: University of Chicago Press.

Masterman, Margaret. 1970. "The Nature of a Paradigm," in *Criticism and the Growth of Knowledge*, Imie Lakatos and Alan Musgrave (eds.) [pp. 58–89]. Cambridge: Cambridge University Press.

Moynihan, Daniel. 1965. *The Negro Family: The Case for National Concern*. Office of Policy Planning and Research, U.S. Department of Labor, March.

Ritzer, George. 1975. *Sociology: A Multiple Paradigm Science*. Boston: Allyn and Bacon.

Staples, Robert. 1986. "Change and Adaptation in the Black Family," in *The Black Family: Essays and Studies*, Robert Staples (ed.) [pp. 20–28]. Wadsworth Publishing.

17

Re-examining the Black on Black Crime Issue: A Theoretical Essay

ROBERT L. PERRY

Robert L. Perry is an Associate Professor of Sociology and Ethnic Studies at Bowling Green State University. He received the Ph.D. degree from Wayne State University.—The Western Journal of Black Studies, *Summer 1989, Vol. 13, No. 2*

Within the last twenty years, politicians, criminal justice personnel, mass media, and the public have become increasingly concerned with crime in the Black community. The recent attention is disconcerting. Black on Black crime is not a new phenomenon; the problem has existed for at least three generations. Why, then, has the condition emerged into national focus only recently?

An association can be made between the Civil Rights Movement of the sixties and the rise of the law and order backlash of the early seventies. During this period, the Civil Rights Movement evolved from the non-violent protest as advocated by Martin Luther King, Jr., to more direct action and "Black Power" defined by Stokely Carmichael, presently known as Kwame Toure, and others. Within these two methodological polemics also emerged James Baldwin's prophetic book, *The Fire Next Time*, and the riots of Watts, Newark, and Detroit. Combined with Black Activism was the renaissance of the cities in the late seventies and the subsequent need for the affluent to move back to the inner city. As a result of the inner city neighborhoods becoming reified, Black crime became an articulated priority of the U.S. Department of Justice. Thus, law and order hysteria has its roots in the conflict resulting from the Civil Rights Movement and Black Activism peaking just as cities were attempting to rejuvenate.

Implicit to the law and order mania is the belief that Blacks are responsible for the surging crime rates. Further, law and order advocates use politics of fear to implant in the minds of the White population the notion that there is a significant chance that they will become the victim of a criminal act perpetrated by

Blacks. This fear has been promoted *ad nauseum* in every large metropolitan area where there is a significant Black population.

The assertion that a majority of crimes committed by Blacks have been to White victims is a myth. Recent research indicates, according to the Justice Department (cited in *Criminal Victimization in the United States, 1985*, 5) that most violent crimes against Blacks were committed by Black offenders (84%). When looking at capital offenses, for example, data based on incidents involving one victim and one offender show that in 1987, 94 percent of the Black murder victims were slain by Black offenders (*Uniform Crime Reports for the United States, 1987*, 9). The law and order clamor has been responsible not for comprehensive programs designed to reduce crime in these communities, but for implementing stop and search, no knock laws, and special strategic units that represent an insult and an attack on the Black community.

The police forces in most urban Black communities have been led and continue to be dominated by White police officers, who are not residents of the areas they police and are often viewed by residents as outside occupation forces. It is police, who have no stake within the communities where they work, who make it relatively common for Black on Black crime to thrive.

There is no absolute cure for Black crime, or for crime in general, primarily because crime is indigenous to American society. Disproportionate crime rates among members of ethnic groups entrapped within ghettoes is a prominent historical fact. Blacks have not historically been the only group to have high crime ratios. The Irish, Italians, Jews, Puerto Ricans, and Cubans, for example, have contributed disproportionately to crime statistics in relation to their population as a result of ghettoization. Blacks have experienced high crime rates for decades. As a result of their lack of vertical mobility, the following conclusions can be drawn: (1) Black on Black crime, then, is not a new phenomenon; (2) recent concern has been misdirected; (3) Blacks are concerned about the high Black crime rate because they comprise a disproportionate number of the victims; (4) disproportionate crime rates have not been peculiar to Blacks; and (5) crime is indigenous to American society. Thus crime is not merely a Black on Black problem, but also an American phenomenon.

The understanding of Black on Black crime cannot be realized outside the study of American social structure and its relationship to the Black American. Any analysis needs to begin with the legacy of slavery and the results of years of Jim Crow legislation. Further, a study of Black migration, the rise of disorder in urban communities, aggression, the use of drugs and alcohol, and policing, all to be incorporated. Discussions of crime in the United States amongst certain ethnic groups without emphasizing how crime is related to the political economy will distort the problem.

The Legacy of Slavery and Jim Crow

A review of the etiology of crime in the Black community needs to begin with slavery, which turned out to be a perennial caste system imposed on Blacks by White American society. Slavery was the vehicle that allowed society to define the Black man as less than a man; it spawned the doctrine that a Black man had no rights a White need respect. This legacy defined interactions between Black and White America. Within this mold, the seeds of self-hate were sown and fertilized. Black culture was defined as aberrant, and the only hope for upward mobility depended on the ability to internalize the values of the dominant culture. Many essential elements of African cultural structures, such as the extended family and religious practices, were altered as a result of the institution of slavery, but many Africanisms remained. The dominant society has condemned these cultural differences, as it has biological differences. Internalizing the dominant culture's values became necessary for Black survival, but the vehicles for cultural acquisition were blocked and the retention of African cultural traits was considered to be uncivilized. It is within this diaspora that self-hate has festered and the crimes against Black communities by Blacks have grown.

Within American culture, more emphasis is placed on property rights than human rights. Those in power enact legislation to protect their own vested property interests (Quinney, 1970; Taylor et al., 1973). Criminal behavior is defined by the powerful and the privileged, and is discriminately used to label the behavior of less powerful races or classes of people. Only acts that violate laws are criminal and whatever the powerful define as criminal is a crime. Statute law exists to protect the interest of the powerful. Thus, as a result, many Blacks feel the law holds no real meaning for them.

Much of the Black "crime" prior to the Civil War was directly related to slavocracy. The Gabriel Prosser Revolt of 1800, Denmark Vesy Revolt of 1822, and Nat Turner Revolt of 1831 were all defined as criminal conspiracies on the part of Blacks. The participants were hanged and their communities severely punished as a result of these revolts. After the Civil War, the South codified vagrancy, and apprenticeship laws were designed to insure a continuous supply of free labor. Because of these laws, former slaveholders were able to retain the work of former slaves. The laws were supported under the guise that Blacks were lazy and ignorant and would not become productive citizens unless trained and forced to work. Jails began to fill with Blacks. This resulted in the development of the Convict Lease System through which plantation owners could lease Blacks convicted of crimes. Since there were few productive jobs for Blacks, they were continuously arrested as vagrants. The ringing of the joyous bells of freedom that came with the Emancipation Proclamation were deadened by *Plessy v. Ferguson* (1896), which held that laws requiring segregation did not violate the Constitution of the United States, solidifying and legitimatizing Jim Crow status for Blacks until the *Brown* decision of 1954. Black self-concept, as well as Black attitudes toward law and order, developed within the context of this legacy. There can be no comprehensive understanding of Black on Black crime outside of the reality of this history.

Black Migration and Disorder in the Cities

There was little significant migration by Blacks from the rural South to northern urban communities between 1790 and 1900. Prior to 1900, 90 percent of the Black population resided in the rural South. The first large northward migration occurred between 1900 and the beginning of World War I. During this period, about five percent of the southern Black population moved to the north-central and north-eastern corridors of the United States into the urban areas of Chicago, Detroit, Philadelphia, and New York. In 1940, the percentage of the Black population residing in the South was 77 percent; by 1974 the figure would drop to below 52 percent. Many Blacks who did not migrate northward moved from rural to urban communities in the South; by 1970, 75 percent resided in urban centers. As Blacks moved to the cities, the "White flight" began, and by 1975, 75 percent of the Whites living in metropolitan communities resided in the suburbs (Ploski and Marr, 1976, 366–368).

Blacks migrated North because their experiences with Whites during Reconstruction had awakened the hope that a more affluent and humane existence might be found in northern cities. Blacks also moved to urban centers because the boll weevil of 1914 destroyed cotton crops. In addition, there was the lure of industrial jobs, and the clarion call of many northern Blacks implied that the North was the promised land of milk and honey. Combined, these attractions were too strong to resist.

The Black migrants were to experience cultural shock as a result of the reception they received in the North. Much of the encouragement to move North had come from the industrial elites, who sought a source of cheap labor. Blacks were often used as pawns to break the backs of the unions. Such misuse of Black labor by management drove a wedge between Black and White relations in the North. White mobs raided Black ghettoes in cities such as Cincinnati, Ohio, and Springfield, Illinois, killing, looting, and burning; Blacks, too, were victims of their own violence. After World War I, Black passivity to the violence perpetrated by Whites changed when Black soldiers began to return home; the Chicago riot of 1919 and Harlem riot of 1935 indicated that Blacks would no longer respond docilely to White violence.

Thus, Black experience within the cities of the North had begun with conflict, corruption, and violence. Consequently, that initial experience has remained constant for many generations of Blacks.

As a result of the American Depression, the population was less economically segregated than before. The Depression was for many a great equalizer; it was a period of stagnation for all of American society. During World War II, the consciousness and expectations of Black people began to rise. The early forties produced the Fair Employment Practices Commission (FEPC) advocated by President Roosevelt, who responded to pressure from Black labor leader A. Philip Randolph. The race riot in Detroit was considered another major incident. The early fifties saw the Korean Conflict and the integration of the armed forces. The latter was to effectively begin the modern-day Civil Rights movement. The *Brown* decision of 1954 put an end to the legal sanctions of "de jure" segregation and "separate but equal." The early sixties were marked by sit-in strikes directed at the integration of public accommodations, riots, and new civil and voting rights acts. The seventies brought repression, law and order, recession, high Black unemployment, regression, and the *Bakke* decision.[1] With this capsulated history of Black experience, several questions come to mind. Why would Blacks not hate themselves? Why would Blacks not be violent with each other? Indeed, why would they not become alcoholics and drug addicts? It is a great testimony to Black strength that *most* Blacks are none of the above. However, it is certainly understandable why the casualty rate is at staggering proportions.

Understanding racism and oppression are integral to understanding violence in the Black community. Institutionalized racism and oppression cause violence in Black communities, destroying the spirit of Blacks, who, in turn, socialize their children into a kind of psychology of despair. The *symptoms* of this despair are self-hate, aggression, alcohol, and drugs. In fact, Black on Black crime is a *victim on victim* crime. There can be no cure through merely attacking the symptoms and blaming the victim. The cure is ultimately in the eradication of racism and oppression.

Aggression and the Use of Alcohol and Drugs

Aggression has been determined by psychiatrists and psychologists to be a common reaction to intense frustration. Frustration and attendant aggression are common denominators in the Western world and not merely the prerogative of any particular group. What precipitates frustration is a unique base in the chemistry of Black crime. Whereas frustration for the dominant groups in American society tends to be individualized, for Black Americans frustration is often in the form of institutionalized racism. Although it is obvious that much crime can be accounted for by various aggression theories, Black on Black crime problems cannot be explained adequately through these theories.

Many displaced aggression theories are psychodynamic approaches, which explain aggressive criminal acts in terms of individual responses to frustration. These theories, however, leave much to be desired in describing the group aggression that is an integral component of subculture violence (Gibbons, 1977, 349–368). To attempt to explain crime in the Black community merely from the point of view of various aggression theories only is to ignore the institutionalized character of the problem. This is a major fault of the work of writers such as Alvin Poussaint (1972), psychiatrist and author of *Why Blacks Kill Blacks*, whose work otherwise is full of insights as to what motivates individuals to commit violence against one another within the Black race. Poussaint's work, however, lacks precise understanding concerning the collective nature of violence. Comparatively, the work of Wolfgang and Ferracuti (1967) attempts to explain how the lessons of violence are learned and transmitted from generation to generation within particular ethnic groups. The problem with both of these individual and subcultural approaches is that neither adequately addresses the dynamic quality of American crime. To get caught up in either extreme, exclusively, is to lose the institutional focus of the American crime problem, with the result being the inability to offer any effective solutions.

There can be no doubt of the magnitude of the crime problem as it exists within the Black community. Black on Black violence and theft can be significantly associated with the use of drugs and alcohol. Drug addicts are responsible for much of all criminal activity that occurs within the urban ghettoes. However, although the use of alcohol and drugs can be associated with crime, one must be careful about asserting causation. Journalistic writers tend to purport that alcohol and drugs cause crime. However, this type of reporting is far from scientific and essentially presents spurious arguments—the substance of which are at best heuristic, peripheral, and superficial. Any meaningful study of Black on Black crime must be holistic if one is to understand the problem, including the use of drugs and alcohol by Blacks, and the relationship of that use to Black on Black crime.

The role of alcohol and its use in American culture is socially acceptable and to some extent obligatory in many circles. Drug use is tolerated by many of the wealthy, who can either obtain drugs legally by getting prescriptions from their "society" doctors, or who can afford to purchase illegal substances from reliable sources. What constitutes alcohol and drug abuse is not normally assessed by the amount one drinks or uses; rather it is defined by the type of use and the circumstances. Thus, the problem of drug and alcohol abuse as it relates to Black on Black crime ultimately can be associated with the economic and social status of the abusers. Most experts agree that there are no significant proportional differences among Blacks and Whites who consume alcohol. However, there are some differences between the races in drinking patterns. Harper (1975), in his article "The Impact of Alcohol on Crime in the Black Community," indicates that Black men tend to be heavier drinkers than White men. He further comments that some Blacks drink heavily on the weekend, that there are cultural social rewards bestowed on heavy drinkers, and that the general knowledge of who sells illegal liquor and narcotics is reminiscent of the slave tradition whereby liquor was given slaves to drown the recollections of an accomplished week's hard work so as to prepare them for another. Without drawing a parallel of patterns with the dominant society, let this observation suffice; patterns of drinking among Blacks are reflections of differences in life history, accessibility to alcohol, and susceptibility to stress. So when looking at drinking in relation to crime, one must consider the genesis of the problem. Needless to say, the results of drinking excessive amounts of alcohol are reflected in the crime statistics of the Black community.

On a lighter note, "Let's get drunk and be somebody," was a phrase uttered often by an acquaintance of this writer. The words, when examined closely, are very significant and point to an attitude that has universal validity within Black ghettoes; to get drunk is to relieve psychic strain, to escape racism and oppression, and to get strength, confidence, and courage to face "The Man." Ray Charles, the blind recording artist, made this matter the subject of his 1960s' tune, "Let's Go Get Stoned." In Blues fashion, he bemoans being unable to do anything right on his job, having marital problems, and being broke. He solicits companionship, in fact, urges everybody to accompany his getting stoned. Yet, after thinking twice, he reminds himself not to overdo escapism for fear of causing bodily harm or damage to others or property. When Blacks succumb to alcohol as an anesthesia, crimes of varied magnitudes result.

Since frustration is acted out on people who are closest in familiarity and proximity, there is little wonder that much wife and child abuse occurs because of excessive drinking on the part of Black males. One of the most serious crimes, which is very often alcohol related, is homicide. This includes vehicular homicides resulting from drunk driving as well as personal homicides emanating from passion and frustration.

The drug abuse problem within the Black community certainly has a root similar to that of alcohol abuse. Drugs contribute enormously to crime, but there are no completely reliable estimates of the cost to society of these drug-related crimes. The scandalous figure of 700,009 arrests (of which 210,298 or 30 percent were Black) cited by the *Sourcebook of Criminal Justice Statistics* (1986, 300) applied merely to drug abuse violations. Unaccounted for in these statistics are the drug related crimes, which include robbery, larceny, and aggravated assault. According to Edmundson et al. (cited by Austin et al., 1977, 24), much criminal behavior is directly related to drug-seeking. A great number of studies have been devoted to this topic, especially in relationship to heroin use. While it is difficult to establish a temporal sequencing that precedes drug addiction or criminality, it seems safe to argue that the need for drugs forces addicts to commit crimes, which generate the means to obtain it (U.S. National Institute on Drug Abuse, 1976, and Weissman, 1979). Prebie (cited by Austin et al., 1977, 162) estimates that heroin users in New York City alone steal $1 million worth of money, goods, and property each day, and suggests that heroin users in slum neighborhoods regularly commit crimes in order to sustain their habits. While many such crimes are property crimes and may not involve the confrontation with victims, many do. In some respects, robbery may seem the most advantageous to drug addicts because the loot is in cash rather than in goods that must be sold at a discount. Contrary to what many believe, most of the victims of drug related crimes are other members of the Black community. Evidence indicates that the risk of incarceration for criminals in these communities is small, as residents tend to look the other way if they themselves are not victims, and police tend to pursue crime less vigorously in poor Black communities than they do elsewhere. Addict criminals are aware of this and do not risk criminal behavior in other communities, where they know that their very presence would raise suspicion. Thus, an apathetic community, combined with non-aggressive police work, promotes Black on Black crime.

Policing the Black Ghetto

There has been little or no improvement in the ability of the police to provide quality service to the Black community despite the so-called war on crime and the creation of the ill-fated Law Enforcement Assistance Administration (LEAA). Issues involving the policing of Black ghettoes continue to be wrought with conflict and controversy. Although millions of dollars have been poured into large, urban, predominantly Black communities through the Justice Department, ostensibly to improve policing, the police, most of whom are White, continue to be viewed by Black ghetto dwellers as hostile, foreign occupying forces bent on oppression rather than service. Many police officers continue to hold racist attitudes toward Blacks as demonstrated by their day-to-day interactions with the Black community. Most of the millions spent on upgrading police forces are earmarked for the purchase of sophisticated hardware, which has done virtually nothing in the last decade to improve police and Black community relations. The Black community continues to have little faith in the police, and the attitudes of policemen toward the inhabitants of these communities have not changed. The blame for lack of progress in these areas lies at the highest policy-making levels of government. The policy on how the war on crime should be fought or what the priorities should be have not been established at either the local or state level, but rather by presidential cabinet level functionaries. Thus, the lack of any real progress in eliminating Black on Black crime is the result of the institutionalized racism that begins at the very top of society. If, for example, the priorities of the Justice Department had been to improve policing through the development of better human relations, one could hypothesize with a high degree of sureness that it would have had a significant effect on Black ghetto and police relationships. The attitudes of the police, and of the administration, must certainly be a reflection of the larger society.

There has been no better description of the attitude of Blacks toward the police than the eloquent statement made by James Baldwin when he wrote:

The only way to police a ghetto is to be oppressive. None of the Police Commissioner's men, even with the best will in the world have any way of understanding the lives led by the people they swagger about in twos and threes controlling. Their very presence is an insult, and it would be, even if they spent their entire day feeding gumdrops to children. They represent the force of the white world, and that world's real intentions are, simply, for that world's criminal profit and ease, to keep the black man corralled up there, in his place. The badge, the gun in the holster, and the swinging club make vivid what will happen should his rebellion become overt. Rare, indeed, is the Harlem citizen, from the most circumspect church member to the most shiftless adolescent, who does not have a long tale to tell of police incompetence, injustice, or brutality...

It is hard, on the other hand, to blame the policeman, blank, good-natured, thoughtless, and insuperably innocent, for being such a perfect representative of the people he serves. He, too, believes in good intentions and is astounded and offended when they are not taken for the deed. He has never, himself, done anything for which to be hated—which of us has?—and yet he is facing, daily and nightly, people who would gladly see him dead, and he knows it. There is no way for him not to know it; there are few things under heaven more unnerving than the silent, accumulating contempt and hatred of a people. He moves through Harlem, therefore, like an occupying soldier in a bitterly hostile country; which is precisely what, and where, he is, and is the reason he walks in twos and threes. And he is not the only one who knows why he is always in company; the people who are watching him know why, too. Any street meeting, sacred or secular, which he and his colleagues uneasily cover has as its explicit or implicit burden the cruelty and injustice of the white domination. (Baldwin, 1961, 65–67)

The continuing problem of policing the Black ghetto is explicit in the scenario presented by Baldwin. White people are aliens in the Black community, and even the Black police officer who, out of necessity, must be socialized to incorporate the values of the dominant group in order to maintain his or her job, is at a loss in terms of being able to change the circumstances that exist within the Black ghetto. With no change occurring in the society as a whole, there is little hope of being able to make much impact on Black on Black crime.

Note

1. A 1978 decision by the Supreme Court, *Regents of University of California v. Bakke*, 438 U.S. 98 S.Ct. 2733, 57 L.Ed.2d 750, held that while the university unlawfully discriminated against a White applicant by denying him admission to its medical school solely on the basis of his race, the university may consider the race of an applicant in its admission procedure in order to attain ethnic diversity in its student body.

References

Austin, Gregory A., Bruce D. Johnson, Eleanor E. Carroll, and Dan J. Lettier (eds.). 1977. *Drugs and Minorities*. National Institute on Drug Abuse. Washington, D.C.: U.S. Government Printing Office.

Baldwin, James. 1961. *Nobody Knows My Name*. New York: Dial Press.

Ebony. 1979. "Addicts Are Responsible for Much of All Criminal Activity," in "Black on Black Crime: The Causes, the Consequences, the Cures," Vol. 34, No. 10, 74–75.

Gibbons, Don C. 1977. *Society, Crime, and Criminal Careers: An Introduction to Criminology*. Englewood Cliffs: Prentice-Hall.

The Guide to American Law: Everyone's Legal Encyclopedia. 1983 ed. "Bakke."

Harper, Frederick D. 1975. "The Impact of Alcohol on Crime in the Black Community," in Lawrence E. Gary and Lee P. Brown (eds.), *Crime and Its Impact on the Black Community*. Washington, D.C.: Howard University Institute for Urban Affairs and Research.

Ploski, Harry A., and Warren Marr II. 1976. *The Negro Almanac: A Reference Work on the Afro-American*. 1776 Bicentennial Edition. New York: Bellwether.

Poussaint, Alvin. 1972. *Why Blacks Kill Blacks*. New York: Emeron Hall.

Quinney, Richard. 1970. *The Social Reality of Crime*. Boston: Little, Brown.

Taylor, Ian, Paul Walton, and Jock Young. 1973. *The New Criminology: For A Social Theory of Deviance*. New York: Harper and Row.

U.S. Department of Justice. 1987. Bureau of Justice Statistics. *Criminal Victimization in the United States, 1985*. Washington, D.C.: Government Printing Office.

_____. 1987. Bureau of Justice Statistics. *Sourcebook of Criminal Justice Statistics, 1986*. Washington, D.C.: Government Printing Office.

_____. 1987. Federal Bureau of Investigation. *Uniform Crime Reports for the United States, 1987*. Washington, D.C.: Government Printing Office.

U.S. National Institute on Drug Abuse. 1976. *Drug Use and Crime: Report of the Panel on Drug Use and Criminal Behavior*. Research Triangle Institute. Washington, D.C.: National Technical Information Service.

Weissman, James C. 1979. *Understanding the Drugs and Crime Connection: A Systematic Examination of Drugs and Crime Relationships*. Madison, Wisconsin.

Wolfgang, M. E., and F. Ferracuti. 1967. *The Subculture of Violence: Towards an Integrated Theory in Criminology*. London: Tavistock.

18

Afrocentricity and the Critique of Drama*

MOLEFI KETE ASANTE

*Molefi Kete Asante is Professor and Chair of the Department of African Ameri-
can Studies at Temple University. He is the leading contemporary proponent of
the concept of Afrocentricity in African American and African Studies.*—The
Western Journal of Black Studies, *Summer 1990, Vol. 14, No. 2*

The emergence of the Afrocentric School of Thought as articulated among the Temple University africologists has served to raise numerous theoreti- cal and methodological questions regarding literary and cultural inquiry.[1] This is particularly true in relationship to the critique of drama and literature. Because Afrocentricity goes beyond the mere demystification of Eurocentricity, the production and critique of drama must also stand beyond the demystifying act. Of course, the self-conscious, autonomous critique of drama or of novels becomes, by virtue of the choice to actualize, a demystification. One does not ignore the Eurocentric critique; one observes its presence and potentiality within a certain, but not universal, context.[2]

The general contours of Afrocentric theory suggest that *location, dislocation,* and *relocation* are the principal metaphors in the critique of drama.[3] *Location* is the cultural position occupied by the writer or critic at the time of creative pro- duction. In effect, it is the intellectual area established by the writer as the place

* This is a version of Molefi Kete Asante's paper presented at the American Studies Association Conference in Toronto, Ontario, on November 4, 1989.

from which the creation will occur. The Afrocentrist argues that it is possible to determine this site, that is, to *locate* a writer by close cosmological, epistemological, axiological, and aesthetic surveying. *Dislocation* exists when a writer seems to be out of synchrony with his or her historical/cultural location. Determining historical/cultural location becomes one of the major tasks of the Afrocentric scholar. *Relocation* occurs when a writer who has been dislocated re-discovers historical and cultural motifs that serve as sign-posts in the intellectual or creative pursuit. The critic's aim, therefore, is nothing more than an adequate location of the dramatist.

Given the political and social history of Africans in the United States, it is essential that the critic of drama is well versed in African American culture and history; otherwise, any critique of drama written from an African American *location* would be relatively off-base. One sees this when movie critics are unable to "get inside" certain African American plays or films, for instance. Both the dramatist and the critic must operate from a similar location in order for congruent criticism, that is, reasonable criticism, to occur.

The Principal Question for the Critic

The principal question that must be answered by the critic of the dramatist's work is, what is the purpose of writing drama? Does it make any difference and if it does, then what is the quality or the nature of the difference being made?

This author has argued in previous essays that the African writer has different purposes, and if that writer is serious, what then is the burden of history for African writers? How does that writer establish a sense of space and what constitutes the uniqueness of the space carved out by the African writer, whether in the continent or in the diaspora? I am convinced that these issues must be dealt with in order to make any sense out of what the critics are saying and certainly what the writers are writing. At the moment, it seems to me that both dramatists and critics are operating in a rather vast and relatively uncharted field with little or no direction.[4] Simply put, neither the African American critics, the critics of the critics, nor the writers have been properly located. If in the end there is location, then we have a better sense of where people are in the heads that give rise to writing in the first place.

Let me be clear: I locate myself within the frames of the historical experiences of African people as a part of human history.[5] I am not unaware of the necessity for the theorist or critic to be *located*. Location is the principal metaphor of an africological analysis. Since I am neither a literary theorist nor a historian, although I am familiar with both disciplines, my purpose is neither literary criticism nor historical criticism, but rather the africological assessment of drama. Only from this viewpoint can I bring an effective analysis to bear on the dramatic creation of African American artists. To do otherwise is to commit the most heinous sin against the ancestral Oguns that make creativity possible in the first place.

Therefore, my aim is to set a proper focus on the condition of writing so that I may be able to ascertain where a dramatist "is coming from." Creating drama, in one way, is a condition much more than it is an art—art forms having certain peculiar meanings within the European worldview. However, for the moment, location carries with it the concept of place, of stand, of positions, of terms. And, to be centrally located within one's cultural and historical context is to know what particular terms and frames are necessary for negotiating the condition. The critic must know these terms and either place herself or himself in these terms or outside these terms. In placing oneself outside of one's historical and cultural terms, however, one relinquishes the appropriate vantage point from which to view reality. This does not mean that you cannot have a view; it simply means that your view is from the margins, the fringes. You can also see from the margins, but it does not give you central, definitive sightings. Perhaps the vision is blurred by mediations that interfere with your own perceptions, comprehensions, of what you see.

Now the African American writing anything—criticism, poetry, fiction, social essays, drama—cannot escape a certain influence of his or her historical experiences. Even the novelist Frank Yerby found that it was necessary, at least on occasion, to "come home" to what he knew as an experience in his background. But this is another story. It is a story of an African trying desperately to find acceptance outside of his own circle. But why should this be necessary? What is the fundamental audience of any European writer, of any Asian writer? What is the imperative of situation that demands an African writer seek to "locate" himself or herself in the circle of the European world-view in order to be taken seriously? This does not happen with the Asian context, for example. That is, African writers are not trying to impress Asian critics or Asian audiences, nor to partake in the Asian world-view, but the writing for European audiences, even more so than for African American audiences, is the emblem of psychological dislocation. The *asili*, the seed, of the problem is the location of the African American dramatist and the critic of the dramatist. Where the writer locates herself or himself is chiefly responsible for the confusion that inheres around the question of audience.[6]

The Black Arts Movement of the 1960s led by Larry Neal, Charles Fuller, Eleanor Traylor, Amiri Baraka, Hoyt Fuller, and Addison Gayle, Jr., understood the need for rescuing the mutilated voices of African Americans through the development of a new aesthetics. According to Floyd Hayes, they "rejected the conventions, values, and myths of the ruling cultural/ideological apparatus."[7] Chief among the young interpreters of this movement in the 1970s was Houston Baker, Jr., who articulated a "counter-hegemonic role" in the most powerful assault on the "universalist" canon.[8] Joined by Henry Louis Gates, Jr., Baker sought to position the Black Aesthetic Movement towards what Hayes refers to as "greater theoretical sophistication and analytical rigor in the examination of the African American cultural tradition."[9]

The principal weakness of the project undertaken by Baker and Gates lies in their inability to transcend the encapsulation of Eurocentric theory.[10] Hayes correctly identifies their flaw as seeking to achieve their goals "by appropriating contemporary European critical theory (especially theories put forward by the late Michel Foucault and Paul DeMan) in the development of a theory adequate for interrogating and assessing African American expressive culture."[11] Afrocentricity is not merely postmodern as a critical instrument, but it is also meta-European. African American critical theory cannot be a reactionary theory in its challenge to European canon hegemony. In effect, it should not assault European critical theories because they exist or because European theorists are having an internal dialogue on the role of criticism. An Afrocentric critique is the African American's response to drama pro-actively and without reference to the European experience except as it relates to the dramatic creation.[12]

Grounded in Historical Situation

It may be true that the condition of writing drama in the African American experience does not suffer from the quality of location as much as I think it does. But it is definitely true that criticism of that literary or cultural condition most often starts at the wrong place. One of Malcolm X's lines became famous and remains true, "you cannot use the oppressor's language and ever think that you can liberate yourself." What this adage conveys is deeper than the lexical items; it is more profound than grammar; it is essentially a point made in connection with terms, terminology in the sense of location. African Americans' ground must be in accordance with their own situation; they must speak of the hard facts of their historical experiences. Only writing that demonstrates the insight to see in a Romare Bearden painting or an Elizabeth Catlett sculpture some of the possible frames of Black experiences, some of the genius of every condition which is entailed in the literary process, can provide African Americans with hope for liberation. I am able to move toward liberation because I reject rejection when it is rooted in playing fields that do not take into consideration the historical experiences of the African American people who know this *place*, the United States of America, as intimately as it can be known. As dramatist or critic, the historical experience of African Americans is simply not an issue and should not be an issue. As a writer, I am all that I need to be in my literary life within the framework of my own culture. This would be so if my cultural/ethnic group comprised one million or one billion people as long as I spoke for and to them out of the centrality of that experience. This is all that I can do. This is all that a writer should be required to do.

African Americans cannot expect and should not expect the White American writer to speak for us; they cannot speak for us; they are not us and do not share our particular experience in this country. They can only speak for themselves, and that they should. They should advocate, criticize, provoke, initiate, and create tragedy and comedy out of their Eurocentric experience. When White critics or authors write scripts or novels that have Blacks in them they always write from their experiences. Consequently, African Americans may say of White writers' books or scripts, "They were all right except for the part where they showed the Black person." This is because the special history of the White writer, be that writer a Joseph Conrad, Eugene Ionesco, or Tennessee Williams, and be that writer considered great and outstanding by the European critics or Afro-European critics, is most often ignorant and sometimes antagonistic toward African life and experience. Now this is so whether one admits it or not. That is the condition of the European cultural location in American society.

The Power of Significations

Signs and significations occur with some locatable content. They are not to be understood apart from what the writer intends. As I write this essay I am fully aware—that is, conscious that I am writing for an audience that will evaluate (judge) me by the significations that I make. I have no doubt that, if I wanted to, I could make some inexplicable statements that would mystify my meanings. The writer has control over the significations, to the extent he or she uses that control to empower the reader or to disarm the reader. African writers who have become known to the world outside of Africa have usually worked within the context of the signs and significations of Europe. Yet, one must know that there are more writers in Africa writing in indigenous languages than are writing in European languages.[13] What does this mean to the American or to the European? What does this say about our story of knowledge of African writers and writings?

We must understand that there are African authors writing in Yoruba, Ibo, Shona, Zulu, Swahili, Gikuyu, Hausa, Wolof, Lingala, and one thousand other languages. And we must suppose, as must be the case, that some of those writers are as skilled as Wole Soyinka, Ama Aidoo, Ngugi Wa Thiong'o, and Chinua Achebe, but can only write in their own language. Since translation of African writers into European languages has not occurred at the rate it should, we are left with the writers who speak to us in English, French, Portuguese, Arabic, or Spanish. Even here, however, the point is that whatever the authors write in these foreign tongues is locatable by virtue of the themes and subjects chosen for the works. I recognize that the ambiguity of location in literature can present some problems, but this is normally taken care of by establishing what the compositional framework is for the work. This may be difficult to establish at first reading, but in the end all of us who write leave a pretty good trail of our whereabouts. In his writing of *Invisible Man*, Ralph Ellison takes one to places that one may have not been before, although most people in 1952 could have imagined what he was talking about; they simply could not *locate* him without establishing the compositional framework from which he functioned.

Determination by Cultural Condition

In the end, it is the cultural condition of the writer that determines what his or her composition will purport to tell. Culture is not subservient to either economics or politics, but is the soul of both. The manner in which the writer conveys a thought, structures a sentence, or decides the solution to a problem is grounded in the culture that is derived from that society. Culture is a complex concept, and while the Marxist argues that economics dictates culture, it seems to me that culture precedes economics and gives us a particular response to literary subjects. To understand what a writer writes, then, one must analyze the cultural components of that writer's society.[14]

But therein is the problem for a people who have been subjected to cultural bombardment backed up by force. What now are the cultural components of such a society? We know that certain elements in the circle of memory, the location of principal mythoforms of a culture, constitute the critical determinants of how a people perform in the midst of circumstances. This is no mysticism; it is the reality of how African Americans have come to know ourselves. The percussive element, for example, in our music is heard and felt whether we are in Chicago or Philadelphia, Atlanta or New Orleans. We could be Baptists or Episcopalians, Jews or Muslims, and yet the percussive elements stir something deep within us. This is the circle of memory.

The Circle of Memory

For the African American, language is the real substance of relationships. There are few places where language does not play the dominant role in the relationships between people. The structure of language contains all of the elements found in the circle of memory; myths walk the syntax, and soul is invested within sentences. Thus, the writer to be located properly must find his or her resources from the recesses of the people's memory. As a writer, I am a reflection of my people, of their sufferings, their joys, their victories, and their myths. Without them, I am nothing and could have no particular reason to speak or to write. Therefore, the African American dramatist can never be outside of the circle and remain relevant. To be outside of the circle of memory means that you might misunderstand some very important messages that are fundamental to appreciating the culture or revealing it. Intercalations that reinforce aesthetic structure in drama through repetition are often key movements around *place* that can only be known if one is inside the culture. To see a play or film produced in America by an American and not be able to identify with anything in the drama is often the experience of Whites who view African American drama or films. This condition is almost impossible *vice versa*. The reason Whites miss the nuances of a film like *School Daze* or a play like *Prince* may have more to do with the inner sanctum of the African American circle of memory than anything else. The most illiterate

African American living in the United States would have understood the movie, *School Daze*, for example, while a White movie or literary critic would be stymied by some of the scenes.

Spike Lee is inside the circle of memory. Radio Rahim is my big brother. Tina is my sister. I know the street in Brooklyn where Sal's Pizza Shop is located. My old man is the Mayor of the block. Mother Sister has given me many readings and I have respected the mysticism of her presence. I have stood on the spot where the police killed Radio Rahim. I am the stutterer with the photos of Malcolm and Martin.

There is more here, however. What Spike Lee brings to us is not just the memory of our places, but of our past. Beyond memory he shows us the possibilities and gives us the options—that is the source of his power with non-Black audiences. They are able to see in his genius the intellectual themes that govern social life in the United States. Thus, he performs a central service for the literary field by showing that to create Afrocentrically does not mean to create negatively, but rather to create from a centered position as an African person. This is our only imperative. What I mean is that the genre and focus of our works give way, always to the inevitability of personal aesthetic choices after the imperative of centeredness.

In a brilliant Afrocentric critique of the writings of Pulitzer Prize Winner Charles Fuller, Nilgun Anadolu Okur remarked that "to apply Eurocentric methods to Ed Bullins or Charles Fuller would be like trying to apply African percussive elements to Korean music. By those standards one could determine that Korean music was underdeveloped rhythmically. However, this would be a false method of analyzing Korean music."[15] Using concepts from the works of Neal, Asante, Molette and Molette, and Harrison, Okur determined that Charles Fuller's dramatic creations bore strong evidence of Afrocentric methods and elements, thereby situating him within the circle of memory.

Afrocentric theory allows a writer to structure both the internal and the external world; they are essentially the same worlds. The difference lies mainly in the way both worlds relate to the investiture of cultural vision—that is, whether or not there is actual difference in vision. Perhaps the only way that the writer can structure both is to see them as one. Of course, this runs one right up against the Parmenidean inheritance of Western philosophy, which infuses difference with qualitative value. The African American dramatist, historically a part of the national society whose difference has been negatively assessed, must reject this particular aspect of the Western tradition. While all Western traditions are not antithetical to the dramatic vision of the African American writer, most drama, as Charles Fuller has demonstrated in his works, has to be centered on achieving balance.[16] An effective and significant dramatist therefore must embody the icons, symbols, and signs of the cultural language of his or her community with the various manifestations in poetry, fiction, and drama.

At this moment of writing, I am totally what I write, even as I write with Coltrane playing in the background on WRTI-FM, Philadelphia. The way the lamp to the left of my monitor throws light on me is a part of the entire moment of my creativity. I abandon myself to myself, but in doing that I do not lose my culture, which is also part and parcel of what I do and am doing. Instead of trying to listen to every beat and every melody of the music, or instead of trying to feel the light on me, I discover important attitudes and ways of being in tune with the rhythms of my culture by just being who I am. And so it is with African American drama and the critique of that drama. Neither the dramatist nor the critic can achieve centrality by self-consciously seeking to escape historical experiences, whether by imitating Eurocentric criticism, which often parades as universal, or by simply attacking Eurocentric theory and criticism.

The Afrocentric theory in history, aesthetics, and culture, as promulgated by the Temple University circle of africologists, remains one of the principal African American intellectual enterprises devoted to the criticism of drama and literature in the tradition of the Black Arts Movement. Like all theory, Afrocentric theory provides explanation and interpretation; *locating* a dramatist or any other writer is fundamental to a proper interpretation. Harmony and balance, the Ma'atian positions, have always served the best in African American aesthetics. Consequently, drama and dramatic criticism are inseparable from culture—just as inseparable as I am from my culture of which I cannot ordinarily be divested.

Notes

1. In addition to the author whose books on this subject include *Afrocentricity* (Trenton, 1988) and *The Afrocentric Idea* (Philadelphia, 1987), other Temple University scholars such as C. Tsehloane Keto, *The Africa Centered Perspective of History* (Blackwood, N. J., 1989); Kariamu Welsh-Asante, *African Aesthetics* (Westport, Conn.: Greenwood Press, forthcoming) and *African Dance* (Trenton, N. J.: Africa World Press, forthcoming); and Daudi Azibo, *Liberation Psychology* (Washington, D.C.: Clarity Press, 1990) have contributed to the theoretical *indaba* on Afrocentricity. In this same tradition have been the works of Maulana Karenga, an original thinker on African American culture; Wade Nobles, the leading Afrocentric psychologist working in the area of culturally consistent models of intervention; Linda James Myers, an Afrocentric scholar who has sought to extend the paradigm to deal with women issues; Dona Richards, one of the seminal scholars in the Afrocentric movement whose analyses of European philosophy and science are significant pieces to the school; Joseph Baldwin, the central figure in the discussion of the impact of racism and oppression on the African American psyche; and Patrick Bellegarde-Smith, whose conceptual works place him in the vanguard of the new scholarship. There are, of course, an increasing number of Afrocentric scholars who have begun to advance the theory and method.
2. See Molefi Kete Asante, *The Afrocentric Idea*, 3–18, for a discussion of the Eurocentric approach to knowledge. Additional information is provided in Asante, *Kemet, Afrocentricity, and Knowledge* (Trenton, 1990).
3. Nilgun Anadolu Okur, *The Artist as Healer: An Afrocentric Analysis of Charles Fuller's Dramatic Works* (Philadelphia, 1989) raises the question of location in reference to Fuller's position within the African American culture. Okur's work is the first serious book-length treatment of the dramatic discourse of Fuller and she advances the critical canon by devoting considerable time to situating the dramatist.
4. Of particular interest are the works of Houston Baker, Jr., *The Journey Back: Issues in Black Literature and Criticism* (Chicago, 1980) and *Blues, Ideology, and Afro-American Literature: A Vernacular*

Theory (Chicago, 1984); Henry Gates, Jr. (ed.), *Black Literature and Literary Theory* (New York, 1984); Addison Gayle, Jr., *Black Situation* (New York, 1970); *The Black Aesthetic* (Garden City, 1972); and Lawrence Hogue, *Discourse and the Other: The Production of the Afro-American Text* (Durham, 1986). One can also see Harold Cruse, *The Crisis of the Negro Intellectual* (New York, 1967) for a profound examination of the dilemma faced by African American scholars, leaders, and artists in a racist society.

5. I write as an African American with all of the potentialities and difficulties of that fact. I embrace the entirety of that truth by rooting myself more firmly in my own historical experiences—becoming more human as a result of such centering.

6. See Asante, *The Afrocentric Idea*, 21–63, for more on audiences.

7. Floyd Hayes, "Communication, Hegemony, and the Production of African American Texts: The Politics of Canonical Improvisation," paper presented to the 7th Annual International Conference on Culture and Communication (Philadelphia, October 5–7, 1989), 48. Hayes has been responsible for raising provocative questions about the imperialism of the Eurocentric approach to knowledge. In this paper he takes on the African American theorists who are still tied to the hegemonic thinking of the European theorists.

8. Houston Baker, Jr., *The Long Black Song: Essays in Black American Literature and Culture* (Charlottes-ville, 1972).

9. Hayes, op. cit., 48.

10. They challenge structuralism and structure and in so doing they challenge order with the aim of over-throwing or suspending it. This is antithetical to the Afrocentric, Ma'atic worldview, which celebrates freedom and creativity within the context of community. To deconstruct European consciousness in the structuralism of texts and preserve order is contradictory in the post-structuralist sense; for the Afrocentric critic, one must fully engage balance and harmony as constituents of order to be taken seriously. This does not mean that deconstruction is an invalid enterprise within the arena of European hegemony of texts, but rather as Nilgun Okur has tried to demonstrate one must deconstruct in order to increase sanity and harmony.

11. Hayes, op. cit., 48.

12. See Maulana Karenga, *Introduction to Black Studies* (Los Angeles, 1985). Karenga establishes the nature of culture within the African American creative community. He argues for the preeminence of a cultural understanding based on references to African American myth, history, ethos, motif, social institutions, political organizations, and economic institutions. This remains the most Afrocentric statement on the cultural subject.

13. Ngugi Wa Thiong'o, *Decolonising the Mind* (London, 1987).

14. Asante, *Afrocentricity and Knowledge*.

15. Okur, op. cit., 7, 8.

16. Charles Fuller, *A Soldier's Play* (New York, 1981), and *We* (New York, 1989).

19

Africentricity in Social Science

Gordon D. Morgan

Gordon D. Morgan is Professor of Sociology at the University of Arkansas, Fayetteville. He received the Ph.D. of Sociology at Washington State University.—The Western Journal of Black Studies, *Winter 1991, Vol. 15, No. 4*

Introduction

Africentricity has been an intellectual theme in Black life since very early times. Its name has changed frequently, and it has been more in favor at some times and places than others. The message, though, that there is continuity in the African heritage is well established. The resurgence of Africentric interest in the past two decades raises important issues about this orientation, which has become a movement and field of study. This paper addresses and clarifies some issues regarding this orientation. Important questions about the scientific status of Africentricity, its thrust toward community, the advocates of this thought, nationalism, gender issues, and the role of Africentricity in comparative studies are all addressed.

The Challenge of Africentricity

Today there are great cleavages in Black American social science scholarship. The cleavages border on hostility, and is as much ideological as theoretical. It is more than just a contest over methods to the attainment of certain theoretical or practical ends. This cleavage is nowhere seen more clearly than in the overall theoretical stances taken by the most visible Black scholars as they present their scholastic postures to their colleagues and to the world.

A part of the cleavage is along lines of age. The tradition in which the older scholars worked, those of the first generation, dating from about the opening of the 20th century, was essentially assimilationist. Scholars such as W.E.B. Du Bois and Carter G. Woodson, representing the social sciences, used their scholastic talents to try to create an atmosphere in which to inform the Black public of their separation from mainstream society that was maintained through the application of segregationist norms. Through the next 50 years, and up to the 1960s, the main thrust of Black scholarship was a press for inclusion, for more rights, for greater awareness of the means to achieve those rights. The development of the National Association for the Advancement of Colored People was assimilationist, for the advancement it proposed entailed movement into mainstream society.

Early scholars reflected their own cultural and intellectual origins by seeing the possibilities and futures of Black Americans as integrated within the framework of a larger America. If anything, self-improvement meant movement closer to the offerings of the mainstream. The work of scholars like Carter G. Woodson (1933), E. Franklin Frazier (1957), and Oliver C. Cox (1948) demonstrated how much pull the mainstream had on Blacks. Woodson, by assiduously teaching and writing Black history, and establishing vehicles for a continuity of that teaching and writing, believed that the more Black people knew about themselves and their culture the better they could understand how to function within the present culture. For Woodson, such knowledge was not incompatible with participation in the mainstream. Indeed, it was projected to help by not having Blacks fantasize and delude themselves often to the detriment of their performances and achievements. Woodson understood the trauma caused by slavery and its aftermath, as well as the divisions within families and communities over issues of color. Kenneth B. Clark's studies (1939), using dolls which showed Black self-hatred emerging by age five or six, only confirmed what had been suspected from as early as the time of Charles Chesnutt's writings on mulattos. The Woodson and Clark studies aimed to show how talent was being destroyed, potential diverted, and lives wasted, proportional to the extent that Blacks were held out of the mainstream because of the lack of self-esteem based on color. Within the tradition of understanding through criticism, established largely by E. Franklin Frazier (1957) and Nathan Hare (1965), it could be seen that middle class Blacks were trying so hard to modify toward the mainstream that sometimes their efforts were seen as a parodying of the classes they attempted to emulate.

As Frazier, Woodson, and Clark critiqued the behavior of individuals, showing it to often be an impediment to Black mobility, Oliver C. Cox began a tradition of critiquing the system of capitalism, charging it with twisting Black minds in the relentless quest for profit. He was abetted by a small coterie of writers, such as Abram Harris (1936) and Claude Lightfoot (1968), and West Indians like Eric Williams (1944), George Padmore (1942), and Frantz Fanon (1963, 1967, 1968). Du Bois, of course, predated them all with his dissertation, *The Suppression of the Atlantic Slave Trade* (1894, 1898), in which he argued about the structure of European society. Europe's long tenure in the Dark Ages enabled it to burst forth as a new lamb in the spring, so filled with its own energy that it recognized no bounds, literally no morality, as it sought to achieve wealth by any means possible.

There had long been a strong Africentric orientation in Black American culture. Paul Cuffee, Martin Delany, Alfred Sam, and Marcus Garvey were proponents of this tradition. They were notable because they decided to mount programs that went beyond talk and to an actual repatriation of Blacks who wanted to return to Africa. Not all of them were successful. The "back to Africa" programs in general were based upon Black rejection by mainstream society. Their prospects for mobility were extremely slim and alternatives had to be sought; returning to the African ancestral home was one of the attractions.

The "Africentric" orientation, on the other hand, did not become academic until the 1960s when the civil rights movement coincided with the independence of many sub-saharan African countries, beginning especially with the Sudan in 1956. Liberia, Haiti, and Ethiopia, of course, had served for long decades as examples of Black political and economic independence. Every schoolboy had at least heard of these Black nations, but few wanted to visit them because economic development there had been stunted. Students were told that the countries were free, but were not told that they were subject to the dictates of former colonial masters. Little was known of Haiti beyond the bravery of Toussaint L'Ouverture. The attitude toward Africa was so conditioned by the exploitative European attitude that few Black youths wished to visit Africa. They did not know much about the continent, but they knew that it was not somewhere they wanted to go.

It was during the 1960s that interest in Africa increased, mainly because more Blacks had the chance to visit the continent in helping roles, whether as missionaries, teachers, or other specialists. There was a demand on campuses that more be taught about the continent. Thus, coincidental with the emergence of Black Studies was a demand that African culture and languages be taught, not only to enlarge the knowledge of the general student body, which seemed to be Eurocentric, but to help Black students who claimed they were being denied knowledge of their heritage. Dashikis, Afros, cornrows, and African names became the rage on campuses as students sought to rediscover their heritage, or at least thought seriously about it. Some of the most vocal of the Africentrists were young persons at that time caught up in the movement; if they made a trip to Africa they were even more convinced of the strength of African culture.

A certain amount of writing by Africans had emerged by this time, which made a large impression on the then youthful scholars. The writings of mainly West Africans on the African personality and negritude were not lost on those persons seeking for viable cultural connections.

Africentricity was assumed as a theoretical orientation among some modern Black scholars for reasons other than that purveyed by scholars of two generations ago. William Leo Hansberry (1974), at Howard University, for instance, conflicted with his professors at Harvard, never receiving his doctoral degree in anthropology or archaeology because he maintained strongly, supported by empirical findings, that the cradle of civilization was most probably in Ethiopia.

George Washington Williams had written an encyclopedic work before the opening of the 20th century on this issue. If Hansberry's and Williams' work are illustrative, they suggest that Africentricity was an empirical issue. The facts, the techniques of their gathering, and the interpretations of their meanings were the debatable issues. Africa was central because many secrets to the human condition were found there. The achievements of Africans were there for all to observe. Timbuctoo, the kingdoms of old Sudan, Benin bronze, and Great Zimbabwe were matters of fact, allowing argumentation only about their interpretations. These physical realities served to give coherency to the Africa continent so that Africentric and Eurocentric explanations found a common ground on which to compete. Interpretations of these facts seemed to take place within an ideological framework, in that they were never independent of the values of the interpreters. The Africentric and Eurocentric interpretations both have agendas, which are located within the interpreters and not so much within the facts themselves. What could be done with the facts always loomed more important than a simple knowledge of the facts.

Is an Africentric Orientation Scientific?

Normal, mainstream social science has moved toward technocratic and technological characteristics, which effectively elbow out of consideration social science not conforming to its methodological requirements. The model of the natural sciences, with techniques for the testing of hypotheses by rigid means, has come to exercise a major influence on social science scholarship. That method of research and theory development were both attacked by Black scholars of the 1960s who maintained that much of the work generated was Eurocentric (ethnocentric), utilizing frameworks and paradigms and reaching conclusions detrimental to Black mobility and psychology. Joyce Ladner (1973), as a representative of that reaction, edited a work entitled *The Death of White Sociology*. The order-equilibrium model, really assimilationist, had held sway for a long time, positing that neither American society nor the Black subculture would be quiescent unless Blacks were assimilated into the mainstream. Majority, normal, European sociology (as a representative of social science work) would not allow that and so Black scholarship reacted by attacking the basic premises of European sociology.

According to Forsythe (1990), Europeans had begun to recognize that a study of society required methods different from those of the natural sciences, but Americans continued to stress the older methods of objectivity and rigid empiricism. Although ample charges of racism and ethnocentrism have been hurled at methodologically sophisticated ethnic studies, and a counter claim made by Africentric Blacks, the issue of the verifiability of Africentric studies itself has not arisen. The inadequacy of Eurocentric social science, even if carefully demonstrated, will not, in and of itself, prove the viability of Africentric social science.

Many scholars call for Africentric approaches, which are thought to liberate Blacks from the constricting hold of Eurocentric thought. But, again, calling for such approaches is not a demonstration that they have other than face credibility. Africentricity may make one feel better about oneself, which undoubtedly is positive for particular individuals, but no orientation solves all of the problems likely to arise within a group. There will be competing paradigms within any theoretical framework and means must be found for resolving the differences. Both Du Bois and Malcolm X were ardent pan-Africanists, but their methods for achieving their ends varied greatly. A methodology appropriate for Africentricity would be no less necessary than one for Eurocentric studies.

Africentric writers seem to assume that the theoretical posture they purvey is without detractors, and that because it is psychologically satisfying to some Blacks, it is somehow more logical and empirically valid than other approaches to an understanding of the Black problem. The Africentric debate, in its classic phase, went on in the 1930s and early 1940s when Howard University sociologist E. Franklin Frazier and Northwestern University anthropologist Melville Herskovits (1941, 1966) clashed on whether Africanisms existed in New World Black culture. Frazier maintained that African culture was destroyed in America during the 250 years of slavery, while Herskovits held that it existed in many forms, which were known only to those having studied cultures in Africa and America to the extent they could recognize similarities in them. In that context a case could be made for continuities. John Blassingame (1972) has identified a few physical culture artifacts from slave days that are traced to West Africa, but most of the artifacts have lost their utility in contemporary society. Lorenzo D. Turner (1949) identified Africanisms in Gullah society in the South Carolina Sea Islands in the 1930s. Basically, though, the argument was not settled (Morgan, 1974).

The adoption therefore of an Africentric orientation was not based upon conclusions that Blacks today are displaced Africans whose behavior, world view, and attitudes belie that fact. Although efforts have been made to reforge ties between New World Blacks and Africans, great gaps yet separate the two groups, though there may be instances of intimacies between individuals representing the two groups.

Unless there are guidelines developed whereby Africentricity has some methodological and theoretical guidelines by which to order its premises, it will be accused of adding little to the understanding of Black problems. Additionally, it will be open to a claim of its own ethnocentricity, a claim its purveyors had already leveled at Eurocentric social science.

Of course, Africentrists argue that the methods of social science were never at issue, only the interpretations produced, holding that Eurocentric conclusions reflected cultural biases detrimental to African peoples, and that part of African history was conveniently overlooked. In this way significant aspects of Black history were lost or misplaced, causing Black youth to develop negative opinions of themselves and their culture. A rediscovery of Black history then became a pressing feature of the Africentric agenda. That rediscovery could take place using the usual tools of scientific inquiry. Often, much positive Black scholarship was present, but never published because of the unwillingness of the majority group publishers to risk the rancor of their colleagues and supporters by promoting positive Black images. Black publishing companies were few and small, and funds did not exist for bringing a more accurate Black history and perspective to public attention.

The most prominent spokesperson for Africentrism, Molefi Kete Asante, does not discuss the methodology of Africentric knowledge. His book, *The Afrocentric Idea* (1987), does not address this point directly. The assumption arises that this method of knowing is one among many and stands in opposition to the Eurocentric method of linear science, which posits that it is the only yet discovered method of producing verifiable knowledge. Africentric knowledge comes from many sources, but it is especially an understanding of and an ability to gain knowledge from, through, and by the use of words. The holders and developers of Africentric knowledge are people who effectively use words. These are the most respected people in the Black community: preachers, teachers, lawyers, advisors, singers, poets, writers. Even medical doctors are highly respected word users, for they convey their diagnoses to their clients in language that suggests not so much that they have technical and scientific knowledge, but a mastery of words. They understand the Africentric fascination with and faith in words, whether written or spoken. The best users of words were the biggest persuaders in the Africentric tradition. Alex Haley (1976) was not the first to discover that the African griot, the person who remembered in detail, sometimes in more than one language, the traditions of his people from the earliest times was highly respected. He was literally the keeper of the word.

Knowledge, whether called scientific, Africentric, or by other names, is verifiable. How one verifies Africentric knowledge appears to be a reasonable question. If Africentric knowledge is basically word mastery, then, when the words themselves are in contradiction, what techniques exist for their resolution? Linear science stresses the resolution of propositions in the use of certain techniques by which data are ordered. This strives for a one-to-one correspondence between data and words, when both are properly used. A proper verbal description will mirror, in all essential details, the physical object or real-life condition. The importance of words as corresponding to reality is also seen dramatically in the case of law. In the courtroom the most important issues of life and death may be debated as if words had three-dimensional reality. There is, of course, drama when watching two well-trained Africentric debaters opposing each other. In their gestures, tones, and deliveries one easily observes the influence of their community training. With both being equally well-trained, and in command of the data before them, resolution of differences between them comes down to their ability to persuade by use of a combination of words and gestures. Debate is essential in the Africentric tradition. It is through the use of words that issues are resolved, and it is learning through the resolution of problems that knowledge is created. When knowledge is verified again and again and found to be dependable, it is transferred over to the realm of tradition and wisdom to be guarded by key persons in the community.

Africentric knowledge involves mythication, religious symbolism, messianism. Myth is thought of as protoscience. Asante believes western science stresses demythification and negates deconstruction. By the latter term is meant the opposite of structural and hierarchical science, which seeks to immobilize values. Thus, bringing values back into the human equation is the essence of deconstruction. Africentric knowledge seems highly deconstructed, if the latter definition of the concept is plausible. Asante states: "In the language of the African-American speaker, myth becomes an explanation for the human condition" (Asante, 1987, 98).

Asante discusses many aspects of the logic and methodology that may be applied to the Afrocentric approach. These are humanism, circularity, self-criticism, spirituality, sensitivity, all of which may be considered pre-Newtonian. Although he issues a call for an Afrocentric paradigm, a world view, a school of thought, none is provided, even in example. The claim is made that such holistic examples are found among groups such as the Wolof and the Ashanti (perhaps). These are sometimes mentioned, but are not demonstrated to exemplify this holistic view, which is thought to hold so much promise.

Africentric methodology faces the same problem as all others seeking to react to Eurocentric ethnocentric methodology. If that is its claim to fame, it amounts to substituting one set of idiosyncrasies for another, leading essentially to a "shouting match" between the methodologies and their practitioners. Eurocentric methodology proves to be too harsh; Africentric too soft.

The Renaissance in Europe proved that a revival of learning and culture based on Greece and Rome really meant that culture was marching backward, as long as it looked for perfection in art and science in the long dead ancient civilizations. The foremost thinkers of the period realized that while much in ancient culture required revival, much was dysfunctional, dogmatic, even wrong, and had to be jettisoned, including much of the thought of wise old Aristotle. The rise of objective, natural science with its values of verification revolutionized thought based upon the paradigms of the ancients, represented by Aristotle. Although he had considerable help in Bruno, Galileo, and Copernicus, it was Isaac Newton, probably more than anyone in the late Renaissance, who called into most serious question the established "truths" of the past.

If Africentricity is a valid method of study and not merely an orientation for discourse, it will revolutionize the way one thinks about the class of phenomena it studies. If it looks back to a golden age of Black achievement in Africa and tries to utilize the method and logic current then, even at the University of Sankore, will it not become burdened down trying to fit knowledge into African frameworks, as Eurocentric thought tried to do during the Renaissance?

Newtonian physics had meaning for an emerging technology, which when applied led to living standard improvements. No less will be required of an Africentric methodology. A crying question will be: How will it aid in getting diasporians out of ghettos and barrios, and motherlanders out of neocolonialism and poverty? A major criticism of Eurocentric science was that it soon moved into the employ of the classes who could best use it for the suppression of those lowest down in the social structure. Nevertheless, it showed that science has more than heuristic utility. The possibility of Africentricity to perform a function such as this—even if features of exploitability are avoided—is imperative.

Community in Africentricity

Social science proposed from its early days that community would decline as urbanization and industrialization increased. These processes were practically universal, though they reached and affected some groups more or less than others and at differential rates. These are not the only processes leading to a decline in community, but they do bear consideration.

It would be instructive to look at Africans on the continent and in the diaspora to determine if community is yet viable. Pan-Africanism, harambee, negritude, ujamaa, Black nationalism, African socialism, and even tribalism could be thought of as strategies for the restoration of community, for they would cohere Africans together for common purposes based on common history. But whether on the continent or in the diaspora, Africentricity and Black community has declined precipitously. Disastrous civil wars and intertribal warfare have been constant features of African life since before independence, and certainly after. Only in a few places was an effective connection maintained between Africans with even the slightest differences between them. Ibo fought Hausa in Nigeria; Baganda battled Banyankole in Uganda; Kikuyu were cool to Luo in Kenya. The conflict between the Watusi and the Bahutu in Rwanda is older than the independence of the two territories they principally inhabit: Rwanda and Burundi. Zulu-Xhosa strife in South Africa prohibited their combining of efforts for a unified thrust toward the eradication of apartheid. And everywhere the Pygmies, Hottentots, and Bushmen, by whatever names they are called, are held in low and exploitable disesteem. Africentricity is unable to cohere these groups. Even the Organization of African Unity, that great hope for the political expression of Africentricity, is moribund.

In the diaspora, and especially in North America, the ultimate expression of Africentricity was "soul," an inexplicable bond between all Black people, a bond forged out of the suffering of the slave experience. It united Blacks of all ranks and statuses and gave them all a common universe of discourse. Under the concept of "soul" the deepest secrets of the most highly placed Blacks could be understood by those farthest down. With "soul" it was not necessary to say anything. A nod of the head, a flashing of the fingers, any recognition at all conveyed reams of understanding to "soul brothers and sisters." Not only was a brother or sister physically safe under the umbrella of soul, but he or she was provided with that rare and irreplaceable psychological security and vitality that enabled survival and integrity in a hostile environment. In polyglot New York City, the author and an Ethiopian walked the streets for dozens of blocks. He was thoroughly impressed with Blacks speaking and nodding recognition of one another, whom they had never seen, and never would again. Even he was included when he thought he would not be. He was further amazed when he was informed this was one aspect of soul. Our hypothesis is that there is a great overlap between Africentricity and soul—behaving and feeling out of a common experience.

Who Are the Believers in Africentric Thought?

As an organized body of knowledge the Africentric idea is relatively new, if the idea is traced in its modern context. It became recognized in the late 1950s and early 1960s with the work of such writers as Leopold Senghor, Aime Cesaire, and Leon Damas, all working in the French intellectual tradition. The continued Africanicity of New World Blacks goes back to even earlier than Marcus Garvey, on the eve of the Harlem Renaissance. Long before the French-speaking Blacks began to write, the movement might have been called Ethiopianism, with a push for the recognition of Blacks as Ethiopians, recognizing that Ethiopia was at one time a powerful political, economic, and military power. Ancient Ethiopia covered much more territory than it does today (Williams, 1944). Perhaps the push to identify Blacks as Ethiopians came to a head when, during the Harlem Renaissance, there was a need to bring coherency for Black Americans in adopting a national Black anthem. Ethiopianism was so strong that Bishop George Alexander McGuire proposed a song called *Ethiopia*, which so competed with James Weldon Johnson's *Lift Every Voice and Sing* that the two men almost came to blows over which composition would become the Black national anthem (Burkett, 1978).

But the idea of Africentrism really is hundreds, even thousands, of years old, for it relates to the recognition of the population of Africa as a people, not merely a collection or conglomeration of individuals having some degree of dark complexion commonality. In that context, Africa was distinguished from the rest of the world by its achievements in important fields: medicine, law, architecture, art, music, religion, and many others. The encroaching sands, the migrations forced by the invasions of others, and amalgamation pushed many Africans, formerly of high culture, into the bush, mountains, and desert where they could escape the ravages of slavery, whether conducted by Christian or Islamic peoples. There they reverted to what is commonly thought of as savagery, the most visible sign of which the West sees as nakedness, scarification, and what appear to be uncivilized social practices.

The social and economic devastation of the continent has continued for literally thousands of years. The odds were much fairer in the period before European penetration in the 19th century. The Asians, variously the Arabs, Egyptians, and Moors, tried to conquer the continent, but could not make much headway beyond the edges, to where they retreated to boats if Africans waged too heavy opposition. The Africans, in general, when pushed beyond their means to resist, retreated to the interior of the continent, where they were protected by forbidding terrain, mosquitoes, wild animals, and diseases against which the outsiders had little immunity.

There was an ebb and flow of African achievement in this process of attacking, counter-attacking, and seeking stability. Africans had been some of the earliest workers in iron, but they did not use this knowledge to make firearms, even when they had access to this technology. The Asians, and later, the Europeans stole a march on the Africans by manufacturing firearms, which enabled them to extend their subjugation of the African continent. With firearms they could move beyond the coastlines and raid into the interior of the continent.

Wherever outsiders could gain a foothold, the raids continued. The hunt for slaves provided the first impetus for raids. The relatively small expeditions the Europeans could put into the field at a given time could be wiped out easily enough, if not by military opposition, then by disease. Another group would then need to be outfitted and the process repeated. Eventually, it became clear to both the Asians and Europeans that the conquest of Africa meant occupying the continent, but the military option was not the only one available. If Africans could be taught the ways of the captors, perhaps they would provide the services and transfer the wealth that the continent had to offer.

The Arabs were not systematic in their attempts to fully exploit the continent—i.e., in their effort to subdue the southern part of it. They sent traders to barter for salt, gold, ivory, and other riches in the south, but the distances back to the north, across the Sahara, were long and arduous traveling. Many Arabs made arrangements with African villages for stopping places, which eventually became acceptable to the villagers. They taught them Arabic as well as Islamic values, and not an insignificant number took African women as their mates, on legitimate as well as concubinage bases. Their children had ties both to the Arabic and African worlds, and their loyalties were often divided. Where the Arabs were not of superior social and economic status, these mixed-blood children more often chose African culture. If the Arabs had social superiority, the offspring frequently identified with the Arabs, rather than with Africans. In time it was difficult to separate African from Arab, even far below the sands of the Sahara. "African" came to connote those Blacks who had most strenuously resisted the acculturating effects of outside influence.

Europeans approached the continent in a more systematic manner. They wanted to explore it, to map it, to learn about its natural features, all toward the end of exploiting wealth, both in regard to nature and people. Dr. Livingston was a prototype of the European explorer. While he might have wanted to learn more about the people in order to help suppress the slave trade, to Christianize, and to civilize the Africans (in his mind), he essentially was performing a valuable service for those Europeans who saw possibilities for taking vast riches from the benighted continent. The Arabs had an earlier start, but the Europeans believed they could catch up easily enough with the application of superior technology. The accounts of Livingston and Stanley, Emin Pasha, Chinese Gordon, Sir and Lady Samuel Baker, etc. (Moorehead, 1960, 1962) are exciting, but reveal more about the intentions of the Europeans to conquer the continent than about African resistance.

After the explorers came the missionaries, and after them the traders and their supporting forces, who literally leveled their guns at African culture. The reconnaissance work had been done; the data were substantially in; and now Europeans could move wholesale to compete with the Arabs for domination of the continent. They began to work with those persons most likely to reject Africentricity, for the invaders were now thinking of true Africans as a barbarous people—people without any connection whatever to European or Islamic civilization. The relatively sedentary Africans, now organized into kingdoms, often in opposition to each other, were the best candidates for Europeanization. They eagerly accepted schools, Christianity, and western behavior as symbols of civility. The values and practices of the traditional African were rejected. It was forgotten that these very values had been the ones that had protected Africans from slavery. It was only because so much of the indigenous population had held onto tradition that the continent had been able to remain as free as it was from enslaving influences.

The Europeans used some of the same tactics as the Arabs to gain the support of people who conceived of themselves as "modernizing." The newcomers were not above allowing a few of their number to move into African villages and to intermix with the population. Again, a sizable class of mulattos and eventually octoroons developed, who felt they naturally should represent the Europeans in the continent. Theirs was a flight from Africentricity paralleling that which had been brought about by the Arabization and Islamicization of millions of Africans. They built schools, churches, hospitals, roads, and opened businesses, which generally utilized Africans in many of the lower positions. For these persons in the money economy and reaping tangible economic benefits, they felt there was no real need to retain their African values. Africentricity was essentially moribund, for it was found mainly among those Africans who had no standing before the newly educated and increasingly westernized people of the Mother continent.

Nationalism and Africentricity

The idea of African peoples having a homeland is a very old one, perhaps the oldest of all indigenous values. As Chancellor Williams has observed, from earliest recorded history, dating to about 6,000 years ago, the people of Ethiopia ruled Lower Egypt, but were gradually pushed farther south and west to finally spread elsewhere over the continent; they always regarded Africa as the province of the Black man. The centuries-long fight, first with the Asians, who finally became Arabicized, and afterwards with the Europeans, was to protect what they thought and assumed to be their homeland. The concept of nationhood did exist at various times in Africa's history, though Westerners were not wont to recognize provinces as such. More often, the largest, best organized, and strongest of the political arrangements were based on several clans sharing common ancestors and values. These groups were often thought of as kingdoms, and not as nations or states of Africa. After the devastation of slavery and colonialism, the sense of Africentricity was severely damaged on the continent and in the diaspora. Probably it was the villagers, mostly out of the reach of modernizing influences, who kept the idea of Africentricity alive.

In Pan-African conferences—which were convened for several years during World War II, led by W.E.B. Du Bois and some future African leaders like Jomo Kenyatta (1963) and Kwame Nkrumah (1957)—the thrust was toward independence of the continent. Africentricity and political liberation seemed almost identical, and the language of Africentricity began to shift after some colonies started to gain freedom. On the continent, as well as in the diaspora, the new word was nationalism, wherein African culture and values could be reaffirmed.

Very soon after independence, however, some colonies fell into serious civil strife. In some cases it was necessary to ask former colonial governments to assure peace and stability by garrisoning military forces in Africa. Thus, these colonialists continued to exercise hegemony over the economic fortunes of their former colonies. But even these measures could fail, as tribalism and political infighting ravaged some lands. Scholars and poets such as Leopold Senghor and Aime Cesaire sounded the call of negritude, literally the spiritual bonding of all African people, hoping this could be used positively. In East Africa, Julius Nyerere of Tanzania was promoting *ujamaa* (family hood), and Jomo Kenyatta *harambee* (pulling together). All were trying to unite the African people, who had lost touch with and feelings for each other over the years of isolation due to slavery and colonialism. There remained a belief that culture and experiential forces bound all Africans together wherever they were (Morgan, 1964). The essence of the internal conflicts in the new countries proved to be based on tribalism, as Africa's most populous new country, Nigeria, burst into flames in the disastrous Biafra War. But this was only the most notable of many conflicts that rent the continent, announcing a serious diminution of independence, nationalism, and, for a time, the much hoped for adherence to Africentricity.

* * *

The Africentric view, while recognized as a cultural reality, does not have a definite origin. There is no way of accounting for its development, nor is there any particular behavior prediction to be made from it. The strength of the view cannot be estimated although it is recognized that individuals may be more or less committed to the view. Even in a society that is quite closed from the standpoint of opportunity, or for the development of a wider viewpoint, some persons will develop an Africentric world view and others will not. The process by which this view comes to predominate is not spelled out by the proponents, nor are they able to show why an Africentric view was so long in developing when Blacks were most severely depressed. A body of literature suggests that Old World or different cultural orientations have a difficult time being maintained in a culture that permits upward mobility into a more affluent mainstream. Immigrants, in general, gave up many of their Old World values and mannerisms as they saw greater possibilities within the wider culture. Is it likely that Blacks follow a similar trajectory?

Any view different from the norm, whether Africentric or otherwise, is a matter of qualitative development, where one sees and understands from a cultural perspective. Scholars such as Harold Isaacs (1975) thought these views to be so deep-seated, through training, that they seemed to be in-born. It is possible that persons without much association with others unlike themselves would soon develop distinctive world views. The opportunity to develop this deep world view may be receding for some Africans and diasporians for they are increasingly a part of a mass society that exposes them to mind-changing processes, which challenge their own notions of the operation of the social world. However, continuing racism does bolster the Africentric initiative.

If Africentricity is merely a challenge to Eurocentricity, its uniqueness does not lie in the challenge, for even Eurocentric thought is not of a whole cloth and must periodically redemonstrate its credibility. The world at one time reached out to the East for religion, science, and high culture. Even today the old religions of the East provide significant challenges to Western Christianity. Attempts to dislodge the Moslems from the Holy Lands were partly grounded in the quest for a shorter route to the fabled Indies in search of the wealth and culture found there. It was important in Europe to borrow from the Orient, for its own technological and general cultural orientation thusly could increasingly benefit in competing on a world scale. One valuable lesson learned by Europe was that isolation was costly and a prescription for stagnation. Consequently, it was not just European science or daring that promoted the events of 1492 and the European rediscovery of the New World; it was the knowledge of the East, coupled with Arabic astronomy and mathematics, that helped create possibilities for Columbus. But more than any of these it was a case of change based on expanded technological knowledge. Until then the West was more enamored of the East than the East of the West. No plan has been devised, which prohibits cultures from borrowing from and sharing with each other; and so it is with Africentricity. It will not be enough to simply point out that there are values and even technology in this world view which the world may utilize; somewhere these must be demonstrable to the extent that they have utility.

Can There Be Comparative Studies under the Africentric View?

Since it is allegedly clear that Africentrism is a unique world view derived from Black people, studies of Black psychology logically utilize that world view. The question of whether or not, indeed, that there is or is not an Africentric view is immaterial; what is important is the introduction of an alternative explanation for Black behavior, which seeks to better explain total behavior and personality. It treats this behavior and personality as authentic and balanced, rather than deviant and schizophrenic.

All research begins with certain basic, essentially unprovable assumptions. These assumptions must be harmonized with the research framework. One way of bringing about this harmony is by defining concepts. Any definition is a construct, a mental rather than a physical reality. Unlike physics, which seeks to neutralize the meaning of concepts by adhering to rigid principles of measurement, social science seeks to harmonize concepts and reality by definition and manipulation of constructs. A psychotic and a member of the lower class are thus defined. A Eurocentric definition of an Afro-American person stresses the differences between the Euro norm and deviation from it. Racial and ethnically comparative research stresses the difference between a Euro norm and differences from it. If the groups are different there is little validity in comparing them. The expectation is that those differences will remain in the sample as in reality. If the groups are not different there is no point in comparing them, for no differences between them are anticipated to be found. It is begging the question to claim that the hunt is for the confirmation or negation of hypotheses. Comparative research of a racial nature can only lead to conflagrations similar to those seen by Azibo (1990, 25–41) when "fat is tossed into the fire." The methodology of Africentrism is well elaborated in that seminal essay.

Summary Comment

The first modern American Black social scientists were assimilationists in that they were prohibited from espousing too much of an African orientation in their teachings and writings. There were exceptions to the case, such as Carter G. Woodson and W.E.B. Du Bois, both far enough out of the mainstream that their teachings did not have to be widely considered. Africa was under colonial rule and diasporians were under economic and professional bondage.

It was only after World War I that they had begun in a serious way to press for Africentric recognition, though Paul Cuffee, Alfred Sam, and Marcus Garvey had been important advocates of Africentricity. Du Bois and future African nationalists had convened PanAfrican congresses in England in the early 1940s. By the late 1950s when African colonies began to gain their independence, Africentricity took the rhetorical form of negritude, harambee, ujamaa, etc. In the diaspora it became crystallized as Black Power.

The late 1960s and early 1970s saw Africentricity move to the universities where the Black experience competed to be taught as a regular part of the curriculum. The popular generic title was Black Studies. These courses often began with African history and experience. Courses were often taught on sections of Africa, and sometimes on the continent as a whole. Even African languages were occasionally taught. Emerging from all this intellectual activity was believed to be a rediscovery of Africans' unique way of looking at the world, currently conceptualized and operationalized as some variety of the term Africentricity.

References

Asante, Molefi K. 1987. *The Afrocentric Idea*. Philadelphia: Temple University Press.
_____. 1988. *Afrocentricity*. Trenton, N.J.: Africa World Press.
Azibo, Daudi Ajani. 1990. "Treatment and Training Implications of the Advances in African Personality Theory," *The Western Journal of Black Studies*, Vol. 14, No. 1, 53–65.
Blassingame, John W. 1972. *The Slave Community: Plantation Life in the Antebellum South*. Oxford University Press.
Burkett, Randall K. 1978. *Garveyism as a Religious Movement: The Institutionalization of a Black Civil Religion*. Metuchen, N.J.: Scarecrow Press.
Chesnutt, Charles. 1968. *Conjure Woman*. Ridgewood, N.J.: Gregg Press.
_____. 1974. *Short Fiction*. Washington, D.C.: Howard University Press.
Clark, Kenneth B., and Mamie Clark. 1939. "The Development of Consciousness of Self and the Emergence of Racial Identification in Negro Preschool Children," *Journal of Social Psychology*, Vol. 10, 591–599.
_____. 1958. "Racial Identification and Preference in Negro Children," in Eleanor Maccoby, et al., *Readings in Social Psychology*, 3rd ed. New York: Holt, Rinehart and Winston [pp. 602–611].
Cox, Oliver C. 1948. *Caste, Class and Race*. New York: Doubleday.
Du Bois, W.E.B. 1894, 1898. *The Suppression of the Atlantic Slave Trade to the United States of America, 1638–1870*. New York: Russell and Russell, 1965.
Essien-Udom, E. U., and Amy Jacques Garvey. 1977. *More Philosophy and Opinions of Marcus Garvey*. Totowa, N.J.: Cass.
Fanon, Frantz C. 1963, 1968. *The Wretched of the Earth*, preface by Jean Paul Sartre, translated by Constance Farrington. New York: Grove Press.
_____. 1967. *Black Skins, White Masks*, translated by Charles L. Markmann. New York: Grove Press.
Forsythe, Dennis (ed.). 1971. *Let the Niggers Burn: The Sir George Williams University Affair and Its Caribbean Aftermath*. Montreal: Our Generation Press.
Frazier, E. Franklin. 1957. *Black Bourgeoisie*. Glencoe, Illinois: Free Press.
Haley, Alex. 1976. *Roots*. New York: Doubleday.
Hansberry, William Leo. 1974. *Pillars in Ethiopian History*, Joseph E. Harris (ed.). Washington, D.C.: Howard University Press.
Hare, Nathan. 1965. *Black Anglo-Saxons*. New York: Marzani and Munsell.
Harris, Abram L., with Sterling D. Spero. 1931. *The Black Worker*. New York: Columbia University Press.
Harris, Abram L. 1936. *The Negro as a Capitalist*. Philadelphia: American Academy of Political and Social Science.

_____. 1968. *The Negro as a Capitalist*. Gloucester, Mass.: P. Smith.
Herskovits, Melville. 1941. *The Myth of the Negro Past*. New York: Harper and Brothers.
_____. 1966. *The New World Negro: Selected Papers in AfroAmerican Studies*, Frances S. Herskovits (ed.). Bloomington: Indiana University Press.
Isaacs, Harold R. 1975. *Idols of the Tribe: Group Identity and Political Change*. New York: Harper and Row.
Kenyatta, Jomo. 1963. *Facing Mount Kenya: The Traditional Life of the Gikuyu*. New York: Vintage.
Ladner, Joyce A. (ed.). 1973. *The Death of White Sociology*. New York: Vintage.
Lightfoot, Claude M. 1968. *Ghetto Rebellion to Black Liberation*. New York: International.
Moorehead, Alan. 1960. *The White Nile*. New York: Harper.
_____. 1962. *The Blue Nile*. New York: Harper and Row.
Morgan, Gordon D. 1964. "Neo-Traditional Africans and Racial Ethnocentrism," *Indian Journal of Social Research* (Bombay).
_____. 1974. "The First Generation Black Sociologists and Theories of Social Change," *Journal of the Association of Social and Behavioral Scientists*.
Nkrumah, Kwame. 1957. *Ghana: The Autobiography of Kwame Nkrumah*. New York: Nelson.
Padmore, George, and Nancy Cunard. 1942. *The White Man's Duty*. N.p.
Turner, Loreno Dow. 1949. *Africanisms in the Gullah Dialect*. Chicago: University of Chicago Press.
Williams, Eric. 1944. *Capitalism and Slavery*. Chapel Hill: University of North Carolina Press.
Williams, George Washington. 1968. *History of the Negro Race in America*. New York: Bergman.
Woodson, Carter G. 1933. *Miseducation of the Negro*. Washington, D.C.: Associated.

20

Beyond Afrocentricism:
Alternatives for African American Studies*

Perry A. Hall

Perry A. Hall *is currently a Visiting Assistant Professor in the Department of Sociology at the University of Alabama at Birmingham. He received the doctorate in Education and Social Policy from Harvard University.*—The Western Journal of Black Studies, *Winter 1991, Vol. 15, No. 4*

I n recent years, Afrocentricity as a belief system, or theoretical perspective, has become nearly synonymous with Black Studies as a discipline. The central idea developed in this essay is that the African American Studies discipline should be conceptualized as a set of theoretical perspectives, rather than as a single theoretical perspective. Among several reasons for this is that, as a tactical matter, it will help in further establishing its institutional legitimacy in the context of American academia if Black Studies is presented as a non-monolithic academic enterprise. Next, because plurality of perspective accurately reflects the evolution of theoretical constructs within the field, as well as the current diversity and variation among both the community of Black scholars and in the African American community itself.[1] Notwithstanding that plurality, indeed because it exists, the disciplinary framework must encompass and reflect a diverse reality. Next, because the presence of alternative perspectives promotes dialogue, which in turn promotes clarity within the discipline. Finally, because honest dialogue leading to greater clarity is paramount in order for Black Studies to come the full circle of its own evolution. Reference is made here to the renewal of Black student activism surfacing on campuses across the nation, led by students who come from crisis conditions in Black communities. They have questions and look to the Black Studies discipline for answers.[2]

*A version of this paper was presented at the Annual Meeting of the National Council for Black Studies, Culver City, California, April 1990. I would like to thank Tommie Lee Lott for his input in developing these ideas, and for allowing the use of his work and ideas in developing this article.

The first point, that more than one theoretical perspective is necessary to comprise a legitimate academic discipline, may be interpreted as over-concern with Eurocentric forms by some who hold that Afrocentrism should be *the* theoretical perspective of the discipline. That is one of perhaps many matters that could, and should, be discussed between those who hold that view and those who do not. What is argued here is that the elements of the discipline must be incorporated so that such discussions can take place. Eurocentric institutions, which house most Black Studies programs, are heavily concerned with the form which academic discourse takes. As long as the discourse takes the proper form and format—i.e., research, scholarship, theory, etc.—and as long as reasoned scholarship is allowed to express any point of view, Afrocentrism, along with other reasoned viewpoints, will be inherently consistent with basic requirements of academic rigor and legitimized within the basic principle of academic freedom.

This is not to be seen as a distortion of the field, because as mentioned, plurality of perspective reflects the historical evolution, and the current variation among Black Studies scholars and the community. Programs which emerged early in the Black Studies movement were often headed and staffed with more or less established Black academics trained in traditional, Eurocentric disciplines.[3] In this article this approach is called academic "integrationism," or a "discipline-based" approach. These labels refer to the work of some Black Studies scholars and, virtually, all other Black related literature from traditional disciplines, in which the aim is to "integrate" the heretofore neglected aspects of Black life into the theoretical and methodological frameworks of so-called "established" disciplines.

The frequent criticism of this perspective has been that—whether it calls itself Black Studies or a traditional discipline—it mirrors the approaches and methodological and theoretical frameworks of traditional disciplines in the study and analysis of the Black experience.[4] The task of disentangling this fragmented knowledge from its mire of intra-disciplinary biases and cross-disciplinary barriers has been said to be too great, and the results not useful.

This approach was strongly opposed by activist elements in the original Black Studies movement, including many who now comprise the field of Black Studies scholars. Although activists were generally united in their opposition to this approach, they argued among themselves as to the shape in which an alternative should be structured. In early years the terms of the alternatives were articulated and debated at the political, rather than the intellectual level (i.e., the Black Nationalist vs. Marxist debate of the seventies and eighties).[5]

In recent years Afrocentrism has emerged as the most visible alternative to the "integrationist" or "discipline-based" approach, as a central theoretical perspective around which to organize the discipline. From the roots of those original activists, Afrocentrism has developed into a paradigm with wide support and many adherents among Black Studies scholars. It has been incorporated into the theme of the National Council for Black Studies' annual conference several times in recent years. It is the expressed theoretical orientation of the only Black Studies Ph.D. program, located at Temple University, and represents a tremendous achievement for the Black Studies movement.

The construction of Afrocentrism has been a vital element in the necessary deconstruction of Eurocentrism. Seminal in the historical construction of Western social science and aesthetic studies, Eurocentric bias and distortion made adequate grasp of the actuality of race in the modern world virtually impossible for Black scholars who grappled with this problem. The need for development of paradigms free of this burden was clear and obvious.

Afrocentrism has been widely embraced, perhaps somewhat uncritically, because it represents this necessary and total deconstruction of the Eurocentric perspective; a "straitjacket"[6] surely designed to restrain those who reach for truth and clarity. Furthermore, the body of knowledge and information emphasized and highlighted by Afrocentrism has been essential in the reconstruction of intellectual perspectives and cultural sensibilities that affirm the historical legitimacy of Blacks while providing an anchor for their consciousness as a people; offering a basis for unified theory construction relative to the study and analysis of Black people and Black communities.

Nonetheless, Afrocentrism, while necessary, is of itself insufficient as a theoretical base from which to address the complete set of issues facing Black Studies scholars. The limitations center around the contention that the Afrocentrist perspective presents a static model that does not adequately address the dynamic interaction of Afrocentric sensibility with Western dominated economic, cultural, and political structures.

The notion of a static versus dynamic model raises an implied discussion of philosophy of culture which is key to the argument raised here. In simple terms, culture is a shared world view. But it is *also the process itself* of creating a shared world view arising out of shared *living* experiences. The traits and trends of commonality in life and experience, referred to as culture, arise from minute as well as all-encompassing aspects of the relation and interaction of humans with themselves, their community, environment, and society. A feeble listing of some of the components of the process of culture—geography, language, community, socialization, family, mythology, magic, ritual, healing, suffering, symbolism, conflict, contradiction, adaptation, synthesis, transformation—begins to reveal complexity belied in the simpler terms of description.

The interaction of minute and all-encompassing elements in the process of culture is like a swelling sea. Molecules and droplets, each with its own direction, momentum, and intensity; meeting, colliding, interacting synergistically; creating ripples, swells; wave action; acting in concert with each other, creating tides that ebb and flow; that reach for the moon and the cosmos; sometimes embodying overwhelming force; changing shorelines and destroying land masses; changing the face of the planet itself.

Because this process produces and sanctions institutions, which in turn sanction culture, it may be perceived as static. For example, the static view of culture, when incorporated into the chauvinist perspective of Eurocentrism, is quick to pronounce the cultural initiatives of Blacks as having melted into the American pot. It creates the idea that the cultural, social, and individual bases of Black experiences are pathological imitations of White culture. It is blind to the continuous process of regeneration of unique reference points and sensibilities which, historically, have characterized African American cultural expression.[7]

Conversely, when incorporated into a rigid Afrocentrist framework, the static view of culture may be also, if not equally, regressive. While its spokespersons deny that Afrocentrism is rigid, they also state that an Afrocentrist quickly rejects, "any thought, action, behavior and value [that] cannot be found in our culture or in our history."[8] Regarding this tendency, the discussion of philosophy of culture above raises the following philosophical question: how is it determined that a thought, idea, or feeling is or is not part of Black history or culture? The dynamics of change in the process of history and culture would, it would seem, make that difficult. Denials notwithstanding, this is one indication of how Afrocentrism replaces Eurocentrism's static concept with its own static view of what Black culture is.

A dynamic view of culture focuses on the fact that, while Afrocentric in origin, Black culture and identity are in constant transformation. In this writer's work in this area, the focus on transformation is overlaid with the theme of duality: that fundamental opposition of cultural sensibilities, first called "double-consciousness" by Du Bois, which shapes, indeed defines, African Americans as a people.[9]

The term transformation implies both change and continuity; change which produces new forms continuous with old forms, carrying something of their essence. At the individual level, personalities and perspectives on life are transformed each day through thoughts, feelings, emotions, experiences, and perceptions. Each night dreams organize these impressions in their consciousness. And each morning they are newly transformed. Yet, their selves are continuous. They are essentially the same person.

The dyadic opposition of sensibilities, expressed in the term duality, pervades the identities, cultural orientations, and communities not only of African Americans, but in fact, those of Africans in all parts of the Diaspora. This was expressed by the South African scholar, Magubane, when he wrote "Neither Africa or Europe alone provides sufficient scope for our collective experience."[10] On all levels descendents of Africa are continually confronted with the contradiction of that dual reality. This is not only the current condition, it is a historical fact. As an analytical construct, duality organizes the internal opposition of sensibilities and seeks to find their synthesis in the transformed ethos of African peoples.

The focus on transformation and duality are the bases of a framework referred to here as a "transformationist" perspective, embodying the basic analytical principle that the interaction of external, objective (systematic) forces on social structure, and the internal, subjective (thematic) forces on cultural sensibility, shapes the lives of individual Blacks and Black communities.[11] It seeks to address issues involved with both the Afrocentrist foundations of Black communities and the forces of transformation with which they interact. Thus, this approach leads to paths of inquiry, and to conclusions, which vary from those proposed by Afrocentrists.

Afrocentrism's seminal objective is revealed in the question posed by Asante: "How can we regain our pre-slavery, indeed our pre-American heritage?"[12] It seeks a reconstruction of perspective that is, in most ways, the specific negation of non-African sensibilities since, it maintains, the absorption of non-African customs and values have had only negative effects.[13] A static view of culture leads Afrocentrism to reject any sign of acculturation as foreign. It seems to beg the question of the need for African Americans to understand and master all aspects of the world of all humans, whether they are considered part of Black culture or not; i.e., Eurocentric training, schooling, etc.

For Blacks to discover who they were is important, but only a part of discovering who they are, who they can be, and where they can go. Therefore, transformation grips the "Afrocentric" view that all of humanity is the progeny of Africa and seeks a reconstruction of perspective which includes, rather than ignores or negates, the presence and impact of other peoples, including Whites, in the transformed global reality of all humans.

For Blacks, knowing one's environment usually means knowing it on two different levels. One level involves the ability to decode the rules, machinations, and processes by which survival is insured and enhanced in this system. The other involves actualizing the political will to collectively transform their environment. Rather than automatically rejecting and hating signs of acculturation in African American personalities, duality puts the internal opposition of cultural sensibility in a perspective in which it can work to their benefit.

A static view of culture and history motivates Afrocentrism to self-consciously construct an Afrocentric mythology as a cultural analog to oppose Eurocentric mythology, using the memories of past Black leaders like Walker, Douglas, Washington, Garvey, Nkrumah, Du Bois, Martin, and Malcolm.[14] Leaders of the past are honored as ancestors and forbearers, and that is well. However, to raise them to the level of prophets, as Afrocentrism proposes, does not seem appropriate.

In view of the discussion of the dynamic concept of culture, it is first of all doubtful whether mythology as such was created out of such self-conscious construction. It also seems that such pre-occupation with static forms and symbols of culture take attention away from some of the important aspects of African American culture as living phenomena. For example, there can be no doubt that the historical river of African American consciousness flows from the South; that the transformed African American cultural framework is based there, and issues from there. In one sense, the more into the deep South one goes, the closer to Africa one gets.

An anecdote from this writer's personal experience is offered to illustrate this. In 1921, the writer's grandmother left the Mississippi delta, came to Detroit, bore 10 children, who had 40 grandchildren, who are giving her lots of great grandchildren, even at this writing. Her sister, named "Ant Modena," stayed in Mississippi and had a smaller, but still ample, brood of children, grandchildren, and great grandchildren. When "Ant Modena" died in 1977, nine carloads of the Detroit branch of the family went down to help bury her in the ancestral soil (along with branches from Chicago, Oklahoma, and other places).

At one point in the service individuals in the congregation began speaking randomly, one at a time, about "Ant Modena": who she was, what she meant to them. Their comments were brief, clear, sincere, and moving. Without visible order, there was visible continuity. When one person stopped talking, another voice came from another direction without loss of a beat. Among all the speakers, one, although sincere in her efforts, was clearly uncomfortable, self-conscious, overlong, and even showy in her remarks. She was White. When she finished, another speaker picked up and it was finished. The service went on.

It all flowed, and it was definitely "in the spirit"—the pure spirit of African communalism—in the framework of the southern African American folk church. Yet, the words "African communalism," would have had no meaning to those who were participating in what the words describe. If those words were spoken to "Ant Modena," when she was alive, or to others in her context, she would have thought them to be rather strange.

Thus, the static view of culture in Afrocentrism leads to an overemphasis on words and language as form at the expense of meaning and communication as substance; as, for example, when Asante states that name changing is "a necessary condition for a new perspective on our place in the world."[15] If not superficial, this view seems at least misprioritized. The dynamic view concludes that a name does not give meaning to a life; rather, a life gives meaning to a name; that the language used is not more important than what the language is used to say; and that a new perspective on the world comes not from new words, but from new ideas.

This presentation should not be interpreted as total opposition to the premises of Afrocentrism. It is intended to suggest that Afrocentrism's limitations not be ignored. A monolithic embrace of Afrocentrism deters not only the Black Studies discipline, but also the development toward further clarity of Afrocentrism itself. That is because the presence of other perspectives promotes dialogue, by raising issues, such as those raised here, for other perspectives to deal with. Even the "integrationist" perspective presents issues and data which cannot be ignored, run from, or simply renamed. For example, William Julius Wilson, whose approach may be characterized as integrationist, or discipline-based (in the sense of the "conventional" or "mainstream" Eurocentric disciplines), despite possible flaws in his analysis, presents issues and data relative to a social and economic crisis that other perspectives should address or account for in some way.[16]

The most important reasons for such dialogue are, as indicated at the outset, related to Black youth and their future. The clarity stimulated from dialogue among different perspectives within the discipline will be especially "relevant"—to borrow a term used frequently in the original Black Studies movement—for students leading a new generation of campus activism. For example, students at Wayne State University in Detroit held a campus administration building for 12 days, in April 1989, in a successful struggle to upgrade the University's Center for Black Studies into a Department of Africana Studies. It was most significant that these students contextualized their struggle with reference to crises conditions in the communities from which they came—specifically, the problems of their own age contemporaries.[17] They seemed to be making the statement that, "if we are going to equip ourselves to effectively serve our communities—ravaged by drugs, violence, joblessness, and hopelessness—we need to have a viable Africana Studies Department."

Similarly, at campuses all over the country students are coming from Black communities with questions and looking to African-American Studies for answers. The emergence of such consciousness among African American students both affirms and vitalizes the value and mission of this discipline. It also heightens the level of responsibility and accountability of scholars in the discipline, in terms of providing students with tools adequate to find their answers and accomplish their mission.

That psychic, emotional, and cultural connection to Africa, Black History, or "Afrocentricity" is important for Blacks and for Black Studies is not argued here; just the means of making that connection—not so much for intellectuals, who by way of material circumstance avoid the worst distractions experienced by ordinary Blacks, but for the most troubled, disadvantaged, and oppressed among them. Those who have time and space in their lives to ponder every thought, idea, or feeling for Afrocentric relevance may well find that it is a useful and cleansing exercise. But likely most Blacks, who basically have to hit the mark from sunup to sundown, are usually preoccupied discovering meaning in more concrete and immediate contexts.

Consider, for example, the issue of rap music. In a hypothetical course, or course unit, on rap, an Afrocentrist might correctly emphasize that rap is a modern form of Nommo—power through the spoken word—and is an expression of the Oral Tradition of Africa and its descendants. However, it may be more relevant, from the point of view of students and their reality, to focus initially on the content, meaning, relevance, or irrelevance of what is communicated in rap music. Rap songs present descriptions of a reality much closer than Egyptian Pyramids. According to one writer, "The voice of Black urban poor people is best represented in Black culture through rap music." Rap artists themselves have sometimes likened their cultural practice to a kind of "black people's television," through which they have "declared war against the dominant ideological apparatus."[18]

Images in rap often reflect an accurate, if harsh, understanding of the conditions under which Black youth must survive, as well as important truths about the larger society where, for example, involvement with drugs and drug trafficking is quite widespread, where police regulate and often profit from drug trade, where violence is regularly used by the government in domestic as well as foreign affairs, and where criminal behavior is common on Wall Street, in Congress, and even in the White House.[19] From their own perspective, they have fewer illusions with mainstream values than many African Americans in Black Studies, or in academia in general, who, whether aware or not, embody those mainstream values.

A similar understanding of similar conditions was involved in the transformation of "Detroit Red," the outlaw and street hustler, to Malcolm X, the revolutionary and leader in Black consciousness evolution. It is no coincidence that rappers and student activists have both been focal points in a rediscovery of Malcolm, currently manifesting among Black youth. An Afrocentrist might approach this issue with the premise that Malcolm's own self-discovery depended on his realization of an Afrocentric perspective. This may or may not be true, depending on how, exactly, an Afrocentric perspective is defined. But, it seems clear that his sense of relevance to Black youth is based more directly on how his street life experiences parallel theirs, creating a concrete context to which they can relate.

Thus, rap and Malcolm are media in which Black youth are communicating messages of self-discovery. While both, especially rap, are associated by some with negative messages, both have "shown the potential to engender a liberating consciousness in Black urban youth."[20] Rappers Blastmaster KRS reached the number one spot with their record "Stop the Violence." According to Detroit rapper D. J. Razor Blayd, a near riot at a recent performance was aborted when someone in the audience shouted the song's main refrain: "Self-destruction. You're heading for self-destruction." Soon, the whole crowd picked up the refrain, and the violence was averted.[21]

This is one small indication of the potential of media within contemporary youth culture as vehicles for consciousness transformation. The African American studies discipline should engage youth on these levels to facilitate this transformation. It is clear that Afrocentrism has a significant role to play in this process. However, to restate once again the theme of this article, more will be needed. Rather than focusing so strongly on the past, there is a need to focus on arriving at an understanding of the present and a direction for the future that ultimately synthesizes, rather than dismantles, the fundamental duality of Black life.

Malcolm is embraced by young and old as a model for Black manhood, political philosophy, and revolutionary courage. But he can also be held up as a model of discipline in his pursuit of knowledge and education. In his self-made prison education Malcolm became very well versed not only in African but also in European history, philosophy, and thought. His final transformation was based not only on awareness of connections to Africa, but of the role of all Africans in a global struggle for human freedom.

Notes

1. John W. Blassingame, "A Model Afro-American Studies Program: The Results of a Survey" [pp. 229–240], in John W. Blassingame, ed., *New Perspective on Black Studies* (Urbana, Illinois: University of Illinois Press, 1973).
2. "WSU Protest Spotlights Black Pride Resurgence," *Detroit Free Press*, April 16, 1989.
3. See Marvin W. Peterson, Robert T. Blackburn, et al., *Black Students on White Campuses: The Impacts of Increased Black Enrollments* (Ann Arbor, Michigan: Institute for Social Research, University of Michigan, 1978), 31–37.
4. Institute of the Black World, *Curriculum Development Project: Final Report*, 1982.
5. Ibid.
6. W.E.B. Du Bois, *The World and Africa* (New York: New World Paperbacks, 1965), 189–197.
7. Perry A. Hall, "Systematic and Thematic Principles for Black Studies," *Journal of Negro Education*, Summer 1984.
8. Molefi Asante, *Afrocentricity* (Philadelphia: Third World Press, 1988), 5.
9. W.E.B. Du Bois, "Our Spiritual Striving," in *The Souls of Black Folk* (New York: Fawcett World Library, 1965 [1898]).
10. Bernard M. Magubane, *The Ties that Bind: African-American Consciousness of Africa* (Trenton, New Jersey: African World Press, 1987), Preface.
11. Perry A. Hall, "Rethinking Racial Group Identity," *Journal of Social and Behavioral Sciences* (forthcoming).
12. Molefi Asante, *The Afrocentric Idea* (Philadelphia: Temple University Press, 1987), 7.
13. Asante, *Afrocentricity*, 5.
14. Ibid., 1.
15. Ibid., 28.
16. William J. Wilson, *The Declining Significance of Race* (Chicago: University of Chicago Press, 1980).
17. "WSU Protest Spotlights Black Pride Resurgence," *Detroit Free Press*, April 16, 1989.
18. Tommie Lee Lott, "Marooned in America: Black Urban Youth Culture and Social Pathology" (unpublished paper).
19. Ibid.
20. Ibid.
21. "Rappers: Bringing the Six O'Clock News," *Detroit Metro Times*, February 17, 1990.

21

A Blueprint for African American Economic Development

Robert E. Weems

Robert E. Weems is an Assistant Professor of History at the University of
Missouri-Columbia. He received the Ph.D. in History from the University of
Wisconsin-Madison.—The Western Journal of Black Studies, *Summer 1993,
Vol. 17. No. 2*

The 1990s appear to have spawned a resurgence of Black nationalist sentiment among African Americans.[1] Moreover, being witnessed is a corresponding resurgence of interest in racial "self-help." Historically, these
complimentary doctrines, Black nationalism and racial self-help, have coalesced
in the promotion of greater (internal) African American economic development.
Unfortunately, for a variety of reasons, previous attempts to develop a truly viable
Black economic infrastructure have failed. Also, some observers have questioned
the efficacy of African Americans' long-time preoccupation with establishing an
independent economic base. This article will both establish the justification for
internal African American economic development as well as offer a program that
may circumvent past failures in this crucial area.

Although most African Americans, historically, have viewed Black business
development as a positive phenomenon, some Black scholars have vehemently
criticized both Black businesspersons and their enterprises.[2] Edward Franklin
Frazier's 1957 study *Black Bourgeoisie* remains, perhaps, the most noteworthy
work associated with the anti-Black business scholarly tradition. Among other
things, Professor Frazier described Black business as "one of the main elements in
the world of make-believe which the black bourgeoisie has created to compensate
for its feelings of inferiority in a white world dominated by business enterprise."[3]

Despite the deceased Frazier's continuing preeminence as a social scientist, his
assertions in *Black Bourgeoisie* concerning Black business were seriously flawed.
First, his direct association of Black business with the Black bourgeoisie appeared
based upon cursory observation rather than census data.[4] Moreover, Frazier's

stated intention *not* to do a comparative study resulted in gross distortion.[5] Having done the comparative research that Frazier failed to do, this writer has discovered that his non-comparative description of Black economic development erroneously implied that attention given internal African American business development represented a pathological condition unique to Blacks.

The Chicago Foreign Language Press Survey conducted by the Works Progress Administration (WPA) in 1942, and currently housed at the University of Illinois-Chicago, gives scholars access to translated versions of newspapers published by a variety of ethnic groups in Chicago during the late 19th and early 20th centuries. As the following examples indicate, most groups viewed internal economic development in positive terms.

The December 14, 1910, issue of *Dziennik Zwiazkowy*, a daily Polish newspaper, featured an editorial entitled "Polish Trade." This ethnic publication asserted:[6]

> Instead of taking our money to strangers and frequently fattening our most bitter enemies, let the Poles take it to their own people, let them support Polish trade and commerce…Other nationalities will not support Polish trade and commerce because they have their own. It depends entirely upon Poles to keep their hard-earned money in Polish hands…We must understand that only through mutual strength and support can we hope to raise industry and commerce in America to a place where it will be at least equal to that of strangers. Let us therefore, patronize Polish businessmen as much as possible and not patronize strangers, because other nationalities do not support us in anything.

The November 21, 1913, *Lietuva*, a weekly Lithuanian newspaper, featured an article entitled "Lithuanian Woman Opens Factory." This article not only praised the efforts of Miss Mary Radzeviciute (the owner of the factory in question) but stated "we urge our Lithuanian women to go to a person of their nationality when in need of goods."[7]

A final example of White ethnic preoccupation with internal economic development appeared in the May 22, 1920, *Ukrania*, a publication of Ukranian-Americans. An article entitled "Ukranian Business in America" included the following:[8]

> A bright spot for the Ukranian immigrant in America is a large, clean Ukranian factory in one of the largest cities, Chicago…It employs a good number of Ukranian people. It is a joy to work in this factory. There they manufacture beautiful lamp phonographs…The inventor of this lovely is Mr. Peter R. Gonsky…This benefactor teaches us that not by speaking, nor by rambling politics, shall we be strong and renowned, but by commerce, trade, manufacturing, and business…Mr. Peter R. Gonsky is a bright living example for us, showing us that we should engage in commerce, manufacturing, and business if we want any power for ourselves and our native country.

This data strongly suggests that, during the late 19th and early 20th centuries, most non-Anglo-Saxon Americans regarded internal economic development as a necessary prerequisite for full acceptance in the United States. The subsequent experience of African and European Americans, however, proved to be quite different. While cultural distinctions among European Americans became blurred due to intermarriage, the African American community remained a distinct, separate enclave. Consequently, while calls for separate Polish, Lithuanian, and Ukranian business development in America have all but disappeared in recent decades, sentiment for internal African American economic development remains strong.

Despite African Americans' historic interest in community-based business, the Black community, collectively, has been unable to establish a viable economic base (notwithstanding the fact that, before the Great Depression, African Americans throughout the United States were relatively successful in establishing a myriad of banks, insurance companies, and retail concerns). Some have claimed that this situation is a consequence of African Americans' general lack of business acumen. Others have argued that American racism has been the primary impediment to Black economic development. Quite frankly, it appears the traditional focus on *obstacles* has unduly influenced Blacks concerning mass-based African American economic development. While it would not be easy, evidence suggests that the Black community can, indeed, exert greater economic self-determination.

The key element in a potential, mass-based revitalization of the African American community revolves around a concept referred to as the "rotating credit association." This economic strategy has been defined as: "An association formed by a core of participants who agree to make regular contributions to a fund which is given, in whole or in part, to each contributor in rotation…In many parts of the non-Western world, this type of association serves or has served many of the functions of Western banks."[9]

According to Ivan H. Light, author of *Ethnic Enterprise in America: Business and Welfare among Chinese, Japanese, and Blacks*, Asian immigrants to the United States brought the rotating credit association concept with them (called "hui" by the Chinese, "ko" by the Japanese). Moreover, prospective Asian entrepreneurs used "hui" or "ko" to circumvent the discriminatory lending practices of White American financial institutions.[10]

Although the rotating credit association concept is found in African tradition (the Yoruba called it "esusu"),[11] African Americans have been unable to use this method of raising capital to the extent that Asians have. Significantly, Ivan Light's description of what makes rotating credit associations *work* provides a clue as to why African Americans have not been able to utilize this economic strategy:[12]

> The advantages of rotating credit depend entirely on the *mutual trust* of members of the clubs; without such mutual trust, neither "hui" or "ko"

could have functioned at all…Moreover, the advantages of rotating credit depended upon *widespread mutual confidence.* Only widespread, institutionalized mutual confidence in the community at large could permit the ready formation of rotating credit associations in response to spontaneous individual needs, and only widespread mutual confidence could encompass enough persons to render the rotating fund large enough to fill commercial needs. If confidence were restricted to very small groups, then the rotating credit associations could not attain great flexibility in formation nor sufficient size to render commercially useful portions. [emphasis mine]

During the period of slavery in North America, transplanted Africans, among other things, lived in an environment that fostered intra-racial mistrust. "House" slaves tended to mistrust "field" slaves (and vice-versa). Moreover, slave revolts or other less spectacular demonstrations of Black self-determination constantly ran the risk of being curtailed because a "faithful" slave would reveal such plans to the authorities.

This unfortunate legacy continues to plague the African American community. Lack of collective direction, or unity, keeps the Black community at a marked disadvantage in American society. It should be pointed out, however, that *unity* and *uniformity* are not necessarily synonymous. This is especially important when one considers the issue of African American economic development.

One of the negative forces that inhibits Black economic empowerment is the fruitless debate as to what represents the "best" means by which African Americans can achieve economic self-determination. Some believe that African Americans' only hope for substantive progress is through the aggressive development of more individually owned Black business enterprises. Others contend that African Americans' best hope lay in the destruction of the capitalist system and the establishment of an egalitarian socialist state.

While Blacks have been arguing among themselves, other groups with more clearly defined goals have made considerable economic inroads in the African American community. For instance, Koreans, using their own version of the rotating credit association, have all but monopolized inner-city business activity in recent decades.

Another sad consequence of African Americans' internal bickering concerning the *means* for achieving Black economic empowerment is the massive waste of economic resources currently available to Black people. Although it has been estimated that African Americans have a collective yearly income of between $250–$300 billion dollars, a relatively miniscule proportion of this sum is being used to promote/support African American commercial enterprise.[13] The rest, significantly, appears to be spent in shiny suburban shopping malls, which further enhances White corporate America's profit margin.

It appears that the rotating credit association concept provides African Americans with a real opportunity to break free from the crippling inertia that keeps them from fulfilling their economic potential. As shall be graphically demonstrated later, it is flexible to the extent that Blacks, who utilize this economic strategy, can focus upon *either* individual entrepreneurial or communal development projects. Moreover, and more importantly, the rotating credit association may, in fact, offer the last and most realistic opportunity to halt the steady decline of African American communities throughout the United States.

A walk or drive through a typical inner-city in contemporary America reminds one of Charles Dickens' classic work, *A Tale of Two Cities*, when he stated: "These were the best of times. These were the worst of times." (A tragic commentary of contemporary African American life is that many Blacks, especially if they do not reside in the inner-city, are quite apprehensive about *walking* around in the "hood.") Although some *individual* African Americans are faring quite well, a significant proportion of Blacks, especially those living in urban enclaves, are literally struggling to survive. In addition, the community pride that existed before the advent of racial integration has been replaced by an apparent apathy concerning the steady deterioration of the Black community's infrastructure. African Americans living in inner-cities generally want to get out. African Americans living outside the inner-city generally want to stay out. Unless African Americans are prepared to witness the virtual extinction of historic Black enclaves (and their traditional institutions), they must devise a means to revitalize their communities. The rotating credit association appears to offer such a possibility.

At this point, it is appropriate to ask: How does a rotating credit association actually operate? Essentially, an "esusu" (the Yoruba name for this phenomenon) enables a group of individuals to pool their resources for either individual or group projects.[14] The following example illustrates this process.

Suppose there is a group of 50 African Americans who want to establish an "esusu," whereby each individual agrees to pay $25 a week into a collective pool for 50 weeks. The total worth of this "esusu" is $62,500. The members of the "esusu" could disburse this sum in a variety of ways. First, the members may decide to pay each member a lump sum of $1,250 on a rotating (weekly) basis during the life of the "esusu" ($1,250 X 50 = $62,500). Second, members of the "esusu" may decide not to take their weekly individual shares; this would provide these individuals with $62,500 to collectively invest in a particular project. Lastly, the members of an "esusu" may decide to take a portion of their individual weekly shares and invest the rest in a group project.

It should be noted that the above scenario represents just *one* "esusu" cycle. Ideally, members of an "esusu" will continue their special relationship on an on-going basis. Tables 1, 2, and 3 illustrate how the "esusu" could work for African Americans from a variety of economic backgrounds.

Although the rotating credit association appears to be a solid, straightforward, and flexible means of accumulating capital, African Americans, because of their unique historical experience, may have difficulty in implementing such a system.

As stated earlier, the rotating credit association cannot exist without mutual trust. Sadly, mutual trust has not been a prevalent historic characteristic of the African American community. Still, considering the seriousness of the situation Blacks find themselves in, they must attempt to transcend traditional internal discord.

Table 1.
The African American "Esusu"*
$10, $25, $50, $100 Weekly Payments
50 Members

	Number of Weeks	Number of Weekly Shares Disbursed	Lump Sum Amount	Total Pool
$10	50	1	$500	$25,000
$25	50	1	1,250	62,500
$50	50	1	2,500	125,000
$100	50	1	5,000	250,000

*The number of weeks listed, along with the number of members, are arbitrary figures for the purpose of illustration. The life cycle of an "esusu" can be less than 50 weeks. Moreover, the number of "esusu" members can be less than 50. Flexibility is one of the strengths of the "esusu."

Table 2.
The African American "Esusu"
$10, $25, $50, $100 Weekly Payments
100 Members

	Number of Weeks	Number of Weekly Shares Disbursed	Lump Sum Amount	Total Pool
$10	50	2	$500	$50,000
$25	50	2	1,250	125,500
$50	50	2	2,500	250,000
$100	50	2	5,000	500,000

Table 3.
The African American "Esusu"
$10, $25, $50, $100 Weekly Payments
500 Members

	Number of Weeks	Number of Weekly Shares Disbursed	Lump Sum Amount	Total Pool
$10	50	10	$500	$250,000
$25	50	10	1,250	625,000
$50	50	10	2,500	1,250,000
$100	50	10	5,000	2,500,000

Perhaps, the ideal vehicle to promote the "esusu" concept within the African American community is through the family. In recent years, large-scale family reunions have proliferated among Blacks. If families used these gatherings to discuss establishing an "esusu," this would represent a giant step in the right direction. Moreover, other groups that share a communal bond, such as churches and fraternal organizations, also appear to be ideal places to establish an "esusu."

In this era of increasing government deficits and decreasing social welfare expenditures, the "esusu" represents an opportunity for the African American community to exercise greater economic self-determination. This is not to say that African Americans should cease relying upon federal, state, and local governments for services (that Black tax payments help fund). The Black community, however, needs to develop a new relationship with governmental bodies.

It is widely acknowledged (and lamented) that adverse circumstances have forced some Blacks to seek government "welfare" for *individuals* (such as General Assistance, Aid For Dependent Children, and Food Stamps). Moreover, African American recipients of this form of government assistance have been stigmatized. On the other hand, American businesses regularly receive *unstigmatized* government "welfare" referred to as tax credits and price supports. While it, unfortunately, appears that a significant proportion of African Americans will continue relying upon government assistance for individuals, a major goal of the Black community should be obtaining more of the government assistance available to businesses. Widespread implementation of the "esusu" could enable African Americans to do just that.

While increased business ownership does not represent a panacea for the African American community, it can assist in the resuscitation of urban Black America. Quite frankly, the non-Black-owned businesses that operate in African American enclaves have no special incentive to revitalize these neighborhoods. Consequently, it should not be surprising that the infrastructure of Black America is crumbling.

Perhaps the only way to prevent the physical (and spiritual) destruction of historic African American enclaves is through a community-based effort centered around the "esusu." In fact, it appears ironic and fitting that African Americans, the most educated and technologically advanced Blacks in the world, may ultimately have to rely upon a traditional African concept, the "esusu," to achieve some semblance of economic self-determination.

Notes

1. For example, an examination of the "rap" lyrics of such popular groups (and individuals) as Public Enemy, KRS 1, and X-Clan reveals numerous unambiguous references to racial unity and positive collective action.
2. Among the African American scholars who have promoted a negative interpretation of Black businesspersons were/are: Abram Harris, *The Negro as Capitalist: A Study of Banking and Business* (1936);

Robert L. Allen, *Black Awakening in Capitalist America* (1969); Earl Ofari, *The Myth of Black Capitalism* (1970); and Manning Marable, *How Capitalism Underdeveloped Black America* (1983).

3. Edward Franklin Frazier, *Black Bourgeoisie: The Rise of a New Middle Class in America* (New York: Collier Books, 1962; originally published, 1957), 129.

4. Although Edward Franklin Frazier and other critics of Black business development have equated this phenomena with an exploitative middle class, actual data, such as the 1929 census of Black business activity, presents a far different picture. This study enumerated 25,701 Black retail enterprises with net sales of $101,146,043. The average net sales for these 25,701 African-American enterprises was $3,935. This compared to annual net sales of over $32,000 for the 1,513,592 White-owned retail enterprises during the same period. These figures strongly suggest that the vast majority of Black businesses were "Mom and Pop" operations run by individuals of limited means. See Charles E. Hall, *Negroes in the United States, 1920–1932* (Washington, D.C.: U.S. Bureau of the Census, 1935), 496–498.

5. Frazier, *Black Bourgeoisie*, 13.

6. The Chicago Foreign Language Press Survey, University of Illinois-Chicago, Microfilm Roll #49.

7. Ibid., Microfilm Roll #42.

8. Ibid., Microfilm Roll #67.

9. Ivan H. Light, *Ethnic Enterprise in America: Business and Welfare among Chinese, Japanese, and Blacks* (Berkeley: University of California Press, 1972), 22–23.

10. Ibid., 20–21, 26–30.

11. Ibid., 30.

12. Ibid., 58–59.

13. David H. Swinton, "The Economic Status of African-Americans: Permanent Poverty and Inequality," in *The State of Black America 1991* (New York: National Urban League, 1991), 28. Significantly, the top 100 African-American enterprises, according to *Black Enterprise* (see June 1992, 102), had combined sales of just under $8 billion dollars in 1991.

14. Eva Krapf-Askari, *Yoruba Towns and Cities: An Inquiry into the Nature of Social Urban Phenomena* (London: Oxford University Press, 1969), 106–107; William Bascom, *The Yoruba of Southwestern Nigeria* (New York: Holt, Rinehart, and Winston, 1969), 27; N. A. Fadipe, *The Sociology of the Yoruba* (Ibadan, Nigeria: Ibadan University Press, 1970), 256.

22

Perception of Power/Control among African Americans: A Developmental Approach

Rudolph A. Cain

Rudolph A. Cain is a Mentor/Professor of Educational Studies and Community and Human Services at Empire State College, State University of New York. He received the doctorate degree in Adult Education Administration with a secondary specialty in Psychology from Columbia University/Teachers College.—The Western Journal of Black Studies, *Fall 1994, Vol. 18. No. 3*

Abstract

This exploratory, cross-sectional study examined the impact of independent variables on the adult developmental cycle of African Americans. Specifically, this research investigated shifts in locus of control and emerging prominent life themes, and the impact of racism on locus of control as it relates to negotiating stages of adult development. A total of 33 African American professionals participated in the study—18 females and 15 males.

Locus of control as a variable defines an individual's perception of control, influenced either by inner strengths or outer influences such as fate. Quantitative measures of this variable in the current study were achieved through the administration of a reconstructed, modified version of the Reid/Ware Locus of Control scale. Responses were obtained across four (4) developmental stages of the Levinsonian paradigm. Thus, participants retrospectively responded to the same scale items four (4) different times. On the other hand, prominent life themes had been identified earlier in a more expanded study, using a modified version of the Malatesta and Culver Life Themes Coding instrument, which had been originally designed for a group of White female graduates of a prestigious, predominantly White institution. As regards the variable racism, five (5) items from the reconstructed, modified Reid/Ware scale, which dealt with aspects of prejudice, discrimination, and racism, were isolated, synthesized, and analyzed.

In this study, it was found that participants were consistently more inner-directed, particularly following young adulthood. The findings also suggests that shifts in perception of control did not reflect the prominence of any particular themes. Rather, certain themes were consistently prominent across the developmental stages in an atmosphere of perceived control. Racism was found to not impact adversely on the group's sense of control over its life. Rather, such encounters served to strengthen inner-directedness.

* * *

Harrington (1985) found that the perception of personal control among "successful" Black women contributes significantly to "success." Success was operationally defined as extraordinary levels of accomplishments in business, academia, or government service. Yet, an important segment of the literature on locus of control focuses on "powerlessness." For instance, Miriels (1970) and Gurin (1969) suggest that externality may be a function of how the individual perceives societal institutions. Furthermore, the findings of Gore and Rotter (1971), Gurin and Epps (1975), on personal efficacy, and Bullough (1972) on political alienation, are noteworthy. They found that because middle-income African Americans tend to express more confidence in their ability to manipulate the social environment, they are likely to cope more effectively with external stressors. Racism as a variable in the current study is considered an external stressor, subjected to individual manipulation and to be problem-solved.

Lefcourt (1976) poignantly notes in his research that "whether people or other species for that matter, believe that they are actors and can determine their own fate within limits, will be seen to be of critical importance in the way in which they cope with stress and engage in challenges." Implicit in Levinson's development stage/age linked theory (Table 1) is the presumption that significant tasks associated with various stages of development may be both stressful and/or challenging situations depending greatly on perception of control. The Levinsonian

Table 1.
Developmental Stages in Early and Middle Adulthood

	65	**LATE ADULTHOOD**	
	60	LATE ADULT TRANSITION	**MIDDLE ADULTHOOD**
	55	Culmination of Middle Adulthood	
	50	Age 50 Transition	
	45	Entering Middle Adulthood	
40		MID-LIFE TRANSITION	
33		Settling Down	**EARLY ADULTHOOD**
28		Age 30 Transition	
22		Entering the Adult World	
17		EARLY ADULT TRANSITION	
CHILDHOOD AND ADOLESCENCE			

model posits a theory about eras and stages of adulthood. The focal theoretical assumption is that growth and development throughout the life cycle proceeds with alternating periods of "structure-building" and "structure-changing," responding continuously to one of three levels of life structures: (1) socio-cultural world, which deals with the individual's relationship to family, peers, and institutions; (2) self and values, which focuses on beliefs, morality, and meaning; and (3) participation in the world, which relates to the quality and extent of one's activities. Throughout each of these stages of adulthood, the individual is confronted with a series of "tasks" (see Table 2). The manner in which individuals respond to tasks (e.g. questioning the existing life structure during the Age 30 transition) during the various eras and stages of adulthood will determine the course and quality of development. Also, quite central to this theory are the role of the mentor and the significance of the Dream; the former, a counselor/ adviser who steers the individual along the career development path, and the latter, constituting a sense of self (i.e., partly fantasy and partly reality) in the world.

Table 2.
Selected Levinsonian Age-linked Stages and Corresponding Tasks

Stage	Tasks

Entering the Adult World 23–27	1. Fashion a provisional structure that provides a workable link between the valued self and the adult society:
	    a. explore possibilities for adult living—keep options open, avoid strong commitments, maximize alternatives; and
	    b. create a stable life structure.

Age Thirty Transition 28–32	1. Questions the provisional structure of "Entering the Adult World." 2. Modify the provisional structure. **Major Sub-Tasks/Novice Period** 1. Forming the dream. 2. Initiating mentoring relationship. 3. Forming peer relationship. 4. Forming occupational choices.
Settling Down 33–39	1. Establishing a "niche." 2. Advancement, progression on a timetable. 3. Settling for a few key choices and building a broader structure around them.

Mid-Life Transition 40–45	1 Come to terms with past; terminate and initiate a new basis on which to live in the future
	2. Terminate the era of Early Adulthood.
	3. Mid-Life individuation
	    a. reappraising the past
	    b. disillusioning

In addition to the likely association of locus of control with the manner in which individuals negotiate tasks of adulthood, locus of control seems closely related to Weiner's (1980) attribution theories of motivation, which describe how the individual's explanations, justifications, and excuses influence motivation.

Life themes are categories of thematic and affective content. Malatesta and Culver (1984) provide the following description:

> We distinguish six (6) types of affiliation: affiliation with an unspecified family member or simple references to the "family"; affiliation with husband/wife, affiliation with lover, and with colleagues, children and relatives. Lack of affiliation was partitioned into loneliness, lack of affiliation with specified family member, lack of affiliation with husband, children, other relatives, lover, and colleagues. For the success and lack of success categories, we distinguished among themes having to do with one's success, that of one's lover, or husband and that of one's children.

Affiliation themes, for instance, focused on references to liking another person, sharing activities, interacting with other persons, comradery, etc....In addition to affiliation themes, affective content themes such as anger/aggression were additional categories of themes.

Racism and its adverse effect on dimensions of growth and development of African Americans are well documented in the literature. The works of Pruitt and Knowles (1969), Kovel (1970), Cross (1970), Grier and Cobb (1968), Comer (1969), Sillen and Alexander (1972), Franklin (1991) and Hacker (1992) are noteworthy. The impact of racism on Black professionals is well documented by Hare (1973), Fleming (1976), Calnek (1970), Hernton (1965), Brown (1980), and Davis and Watson (1982). Importantly, Shirely Teper (1977) reminds us that "if one is a member of the society's majority culture, institutions continually reinforce one's sense of self. But people of a minority culture may get little or no confirmation of their group worth from the institutions that mediate the society for them." She further observes that "ethnicity is a prism through which human behavior is both shaped and perceived. We have paid little attention to its pervasiveness in determining perceptions, values, attitudes and behavior, as well as its effects on social institutions." Also, the recent work of Cross (1991), which provides a sterling historical record of research on "black identity," offers a plethora of implications about the likely impact of racism on shaping self-concept. However, noteworthy is Ruffin's (1989) observation that "although several models (e.g., Cross, 1978; Harrell, 1979) have been proposed to clarify the patterns used by Blacks in adapting to racial situations, none discussed adaptive patterns vis-à-vis adult development." Consequently, the struggle to confront racism may constitute a significant developmental task for African Americans.

Therefore, the purposes of this study are twofold: (1) to examine the direction of locus of control across developmental stages and the corresponding emergence of prominent life themes; and (2) to explore the impact of racism on perception of control. Consequently, it is hypothesized that perception of control will reflect shifts in the prominence of life themes, and that racism will impact adversely on perception of control.

Method

Study Participants

The participants in this study were 18 females and 15 males, all volunteers. They were recruited through the professional and personal contacts of the investigator, himself an African American. The age range for this group was 28–55 and all participants were residents of the New York metropolitan area.

Though the sample was not randomly chosen and small in size, thus raising questions of representation and generalizability, the acquisition of some important baseline data outweighs these limitations. For instance, with the exception of the research works of Levinson (1978), Gooden (1981), Harrington (1985), and Ruffin (1989), African Americans have been almost totally absent in the literature on adult development. The thrust of most studies have been on a White, middle class cohort. In addition, there is a dearth of research that assesses locus of control among African American adults. To this researcher's knowledge, there is no known research that examines shifts in locus of control across developmental stages.

All study participants were middle income persons who would likely reflect middle class values in terms of education and general life style. This cohort had been identified in order to provide a basis for any type of subsequent comparative analysis with benchmark studies that have concentrated primarily on a middle class cohort.

A Cover Letter, Background Questionnaire, and Survey Response to Levinson's stages and corresponding tasks, and the reconstructed, modified Reid/Ware Rotter Scale, were mailed to all participants.

Table 3 presents selected demographic characteristics of the group. A separate category for Occupation was not included primarily because occupations clearly clustered around three broad areas—teaching/counseling, social work, and managerial related professions. Exceptions were Physician (1), Lawyer (1), and Law Enforcement Officers (2). On the other hand, the reader might question the inclusion of Religion/Church affiliation. However, the role and influence of the Black church in the African American community is indisputable, and therefore, provides relevant background information.

Study participants were interviewed, averaging four to five hours. Therefore, considering the needed time for the completion of all research related activities, participants invested a minimum of 6–8 hours. This reported research focuses on several dimensions of a larger study.

Instruments and Procedures

In this study, the modified Reid/Ware version of the locus of control scale was used because the literature individuates extensive use of this scale. Permission

Table 3.
Selected Background Characteristics of Study Participants
N = 33
Age Range–32–55; Average Age–43

	Males (15)	Female (18)
Marital Status		
Never Married	5	7
First Marriage	8	6
Divorced/Widowed	3	5
Age at first time of marriage		
under 18	0	3
18–21	4	4
22–25	6	7
26–29	2	2
over 29	3	2
Education (highest level)		
Some College	4	5
Undergraduate degree	1	5
Graduate degree	10	8
Income		
No income	0	1
Under $15,000	2	3
$15,000–$24,000	7	8
$25,000–$34,000	3	3
$35,000 and over	3	3
Religious/church affiliation during pre-adult period		
Great influence	7	8
Some influence	6	8
Little or no influence	2	2

had been obtained in writing from the developers of the scale to further modify it in order to include items that would more aptly elicit responses regarding perceptions about discrimination, prejudice, and racism. This scale originally consisted of approximately 23 forced-choice paired items, each set representing a perception of internal or external control. Ultimately, a reconstructed version was designed to both include additional items as well as elicit responses to the same sets of statements across four (4) developmental stages. Both the Reid/Ware and the Reconstructed scales were field tested on two different groups of African American professionals, who resembled the SES profile for the study cohort. This procedure, part of the larger study, produced a finding of no significance in the mean scores on both instruments, thus establishing validity of the reconstructed scale. Subsequently, the reconstructed modified Reid/Ware was completed by each study participant, with instructions that he/she mentally imagine how he/she would respond at each hypothetical stage. Though reliance on recall and introspection were critical, recall has been effective in certain methodologies such as the Critical Incident Technique. The works of Flanagan (1954) and Cain (1977) are noteworthy. Also, corroborating the results from the locus of control scale with observations culled from narrative interviews, is a good test of validity. Using a median split method as a means of insuring uniformity across stages, a grand mean of 6.75 was computed. That is, scores below 6.75 were considered internal; and those above 6.75, were deemed external. Thus, standard deviations and two-tail tests of significance were computed for each stage; the latter enabling a determination of the significance of differences between means.

Once the direction of control for each stage was determined, the ultimate objective was to examine corresponding life themes for each stage. Prominent life themes had been identified earlier by a Panel of Professional Coders, using an expanded (i.e., 35 to 47 items) version of the Malatesta and Culver scale/Coding for Life Themes Manual, since the scale had been originally designed for a different cohort. The expanded version included items/themes (e.g., oppression) that were considered reflective of some perceived experiences of African Americans. These additional items had been rated by a Panel of Professional Coders and necessary changes made. Subsequently, a worksheet, listing the 47 themes under each of the four developmental stages under investigation, was prepared to facilitate the tallying process, and the ultimate ranking of themes for each stage. For the purposes of the current study, only those six (6) themes dealing with racism and its machinations were analyzed. Baldwin (1965) and Haviland (1983) found that the frequency of the appearance of a theme in narrative materials is an index of the dynamic.

In terms of instrumental and procedural techniques used to assess the impact of racism on developmental tasks, anecdotal observations from narrative interviews, an analysis of responses to relevant items from the reconstructed Reid/Ware modified Rotter scale, and the strength and prominence of relevant life themes were synthesized and analyzed.

Results

Locus of Control

The results shown in Table 4 reflect comparisons made between the various stages/age groups. A two-tail test of significance was used to analyze the data.

For the first two comparisons (I vs. II, and II vs. III), the mean differences were significant at the .001 level, which indicated an overall tendency to move toward internality. That is, as young adults, there was an initial proclivity to be more externally oriented or outer-directed; thus, supporting the findings of Gurin (1969) and Strickland (1965). As expected, Stage III vs. IV showed no

Table 4.

Mean Differences for Stage Comparisons on the Reconstructed
Modified Reid/Ware Scale (Locus of Control)

Stage/Age	N	X̄	S.D.	P-value
I. (22–27)	33	11.55	5.39	t = 3.62
II. (28–32)	33	7.93	4.90	p = <.001
II. (28–32)	33	7.93	4.90	t = 3.15
III. (33–39)	33	6.48	4.69	p = <.001
III. (33–39)	33	6.48	4.69	t = 1.60
IV. (40–45)	33	4.10	2.50	p = >.02

significance between means (t = 1.60, p = > .05). Those individuals were already operating at an internally oriented mode of locus of control.

Table 5 presents mean differences comparisons between stages for females. In the first set of comparisons (Stage I vs. Stage II), there was a significant difference found that indicated that during the age of 23–27, study participants tended to be more externally oriented than as older individuals (ages 28–32).

This suggests that a sense of internal control begins to emerge and become established somewhere between ages 28 and 32 years old. Corroborated evidence for this assumption is reflected by non-significant mean differences for the remaining stage comparisons (Stage II vs. Stage III, and Stage III vs. Stage IV). Simply put, Stages II through IV consisted of individuals who were internally oriented. The data also show that the individual's preference for an internal locus of control is stabilized throughout those stages.

Mean difference comparisons for males are shown in Table 6. Examination of this table indicates that at Stage I, study participants were externally oriented. No real difference was found between Stage II and Stage III. Somewhat surpris-

Table 5.

Mean Differences for Stage Comparisons for Females on the
Reconstructed Modified Reid/Ware Scale (Locus of Control)

Stage/Age	N	X̄	S.D.	P-value
I. (23–27)	18	11.00	4.80	t = 3.14
II. (28–32)	18	6.41	3.48	p = <.05
II. (28–32)	18	6.41	5.83	t = 1.8
III. (33–39)	18	3.46	3.16	p = >.05
III. (33–39)	18	5.83	4.50	t = 1.96
IV. (40–45)	18	3.16	2.65	p = >.05

ing, however, was the significant difference between means for Stage III vs. Stage IV. For the male participants in this study, this finding suggests that males were much more internally oriented at ages 40–45, than they were at 33–39 years old. It would be interesting to know whether this trend continued in the next stage, middle adulthood (ages 46–51); a subject for a possible extended study.

As Table 7 shows, as younger individuals, study participants, both females and males, were usually external in their attitude toward the world. The important finding here is the fact that no significant difference was found across the four stages. It appears from the data that the experiences of African American

Table 6.

Mean Differences for Stage Comparisons for Males on the Reconstructed Modified Reid/Ware Scale (Locus of Control)

Stage/Age	N	X̄	S.D.	P-value
I. (23–27)	15	9.60	8.07	t = 2.08
II. (28–32)	15	5.83	4.80	p = <.05
II. (28–32)	15	8.07	6.07	t = 1.56
III. (33–39)	15	4.80	3.16	p = >.05
III. (33–39)	15	6.07	4.11	t = 2.13
IV. (40–45)	15	3.16	2.24	p = <.05

Table 7.

Mean Differences for Stage Comparisons between Females and Males on the Reconstructed Modified Reid/Ware Scale (Locus of Control)

Stage/Age	N	X̄	S.D.	P-value
I. (23–27) – Females	18	11.00	4.80	
I. (23–27) – Males	15	9.64	5.83	
				t = 1.35
				p = >.05
II. (28–32) – Females	15	6.41	3.46	
II. (28–32) – Males	15	8.07	4.80	
				t = 1.48
				p = >.05
III. (33–39) – Females	18	5.83	3.16	
III. (33–39) – Males	15	6.07	3.16	
				t = .24
				p = >.05
IV. (40–45) – Females	18	4.50	2.65	
IV. (40–45) – Males	15	4.11	2.24	
				t = .95
				p = >.05

female and male participants in the study are not that much different from each other. Consistent with the previous tables (4–6), the onset of an internal orientation, at least for these study participants, occurs at Stage II (between ages 28 and 32 years old).

Prominent Life Themes

The ranking of prominent life themes was facilitated in the larger study. However, it was found that the prominence of certain themes varied across developmental stages. For instance, Success/Recognition and Competence/Lack of Competence were quite prominent as participants "Entered the Adult World" (ages 22 to 27). Yet, during the Mid-Life Transition (ages 39–45), the theme "Acceptance/Rejection" is quite prominent. Thus, there was not a consistent pattern in terms of the prominence of themes across developmental stages. However, one exception was the strong presence of Competence/Lack of Competence during the "Age 30 Transition (ages 28 to 32)" as was the case during the stage, "Entering the Adult World."

Impact of Racism

Encounters with prejudice, discrimination, and racism have been intricately woven into the experiences of African Americans. Consequently, it was expected that prominent themes such as Equalitarianism/Racism and Oppression/Alienation/Victimization would have been prominent themes among the study participants. However, based on the coding of themes and subsequent ranking by a Professional Panel of Coders, these themes were found not to rank high. Also, two (2) additional findings are particularly noteworthy: (1) the final question on the Background Information Survey, which was initially distributed to study participants, asked the question, "What would you consider to be the most negative factor that has influenced your development as an adult?" Subsequently, a content analysis of all open ended responses to this question revealed that racism was not an important factor. As a matter of fact, only two (2) respondents, both males, alluded to the negative impact of racism on their development; and (2) an analysis of five (5) paired items from the Reconstructed, modified, Locus of Control scale, which dealt specifically with attitudes and perceptions about racism, revealed a proclivity of study participants to not use or blame the system of institutionalized racism for any personal lack of opportunity, accomplishments, or success. Furthermore, observations from the interviews suggest an unabiding awareness of racism; yet, an over-riding motivation and drive to take charge of one's life in spite of racism. Rather vivid anecdotal content about prejudice, discrimination, and racism in the military, police department, and academia was provided by study participants. For instance, a seasoned police officer made the following observation:

There are certain assignments that I just will not get. The Police Brass don't give them to me based on my tendency to speak up. I am labeled militant; I am a bad guy. Therefore, "Watch him."

Another respondent, a Ph.D. college professor, relates the issue of competence/lack of competence to racism, when he observes:

When Blacks are competent and effective, Whites are often threatened and will frequently react through character assassination. Consequently, those Blacks who are pro-Black, yet, described by some Whites as anti-White, may never realize their fullest potential.

Though in both instances, there is a recognition of perceived racism, additional observations from the interviews with these respondents indicate that they were not fixated or obsessed with outer-directed influences such as racism, but were more focused on creating adaptive and coping strategies that were more inner-directed.

Discussion

Locus of Control and Prominent Life Themes

An analysis of the mean scores between stages suggests a consistent inclination toward internality. The observation is vividly reflected in the dominance of certain themes during stages in which participants perceived control or a lack of control. Furthermore, the mean scores indicate a consistent inclination toward internality as respondents moved through and between stages. It would seem that if this pattern continued (i.e., beyond the Mid-Life Transition, 39–45 years old), some interesting questions and issues should surface about dependency, powerlessness, and coping strategies among middle-aged and older African Americans. Of course, this would be a topic for another research project to evaluate; for instance, whether there is a continuing inclination toward internality or an emerging multi-dimensionality in locus of control.

First, let us take a look at the early stages corresponding themes and perception of control. During the "Entering Adult World" stage, there is a movement toward internality, with a corresponding dominance of the themes "Success/ Recognition" and "Competence/Lack of Competence." For most of the study participants, this period represented concrete evidence of achievement (e.g., college degree), thus providing impetus for assuming greater control of one's life and destiny.

The "Competence/Lack of Competence" theme continues to dominate during the "Age 30 Transition"—a period of introspection, evaluation, questioning, and assessment. The narrative interviews generally reflected a preoccupation with professional and career development concerns. At this particular junction, there is a realization of the need to expand one's options, both educationally and career-wise. Yet, there is also some stress and conflict associated with self-percep-tions—for instance, one's ability to compete with White counterparts.

On the other hand, during the "Settling Down Period," regarded as an opportunity to "come to grips" with what exists, there is a kind of acceptance and acquiescence regarding one's strengths and abilities to compete. Thus, the prominence and strength of the theme "Acceptance/ Rejection."

What is particularly noteworthy is the dominance of the theme "Hopeful/ Desperate" during the Mid-Life Transition, at which time most study partici-pants were gravitating back to external control. This observation may reflect some disillusionment with real or perceived control of one's destiny. Some respondents referred to the collective status of African Americans in terms of the dissonance between the promise of equal opportunity and the political reality, characterized by systematic racism and oppression at various levels and sectors of American society. During this period, there seems to have been a preoccupation with not only assessing one's own growth and development, but reassessing the collective gains of the race.

Though evidence suggests that collectively and individually the group felt an increasing sense of control over their lives, many experienced what Levinson calls the "process of 'disillusionment.'" Critically reassessing the past within the con-text of impacting on their own destinies and the destiny of their people might be considered an additional developmental task for African Americans. This aspect is particularly critical since many study participants see themselves as products of the social movements of the 1950s and 1960s and envisioned significant change, and saw themselves taking some responsibility for whatever change occurred. For instance, a male respondent noted:

> As a welfare worker, I got caught up in the whole social revolution—we were like doing things in welfare for the "power to the people" and the whole struggle for welfare rights. Yet, I wonder now what all of that meant, when we now witness hundreds of thousands of people in poverty and homelessness.

Then, there was the female respondent who reflected on the challenges of the period by commenting:

> We were excited about the possibilities of the 60s in terms of social change. My involvement in the African American Teachers' Association was an opportunity to challenge the conditions under which Blacks were educated [miseducated] in the New York City School system. Now, over 25 years later, the system is worst than ever.

Consequently, though many perceived themselves as being confronted with what is little or no change, yet many remain hopeful and some see the necessity for continuing struggle. The comments of one respondent, an activist during the 1960s, are noteworthy:

I have become mature about politics. You don't expect to see a political movement today and the results next week. That's what I have learned. The result
of what you're seeing now, our children will benefit from. That is political
maturity.

As noted earlier in the reporting of results, mean differences among females
were only significant between the stages "Entering Adult World" and "Age 30
Transition." In the former, the important tasks included exploring options and
choices and creating a stable life structure. In the latter, the individual is usually
confronted with modifying the provisional structure established in the former.
This finding is consistent with results from the field testing of the Reid/Ware
modified scale and the Reconstructed Reid/Ware modified scale. Also, noteworthy is the similarity between these reported results and those of Harrington
(1985), who found that successful Black women of poor background were often
more internally controlled than those of middle class background. Bear in mind
that during the "Settling Down Period" there is a focus on career advancement,
and during the "Mid-Life Transition" the individual reappraises the past and
undergoes the "process of disillusionment." Two (2) factors are particularly poignant: (1) the general profile of Harrington's successful women of poor background resembles the background profile of women in the current study (i.e.,
both groups were products of poor or working class background, holders of college degrees, and highly achievement-motivated), though Harrington's sample of
Black women had achieved significantly in their respective careers; and (2) the
age range for Harrington's sample was 40–45 and 32–55 for the current group of
study participants. The significance of the finding (i.e., internal orientation) in
the current study is that mean differences for locus of control were determined by
an examination of possible statistical differences between developmental stages.
Furthermore, noteworthy is the observation that Harrington's findings emerge
from a statistical analysis of locus of control within the context of his sample's
present or existing perception. Thus, as in the case of the current research, his
assessment of locus of control does not provide a retrospective and developmental
perspective, thus capturing possible changes or shifts in locus of control between
stages of development.

An analysis of the results for male study participants suggests that males,
like females, tended to be more outer-directed or external, until they reached
the "Settling Down" stage. It might also be noted that mean differences between
the "Settling Down" stage and the "Mid-Life Transition" stage were found to be
significant in terms of internality for this male cohort.

What is particularly interesting and noteworthy about the male cohort is
that narrative data revealed a more pronounced tendency to vacillate between
externality and internality, thus supporting the multi-dimensional possibilities
of locus of control.

The results of comparing the significance of mean differences between females and males across developmental stages support the stability of measures of internality and externality in that no real male/female differences emerged. This finding may suggest that the scale is a good reliable measure in this study. Gender differences would have suggested the presence of situational variables. Also, in looking at females and males separately, both showed significant differences between stages. Thus, one would expect no real differences between males and females across stages.

Over-all, the findings for both females and males reveal a general tendency toward internality, particularly following the "Entering the Adult World" stage. Interestingly, there were isolated instances revealed in the content of narrative interviews that were clearly indicative of externality rather than internality, which may suggest and support the multi-dimensionality of locus of control. Thus, it seems possible that in individual cases, the direction of control may change (i.e., within a particular stage), depending on the nature of the task. For instance, a 38-year-old single female, school teacher, who holds a Masters degree in Special Education, noted the following:

> I have reconciled myself to the fact that if I am to get married, fate will determine it as well as other paths in my life. And I think that if I am meant to get married, at some point in time, then that is what will happen.

Yet, during the same period of struggling to confront the marital issue, this individual was much more inner-directed in the area of career development.

Then, on the other hand, the comments of a male, Ph.D. college administrator, who admitted to being "gay" at the time of the interview, seem poignant:

> Following a serious prostate condition at age 30, my sexual activities were severely limited. Bouts of hemorrhaging had not been uncommon. I recalled that during this period of debilitation, I perceived my problems as punishment for being gay. I always thought that people did not know all the pain that I was going through: I saw my life as being cursed, not having had a father figure. I felt a fatalistic view of myself at the time, but nothing was ever going to go right in my life, which in my worst moments, is what I feel. Oh, I blamed God…I had a lot of arguments with Him, and I said, "If there is a God and I get up to heaven, He and I are going to have quite a few words."

At the same time that this individual was experiencing a severe medical crisis, responding with an external orientation, he was experiencing encounters with racism in graduate school. Yet, he had taken charge of his educational aspirations and completed the Ph.D., supporting an inner-directed or internal orientation.

Therefore, the above scenarios suggest that the nature of circumstances and events in the lives of people may determine the locus of control orientation, even within the same stage of development. Consequently, situations, rather than specific stages, may impact more significantly on the direction of locus of control.

The general finding regarding locus of control—that is, the propensity of the study group toward internality during adulthood—seems consistent with the success patterns of this population. Given the awareness of institutionalized racism, this group seems to have clearly determined that it must take responsibility for what happens to it. Otherwise, a less encouraging pattern of success might be the rule. Furthermore, the data in this study that is narrative and statistically descriptive, strongly support the assumption that the perception of power and control among middle class African Americans may greatly determine the qualitative responses to specific tasks associated with various stages of development. Therefore, if one is to fully understand and appreciate the range of behavior responses of African Americans to developmental tasks, this understanding must be grounded in a realistic appraisal of power or powerlessness in affecting behavior. Also, confronting racism from the "cradle to the grave" may constitute an additional developmental task for African Americans, thus necessitating the expansion of Levinson's tasks.

More importantly, as previously noted, throughout the adult developmental stages, there was a general tendency toward internal control (i.e., no real observable shifts in locus of control). Therefore, the hypothesis that shifts in perception of control reflect the prominence of certain life themes is not supported by the data, primarily because again, there were no real observable shifts. Rather, it was found that certain themes—Success/Recognition, Competence/Lack of Competence, and certain affiliation themes—were consistently prominent across the developmental stages in a consistent atmosphere of perceived control. Consequently, one can merely speculate that had there been real observable shifts in locus of control, prominent themes might have been different.

Impact of Racism

Viewed as a theoretical hypothesis within the context of its adverse affect on creating a sense of powerlessness, racism and its impact on this study group was not supported in the study—particularly in terms of accomplishing basic developmental tasks. Yet, across developmental stages, the pervasiveness of racism and its machinations tended to generate additional developmental tasks for African Americans, requiring a cornucopia of coping strategies. Ruffin (1989) found similar results. For instance, in the formative stages of development, anger and rage were sometimes the response to subtle or blatant forms of racism, ultimately transforming anger and rage into motivation for taking greater control of one's life and destiny. Therefore, the respondents in this study tended to see racism as having less of an adverse affect on negotiating developmental tasks than their own ability, capacity, and determination to achieve and succeed. This finding is somewhat confirmed by Edwards and Polite (1992) when they note the following:

> Though they will certainly experience racism, successful blacks seldom give into the thinking of racial victim. They neither expect the Man to save them,

nor blame the Man for all the problems and injustices in society. They recognize racism's reality and its virulence, but just don't give into its debilitation.

Conclusion

The reader should be cautious about drawing definitive inferences and conclusions from this study, primarily because of a number of real or potential limitations. First, the sample is one of convenience, and thus may not be representative. Second, clearly a cross-sectional method used in assessing developmental patterns cannot capture reliable variations over time that would strengthen the validity of findings. Third, the possibility of multidimensionality of the locus of control instrument camouflaging real differences and variations exists. Yet, there appears to be numerous possibilities for future research. For instance, the finding that during the mid-life transition (40–45) there is a strong presence of internality among both males and females, may suggest a peak in locus of control. This poses an interesting question in light of economic and other social indicators, which often necessitate, for instance, career changes during this stage.

However, for those in the helping professions such as counseling and mental health, the findings may provide some valuable insights that might be used as diagnostic markers for presenting problems, and ultimately the creation of strategies and techniques for various forms of supportive intervention.

Acknowledgements

The author wishes to acknowledge the invaluable support and assistance of Dr. Andrew Henderson, research consultant, and the Panel of Professional Coders—Dr. Joelle Carroll, Dr. Vincent Wallace (posthumously), Dr. Raymond Weston, and Ms. Christine Perry. He expresses indebtedness to two colleagues, Dr. Timothy Lehman and Dr. Miriam Tatzel, who provided critical comments on very early drafts of this paper. Also, he is most grateful for the interest, candor, and trust of the Study Participants.

References

Baldwin, A. 1965. "A Method for Investigating the Single Personality," in E. A. Southwell and M. Merbaum (eds.), *Personality: Readings in Theory and Research*. Belmont: Wadsworth.

Browne, R. 1980. "The Black Middle Class Defined," *Ebony*, September, 44–49.

Bullough, B. 1972. "Alienation in the Ghetto," in C. Bullock and H. Rogers (eds.), *Black Political Attitudes*. Chicago: Markam.

Cain, R. 1981. "Critical Incidents and Critical Requirements in Mentoring," *Alternative Higher Education*, Vol. 6, 111–127.

Calnek, M. 1970. "Radical Factors in the Counter-Transference: The Black Therapist and Black Client," *American Journal of Orthopsychiatry*, Vol. 126, 802–806.

Comer, J. 1969. "White Racism: Its Root, Form, and Function," *American Journal of Orthopsychiatry*, Vol. 126.

Cross, W., Jr. 1970. "The Black Experience Viewed as a Process: A Crude Model for Black Selfactualization," a paper delivered at the twenty-fourth annual meeting of the Association of Social and Behavior Scientists, Tallahassee, Florida, April 23–24.

_____. 1978. "The Thomas and Cross Models of Psychological Nigrescence," *Journal of Black Psychology*, Vol. 5, 13–31.

_____. 1991. *Shades of Black*. Philadelphia: Temple University.

Davis, G., and G. Watson. 1982. *Black Life in Corporate America*. New York: Doubleday.

Flanagan, J. 1954. "The Critical Incident Technique," *Psychological Bulletin*, Vol. 2, 327–345.

Fleming, J. 1976. *The Lengthening Shadow of Slavery: A Historical Justification for Affirmative Action for Blacks in Higher Education*. Washington, D.C.: Howard University Press.

Franklin, R. 1963. "Youth's Expectations about Internal Control of Reinforcement Related to N Variables," *Dissertation Abstracts*, Vol. 24.

Gooden, W. 1981. "Black Male Development," unpublished doctoral dissertation, Yale University.

Gore, P., and J. Rotter. 1971. "A Personality Correlate of Social Action," in R. Wilcox (ed.), *The Psychological Consequences of Being a Black American*. New York: John Wiley.

Grier, W., and P. Cobbs. 1968. *Black Rage*. New York: Basic Books.

Gurin, P., et al. 1969. "Internal-External Control in Motivational Dynamics of Negro Youth," *Journal of Social Issues*, Vol. 43, 29–53.

Hacker, A. 1992. *Two Nations Divided: Black and White*. New York: Macmillan.

Hare, N. 1973. *Black Anglo-Saxons*. New York: Macmillan.

Harrell, J. 1979. "Analyzing Black Coping Styles: A Supplemental Diagnostic System," *Journal of Black Psychology*, Vol. 5, 79–84.

Harrington, C., et al. 1985. "Successful Women: A Psychological Investigation of Family, Class and Education Origins," a report of the Institute for Urban and Minority Education, Teachers College, Columbia University.

Hernton, C. 1965. *Sex and Racism*. New York: Grove Press.

Kovel, J. 1970. *White Racism: A Psychohistory*. New York: Pantheon.

Lefcourt, H. 1976. *Locus of Control: Current Trends in Theory and Research*. Hillsdale: Lawrence Eribaum Associates.

Levinson, D., et al. 1978. *Seasons in a Man's Life*. San Francisco: Jossey-Bass.

Malatesta, C., and C. Culver. 1984. "Thematic and Affective Content in the Lives of Adult Women: Patterns of Change and Continuity," in Malatesta and C. Izard (eds.), *Emotion in Adult Development*. Beverly Hills: Sage Publications.

Miriels, H. 1970. "Dimensions of Internal versus External Control," *Journal of Consulting and Clinical Psychology*, Vol. 36, 40–41.

Pruitt, K., and L. Knowles (eds.). 1969. *Institutional Racism in America*. Englewood Cliffs: Prentice-Hall.

Reid, D., and E. Ware. 1969. "Multidimensionality of Internal versus External Locus of Control: Addition of a Third Dimension and On-Distinction of Self versus Others," *Canadian Journal of Behavior Science*, Vol. 6, 131–142.

Ruffin, E. 1989. "Stages of Adult Development in Black Professional Women," in R. Jones (ed.), *Black Adult Development and Aging*. Berkeley: Cobb and Henry.

Sillen, A., and W. Alexander. 1972. *Racism and Psychiatry*. New Jersey: Citadel Press.

Strickland, R. 1965. "The Prediction of Social Action from a Dimension of Internal-External Control," *Journal of Social Psychology*, Vol. 22, 108–112.

Teper, S. 1977. *Ethnicity, Race, and Human Development*. New York: American Jewish Committee.

Weiner, B. 1980. "The Role of Affect in Rational (Attribution) Approaches to Human Motivation," *Educational Research*, Vol. 9, 4–11.

23

Towards an Africological Pedagogical Approach to African Civilization

Victor Oguejiofor Okafor

Victor O. Okafor is an Assistant Professor of African American Studies in the Department of African American Studies at Western Michigan University. He obtained the Ph.D. in African American Studies from Temple University in 1994. He received both a Master's degree in Public Affairs (1988) and a Bachelor's degree in Journalism with a Business minor (1986) from Indiana University.—The Western Journal of Black Studies, *Fall 1996, Vol. 20, No. 3*

Abstract

Within academic circles, subjects such as African Civilization, African Philosophy, African Religion, etc. have continued to evoke controversial questions about their legitimacy and historical groundedness even in the face of what looks like an explosion in scholarship pertaining to the African World. This paper accomplishes two broad objectives: (1) it presents a case study of such controversies, particularly as they relate to the subject of African Civilization; and (2) it makes a case for an Africological pedagogical approach to African Civilization.

First, the paper takes a synoptic look at the nature and sources of the challenges that, historically, have been mounted against subjects such as African Civilization, African Philosophy, and African Religion. It then counter-balances this with a survey of the kinds of scholarly arguments and data that proponents of those subjects have advanced over the years. The paper contends that while debates and questions on any subject or issue are a normal and needed part of academic life, the cynicism that apparently persists in certain sections of the academy towards Africa and civilization/philosophy serves as a useful key to unlocking the impact of *hegemonic intellectualism.*

The paper proposes that the title, *African Civilization*, with its inter-connected constituent centers, as opposed to *African Civilizations* (which appears to be the preference of "academic anthropology" and reflective of a rather reactive tendency in Africological scholarship), more realistically reflects the fact that the study is about the African place in the comity of World Civilizations even though that place itself is mosaic in character.

* * *

Critical questions examined by this paper include as follows. What is the most appropriate place for African Civilization in an Africological curriculum? What is the role of African Civilization in the larger American university curriculum?

Professor Theophile Obenga's latest book, *A Lost Tradition: African Philosophy in World History* (1995) significantly broadens and deepens our understanding of the factual concept of African historical continuity. Like the contributions of his late associate, Cheikh Anta Diop, Obenga in *A Lost Tradition*, which had been eagerly awaited, sheds immense light on a subject in the academy that has been highly disputed territory and on which debate continues. This illuminating study of the anteriority and evolution of African Philosophy from antiquity to the present era reminded one of that chapter of Cheikh Anta Diop's *Civilization or Barbarism* rhetorically entitled, "Does an African Philosophy Exist?" While Diop answered his question affirmatively by essentially taking his reader on a journey through ancient Egyptian cosmogony in juxtaposition with comparative cosmogonies in Africa, Obenga took a step ahead by persuasively making a case for an African Philosophy that is not merely rooted in antiquity, but one that is both organic and continuous even in the face of disastrous interventions in African Civilization itself.

Along with a bold approach to the subject of African Philosophy, a boldness that stands dramatically apart from the anthropological squabbles that usually characterize discussions of African Philosophy,[1] Obenga presents us with an unequivocal stance on the vexed question of African historical continuity. In doing so, Obenga reminds one of another vexed question: Does an African Civilization exist? Is there an African Civilization, or do we simply have a set of culturally-isolated civilizations on the African Continent? On the surface, this might come across as a semantic question, but this writer shall demonstrate that it represents a serious conceptual issue in African historiography. This issue came to the fore, a little while ago at a Southern university, during a debate on the subject of African Civilization. A big question arose as to the legitimacy of the category, African Civilization. Let it be known that we did prevail in that debate. However, a review of the major questions and contentions that surfaced during that debate is relevant and potentially useful to on-going discussions on academic diversity, curricular and multicultural issues across the campuses of the nation. Is there an African Civilization, or are there a multiplicity of cul- turally-disconnected civilizations in Africa? That was the big contention. An anthropological school of thought contended that Africa, as it put it, is such an "incredibly diverse continent that the talk of an African Civilization is a misnomer." By making a case for an African Civilization, we were told, we were engaging in what was described as an incredible act of homogenization. I was accused, to my amusement, that by proposing a course on African Civilization, I was "trying to turn Africa into a continent." That was quite a lesson for me, for I had never known, until then, that Africa is not a continent. It was further contended that Africa is in reality a creation of Europe—a somewhat twisted echo of V. Y. Mudimbe's *Invention of Africa.*

The implied notion that, in general, Africans of the pre-colonial era hibernated in closed-off clan or ethnic enclaves and remained unaware of Africans based in other regions of the continent is belied by two examples of long and extensive intra-African socioeconomic exchanges during the medieval period of African Civilization. The first is the trans-Saharan trade involving West Africans and North Africans from about 600 AD to 1600 AD—a trade that flourished alongside three gigantic empires—Ghana (622–1203 AD), Mali (1235–1500 AD) and Songhai (1475–1600 AD). (Jackson, 1970; Davidson, 1991; Ohaegbulam, 1990). Among the goods exchanged at the trans-Saharan trade centers of Kumbi Saleh, Awdaghost, Timbuktu, Jenne, Walata and Gao were gold, salt, ivory, pepper, cloth and kola nuts (Ohaegbulam, 1990, p. 71). One of Mali's emperors, Mansa Musa, paid a famous pilgrimage to Mecca in 1324–1325—a pilgrimage during which Emperor Musa lavishly gave away so much gold in alms that Mali's fame rose to an all-time high (p. 77). The second example of a large-scale, pre-colonial intra-African socioeconomic commingling took place in the southeastern sector where from about the 10th century AD until the 17th, coastal cities such as Kilwa, Mombassa, Sofola, Malinda and Zanzibar brokered gold exports from the southern-based Monomotapa Empire to Arabian, Indian and Chinese merchants. This trade contributed immensely to the internationalization of KiSwahili (Jackson, 1970, p. 281). Swahili itself is a language and name of Africans on the coast of Kenya, Tanganyika and the Island of Zanzibar (Davidson qtd. in Jackson, p. 280). In sum, what I have tried to demonstrate here is the fallacy of the notion that colonial rule necessarily elevated Africans from a point of provincialism to one of continental or regional African consciousness—a Eurocentric notion that Professor Anthony Kwame Appiah echoes in his controversial book, *In My Father's House* (1992).

Interestingly, however, this same anthropological school of thought that had contested the existence of African Civilization, as opposed to African Civilizations, was quick to point to a set of historical and living evidence of the category, Western Civilization. It was argued that the democracies and stable governments and societies of the West testify to the existence and legitimacy of Western Civilization. By implication, that contention draws attention to the instability that characterizes the contemporary African political scene. At this junction, let it be known that this writer does not dispute the existence of Western Civilization. While it is a fact that contemporary Africa reels under the suffocating weight of political instability and economic insecurity, a fact of life attributable to complex internal and external variables, that reality does not negate another fact: that a distinctly African voice constitutes a part of the matrix of the cosmologies, epistemologies, axiologies, cosmogonies and ethos that make up the global scheme of things.[2] This writer described this global humanity as a matrix for the simple fact that despite our, by and large, phenotypical and geo-environmental differences, we are inter-related by virtue of belonging to a common species called human beings. On this basis, we can talk about world history, or what Maulana Karenga describes as "the struggle and record of humans in the process of humanizing the world, i.e., shaping it in their own image and interests" (Karenga, 1993, p. 70). Africa's collective contribution to this process of humanizing the world, variegated across space and time, constitutes the essence of African Civilization, unless a case could be made, as Hegel and his disciplines had unsuccessfully tried, that there is no such African contribution to the global superstructural landscape.

Nascent scholarship increasingly points to the commonalties of African cultural centers.[3] The fact of the existence of more than a thousand linguistic groups on the vast continent of Africa (Ramsay, 1995, p. 3) apparently tends to cast a shadow on the linkages that bind African cultural centers as one people. In his *African Civilization Revisited* (1991), Basil Davidson, that energetic British scholar and one of the few non-African historians who, to significant extents, have recorded and interpreted African history through the eyes of Africans, traces the origins of Pan-Africanism back to two major historical epochs: the emergence of an Iron Age culture and the gradual drying up of the Sahara region of Africa into a desert, as from 2500 B.C.E. The invention of the iron-pointed spear enabled some groups to impose their wills on others, ultimately resulting in the emergence of a great variety of distinct peoples from the "ancestral stocks." At the same time, as the Sahara region dried up, desertification generated a massive pressure on available food supplies, prompting Africans to disperse in southerly directions. Davidson writes:

> In this long and complex disintegration of the Neolithic pattern and its reconstruction within an Iron Age framework we can find the origins of modern African societies, showing as these do, in a multitude of ways, a diversity that is none the less rooted in a profound and ancient unity. (p. 16)

He goes on to observe that "this large theme of unity-in-diversity runs throughout subsequent African history." This theme bears such a great significance that "little about the African past (and therefore about the African present) can be understood apart from it." Although Pan-Africanism as a movement came to life in modern times, and Davidson does recognize that fact, its psycho-cultural roots are traceable back into the distant neolithic past (p. 16).

Given this backdrop of the emergence of African ethnic groups from a common background of deep, ancient unity, as Davidson's work testifies, there exits, therefore, a scientific basis for the category known as African History. As Obenga's (1995) latest work demonstrates, this history has had a continuous life despite anthropological protestations to the contrary. Armed with ample evidence and following in the footsteps of Diopian scholarship, Obenga writes:

> A careful and serious study of African history, from antiquity through the present era, reveals a deep genetic linkage: from Ancient Egypt's impact on the culture of the rest of the African continent to the unity of all African languages, African history is one continuous, unbroken narrative of a people with a shared consciousness. (p. v)

That quotation from Obenga's book reflects a holistic approach to African historiography, which is in sync with Africological methodological emphasis on synthesis. In *Kemet, Afrocentricity, and Knowledge*, Asante (1990) articulates a pathway to synthesis in Africology. He frames it in the following words.

> A person who seeks the road to Ma'at must come by the column of unity. This, of course, is no miracle because consciousness precedes unity. The person who wants to analyze anything for the purpose of synthesis will find that the first rule is to examine the object, thing, person, speech for unity. As Afrocentricists, that is our first obligation because it is the first step on the road to Ma'at. (p. 98)

The issue of consciousness raised in the preceding passage needs to be singled out for mention, for it touches upon an aspect of contemporary African life and scholarship that remains problematic. I mean to say that a mind still enshackled by the slave or colonial mentality may find it difficult to see beyond the imperial boundaries, imperatives, strategies and tactics that had worked to limit the intellectual possibilities of the Africanist project—a project that appears to be searching for legitimacy in the wake of the demise of the Cold War that had sustained it in the first place. The fact that such enshackled minds are still well and alive in African scholarship apparently prompted Obenga's observation that "contemporary African philosophy deals constantly with issues and outlooks from the vantage point of the Western academic anthropology" (p. 14). As a mirror of the African cultural world, Africological synthesis represents one of the fundamental distinctions between the Africanist project, still entrapped in the limiting conceptual framework of academic anthropology, and the Africological enterprise. A more incisive portrayal of the distinctions between the anthropological Africanists and Africologists comes from Asante. The anthropological Africanists, he writes, are "blinded by their own sense of Africa as a divided continent with innumerable cultures" (Asante, 1993, p. 19), a conceptual blindness that they inherited from "the hostile writings of early European scholars." In consequence, "anthropologists have argued the disunity of African culture while arguing the unity of European culture."

In his *Civilization or Barbarism* (1991), Cheikh Anta Diop provides a definition of African History that I find to be pertinent to the unfolding discussion on a new pedagogy for African Civilization. He defines African History as a two-layered category. Taking off characteristically with a rhetorical question, "What can we call African history?" (p. 213), Diop identifies two major constituent parts of African History: (1) a *general African history*, "further off in time and space and including the totality of our peoples" (p. 213); and (2) a second layer consisting of the *local histories* of segments of African peoples dispersed by such external forces as slavery and colonialism. Using this historiographic map, the category African History then becomes a matrix, an umbrella, under which are embedded ancient African history, North African history, West African history, Southern African history, East African history, African American history, African European history and African Asian history. Such an approach synchronizes with Molefi Kete Asante's concept of an African Cultural System, which is both diverse and dynamic but derived from a common historical and cultural heritage. Tsehloane Keto's (1995) *time map of Africa*, which delineates four periods during which African achievements excelled in history, provides an additional conceptual grid for African Civilization. The time map identifies the following epochs:

> (1) the first period before the fourth millennium B.C.E. in Kemet [Egypt] that followed the creation of human cultures;

> (2) the second period between 600 to 1600 [A.D.] in West Africa that witnessed the concentration of state power and the formation of gigantic states like Ghana, Mali and Songhai;

> (3) the third period from 1800 to 1890 that saw the attempt to rebuild defensive redoubts through the unification of existing societies throughout the African world among the Baganda, in Haiti, in Ashanti, among the Fulani, in Ethiopia, among the Zulu and among the Lunda;

> (4) the emergence of African people in the post-1960 period through the Civil Rights Movement in the United States and through the struggle for political independence in Africa and the Caribbean. (p. 138)

I have found this conceptual grid effective in the formulation of syllabi for the course on African Civilization. However, in using it, I modified it to incorporate the most primary development in the earthly world—the emergence of the human species in Africa. Keto's time map of African history reflects a philosophy of history best illustrated by Obenga's (1995) observation that "Africans, from classical times to the present, belong to the same cultural universe, linked by the same traditions" (p. vi). As a clear-cut contrast to the Africanists' protocol that separates African people (Asante, 1990, p. 15), we, as Africologists, have before us, a conceptual framework by which we can take up a challenge from Obenga: "In this century, at this moment, it must be our decision to recognize and act upon" (p. vi) the fact of the oneness of African Civilization.

Whereas African history and African Civilization are inter-connected subjects and the latter springs out of the former, they are not necessarily synonyms. While African history is concerned chiefly with the chronological records and analyses of past events in the lives and affairs of African people, I contend that African Civilization focuses on the intellectual and material tools and institutions developed by Africans, across space and time, in order to satisfy their biological, social, political and economic needs as well as to adapt themselves to their changing social and geographical environments. I adapted this conception of civilization from what Festus Ugboaja Ohaegbulam (1990) defines as culture (p. 88) in his *Towards an Understanding of the Experience: From Historical and Contemporary Perspectives.*

In zeroing in on centers of African Civilization such as ancient Egypt, Nubia, Axum, Ghana, Mali, Songhai, Kilwa, Sofola, Malinda, Monomotapa, etc., along with a preface that human life itself began in Africa (as paleontology has demonstrated from time to time), a student needs to examine the commonalties that those centers share in the midst of linguistic and other kinds of diversity. The title, *African Civilization*, with constituent centers—as opposed to *African Civilizations*, which is the preferred title from both the standpoint of what Obenga aptly describes as "academic anthropology" (p. 6) and what I have chosen to characterize as a reactive tendency in African scholarship—more realistically reflects the fact that the study is about the African place in the comity of World Civilizations even though that place itself is mosaic in character. Academic anthropology's apparent preference for "African Civilizations" appears to stem from an old and discredited claim, but one that remains an article of faith in some academic circles, namely that North Africa is historically Caucasian. Asante (1990) sheds light on the source of this hegemonic Eurocentric claim:

> To prosecute the maligning of Africa it was necessary for [Georg] Hegel to advance a false division of the continent, a division superimposed on the land, not by the people of the continent themselves, but by European historians, anthropologists, and colonial administrators who said Africa consisted of Asian Africa, European Africa, and Africa proper. In *Philosophy of History*, [Georg Hegel] explained that Africa proper was the territory south of the Sahara; Egypt was the part of Africa connected to Asia. (p. 33)

Addressing this still-controversial subject in the chapter aptly titled, "Modern Falsification of History" in *The African Origin of Civilization: Myth or Reality*, Diop reports:

> We can invoke archeological and historical documents unanimously attesting that [North Africa] was always inhabited by [Black Africans]…At the end of the Paleolithic, in the province of Constantine, Algeria, five layers of fossilized men were found. Among these, several [Africoids] presenting affinities with the Nubians of Upper Egypt are mentioned. During the historical epoch, Latin documents testify to the existence of Blacks throughout North Africa. (1974, p. 65)

As an addition to Asante's and Diop's historical observations, let me also point out that the alleged whiteness of North Africa in antiquity ignores a basic historical fact that Arab migration to Africa began in the 7th century of the present era. Of pertinence here is that label known as Sub-Saharan Africa. It represents a conceptual trick, a conceptual dissection of the Nile Valley centers of enlightenment from African Civilization. It is a flawed and political conception for two major reasons: (1) the large territory in North Africa that we identify as the Sahara Desert had been a wet region prior to about 2500 BCE. Even as we gather here today, the southerly direction of desertification continues to eat up arable land in Africa. Thus, the Sahara encompasses several African societies that are, by and large, culturally connected and, therefore, does not represent a barrier that culturally cuts North Africa from what is often described as Sub-Saharan Africa. To argue for an African Civilization with the African continent as its geographical and cultural base is by no means a suggestion that African culture itself is monolithic. In the same breadth, a course on Western Civilization cannot be seen as implying that the French culture replicates British culture, German culture, or other European cultures which it subsumes. The fact that those cultures are embedded in the course on Western Civilization has not, to my knowledge, prompted a demand that the title of the course be changed to "Western Civilizations."

The linguistic heterogeneity that characterizes the African cultural plane obscures an underlying genetic linguistic unity, which is increasingly coming to the fore through emerging linguistic research. For example, a 1989 study by F. Niyi Akinnaso finds that the more than four hundred African languages spoken in Nigeria, West Africa, share a "structural similarity" (p. 137). Diop's *The African Origin of Civilization: Myth or Reality* (1974), *Civilization or Barbarism* (1991), and *Precolonial Black Africa* (1987) not only demonstrate linguistic parallels between the Senegalese language of Wolof and the ancient Egyptian language *Mdw Ntr* (Diop, 1974, p. 153), they also identify parallels that criss-cross African societies of West, South, East and North Africa, including ancient Egypt, in such specific cultural subjects as cosmogonies, totemism, circumcision, kingship, social organizations, political organizations, matriarchy, economic organizations and languages. Among them are parallel concepts and beliefs between ancient Egypt and the Dogon of Mali, including the concept of an androgynous God. The ancient Egyptian god of evil, Seth, and the Dogon counterpart, Yurugu, are symbolized by the same animal form. Diop also found that a common belief existed in the cosmologies of the ancient Egyptians, the Woyo of Equatorial Africa, the Yoruba of Nigeria, and the Nyambism of Zaire that *the number* constituted the basis of creation (Diop, 1991, p. 320). In the area of political leadership, the vitalist concept, requiring the regeneration of kings through ritualistic killing, was characteristic of African monarchies, including pharaohnic Egypt (p. 323). In a linguistic examination of the relationship between *Maat* and Modern Thought, Obenga finds that *Maat*, or truth, plays a "fundamental role" in a fairly long list of African languages that crisscross the continent. These are *Mdw Ntr* of ancient Egypt and Coptic of contemporary Egypt; *Caffina* of Ethiopia; *Ngbaka* of the Central African Republic; *Fang* of Equatorial Guinea, South Cameroon and Gabon; *Mpongwe* of Gabon; *Yoruba* and *Hausa* of Nigeria; *Mada* of North Cameroon; and *Nuer* of Nilotic Sudan (p. 72). Let me add that in my language of *Igbo*, Maat radiates prominently in our saying that *eziokwu bu ndu* (literally translated as "truth is life"). *Eziokwu bu ndu* means that truth sustains life. In the Igbo culture of Nigeria, when we make that statement to a person, we seek to accomplish two closely-tied objectives: (1) to admonish him/her for saying what we deem to be less than the truth of a situation; and (2) to encourage her/him to speak truthfully. The encouragement lies in our reminder to the person that truth is like a seed to life.

Another critical point relates to cynicism about African Civilization or its constituent part, African Philosophy, which has tended to derive from an impression that Africa of the past lacked the skill of writing, that Africa was almost peculiarly an oral culture—a cynicism that persists despite that fact that "it is a typically [African] language that has been the oldest written language in the history of humanity. It began 5,300 years ago, in Egypt" (Diop, 1991, p. 215). That of course is not to suggest that writing was ever widespread in ancient Africa or elsewhere.

Acceptance of the preceding conceptualization of African Civilization could lead to a better understanding of the foundational role that African Civilization plays in an Africological curriculum or what we commonly refer to as African American Studies or Black Studies. In fact, a critical look at three major definitions of Africology will illustrate my point. In *Kemet, Afrocentricity, and Knowledge*, Molefi Asante (1990) defines African American Studies as a human science designed to discover in historical and contemporary human affairs, "all the ways African people have tried to make their physical, social, and cultural environments serve the end of harmony" (p. 7). Consider also Winston A. Van Horne's (1994) definition of Africology as "a normative and empirical inquiry into the life histories and prospects of peoples of primary African origin and their descent trans-generationally, transmillennially and universally" (p. 1). The third definition comes from Maulana Karenga (1993). He defines Black Studies as "the systematic and critical study of the multidimensional aspects of Black thought and practice in their current and historical unfolding" (p. 21). A common thread binds those pivotal definitions of Africology together: they posit the discipline as one whose areas of inquiry encompass the African or Black world, from historical and contemporary perspectives—a world that revolves around the continent of Africa as its springboard. Asante contends that the grand focus of Africological multidimensional inquiry hinges upon African peoples' strive towards harmony in human affairs. For an illustration of the factor that Asante describes as harmony, this writer will turn to Ohaegbulam who writes that "communities of traditional African societies were human centered and regarded human need as the supreme criterion of behavior" (p. 23). I contend that a comprehensive Africological curriculum ought to take off with a critical and systematic study of the evolution of African Civilization from antiquity. Using ancient Egypt or Kemet as a paradigm, the high point of African Civilization in antiquity, as a rather long list of contemporary Africological scholars have argued (Asante, 1990; Diop, 1974; Karenga, 1993; Keto, 1989 and 1995; Obenga, 1995), a student of African Civilization could investigate a representative sample of centers of that civilization in order to ascertain, among other questions, how they went about the pursuit of harmony, or *Maat*, in human relations. That is to say, African Civilization idealizes the spiritual/ethical dimension of human beings. That ethical dimension lies at the core of what it is to be human, from the standpoint of African Civilization (Karenga, 1993b, p. 385). Maat was at the center of ancient Egyptian life for more than 3,500 years. Obenga contends that life without the pursuit of truth, justice and love or what are collectively described as Maat would have been unthinkable for the ancient Egyptians (p. 15). In fact, the ancient Egyptian society is one that believed in the ultimate possibility of a just society—a society that could be established on the basis of seven cardinal principles: truth, justice, propriety, harmony, balance, reciprocity and order (p. 391). Of course, the extent to which Africans of today, in the diaspora or on the continent, approximate that kind of humanistic philosophy of life remains a point of disputation. To what extent has a long and sustained encounter, under situations of powerlessness, with a worldview that places a premium on power, destruction and control infected our minds? The challenge of reconciling the African with his past should not be viewed as an easy task, given the exigencies of an exploitative and might-is-right world order that appears to prevail at the moment.

As this writer indicated at the beginning, Obenga's (1995) latest work, like his 1974 United Nations-sponsored, joint presentation in Cairo together with the late Cheikh Anta Diop on ancient Egypt, represents a significant contribution to Africological scholarship. The great question, "Who were the Egyptians," posed by Diop in his *The African Origin of Civilization: Myth or Reality* served and continues to serve as a reminder of the fact that segments of the academy have continued to disbelieve that ancient Egypt was primarily a black civilization despite abundant historical evidence to that effect (Ben-Jachannan, 1988; Bernal, 1987; Diop, 1974; J. G. M. George, 1976; Obenga, 1995). Resistance to the inclusion of ancient Egypt in a survey course on African Civilization often surfaces through oblique misapplications of historical facts. For instance, during the debate that this writer recalled earlier, a professor had suggested to me that what I really needed to do was to focus on West Africa which, he explained, was the main source of the African captives who were transplanted to the New World between the 16th and 19th centuries. In other words, the professor did not see and, perhaps, would not recognize the indispensable place of ancient Egypt in any discourse on African Civilization. On the other hand, ancient Greece constitutes the backdrop of the course on Western Civilization. Let me cite just one example. The introductory chapter of a University of Chicago text on Western Civilization starts off with the following line: "The polis, or city-state, was the characteristic political form in Greece when the Greeks learned to write in the late 8th century B.C., and for the next four hundred years it remained the environment in which most Western literature was produced" (Adkins and White, 1986, p. 1). However, do we require instructors of Western Civilization to prove that European Americans had all migrated from Greece in order to justify its paradigmatic role in the course? In fact, is it not a major irony of history that despite the mainstream's romanticization of the Greek heritage, there had been a strenuous white national movement within the United States in the late part of the 19th century and well into the first quarter of this century for the exclusion of Southern Europeans, including Greeks, from the United States. Driven by ethnocentric theories of "higher and lower" grade Europeans, the movement succeeded in pushing through the 1924 National Origins Act, which was expressly targeted against Southern and Eastern Europeans, along with the Chinese and Japanese. In fact, it was not until 1965 that the law was replaced (Wong, 1985, p. 45). One wonders what would have been the response of my professor friend, who questioned the relevance of ancient Egypt to African Americans, if one had brought this paradox to his attention. Ignore the fact that the introductory chapter of the book on Western Civilization did not tell us who taught the Greeks how to write although it acknowledged that they did, in fact, learn how to write as opposed to saying that they had invented writing, which, as we learned earlier, had been in vogue in ancient Egypt more than five thousand years ago. This writer's point is to demonstrate that the questioning of the relevance of African antiquity to African Americans that one encounters in discussions about contemporary university course offerings hardly comes up in respect of ancient Greece and European Americans, despite the irony in the history of a people who have simultaneously romanticized ancient Greece and then pushed for the exclusion of Greeks from the United States.

The preceding pages have demonstrated a historically factual basis for a holistic pedagogical approach toward *African Civilization*. This holistic pedagogy rejects the traditional title of *African Civilizations* because while it reflects a historical reality that in the past significant cultural, social, political, economic and technological developments took place in various regions of Africa, it, unwittingly, plays into the hands of an ahistorical, neo-Hegelian perspective that denies African historical continuity and the resultant historical consciousness. On the other hand, the concept, *African Civilization*, is affirmative of the agency, the voice, of African peoples in world history and their identifiable signature mark on it. It is striking to note that St. Clair Drake (1993) underscores this position in his comments on Leopold Senghor and Negritude. "Senghor has emphasized the point repeatedly that [African Civilization] must be viewed as having a distinctive contribution to make to the culture of the universal, which is made up of diverse strands" (p. 465).

"African Civilization," as a category, does not by any means deny, or seek to deny, the diversity that characterizes African societies, but it recognizes their fundamental cultural commonalities as well as their unique historical experiences and ecologically induced psycho-social orientation—cultural commonalities and historical experiences that, on the one hand, serve as the basis of their common identity as Africans, and on the other hand, distinguish them from other segments of the human family. Apart from unique historical and cultural experiences that are deemed to have helped to shape what amounts to an African perspective in the multi-centric world,[4] there is also the psycho-social factor—considered to be a function of the effect of the ecological environment itself on human social evolution. Cheikh Anta Diop's "two-cradle theory" is most significant in this respect. Based on two models of human ecology, which he identified as the Southern cradle and the Northern cradle, Diop (1974) writes:

> The history of humanity will remain confused as long as we fail to distinguish between the two early cradles in which Nature fashioned the instincts, temperament, habits, and ethical concepts of the two subdivisions before they met each other after a long separation dating back to prehistoric times. (p. 111)

He goes on to explain that the Southern cradle had been shaped along the valley of the Nile, from the great lakes region of Africa (where the earliest human fossils have been found) to the Nile delta. Marked by surplus essential resources, the sedentary and agricultural way of life in this physical environment generated a human outlook characterized by a gentle, idealistic, peaceful nature, laced with a spirit of justice and gaiety. Daily coexistence with fellow human beings in the northern part of this cradle necessitated and reinforced those virtues (p. 111). Remember the saying that necessity is the mother of invention.

In contrast, the Northern cradle crystallized in the Eurasian steppes whose barrenness and extreme coldness engendered not only certain instincts in the human being that were necessary for sheer survival, but also instincts for conquest, for aggression driven primarily by a need to escape from a hostile climate. Let me recapture the details through the very words of Diop (1974) himself.

> Here, Nature left no illusion of kindliness: it was implacable and permitted no negligence; man must obtain his bread by the sweat of his brow. Above all, in the course of a long, painful existence, he must learn to rely on himself alone, on his own possibilities. He could not indulge in the luxury of believing in a beneficent God who would shower down abundant means of gaining a livelihood; instead, he would conjure up deities maleficent and cruel, jealous and spiteful. (p. 112)

When one ponders the major tragedies of the last five hundred years, even as we celebrate its technological breakthroughs, one is persuaded to view Diop's two-cradle model of human social evolution with all seriousness. Is it safe to assume that as the techo-materialistic aspect of contemporary human society advances, almost at an exponential rate, less and less premium has come to be placed on humanistic values? Is it safe to assume that the quality of human relations seems to be deteriorating, that commercial mass media increasingly valorize those kinds of thought, experiences and conduct that negate the sacred principles that make for positive human relations? Is it safe to ask, rather rhetorically, whether those kinds of instincts that Diop traced to the Northern cradle are increasingly creeping into general human consciousness, that those kinds of instincts are gradually gaining ascendancy in human affairs as we glide towards the 21st century? These kinds of questions and assumptions can guide us in evaluating the relevance of African Civilization to the contemporary world.

Notes

1. An illustration of what I characterized as anthropological squabbles can be seen in certain areas of the discourse that has been going on within a circle of African scholars who identify themselves as professional philosophers. Although they have been prolific and robustly critical, they have, in general, failed to connect their works on African Philosophy with ancient Egyptian Philosophy. In fact, this school of thought views African Philosophy as an entity that is of recent origin. In an essay titled, "The Question of African Philosophy," Peter O. Bodunrin, one of such professional philosophers, identifies three others as belonging to the African school of professional philosophers: Kwasi Wiredu, Paulin Hountondji, and Henry Odera Oruka. However, the works of Lancinay Keita, who belongs to this class of scholars, represent an exception in terms of his recognition that ancient Egypt belongs to the African philosophical tradition. For details, the reader is referred to *African Philosophy: The Essential Readings* (1991), edited by Tsenay Serequeberhan, and *African Philosophy* (1984), edited by Richard Wright.
2. Pertinent works that readers may consult include Anthony Browder's *Nile Valley Contributions to Civilization,* Vol. 1, Washington, D.C.: Institute for Karmic Guidance, 1992; Basil Davidson's *African Civilization Revisited,* Tenton: Africa WP, 1991; Cheikh Anta Diop's *The African Origin of Civilization: Myth or Reality,* Westport: Lawrence Hill, 1974; Diop's *Civilization or Barbarism,* Westport: Lawrence Hill, 1991; Diop's *Pre-Colonial Black Africa,* Westport: Lawrence Hill, 1987; Martin Bernal's *Black Athena: The Afro-Asiatic Roots of Classical Civilizations,* Vol. II, New Brunswick: Rutgers, 1991; James George's *Stolen Legacy,* San Francisco: Julian Richardson, 1976; John G. Jackson's *Introduction to African Civilizations,* Secaucus: Citadel, 1970; Ivan Van Sertima's *Black Women in Antiquity,* New Brunswick: Transaction Books, 1989; Sertima's *Blacks in Science: Ancient and Modern,* New Brunswick: Transaction Books, 1992; and Chancellor Williams' *The Destruction of Black Civilization,* Chicago: Third World, 1974.
3. See Cheikh Anta Diop's *The Cultural Unity of Black Africa, Precolonial Black Africa,* and *Civilization or Barbarism;* Molefi Kete Asante's *African Culture: The Rhythms of Unity;* Basil Davidson's *African Philosophy;* as well as Kwame Gyeke's and Theophile Obenga's works in the area of African Philosophy, a constituent element of African Civilization.
4. Pertinent works include Molefi Kete Asante's *Afrocentricity* (1988), *Kemet, Afrocentricity, and Knowledge* (1990), *The Afrocentric Idea* (1987); C. Tsehloane Keto's *Vision, Identity and Time: The Afrocentric Paradigm and the Study of the Past* (1995); and Dona Marimba Richards' (now Ani) *Let the Circle Be Unbroken: The Implications of African Spirituality in the Diaspora* (1980).

References

Adkins, Arthur W. H, and Peter White (eds.) (1986). *University of Chicago Readings in Western Civilization: Vol. 1, the Greek Polis.* Chicago: University of Chicago Press.
Akinnaso, F. Niyi (1989). "One Nation, Four Hundred Languages: Unity and Diversity in Nigeria's Language Policy," *Language Problems and Language Planning*, Vol. 13, No. 2, 29–61.
Appiah, Anthony (1992). *In My Father's House: Africa in the Philosophy of Culture.* New York: Oxford University Press.
Asante, Molefi Kete (1985). *African Culture: The Rhythms of Unity.* Westport: Greenwood Press.
_____. (1987). *The Afrocentric Idea.* Philadelphia: Temple University Press.
_____. (1988). *Afrocentricity.* Trenton: African World Press.
_____. (1990). *Kemet, Afrocentricity, and Knowledge.* Trenton: Africa World Press.
_____. (1993). *Malcolm X as Cultural Hero and other Afrocentric Essays.* Trenton: Africa World Press.
Bodunrin, P. O. (1984). "The Question of Culture, " in Richard Wright (ed.), *African Philosophy: An Introduction* [pp. 1–24]. New York: University Press of America.
Davidson, Basil (1991). *African Civilization Revisited: From Antiquity to Modern Times.* Trenton: Africa World Press.
Diop, Cheikh Anta (1974). *The African Origin of Civilization: Myth or Reality,* Mercer Cook (trans.). Westport: Lawrence Hill.
_____. (1991). *Civilization or Barbarism: An Authentic Anthropology,* Yaa-Lengi Meema Ngemi (trans.). Westport: Lawrence Hill.
_____. (1987). *Precolonial Black Africa.* Westport: Lawrence Hill.
_____. (1989). *The Cultural Unity of Black Africa: The Domains of Patriarchy and Matriarchy in Classical Antiquity.* London: Karnak House.
Drake, St. Clair (1993). "Diaspora Studies and Pan-Africanism," in J. Harris (ed.), *Global Dimensions of the African Diaspora* [pp. 451–518]. Washington, D.C.: Howard University Press.
Jackson, John G. (1970). *Introduction to African Civilizations.* New York: Carol Publishing.
Karenga, Maulana (1993). *Introduction to Black Studies.* Los Angeles: University of Sankore Press.
_____. (1993b) "Towards a Sociology of Maatian Ethics: Literature and Context," in Ivan V. Sertima (ed.), *Egypt Revisited* [pp. 352–398]. New Brunswick: Transaction Books.
Keto, C. Tsehloane (1989). *Africa Centered Perspective of History.* Blackwood: K. A. Publications.
_____. (1995). *Vision, Identity and Time: The Afrocentric Paradigm and the Study of the Past.* Dubuque: Kendall/Hunt.
Mbiti, John S. (1989). *African Religions and Philosophy,* 2nd ed. Portsmouth: Heinemann.
Mudimbe, V. Y. (1988). *The Invention of Africa: Gnosis, Philosophy, and the Order of Knowledge.* Bloomington: Indiana University Press.
Obenga, Theophile (1995). *A Lost Tradition: African Philosophy in World History.* Philadelphia: Source Editions.
Ohaegbulam, Festus Ugboaja (1990). *Towards an Understanding of the African Experience: From Historical and Contemporary Perspectives.* New York: University Press of America.
Ramsay, Jeffress F. (1995). *Global Studies: Africa.* Guilford: Dushkin and Benchmark.
Richards, D. M. (1980). *Let the Circle Be Unbroken: The Implications of African Spirituality in the Diaspora.* New York: Djifa.
Serequeberhan, Tsenay (ed.) (1991). *African Philosophy: The Essential Readings.* New York: Paragon House.
Van Horne, Winston (1994). "Africology: A Discipline of the Twenty-First Century." Paper presented at the Sixth Annual Cheikh Anta Diop Conference, Temple University, Philadelphia, October.
Willet, Frank (1971). *African Art: An Introduction.* New York: Praeger.
Wright, Richard (ed.) (1984). *African Philosophy: An Introduction.* New York: University Press of America.
Wong, Morrison G. (1985). "Post-1965 Immigrations: Demographic and Socioeconomic Profile," in Lionel Maldonado and J. Moore (eds.), *Urban Ethnicity in the United States: New Immigrants and Old Minorities,* Vol. 29 [pp. 51–71]. Beverly Hills: Sage Publications.

24

Towards a Grand Theory of Black Studies: An Attempt to Discern the Dynamics and the Direction of the Discipline

ARTHUR LEWIN

Arthur Lewin, Ph.D., is Associate Professor of Black and Hispanic Studies at Baruch College of the City University of New York.—The Western Journal of Black Studies, Summer 2001, Vol. 25, No. 2

Abstract

This paper attempts to develop a grand theory of Black Studies by drawing on the works of some of the foremost writers in, and critics of, the field. It uses the history of the Black intellectual tradition as a frame and places Black Studies in the context of multicultural studies, the contemporary academy, and the development of the global economy and culture.

* * *

One of the things missing in Black Studies is a compelling radical paradigm, a grand theory that gives guidance, shape and direction to where Black Studies is headed. This simply does not exist. (Lusane, 1997, 14)

Usually, a discipline develops in tandem with the theory of the discipline. Black Studies, though, appears to have burst full-blown upon the academic scene a generation ago; 30 years later it still does not have a coherently stated rationale.

Nonetheless, there are today more than 300 departments and programs in Black Studies (Karenga, 1993, 488–505). If the discipline can advance this far without an idea of itself, what might it accomplish if it had one?

"A discipline by definition is a self-conscious, organized system of research and communication in a defined area of inquiry and knowledge" (Karenga, 1993, 489). The Black Studies area of inquiry is quite expansive. It offers an alternate version of courses in every discipline. Black Studies is perhaps the most oppositional of the multicultural studies; African Americans being the most excluded cultural element in American society. Therefore, to develop a theory of Black Studies is also to develop a theory of multiculturalism, a theory of the academy, and a theory of the society.

One way to encapsulate the dynamic of Black Studies is to focus on the dialectic at the heart of the discipline. The pivot, around which the discipline revolves, appears to be the sharp and bitter divide between its nationalist and inclusionist elements.

Nationalists vs. Inclusionists

Though it appears as if it were a relative newcomer, the roots of Black Studies run deep. "Behind the concept of African American Studies is essentially the Black intellectual tradition, the critical thought and perspectives of intellectuals of African descent and scholars of the African diaspora" (Marable, 1996, 3). The central division in Black Studies may be seen as that between the "inclusionists" and the "nationalists" (Marable, 1998, 3–8) rooted in the traditional divide in the Black intellectual tradition, assimilation and separation (Cruse, 1984; Lewin, 1984). These two schools, nationalist and inclusionist, are interdisciplinary, deeply theoretical, and critical of the status quo and of each other.

The inclusionists seek to work within the academy, as they study the history and development of Africans in America and advocate for their closer integration into this society. The nationalists put Africa first in their study of the history, and development, of African Americans. They advocate a divorcement from Eurocentric thought and institutions.

It was during the sixties, during the last cycle of Black activism (Brisbane, 1974) that Black Studies raucously breached the Ivory Tower. As that activist cycle inevitably waned, college officials began turning to those with inclusionist philosophies to develop and staff these programs. The pioneering nationalist figures have come to see the later-comers as eroding the original thrust of the discipline. "Black Studies was (essentially) a mass movement and a mass struggle based on the notion that education belongs to the people and the idea is to give it back to them" (Hare, 1972, 33).

The inclusionists not surprisingly see things differently. They see themselves as "rationally," "scientifically" setting about establishing the field. They picture the nationalist thinkers today, and the student protesters of yesterday who institutionalized the discipline, as overly emotional (Appelbome, 1996).

One of the premier nationalist departments is the one at Temple University founded by Molefi Kete Asante who developed the concept of "Afrocentricity." One of the foremost inclusionist departments is the one at Harvard headed by Henry Louis Gates. Here the professors have joint appointments with other academic departments reflective of their focus on inclusion.

The Temple School (Afrocentricity) says that it retains the challenge to the prevailing attitudes and beliefs of the academy embodied in the student protests that led to the creation of departments of Black Studies. The Harvard School contends that it represents the maturing, the firmer grounding, of the field in academia.

The inclusionists see Afrocentrists and other nationalists as making exaggerated, romantic claims about Africa. Gates says, "There's a lot of energy these days in African American Studies, but there is a lot of wishful thinking too. You can't make it up, man. You have to do the archival work" (Appelbome, 1996, 26). The Afrocentrists, however, see the inclusionists as overly emphasizing rationality and of being actually Eurocentric. Says Victor Okafor commenting on Kwame Anthony Appiah, a member of the Harvard School:

> I believe that Appiah's work represents a notable theoretical contribution to African/African American studies. It qualifies to be classified as a Eurocentric model for African/African American Studies, in contrast to the Afrocentric model...As would be expected given the Eurocentric bias of [Appiah's book] *In My Father's House* major Euro-American media have published sympathetic reviews of his work. (Okafor, 1993, 209–210)

So we see that it is a heated discourse indeed. However, this vigorous, oftentimes harsh, debate is perhaps crucial to the discipline:

> One of the most important achievements of Black Studies scholars is to have put forth contestation in Africana Studies as a fundamental mode of understanding society, self and the world...Thus if it holds true to its academic and social mission, Black Studies is compelled to practice internally what it demands externally—i.e., self-criticism and self-correction. (Karenga, 1993, 40–41)

However, it is believed that the "success or failure of Black Studies programs and departments will depend to a large degree on the resolution of ideological struggles within Black Studies" (LeMelle, 1984, 60). A theory of Black Studies, though, could not favor one ideology over the other; in fact, to the extent that it did, it would be a nationalist or inclusionist theory, not a theory of the discipline.

How can a comprehensive theory of Black Studies resolve the ideological struggle without taking sides? There is only one way. *The theory of Black Studies must assert that the nationalists and the inclusionists are equally valid.* Hence, it must hold that *each is right that the other is wrong*. It must postulate that all America (and all humanity) is one, but it must also note that to be color-blind in a caste-ridden, racially polarized society is in a sense to acquiesce to subordination. It must assert that the African in America can never be a part of the whole, but the African cannot live in America apart from the whole.

Curiously, this somehow parallels the paradox of quantum theory (Light, as you may recall, is a particle and a wave, even though particles, by their very nature, cannot be waves and vice versa.) Quantum theory in discovering the "uncertainty principle" undermined the rational basis of physics and the mathematical sciences. Multiculturalism, of which Black Studies is a key element, embodies the uncertainty principle in the study of society.

Black Studies and the Multicultural Movement

"World culture is repositioning itself to accept a completely different perceptive mode—the mode of the dynamic many-centered…holism, the idea that there is no cardinal center, just many centers floating in a cosmic system which honors only diversity" (McLuhan and Power, 1989, ix). The multicultural movement and the "third world" liberation struggles emerged in the vacuum created by the collapse of the European powers in the wake of the world wars:

> After World War II, the process of decolonization changed the world map… a new model is now required in the reconstruction of world history: a multicultural model, in which different centers and different political and cultural strategies are all granted equal attention and merits as due…Scholars from universities and other cultural institutions in Europe and America, Asia and Africa are working on this model, making use of different methodological tools, and, of course, laboring under biases produced by their own cultural backgrounds. (Liverani, 1996, 423)

The world wars destroyed the European imperial power centers, unleashing a series of colonial conflagrations. These wars of liberation reverberated in the internal colonies of forcibly assimilated peoples within Europe and America. The wholesale slaughter of the world wars was proof-positive that rationalism was not sound. This spawned the existentialist movement and postmodernism, all of which gave great impetus to the Multicultural movement. Schools of thought like Afrocentricity were advanced that provided theoretical ammunition for the further assault on the remnants of rationalism, as they fostered the colonial rebellions, and were sustained by them.

Today, fifty years after the second world war, the hopes of the newly liberated nations of Africa, Asia, the Caribbean and Latin America have dimmed, as the revolutionary consciousness of African Americans has waned. Meanwhile, the United States has emerged as the colossus enforcing a new political, economic and cultural order on the world stage.

However, just as America, and things American, are at the heart of the whole that is the world, African America and things African American are at the heart of the whole that is America. The culture that America exports: its music, its sports, its fashion, its idiom, is largely African American, as is much of its television and movie fare. And it is these cultural products that Hollywood and Madison Avenue are using to break down the cultures of every nation on earth, fashioning them all into one homogenous global culture with a distinctly American flavor, that is heavily African American.

Black Studies and the Global Paradigm

Marshall McLuhan observed that "today after a century of electronic technology, we have extended our central nervous system itself in a global embrace, abolishing space and time." Continuing the analogy, if all the world is one, one entity, one being, then what governs its behavior? What is its "mind" so to speak?

Its actions appear governed by the philosophy, the mindset, that constructed the Global Village, namely the Western scientific tradition. Those operating from an Afrocentric perspective, however, stubbornly insist that African thought is the bedrock basis of Western thought. African thought and tradition would then be at the center of the World Entity's "Mind." Which is right? Is African or Western thought the "Mind of the World"?

However, would not the World Being, if it be sentient, like any other intelligent mind, have two parts: a conscious and an unconscious? Does the Western tradition represent the conscious mind that represses its base, that is, the African Source?

The conflict, though, is not between the two traditions. They complement each other. The European tradition is built upon the African tradition. It is their ethnocentric variants, Eurocentricity and Afrocentricity that are at war.

Afrocentricity vs. Eurocentricity

"The philosophy that African American thinkers like Molefi Kete Asante extract from Diop's interpretation of ancient African texts is called 'holism.' This view which has come to be called 'Afrocentrism,' claims that all reality is a unity" (Verharen, 1995, 65). One might ask how a philosophy that has "Afro" in its name can claim to speak for the whole? Verharen says that "under the holism of Afrocentrism all humans are African peoples" (Verharen, 1995, 71). According to Asante:

> The Afrocentric analysis reestablishes the centrality of the ancient Kemetic [Egyptian] civilization and the Nile Valley cultural complex as points of reference for an African perspective in much the same way as Greece and Rome serve as reference points for the European world. (Asante, 1990, 9)

Is Asante saying that Afrocentricity is but the mirror image of Eurocentricity? How can that be, though, if Africa, and African civilization, is truly primary for all others?

Asante seems to be aware of these difficulties when he declares: "Perhaps what is needed is a post-Western or meta-Western metatheory to disentangle us from the consuming monopoly of a limited intellectual framework, but first let us establish the idea of an Afrocentric metatheory" (Asante, 1987, 34). Today, more than a decade later, now that Afrocentricity has been established and developed, it may be fruitful to explore what a "post-Western or meta-Western metatheory" might actually look like. Perhaps it will provide a broader "intellectual framework," one in which we can ground a grand theory of Black Studies.

Towards a Grand Theory of Black Studies

Humanity had an African genesis (Diop, 1991), and so too did civilization (Diop, 1974). When there were only Africans there was no Afrocentricity since there was no "Other." There was no need for Africans to be centered in their culture since there was no other culture for them to possibly be centered in.

The European tradition appreciated its African roots; that is, until the Age of Empire with its subjugation of Native Americans and enslavement of Africans. In order to rationalize the barbaric treatment of others, a virulent Eurocentrism was spawned that distorted and denigrated non-European cultural forms and fabricated history (Bernal, 1987; Bernal, 1991). Afrocentricity developed as a counter to Eurocentricity, as a reaction to it.

For example, Marimba Ani's Yurugu, "the most powerfully argued, as well as most extensive, presentation of the essential features of an Afrocentric worldview" (Howe, 1998, 247) begins thusly:

> This study of Europe is an intentionally aggressive polemic. It is an assault upon the European paradigm; a repudiation of its essence. It is initiated with the intention of contributing to the process of demystification necessary for those of us who would liberate ourselves from European intellectual imperialism (Ani, 1994, 1)

Afrocentricity *is* the mirror image of Eurocentricity in every sense of the word. Afrocentricity is a thoughtfully constructed philosophy; Eurocentricity something few would even admit to. The minority group's ethnocentrism is openly stated, in fact, celebrated. The majority's ethnocentrism is quieter, yet nonetheless the dominant, governing force. However, confronted with its own reflection, Eurocentricity gradually gives ground.

The institution of Black Studies programs and departments 30 years ago, in the wake of the nationalist movement of the sixties, was an example of Eurocentricity giving ground. Articles in the popular press admitting humankind's African origins and picturing Adam and Eve as Black (Tierney, 1988), and pieces stating that the founders of the Pharonic dynasties were Black (Kantrowitz, 1991), also exhibited Eurocentricity pulling back. The same can be said about the broad hearing given Bernal's *Black Athena*.

However, there was a sharp counterattack. In 1996, Mary Lefkowitz wrote a book, and co-edited another (Lefkowitz, 1996; Lefkowitz and Rogers, 1996), that specifically targeted Bernal's work. Two years later, Stephen Howe's *Afrocentrism: Mythical Pasts and Imagined Homes* delivered a detailed, hostile critique of nationalist Black Studies (Howe, 1998). However, even these books contained major admissions conceding the primacy of the African tradition:

> Apparently he (Herodotus) was so impressed by the antiquity and complexity of Egyptian culture that he wanted to establish connections with Greek customs wherever he could...These first century priests (Strabo and Diodorus) seem to have been particularly eager to point out to visitors instances of what the Greeks had learned from Egypt...The Greeks as we have seen were eager to connect themselves in any way they could to Egypt...The Greeks had such a high regard for Egyptian religion and laws, because they understood so little about them; quite unrealistically, they thought of the country as a utopia. The Greeks respected Egypt for the great antiquity of its civilization...But even if the Greeks had been able to take advantage of Egyptian expertise in certain areas, that would not mean that they had "robbed" Egypt of her knowledge, because knowledge (and culture) cannot be "stolen," like objets d'art. (Lefkowitz, 1996, 62, 72, 84, 85, 89)

> For sheer weight, intensity, persistence of negative prejudice, maybe no human group has been so burdened by others' attitudes as have Africans... Virtually every European state and ethnic group has drawn on and abused the discipline of archaeology in its search for historical roots, often involving straightforwardly racist ideas about the origins and destiny of itself and its neighbors. (Howe, 1998, 23–27)

Also, on the dust jacket of Howe's book we read: "For centuries, racist, colonial and Eurocentric bias has blocked or distorted knowledge of Africans, their histories and cultures. The challenge to that bias has been one of the greatest intellectual transformations of the late twentieth century." Why then is the book titled, *Afrocentrism: Mythical Pasts and Imagined Homes*? The revealing answer is found in the very next sentence on the dust jacket. "But alongside this necessary redressing has arisen a counter mythology, proclaiming the innate superiority of African-descended peoples."

Howe confuses cause and effect. Afrocentricity did not arise "alongside this necessary redressing"; rather it is the catalyst causing the necessary redressing. Afrocentricity developed as a counter to Eurocentricity, as a reaction to it. Whatever its flaws, it holds a mirror to Eurocentricity and Eurocentricity shrinks in the face of its own reflection. Afrocentricity is potent in that it attacks and destroys Eurocentricity, but it is necessarily flawed because it is necessarily ethnocentric.

In a relentlessly racially charged atmosphere, Afrocentricity and other nationalist Black Studies attack the admitted bias of the academy with, not surprisingly, relentlessly racial arguments. This has sparked a spirited debate, spurred on the development of a countervailing inclusionist wing to the discipline, and has spun off books like *Black Athena*.

The debate has yielded key concessions and inclusionist Black Studies has brought new resources and perspectives to the discipline. *Black Athena* has altered the academy's consensus on ancient history. Just as Martin Luther King would not have been successful without the specter of Malcolm X, the resources and facilities being poured into inclusionist Black Studies would hardly have been forthcoming without the challenge posed by nationalist Black Studies.

And while it is true that the inclusionist wing is a departure from the original thrust of the discipline, the original thrust was not, and could not have been, maintained. The activism that produced nationalist Black Studies characteristically comes in waves (Brisbane, 1974), and accommodation is as common a response as separation to the "crisis of the negro intellectual" (Cruse, 1984) and the fundamental challenge facing the African in America. The establishment's sponsoring of inclusionist Black Studies, though perhaps an attempt to blunt Afrocentricity and other nationalist Black Studies, still adds weight to multiculturalism.

Whereas the inclusionists are funded by the establishment, and, hence, have greater access to the American public, including the Black public, the nationalists have far more impact on the historical, the theoretical, and above all the moral development of the field (Asante, 1987; Asante, 1990; Karenga, 1993). After all the inclusionists are trying to, as their name implies, meld the field into the mainstream academy (Note their penchant for joint appointments in Black Studies and other older disciplines.)

Essentially, nationalist Black Studies articulates the African demand, and the inclusionists mediate the establishment's response. For example, note *The Encyclopedia of the African and African American Experience* (Gates, 1998) and its accompanying CD ROM funded by Microsoft. Also, note Henry Louis Gates' multipart PBS special on Africa, aired in late 1999, and the reaction to it on the internet and elsewhere. The strongest, most vociferous critique of these two projects has come from nationalist Black Studies circles, and the Black intellectual community, as a whole, seems to be siding with the nationalists. Doubtless, future editions of these projects will be modified to make them more palatable. And they will be criticized again, and modified again, in a complex, ongoing negotiation.

Will the two, nationalists and inclusionists, ever reach agreement? If they did, they would merge, and Black Studies and the mainstream academy would also become one. There would no longer be a need for "Black" Studies because the academy would have abandoned "White" Studies.

Other Lines of Thought

In this paper we presented a theory of Black Studies that focused on the discipline in terms of the fundamental contradiction of its two opposing wings, the nationalist and the inclusionist. However, there are other contradictions that others may see as equally important. For example, there are contradictions concerning race, gender, activism, multiculturalism, and orthodoxy.

Race: a fundamental construct or accident of identity?

> "Race is an invention of the white…I have not exactly seen, as asserted by Professor Spencer, how latching on to a bunch of worn out, discredited theories of biology and culture can save black folk." (Early, 1993, 57–58)

> "Theoretically, race is an indefensible category; practically, it is an inescapable aspect of American social reality." (Smith, 1993, 76)

Can orthodoxy of any kind be justified?

> "The new breed of 'color-blind' African American sings a refrain that is distressingly as simple as it is symptomatic. 'Rather than cast our lot with the race, we race to leave the caste.'" (Spencer, 1993, 47; Pollard, 1993)

> "What angers me is the inability many black people sometimes exhibit to accept nuances of thought and gradations of position as reasonable intellectual responses to the extraordinary profundity of our position in this society." (Early, 1993, 58).

Should commitment to race necessarily supersede commitment to gender?

> "The manipulation of the idea of an essential black identity around which we must all rally has been used to foster both racial solidarity and as a method of controlling African Americans. Consider for example, the effects of subordinating Black women's issues to the concerns of Black men." (Collins, 1993, 54)

Is Multiculturalism a friend to, or a competitor of, Black Studies?

> Throughout this paper we have seen multicultural studies as a broad rubric under which Black Studies can be included. Similarly, others may see it as an associated or allied field. However some view it as an outright danger. "The umbrella of multiculturalism is so broad that no ethnic group or lifestyle faction can be excluded from it…Its lack of distinctions causes it to include even what it intends to oppose." (Smith, 1993, 76)

Should thought (theorizing) or action (activism) be the goal?

> "Scholars have an obligation not just to interpret, but to act" (Marable, 1998). Knowledge for its own sake "may be unfashionable, and even unrealizable; but it should command our respect all the same." (Gates, 1998)

A theory of the discipline, I felt, should be structured, for elegance sake, around one central division, and inclusionism vs. nationalism, because of its centrality in the Black intellectual tradition, was selected as the frame in this paper. However, others might argue for a more complex, multifaceted scaffolding perhaps employing some, or all, of the above concerns.

Conclusion

No matter how a theory of Black Studies is constructed, though, can it really be expected to "give guidance, shape and direction to where Black Studies is headed?" Do disciplines develop this way, from the inside, from the self-conscious ruminations of its practitioners, or from external exigencies?

Foucault notes how behavioral sciences developed over centuries. As European royalty gradually lost its power and authority, the populace gradually began to internalize an increasingly sophisticated set of categorizations to govern their actions. Hence, sciences of behavior gradually came into being (Foucault, 1994). This was a rational process. One system of thought inevitably, inexorably supplanted another.

But Black Studies, and other multicultural studies, occur in post-rational, post-modern, times. Things move much, much faster. In fact, everything seems to be happening at once. Not only is the academy changing, every aspect of society is being rapidly transformed. Peoples, cultures and institutions are compressed, and the nature of society (community) changes at an accelerating rate (Toffler, 1970; Naisbitt, 1982). Some of these processes contradict, and some reinforce, each other. And some processes seem to be waxing and waning simultaneously. For example, the internet seems to be both centralizing and decentralizing authority. It increases the ability of government, and other institutions, to obtain information about the individual, while at the same time, the internet also increases the ability of individuals to access, and disseminate information. It is useless to only look at these changes in purely linear, rational, fashion. They must also be seen as a whole.

As America's power over the world grows, the American populace increasingly looks like the world's people. And as America's culture becomes the world's culture, a multicultural movement grows within America. It is largely over this multicultural movement, and the demographic changes that generate it, that a "culture war" rages within America's shores. At the heart of this conflict we find, not surprisingly, the political and economic struggle of the African.

If it can be said that people the world over made America, then none more so than the African. It was the labor of the African, and the trade in Africans, that generated the wealth that launched the Industrial Revolution, on both sides of the Atlantic (Williams, 1992). It was to a large extent over the land of the African that the world wars were initiated. America inherited its power from the war-shattered nations of Europe. Later, it employed the hypnotic power of its culture, largely recycled African American culture, to enthrall the world with the American Dream.

The theory of Black Studies that we have espoused points to incremental change in academia's, and the public's, perception of Africa and the history of Africa. We also noted that multicultural values are increasingly becoming the norm.

However, the educational system, on every level, continues to spew out false information. Also, as Black families grow more middle class, the Black family weakens (Lewin, 1990), and the Black prison population rises. And as Black artists and Black athletes make more and more money, negative stereotypes are increasingly broadcast around the world, shaping others' perceptions of African Americans, and Black youth's perceptions of itself (Lusane, 1997).

This certainly is the best of times for Africans in America, but doubtless it is also the worst. And when all is said and done, will the African still exist, literally, let alone culturally? And what role can Black Studies play, should Black Studies play, if any, in all of this? Manning Marable and Henry Louis Gates framed the issue well. "Scholars have an obligation not just to interpret, but to act" (Marable, 1998). Knowledge for its own sake "may be unfashionable, and even unrealizable; but it should command our respect all the same" (Gates, 1998). Doubtless they are each right that the other is wrong.

References

Ani, M. (1994). *Yurugu: An African-Centered Critique of European Cultural Thought and Behavior.* Trenton: Africa World Press.

Appelbome, P. (1996). "Can Harvard's Powerhouse Alter the Course of Black Studies?" *New York Times,* November 3, Section 4A, 241.

Asante, M. K. (1987). *The Afrocentric Idea.* Philadelphia: Temple University Press.

_____ (1990). *Kemet, Afrocentricity, and Knowledge.* Trenton: Africa World Press.

Bernal, M. (1987). *Black Athena: The Afroasiatic Roots of Classical Civilization, Volume I, Fabrication of Ancient Greece, 1785–1985.* New Brunswick: Rutgers University Press.

_____ (1991). *Black Athena: The Afroasiatic Roots of Classical Civilization, Volume II, Archaeological and Documentary Evidence.* New Brunswick: Rutgers University Press.

Brisbane, R. H. (1974). *Black Activism: Racial Revolution in the United States, 1954–1970.* Valley Forge: Judson Press.

Collins, P. (1993). "Setting Our Own Agenda," *The Black Scholar,* Vol. 23, No. 3 and 4, 54.

Cruse, H. (1984). *Crisis of the Negro Intellectual: A Historical Analysis of the Failure of Black Leadership.* New York: William Morrow.

Diop, C. A. (1974). *The African Origin of Civilization: Myth or Reality.* Chicago: Chicago Review Press.

_____ (1991). *Civilization or Barbarism: An Authentic Anthropology.* Chicago: Chicago Review Press.

Early, G. (1993). "A Brief Response to Michael Spencer," *The Black Scholar,* Vol. 23, No. 3 and 4, 58.

Foucault, M. (1994). *The Order of Things: An Archaeology of the Social Sciences.* New York: Vintage.

Gates, H. L., Jr. (1998). "A Call to Protect Academic Integrity from Politics," *New York Times*, April 4.

Howe, S. (1998). *Afrocentrism: Mythical Pasts and Imagined Homes*. London: Verso Books.

Kantrowitz, B. (1991). "Afrocentrism: Was Cleopatra Black? Fact or Fantasies—A Debate Rages over What to Tell Our Kids about Their Roots," *Newsweek*, September 23, 42–50.

Karenga, R. (1993). *Introduction to Black Studies*. Los Angeles: University of Sankore Press.

Lefkowitz, M. (1996). *Not Out of Africa: How Afrocentrism Became an Excuse to Teach Myth as History*. New York: Harper Collins.

_____, and G. M. Rogers (eds.) (1996). *Black Athena Revisited*. Chapel Hill: University of North Carolina Press.

LeMelle, T. (1984). "The Status of Black Studies in the Second Decade: The Ideological Imperative," in *The Next Decade: Theoretical Research Issues in Africana Studies*, James Turner (ed). Ithaca: Cornell University Press.

Lewin, A. (1984). "The Struggle for Authority in Black America," *The Western Journal of Black Studies*, Vol. 8, No. 4, 206–13.

_____ (1990). "A Tale of Two Classes: The Black Middle Class and the Black Poor," *The Black Scholar*, Vol. 21, No. 3, 7–13.

Liverani, M. (1996). "The Bathwater and the Baby," in *Black Athena Revisited: How Afrocentrism Became an Excuse to Teach Myth as History*, Mary Lefkowitz and Guy MacLean Rogers (eds.). Chapel Hill: University of North Carolina Press.

Lusane, C. (1997). "Interdisciplinary Perspectives on African American Studies," *Race and Reason*, Vol. 4 [1997–98].

Marable, M. (1998). "A Plea the Scholars Act Upon Not Just Interpret Events," *New York Times*, April 4.

McLuhan, M., and B. R. Powers (1989). *The Global Village: Transformations in World Life and Media in the 21st Century*. Oxford: Oxford University Press.

Naisbitt, J. (1982). *Megatrends: Ten New Directions Transforming Our Lives*. New York: Warner Books.

Okafor, V. (1993). "An Afrocentric Critique of Appiah's *In My Father's House*." *Journal of Black Studies*, Vol. 24, No. 2, 196–212.

Pollard, A. B., III (1993). "The Last Great Battle of the West: W.E.B. Du Bois and the Struggle for African America's Soul," in *Lure and Loathing: Essays on Race, Identity and the Ambivalence of Assimilation*, Gerald Early (ed.). New York: Penguin.

Shlain, L. (1998). *The Alphabet Versus the Goddess*. New York: Viking.

Smith, D. L. (1993). "Let Our People Go," *The Black Scholar*, Vol. 23, No. 3 and 4, 76.

Spencer, J. M. (1993). "Trends of Opposition to Multiculturalism," *The Black Scholar*, Vol. 23, No. 2, 2–5.

Tierney, J. (1988). "The Search for Adam and Eve," *Newsweek*, January 11, 46–52.

Toffler, I. (1970). *Future Shock*. New York: Random House.

Verharen, C. C. (1995). "Afrocentrism and Acentrism: A Marriage of Science and Philosophy," *Journal of Black Studies*, Vol. 26, No. 1, 62–76.

25

Africana Womanism: The Flip Side of a Coin

Clenora Hudson-Weems

Clenora Hudson-Weems, *Professor of English at the University of Missouri-Columbia, is the author of* Africana Womanism: Reclaiming Ourselves, *a seminal family centrality paradigm prioritizing race, class, and gender for all women of African descent, and* Emmett Till: The Sacrificial Lamb of the Civil Rights Movement, *which grew out of her 1988 doctoral dissertation, the first to take the position of Till's brutal lynching on August 28, 1955, as the true catalyst of the modern Civil Rights Movement. She is co-author of* Toni Morrison, *the first book on this Nobel Prize-winning author. Her forthcoming edited book is* Contemporary Africana Theory and Thought. *Her film script,* Emmett, *is with a major Hollywood producer, and a PBS Docu-film by Firelight Media in New York, based on her* Till *book, will begin its shooting this spring.*—The Western Journal of Black Studies, *Fall 2001, Vol. 25, No. 3*

Abstract

Africana Womanism is a paradigm designed for all women of African descent, prioritizing race, class, and gender, and is an antidote to stress affecting Black females as sisters and, moreover, Black male/female relationships, the foundation of the Black family, and the key to Black survival. "Africana Womanism" takes its models from African women warriors and creates a paradigm relative to this age-old legacy of Africana women's activism.

* * *

With the weight of racial pressures in the 20th century, the strained relationships among Black women emerged as well. Addressing these concerns, Africana Womanism became an antidote to the stress currently confronting both Black women as sisters, as well as Black male/female relationships. Nobel Prize-winning author, Toni Morrison, captured the strain of female relationships in particular in her commencement address, "Cinderella's Stepsisters," which she delivered at Barnard College in the 1980s. As you entertain Morrison's insights, just for the moment, I would like for you to substitute any particular group for women/mothers/sisters here, such as Blacks, Native Americans, Asians, Latinas, Jews, differently abled, men, etc. who, in much the same way as the women or the "stepsister" here could be discriminated against simply because of their differences:

> I am alarmed by the violence that women do to each other: professional vio-lence, competitive violence, emotional violence. I am alarmed by the willing-ness of women to enslave other women. I am alarmed by a growing absence of decency on the killing floor of professional women's worlds…
>
> I want not to ask you but to tell you not to participate in the oppression of your sisters. Mothers who abuse their children are women, and another woman, not an agency, has to be willing to stay their hands. Mothers who set fire to school buses are women, and another woman, not an agency, has to tell them to stay their hands. Women who stop the promotion of other women in careers are women, and another woman must come to the victim's aid. Social and welfare workers who humiliate their clients may be women, and other women colleagues have to deflect their anger…
>
> I am suggesting that we pay as much attention to our nurturing sensibili-ties as to our ambition. We are moving in the direction of freedom and the function of freedom is to free somebody else. You are moving toward self-ful-fillment, and the consequences of that fulfillment should be to discover that there is something just as important as you are and that just-as-important thing may be Cinderella—or your stepsister…
>
> In your rainbow journey toward the realization of personal goals, don't make choices based only on your security and your safety. Nothing is safe… But in pursuing your highest ambitions, don't let your personal safety dimin-ish the safety of your stepsister. In wielding the power that is deservedly yours, don't permit it to enslave your stepsisters. Let your might and your power emanate from that place in you that is nurturing and caring.

Here Morrison comments on her amazement at the cruel manner in which women treat each other every day, particularly in the workplace. Her statement offers profound insights into the nature and source of the absence of sisterhood on the part of many women toward each other, an unfortunate phenomenon which violates the very foundation of female relationships. Genuine Sisterhood, which is one of the eighteen characteristics of Africana Womanism as I defined in *Africana Womanism: Reclaiming Ourselves* (1993), is one of the key components for human survival, for the security and harmony of women undergird the strength and structure of society and all its participants. Other Africana Womanism descriptors are self-namer and selfdefiner, strong, in concert with male in struggle, whole, authentic, flexible role player, respected, recognized, spiritual, male compatible, respectful of elders, adaptable, ambitious, and mother and nurturing.

Commenting on the overall element of human survival, let me divert for a moment to the flip side of the coin, that is the plight of the Africana man, because our destinies are, indeed, intertwined. The dilemma of the Africana man, then, here symbolized in the horrific Till murder case, draws upon the interconnected experiences, interestingly demonstrating the critical need for a continued concerted struggle with both Black men and women together aiming at eradicating their shared oppression. One of the most graphic examples of racial violence and cultural dominance staring us in the eye is the August 28, 1955, brutal lynching of the 14-year-old Black Chicago youth, Emmett Louis "Bobo" Till, who naively whistled at a 21-year-old white woman, Carolyn Bryant, in Money, Mississippi, three months prior to Rosa Parks' December 1, 1955, refusal to relinquish her bus seat to a white man in Montgomery, Alabama, thereby becoming the true catalytic event of the modern Civil Rights Movement of the fifties and the sixties, as it undoubtedly set the stage for the Montgomery Bus Boycott. No one tells the Till story more vividly than does Rayfield Mooty, a civil rights activist, Labor Union leader, and my chief informant during my research, who was responsible for bringing this case to public attention. Till's second cousin by marriage contends that:

> No one who was old enough to be aware could forget that quiet Sunday morning, August 28, 1955, when the flame in the Civil Rights Movement that was burning low suddenly blazed following the reports of every newscaster on TV and radio and of telephone calls from friend to friend that Emmett Louis Till, fourteen, had been dragged from Moses Wright's (his uncle's) home in Money, Mississippi, by two white men in the middle of the night at gunpoint. One kidnapper's wife had accused Till of "wolf-whistling" at her in a grocery store. Four days passed, as blacks hoped that what seemed all too familiar and true, would prove to have been a nightmare. But on that fourth day, grim reality surfaced—Southern style. In an area where it suddenly runs 30 feet deep, the Tallahatchie River had become sick of something it was forced to swallow and heave up—the mutilated body of Emmett Till. A seventeen-year-old white fisherman, Robert Hodges, saw the feet sticking up. He got a motor boat, rode to the corpse and pulled it out. Till had been lynched, shot through the head and tossed, naked, into the river with a seventy-pound cotton gin fan tied around his neck with barbed wire. (Hudson-Weems, *Till*, 131–132)

Having said that, I would like to now go back to the original side of the coin— The Africana Woman and her triple plight. What is Africana Womanism?

> Neither an outgrowth nor an addendum to feminism, *Africana Womanism* is not Black feminism, African feminism, or Walker's womanism that some Africana women have come to embrace. *Africana Womanism* is an ideology created and designed for all women of African descent. It is grounded in African culture, and therefore, it necessarily focuses on the unique experiences, struggles, needs, and desires of Africana women. It critically addresses the dynamics of the conflict between the mainstream feminist, the Black feminist, the African feminist, and the Africana womanist. The conclusion is that *Africana Womanism* and its agenda are unique and separate from both

White feminism and Black feminism, and moreover, to the extent of naming in particular, *Africana Womanism* differs from African feminism. (Hudson-Weems, *Africana Womanism*, 24)

Note the importance of terminology—Africana womanism not feminism nor womanism, particularly as womanism is often misconstrued as being the same as Africana womanism, in spite of the fact that Walker defines a womanist in the introduction of her book, *In Search of Our Mothers' Gardens*, as:

A black feminist or feminist of color...who loves other women, sexually and/or non-sexually. Appreciates and prefers women's culture...[and who] sometimes loves individual men, sexually and/or nonsexually. Committed to survival and wholeness of entire people, male and female...Womanist is to feminist as purple to lavender. (xi, xii)

The culminating factor for Womanism and the womanist in the context of feminism and the feminist is that of a shade differentiation whereas Africana womanism offers an entirely different agenda with an entirely different set of priorities for the Africana womanist. Perceptively, the editors of *Call and Response: The Riverside Anthology of the African American Literary Tradition* see that "there is little differentiation between the womanist [Walker's] and the black feminist," and to a varying degree the feminist as well, in terms of their female-based agendas (1378–1379). Hence, the definition of the above terms are established. Once this is accomplished, it should be noted that in identifying with a particular terminology, you are automatically buying into its agenda as well.

In African cosmology, the term *nommo* means the proper naming of a thing which brings it into existence. Africana people have long been denied the authority of not only naming self, but moreover, of defining self. Morrison's *Beloved* reflects on this peculiar predicament for the enslaved—"Definitions belonged to the definers, not the defined" (Morrison, 190). As Black powerlessness during slavery should be a thing of the past, it is now of utmost importance that we seize the opportunity of taking control over both of these determining interconnected factors in our lives today if we hope to avoid degradation, isolation, and annihilation in a world of greed, violence, and pandemonium.

Why Africana Womanism and what is its relativity to modern-day feminism? To begin with, the priorities of Africana women are different from those of white women feminists. Africana womanism is family-centered, whereas feminism is female-centered. Our priorities are race, class, and gender, while the feminist concentrates on gender issues. We strive for race empowerment; the feminist, no matter what form of feminism, strives for female empowerment. White feminist Bettina Aptheker objectively analyzes these basic differences between Black and white women in her recognition that the first line of order for Black women and their communities is to address the race factor. Her accurate assessment of the situation is as follows:

When we place women at the center of our thinking, we are going about the business of creating an historical and cultural matrix from which women may claim autonomy and independence over their own lives. For women of color such autonomy cannot be achieved in conditions of racial oppression and cultural genocide... In short, "feminist," in the modern sense, means the empowerment of women. For women of color, such an equality, such an empowerment, cannot take place unless the communities in which they live can successfully establish their own racial and cultural integrity. (Aptheker, 19)

She makes it clear that addressing race issues for the Black women is a prerequisite for addressing gender concerns.

The recognition of the differences in the specific struggle of white women against white male domination both inside and outside of their private domain and Black women in a concerted liberation struggle with their male counterparts becomes crucial for discussion. Linda LaRue, voicing her positions some five years before Aptheker, understood this varying degree of white male domination relative to Black men and women verses white women. LaRue says:

Blacks are oppressed and that means unreasonably burdened, unjustly, severely, rigorously, cruelly and harshly fettered by white authority. White women, on the other hand, are only suppressed, and that means checked, restrained, excluded from conscious and overt activity. And this is a difference. (LaRue, 218)

Taking LaRue's concept to yet another level eight years later was Audre Lorde, who cautioned us of the dynamics of the discriminating phenomenon of Black women/white women, Black women/Black men, and Black/white interrelationships. This is particularly the case wherein Black women erroneously accept the notion that they have a shared commonality with white women as being equally subjugated by their male counterparts, which is a commentary on how the psyche of Black women, who buy into this notion, can negatively impact the Black community. Black women share oppression proportionally more with Black men in society than they do with white women. According to Lorde:

Black women and white women are not the same. For example, it is easy for Black women to be used by the power structure against Black men, not because they are men, but because they are Black. Therefore, for Black women, it is necessary at all times to separate the needs of the oppressor from our own legitimate conflicts within our communities. This same problem does not exist for white women. Black women and men have shared racist oppression and still share it...Out of that shared oppression we have developed joint defenses and joint vulnerabilities to each other that are not duplicated in the white community. (Lorde, 118)

This phenomenon of "shared racist oppression" is dramatized in Morrison'
Beloved, which I explore in *Africana Womanism*:

> Sethe and Paul D. unquestionably share a common bond, as "her story was
> bearable because it was his as well—to tell, to refine and tell again"...They
> have both been victimized in similar ways—both used as work horses and
> abused as grantees of the sexual whims of their oppressors. As readers are well
> aware that the women in *Beloved* represent the victims of "the 'unspeakable'
> fate to which most female slaves were heiresses," so are readers aware that
> this fate is one not experienced by the slave woman alone...On the contrary,
> Africana men, too, experienced sexual exploitation by their slave-holders,
> thereby validating this author's thesis that sexual exploitation and racism
> more closely identify the dynamics of the Africana experience during slavery
> than does the notion of sexual exploitation and gender. (Hudson-Weems,
> *Africana Womanism*, 99, 124)

For the moment, let us review the caustic beginnings of feminism for Blacks
in the mid 19th century when racial segregation and its attendant, oppression,
were the order of the day. Feminism and the Woman Suffrage Movement had
its beginnings with a group of liberal white women, who were concerned with
abolishing slavery and granting equal rights for all people regardless of race, class,
and sex. However, when the Fifteenth Amendment to the Constitution of the
United States was ratified in 1870, granting Africana men voting rights, while
denying that privilege for women—white women in particular—the attitudes
of those white women toward Blacks shifted. Unlike Black women, who were
jubilant with this victory for the Black race, as they knew that a vote in the Black
community could only improve things for them in general, white women were
disappointed, and justifiably so, having assumed that their benevolence toward
securing full citizenship for Africana people would ultimately benefit them.
Hence, an organized movement among white women from the 1880s on shifted
the pendulum from a liberal posture to a radically conservative one.

The National American Woman Suffrage Association (NAWSA) was
founded in 1890 by northern white women; however, "southern women were
also vigorously courted by that group" (Giddings, 81), which demonstrated the
growing race chauvinism of the late 19th century. Departing from the original
women's suffrage posture of Susan B. Anthony, the organization brought together
the National Woman Suffrage Association and the American Woman Suffrage
Association, protesting that middle-class white women's vote must aid their male
counterparts in preserving the virtues of the Republic from the threat of Black
men, unqualified and biological inferiors, who, with the voting power, could
acquire political power within the American system. Carrie Chapman Catt, a
staunch conservative suffragist leader, and other women in her camp, insisted
upon strong Anglo-Saxon values and white supremacy. They wanted to band
with white men to secure the vote for pure whites, excluding both Black and

white immigrants. In Peter Carrol and David Noble's *The Free and the Unfree* Catt is quoted thusly:

> There is but one way to avert the danger. Cut off the vote of the slums and give it to [white] women...[White men must realize] the usefulness of woman suffrage as a counterbalance to the foreign vote, and as a means of legally preserving white supremacy in the South. (296)

Embracing a firm belief in inherent Black inferiority, these women felt that Blacks should not be allowed the right to vote before white females, which did not come until passage of the Nineteenth Amendment in 1920. Thus, while it is understandable how white women felt regarding their exclusion from the voting rights agenda, their racist hostility and racist attitudes toward Africans were unjustifiable and hence cannot be overlooked.

As feminism is an agenda designed to meet the needs and demands of white women, it is plausible for that group, who are themselves victims of gender oppression primarily, to tailor a theoretical construct for the purpose of addressing those needs of eradicating female subjugation first. However, placing all women's history under white women's history, thereby assigning the definitive position to the latter, is rather presumptuous. It demonstrates the ultimate in racial arrogance in suggesting that authentic women activity resides with them alone. It is important here to establish the true role of the Africana woman as not a participant in a separate struggle, but rather as co-partner with the Africana man in this tremendous struggle between the races. To be sure, Frederick Douglass, himself a strong supporter of feminism prior to the 1863 signing of the Emancipation Proclamation, understood this well, as reflected in his opinions on women's rights:

> I have always championed women's rights to vote; but it will be seen that the present claim of the Negro is the one of the most urgent necessity. The assertion of the right of woman to vote meets nothing but ridicule. There is no deep-seated malignity in the hearts of the people against her; but name the right of the Negro to vote, all hell is turned loose and the Ku Klux and Regulators hunt and slay the unoffending black man. The government of this country loves women. They are the sisters, mothers, wives, and daughters of our rulers. (Douglass, 84)

Clearly, his loyalties shifted when the question of the Black man's right to vote became central to the overall picture of political power in the Black community. It is, therefore, ludicrous to include as feminists such Africana women activists as Lucy Terry, Maria Stewart, and Frances Watkins Harper; or leading abolitionists such as Sojourner Truth, militant abolition spokesperson and universal suffragist, or Harriet Tubman, the Underground Railroad conductor; or Ida B. Wells, the early 20th century anti-lynching crusader; and even to some degree, Anna Julia Cooper, who at least acknowledges in *A Voice from the South* that "woman's cause is man's cause: (we) rise or sink together, dwarfed or godlike, bond or free" (Cooper, 61). Moreover, Mary Church Terrell, president of the National Association of Colored Women, asserted that:

> Not only are colored women…handicapped on account of their sex, but they are almost everywhere baffled and mocked because of their race. Not only because they are women, but because they are colored women. (Freeman, 531)

The end result is reflected in Iva Carruthers' assertion, which rescued Parks in particular from the feminist arena years ago in the early eighties, contending that:

> In the American experience the feminist movement had effectively displaced Black unity whether in the context of the Abolitionist movement, the right-to-vote movement or the civil rights movement. And so we sit idly by and let whites turn Harriet Tubman and Rosa Parks into supporters of white feminism as opposed to race defenders. (Carruthers, 18)

Collectively, all these assertions here strongly anticipate that of a Nigerian activist, Taiwo Ajai, who holds that Africana women's "emancipation is unattainable until the basic rights are provided all [Black] people" (quoted in Ntiri's *One Is Not a Woman*, 62–63).

It is equally unjustifiable to consider Black women writers and their female characters as (Black) feminists. According to internationally acclaimed Nigerian novelist, Buchi Emecheta, author of *The Joys of Motherhood*:

> Women authors are frequently still being ignored by male critics or put into a separate category as "feminist" which means that their works are not evaluated in the same way as those of male authors. My novels are not feminist; they are part of the corpus of African literature and should be discussed as such…I deal with a variety of topics in my novels which are certainly not feminist: war, colonialism and the exploitation of Africa by the West, and many others…I have not been relating well with Western feminists and have found myself at loggerheads with them from time to time. They are only concerned with issues that are related to themselves and transplant these onto Africa…Western feminists are often concerned with peripheral topics and do not focus their attention on major concerns…They think that by focusing on exotic issues in the "third world" they have internationalized their feminism. (50)

There is also Zora Neale Hurston's *Their Eyes Were Watching God* and the protagonist, Janie Mae Crawford, who engages in a twenty-five-year quest for the right man, which is certainly not a feminist agenda. The protagonist, believing that her soul mate is off with some other women, pleas,

> And God, please suh, don't let him love nobody else but me. Maybe Ah'm is uh fool, Lawd, lak dey say, but Lawd, Ah been so lonesome, and Ah been waitin', Jesus. Ah done waited uh long time. (180)

Then there is Mariama Bâ's *So Long a Letter* and protagonist Ramautoule, who insists on the centrality of family:

> I am one of those who can realize themselves fully and bloom only when they form part of a couple. Even though I understand your stand, even though I respect the choice of liberated women, I have never conceived of happiness outside marriage [56]…I remain persuaded of the inevitable and necessary complementarity of man and woman…The success of a family is born of a couple's harmony, as the harmony of multiple instruments creates a pleasant symphony…The success of a nation therefore depends inevitably on the family. (88–89)

Also, there is Paula Marshall's *Praise Song for the Widow* and protagonist Ava Johnson, who, as the Africana womanist, comes to accept her authentic name—Avatara. Toni Morrison's *Beloved*, too, adds to this list, wherein the author speaks of positive male-female relationship via one of her male characters, Sixo:

> She is a friend of my mind. She gather me, man. The pieces I am, she gather them and give them back to me in all the right order. It's good, you know, when you got a woman who is a friend of your mind. (272–273)

And finally, there is Terri McMillan's *Disappearing Acts* and protagonists Zora and Franklin, whose lives end on a positive note of male-female togetherness.

All represent that body of Black women writers/novelist who should not be considered feminists or as having a feminist agenda.

A poignant example of the primacy of family and the need for prioritizing for human dignity and racial parity is the story of Ruth Mompati, the South African activist, who relates her experience of going into a large auditorium and witnessing countless decomposed bodies of children who had become victims of apartheid. She asserts that:

> The South African woman, faced with the above situation, finds the order of her priorities in her struggle for human dignity and her rights as a woman dictated by the general political struggle of her people as a whole. The national liberation of the Black South African is a prerequisite to her own liberation and emancipation as a woman and a worker (*One Is Not a Woman*, 112–113).

To be sure, this quotation is a firm representation of the opinion of Daphne Ntiri, an astute African scholar who specializes in women's issues. She contends that "human discrimination transcends sex discrimination…the costs of human suffering are high when compared to a component, sex obstacle" (Ntiri, 6).

Echoing that idea is Chioma Steady in *The Black Woman Cross-Culturally*, who holds that for the black woman in a racist society, racial factors, rather than sexual ones, operate more consistently in making her a target for discrimination and marginalization:

This becomes apparent when the "family" is viewed as a unit of analysis. Regardless of differential access to resources by both men and women, white males and females, as members of family groups, share a proportionately higher quantity of the earth's resources than do black males and females. There is a great difference between discrimination by privilege and protection, and discrimination by deprivation and exclusion. (27–28)

Here her assessment addresses the source of discrimination—racism—that Africana women continue to endure.

According to Hudson-Weems:

There is the oppression of the South African woman who must serve as maid and nurse to the white household with minimum wage earnings, the Caribbean woman in London who is the ignored secretary, and the Senegalese or African worker in France who is despised and unwanted. There is the Nigerian subsistence farmer, such as the Ibo woman in Enugu and Nsukka, who farms every day for minimum wages, and the female Brazilian factory worker who is the lowest on the totem pole. Clearly, the problems of these women are not inflicted upon them solely because they are women. They are victimized first and foremost because they are Black; they are further victimized because they are women living in a male-dominated society. (*Africana Womanism*, 30)

Be that as it may, the problems of Africana women beyond racism, including physical brutality, sexual harassment, and female subjugation in general perpetrated both within and outside the Africana community, ultimately have to be resolved on a collective basis within their communities. Because "Africana men have unfortunately internalized the patriarchal system to some degree," they must come together with their female counterparts and work toward eliminating racist influences in their lives first, with the realization that they can neither afford nor tolerate any form of subjugation, female subjugation included (Hudson-Weems, *Africana Womanism*, 63). Along those same lines, Ntiri summarizes Mompati's position that sexism "is basically a secondary problem which arises out of race, class and economic prejudices" (quoted in *Africana Womanism*, 5) Although Steady fails to properly name herself, she does, however, demonstrate a strong sense of priorities in the following quotation, which is clearly in alignment with the sense of prioritizing race issues inherent in Africana womanism:

Regardless of one's position, the implications of the feminist movement for the black woman are complex...Several factors set the black woman apart as having a different order of priorities. She is oppressed not simply because of her sex but ostensibly because of her race and, for the majority, essentially because of their class. Women belong to different socio-economic groups and do not represent a universal category. Because the majority of black women are poor, there is likely to be some alienation from the middle-class aspect of the women's movement which perceives feminism as an attack on men rather than on a system which thrives on inequality. (*The Black Woman Cross-Culturally*, 23–24)

Moreover, in her article in *Women in Africa and the African Diaspora*, Steady further asserts:

For the majority of black women poverty is a way of life. For the majority of black women also racism has been the most important obstacle in the acquisition of the basic needs for survival. Through the manipulation of racism the world economic institutions have produced a situation which negatively affects black people, particularly black women…What we have, then, is not a simple issue of sex or class differences but a situation which, because of the racial factor, is castlike in character on both a national and global scale. ("African Feminism," 18–19)

In reflecting exclusively on the question of gender for the Africana woman, it is naive for Africana women to believe that whenever they address gender issues, they are engaging in feminist activity, and hence, because gender problems are serious issues for them, too, they see themselves as needing feminism as a means of confronting this concern. In fact, some Africana scholars take it a step further, claiming that they are the "original feminists," insisting that Black women were feminists long before feminism, as if the term itself is so inherently sacred that they must be identified or connected with it. They vow that they will not let white women have feminism, herein engaging in a ludicrous battle for turf that clearly does not belong to them and which many Black women insist that they do not need anyway for various reasons. Be that as it may, Africana womanism, too, deals with gender issues, as the feminist has no exclusive on gender issues. As we are yet operating within a patriarchal system, attacking gender biases does not translate into mandating one's identification with or dependency upon feminism/ Black feminism as the only viable means of addressing them, which is obviously the practice of many staunch Black feminists in their attempts to validate their identity. Be that as it may, noted Black psychologist Julia Hare, in the 1993 *Black Issues in Higher Education*, asserted that:

Women who are calling themselves Black feminists need another word that describes what their concerns are. Black Feminism is not a word that describes the plight of Black women…The white race has a woman problem because the women were oppressed. Black people have a man and woman problem because Black men are as oppressed as their women. (Hare, 15)

Obviously Hare was not cognizant of the fact that another word had already been put forth in the public arena in several papers on the Black womanism/Africana womanism paradigm that I presented at national conferences, such as the National Council for Black Studies in March, 1986 and 1988, the African Heritage Studies Association in 1988, as well as the 1987 and 1988 National Women Studies Association Conference. These public presentations culminated in two

1989 articles—"Cultural and Agenda Conflicts in Academia: Critical Issues for Africana Women's Studies" in *The Western Journal of Black Studies*, and "The Tripartite Plight of Black Women in the Works of Hurston and Walker" in *The Journal of Black Studies*.

The truth of the matter is that the majority of Black women are not feminists/ Black feminists, but rather Black women activists whose activities are best characterized by race-based activities as outlined by Africana womanism. According to Patricia Liggins-Hill, general editor of *Call and Response*, "of all the theoretical models, Hudson-Weems's best describes the racially based perspective of many black women's rights advocates, beginning with Maria W. Stewart and Frances W. Harper in the early 19th century" (1370). In fact, Africana women activists can be seen as blueprints for framing other gender theories to some degree. For example, Black women have been neither silent nor voiceless as seems to have been the case of feminists in general, who aspire to this quality, and thus, "breaking silence" and "finding voice" have become a major goal for them. This need is expressed in Betty Friedan's *The Feminist Mystique*, in which she describes the feeling of disenchantment with household drudgery on the part of white women and their desire to be free, asserting that there was a

> strange stirring, a sense of dissatisfaction, a yearning that women suffered in the middle of the twentieth century in the United States. Each suburban wife struggled with it alone as she made the beds, shopped for groceries, matched slipcover materials, ate peanut butter sandwiches with the children, chauffeured Cub Scouts and Brownies, lay beside her husband at night—she was afraid to ask even of herself the silent question—is this all? (Friedan, 11)

This would hardly be the reaction of Black women, who would readily respond that if this is all that they could expect out of the relationship, then the relationship would be in trouble.

In spite of the overall position in the academy, Africana women do not see their male counterparts as their primary enemy as does the white feminist, who is carrying out an age-old battle with her counterpart for subjugating her as his property. According to Nigeria's first woman playwright, 'Zulu Sofola:

> It [the dual-gender system between African men and women] is not a battle where the woman fights to clinch some of men's power [which] consequently has set in motion perpetual gender conflict that has now poisoned the erstwhile healthy social order of traditional Africa. (quoted in *Africana Womanism*, 47)

Moreover, contrary to the white feminists' need to be equal to men as human beings, Black women have always been equal to their male counterparts, in spite of some Africana men's attempts to subjugate them on some levels. According to Angela Davis in *Women, Race and Class*:

> The salient theme emerging from domestic life in the [American] slave quarters is one of sexual equality. The labor that slaves performed for their own

sake and not for the aggrandizement of their masters was carried out on terms of equality. Within the confines of their family and community life, therefore, Black people transformed that negative equality which emanated from the equal oppression they suffered as slaves into a positive quality: the egalitarianism characterizing their social relations. (18)

In addition, during American slavery, Africana women were as harshly treated, physically and mentally, as were their male counterparts, thereby invalidating the alignment of Africana women and white women as equals in the struggle. One need only to reflect on Sojourner Truth's 1852 "Ain't I a Woman" oration, which she unsolicitedly delivered at the all-white Women's Rights Convention in Akron, Ohio:

Well, chullun, whar dar is so much racket, dar must be something out okilter. I t'ink dat 'twixt de niggers of de Souf an' de women at de Norf' all a'talkin' bout rights, de white men will be in a fix pretty soon. But what's all dis here talkin' 'bout?

Dat man ober dar say dat women needs to be helped into carriages, and lifted ober ditches, and to hab de best place everywhere. Nobody eber helped me into carriages, or ober mud puddles, or gibs me any best place. And ain't I a Woman? Look at me! Look at my arm! I have ploughed, and planted and gathered into barns and no man could head me! And ain't I a woman? I could work as much and eat as much as a man—when I could get it—and bear de lash as well! And ain't I a woman? (Truth, 104)

Indeed, the endless chores of the Africana woman awaited her both inside and outside the home. To be sure, Africana men and women have been equal partners in the struggle against oppression from early on. Again, they could not afford division based on gender. Granted, in some traditional societies, male domination was a characteristic; but in the African-American slave experience, Africana men and women were viewed the same by the slave owners, thereby negating traditional (African and European) notions of male or female roles.

Black sociologist Joyce Ladner in *Tomorrow's Tomorrow* also comments on the Black woman's opinion of the Black man as not her primary enemy:

Black women do not perceive their enemy to be black men, but rather the enemy is considered to be oppressive forces in the larger society which subjugate black men, women and children. (277–278)

Therefore, the Black man has no institutional power to oppress his women or anyone for that matter to the same degree as do white men in the case of their women and people in general. In the final analysis, the Africana "females and males were equal in the sense that neither gender wielded economic power over the other" (Boulin-Johnson and Staples, 49). Given these realities, Germaine Greer's contention that "Men are the enemy. They know it—at least they know there is a sex war on, an unusually cold one" appears inapplicable to the circumstance of Africana women and the overall Africana community (Lashmar, 33).

Today, Africana women must insist that they are equal partners in a relationship in which passive female subjugation neither was nor is the norm in their community. According to Morrison in "What the Black Woman Thinks about Women's Lib,"

> for years black women accepted that rage, even regarded that acceptance as their unpleasant duty. But in so doing they frequently kicked back, and they seem never to have become the true slaves that white women see in their own history. (63)

Indeed, Africana women have not had that sense of powerlessness that white women speak of, nor have they been silenced or rendered voiceless by their male counterparts, as is the expressed experience of white women. The labels "Black Matriarch," "Sapphire," and "bitch" appended to the Africana woman to describe her personality and character clearly contradict the notion of the Africana woman as voiceless or powerless. Moreover, unlike the white woman, the Africana woman has been neither privileged nor placed on a pedestal for protection and support.

In conclusion   s I reflect on the embryonic stage of "Africana Womanism" in the mid eighties, which I earlier referred to as "Black Womanism," I found it necessary to name and define the true concerns, priorities, and activities of Black women. As I participated in international dialogues at international conferences, serving on panels relative to Africana women and their true role within the constructs of the modern feminist movement, it became clear to me that Africana women globally, both in their private and public lives, engage in supporting their male counterparts for the safety and security of their families and communities as a number one priority. Reflecting on the history of Africana people and women in particular, my conclusion was that for centuries Africana women have been engaging in Africana womanist activities, demonstrating a prioritizing of race as collective activists and that this legacy dates back to the rich legacy of African womanhood. Thus, the existence, not the name itself, of this phenomenon—Africana womanism—is not new, but rather a practice that dates back to Africa. To be sure, *Africana Womanism* takes its models from African women warriors and moves on to create a paradigm relative to this age old legacy of Africana women activism. The results, in the words of Delores Aldridge, in "Towards Integrating Africana Women into Africana Studies," is a "revolutionary work on Africana womanism [that]…has no parallel as a new way of understanding Africana women" (196). And so, in returning to the collective struggle and leadership of Africana people globally for the survival of our entire family/community, let us not forget our past strengths, indeed, the rich legacy of our glorious African ancestry, and indeed, the rich legacy of Africana womanhood.

References

Ajai, T. (1981). "The Voluptuous Ideal," in *One Is Not a Woman, One Becomes: The African Woman in a Transitional Society*. Daphne Ntiri (ed.). Troy, MI: Bedford.

Aldridge, D. (2000). "Towards Integrating Africana Women into Africana Studies," in *Out of the Revolution: Studies in Africana Studies*. Delores Aldridge and Charlene Young (eds.). Lanham, MD: Lexington Books [191–202].

Aptheker, B. (1981). "Strong Is What We Make Each Other: Unlearning Racism within Women's Studies," *Women's Studies Quarterly*, Vol. 1, No. 4.

Bâ, M. (1980). *So Long a Letter*. Oxford, England: Heinemann.

Boulin-Johnson, L., and R. Staples (1993). *Black Families at the Crossroads: Challenges and Prospects*. San Francisco: Jossey-Bass.

Carroll, P. N., and D. W. Nobel (1977). *The Free and the Unfree: A New History of the United States*. New York: Penguin Books.

Carruthers, I. E. (1980). "Africanity and the Black Woman," *Black Books Bulletin*, Vol. 6, 14–20, 71.

Cooper, A. J. (1988). *A Voice from the South* [1892]. Reprint, New York: Oxford University Press.

Davis, A. (1983). *Women, Race and Class*. New York: Vintage.

Douglass, F. (1976). *Frederick Douglass on Women's Rights*. Philip S. Foner (ed.). Westport, CT: Greenwood Press.

Freeman, J. (ed.) (1995). *Women: A Feminist Perspective*. Palo Alto, CA: Mayfield.

Friedan, B. (1963). *The Feminine Mystique*. New York: Dell.

Giddings, P. (1984). *When and Where I Enter: The Impact of Black Women on Race and Sex in America*. New York: Bantam.

Hare, J. (1993). Quoted in "Feminism in Academe: The Race Factor," Ellen Crawford in *Black Issues in Higher Education*. Vol. 10, No. 1, 12–15.

Hill, P. L. (1997). *Call and Response: The Riverside Anthology of the African American Literary Tradition*. Boston/New York: Houghton Mifflin.

Hudson-Weems, C. (1989). "Cultural and Agenda Conflicts in Academia: Critical Issues for Africana Women's Studies," *The Western Journal of Black Studies*, Vol. 13, No. 4, 185–189.

―――――. (1993). *Africana Womanism: Reclaiming Ourselves*. Troy, MI: Bedford.

―――――. (1994). *Emmett Till: The Sacrificial Lamb of the Civil Rights Movement*. Troy, MI: Bedford.

Hurston, Z. (1978). *Their Eyes Were Watching God*. Urbana: University of Illinois Press.

Ladner, J. (1972). *Tomorrow's Tomorrow: The Black Woman*. Garden City, NY: Anchor.

Lashmar, P. (1996). "The Men's Gloom," *New Statesman and Society*, Vol. 9.

Lorde, A. (1984). *Sister Outsider*. Freedom: Crossing Press.

Mompati, R. (1981). "Women and Life under Apartheid," in *One Is Not a Woman, One Becomes: The African Woman in a Transitional Society*. Daphne Ntiri (ed.). Troy, MI: Bedford.

Morrison, T. (1971). "What the Black Woman Thinks about Women's Lib," *The New York Times Magazine*, August.

―――――. (1987). *Beloved*. New York: Alfred A. Knopf.

―――――. (1993). "Cinderella Stepsisters," in *Issues across the Curriculum*. Seattle, WA: Impact Communications.

Ntiri, D. W., (ed.) (1982). *One Is Not a Woman, One Becomes: The African Woman in a Transitional Society*. Troy, MI: Bedford.

Ravell-Pinto, T. (1985). "Buchi Emecheta at Spelman College," *Sage*, Vol. 2, No. 1, 50–51.

Sofola, Z. (1993). Quoted in *Africana Womanism: Reclaiming Ourselves*, by Clenora Hudson-Weems. Troy, MI: Bedford.

Steady, F. C. (ed.) (1981). *The Black Woman Cross-Culturally*. Cambridge, MA: Schenkman.

―――――. (ed.) (1987). *Women in Africa and the African Diaspora*. Rosalyn Terborg-Penn, Sharon Harley, and Andrea Benton Rushing (eds.). Washington, D.C.: Howard University Press.

Truth, S. (1968). "And Ain't I a Woman," in *Narrative of Sojourner Truth*. New York: Arno and *The New York Times*.

Walker, A. (1983). *In Search of Our Mothers' Gardens*. San Diego: Harcourt Brace Jovanovich.

Africana Studies and Gender Relations in the Twenty First Century

DELORES P. ALDRIDGE

Delores P. Aldridge (Ph.D., Purdue University) is the Grace Towns Hamilton Professor of Sociology and African American Studies, Emory University. She served as the founding director of African American and African Studies at Emory in 1971 as well as the first African American woman faculty member at the institution. Aldridge became the unprecedented two-term elected president of the National Council for Black Studies under whose leadership the organization received major funding for numerous projects. One of these projects that she directed focused on collection, analysis, and dissemination of information regarding the presence and nature of Black Studies on 1,600 college and university campuses, the findings of which were the impetus for much of her prolific scholarship on cultural democracy, gender relations, and Africana Studies over the last decade including this article.—The Western Journal of Black Studies, Fall 2003, Vol. 27, No. 3

Abstract

There must be complementarity in gender relations in Africana Studies in the 21st century for the continued survival and healthy development of the discipline. Reasons for promoting gender equity are explored, and common grounds for male and female scholars as well as external forces impinging upon the destiny of African peoples and their scholarship are presented. Finally, strategies are offered for integrating Black women into an Africana Studies curriculum.

Introduction

African people are the genesis of human kind and over the ages men and women have complemented each other in work, family life, and goals. This complementarity in gender relations must be kept for a healthy continued development in a discipline that maintains a dual mission of academic excellence and social responsibility. Focusing on its intellectual discourse, the question needs to be asked insistently and consistently: What would promote strong and positive gender relations in demonstrated intellectually sound scholarship? And, how does the discipline nurture this kind of development? Much of the African world might agree on an approach to the discipline that promotes and enhances equity, is balanced with and by work of both genders, offers rewards to both, and functions in a sustainable relation to the academy's other entities or disciplines. Determining whether this is the case and how such an equitable discipline might be developed are enormous questions Africana scholars should be considering. Indeed, Africana scholars have the ability to create a much better discipline than we have yet succeeded in establishing.

Africana womanist scholars urge the redefinition of the partnership between Africana men and women in pursuit of intellectual and political objectives (see Henry and Foster, 1982; Gordon, 1987; Hudson-Weems, 1989, 1997; Aldridge, 1992). Proponents of this view generally identify with and contribute to the overall efforts to develop Africana Studies as a discipline rather than aligning with Women's Studies departments and programs without affiliation to Africana Studies units.

In this article I focus on the future of Africana Studies in American higher education and more specifically on promoting gender equity in Africana Studies and its implications for the survival of the discipline. I believe both Black men and women must play crucial roles in the promotion and development of Africana scholarship and in the promotion of models for empowerment of Black people. I strongly believe that a large, strong, and united intellectual constituency of men and women is essential for the development and implementation of pedagogy and scholarship focusing on the lives of people of the African Black World.

As is well known, there has been increasing focus on women and race in recent years, but women issues seem to be overshadowing much of the Black issues, be they male or female, in the new dialogue within many institutions of higher education. And, within the ranks of Africana Studies, there is need for careful attention to efforts to offset fragmentation, which can serve to dilute the full attention to the overall group. Put another way, a vision of the American academy that highlights gender differences as complementary among Africana scholars (as well as the commonalities) can be useful in capturing the need and appreciating the potential of mutual intellectual as well as political support as a unified group.

I argue that gender complementarity increases the political effectiveness and intellectual necessity of the thrust of Africana Studies as a whole. But I also wish to demonstrate that the likelihood of gender political cooperation could increase if we could persuade women and men to focus more on the interests that they hold in common. Although there are many similarities in interest between the two groups in the academy, I believe that the most powerful force for positive group action and complementarity resides in increasing the intellectual visibility of women that can occur from their integration in all phases of the Africana scholarly enterprise, including attention to theory building.

As I make the case for a genuine marriage or political coalition with a broad-based intellectual agenda, I also am interested in an enterprise that includes a male-female focus that would encourage gender cooperation and offset tension. This inclusion is an essential aspect of any united effort that seeks to promote equity in scholarship and visibility in Africana Studies, without alienating male supporters. It is refreshing to note that when common survival is concerned, individuals can come together. For example, recently, business consultant Paul Hawken conducted a workshop with middle level managers in a big corporation that produces, among other things, pesticides and herbicides. Early in the discussion, the group of managers—engineers and MBAs—strongly rejected the idea that creating full social justice and resource equity in American society is essential to the long-term viability of business and the nation itself. Then, these managers were given an exercise asking them, in five groups, to design a spaceship "that would leave the Earth and bring its inhabitants back, alive, happy, and healthy 100 years later." After this, the managers voted on which group's spaceship design was best. The winning design was comprehensive. It included important beneficial insects, so no pesticides were required. Recognizing the importance of photosynthesis, the winning group decided that "weeds were important in a healthy ecosystem and banned herbicides on board. Their food system, in other words, was totally organic. This group of engineers and MBAs also decided that as a crew, they needed lots of singers, dancers, artists, and storytellers, because the CDs and videos would get old and boring fast, and engineers alone did not a village make." Most strikingly, these same corporate managers decided for justice and equity. When they "were asked if it was OK if 20 percent of the people on the spaceship controlled 80 percent of the resources on board, they immediately and vociferously rejected that notion as unworkable, unjust, and unfair" (1999).

This suggests that any group contributing to an enterprise will wish to equitably share in the benefits and rewards. Of course, this is instructive for those in Africana Studies and in higher education, where Black women are matriculating in greater numbers than Black men. Can a developing discipline afford to ignore them? Or, must it nurture and cater to them?

Africana Studies: A Look at Its History

Africana Studies must not ignore its history with its reformist-radical roots. Forerunners or precursors of the modern Africana Studies movement were men such as W.E.B. Du Bois and Carter G. Woodson and women such as Anna Julia Cooper and Ida Wells Barnett. Contemporary Africana Studies pioneers were men such as Nathan Hare, John Henrik Clarke, James Turner, Leonard Jeffries, James Stewart, Maulana Karenga, Molefi Asante, William Nelson, Howard Dodson, Sinclair Drake, and Vincent Harding. Women in the ranks of pioneers include among others, Delores P. Aldridge, Angela Davis, Frances Beale, Mary Frances Berry, Bertha Maxwell, Carlene Young, Vivian Gordon, Sonia Stone, Charsye McIntyre, Barbara Woods, Shirley Weber, and Barbara Sizemore. The original mission of the movement must be continuously reaffirmed—liberation of our people through intellectual excellence and social responsibility. At the beginning there were both men and women fighting side by side for the liberation of Black people. There was no fighting for women or fighting for men but fighting for the group. From this beginning, a Black male hegemony focus and a counter Black Women's Studies Movement emerged.

However, the major scholarship, theorizing, and orientation of the field became dominated by males. Some women felt it necessary to wage a battle for gender recognition as a field worthy of being studied. Out of this perceived rejection, a move to revitalizing and creating scholarship by and about Black women has emerged often within Women Studies or separately. But, the move to Women's Studies has not been without its tensions and disappointments. Many Black women have felt their interests were not at the center of the discourse. Bell Hooks (1984) dealt with this in her work, *Feminist Theory: From Margin to Center*. However, to envision Black women becoming the center of a field dominated by white women stretches the imagination. Moreover, is it more natural to move to the center of Africana Studies with equal status to that of Black males and their scholarship? Would such a move not be in keeping with recovery of the original mission of Africana Studies—a disclaimer of Euro-male centered scholarship?

Africana womanism and African centered Afro-centricity, if truly embraced, is a means toward recovering the initial thrust and roots of equity and justice in Africana Studies. Neither of these orientations or schools of thought advocates separatism of Black men from Black women, but rather encourages togetherness so that they and their families may forge ahead. The big questions or issues need to be raised so as to bridge the divide and ensure a future for Africana Studies. Will the Black male be open to recovery of the mission, given that they appear to be under siege? Can we work on the issues of divide and conquer? Where are our relevant studies on the impact of racism? Where are our relevant studies on the impact of sexism? Should the group be moving together to study these major issues?

In laying out the arguments in this presentation, I am reminded of the words of Carlene Young in a speech given at Emory University in February, 2002. Commenting on strategies to combat Black gender inequality in the academy, she stated:

> I hope that Black scholars in the academic community will begin to recognize and appreciate the need for broad-based institutional organizing to create the kind of collective consciousness to pull us together. I fear that too many are not

convinced that it can be done, but what we need is the constituency—those who are willing to think hard about how to create, sustain, and energize Black men and women scholars to work for a discipline that is truly ours.

I am also reminded of work done with three male colleagues (Hare, Stewart, Young, Aldridge, 2000), who in examining the historical background and contemporary status of, and the future directions and challenges to Africana Studies, used the idea of an Africana village, metaphorically, to describe the variety of scholarly activity in the field. Long before the oft quoted statement "It takes a village to raise a child" became popular, those of us familiar with the African example knew that the village indeed rears the child. So is it unreasonable to ask or expect that "It takes a village to raise a discipline"? Just as a village has complementing and competing components, so does the field of Africana Studies consist of a variety of intellectual traditions, which differ in approach even as we share the forward garnering of knowledge about, and advancement of, the Africana community as our objective. In short, Africana Studies is an academic area in which a wide variety of activities takes place under a broad ideological umbrella and under a variety of structural arrangements (such as departments, programs, and centers). While such units are usually located on the university campus, some are community based. A few university based units sponsor overseas travel and/or study abroad programs (Hare, Stewart, Young, and Aldridge, 2000, 126).

Specifically, I envision women and men committed to advancing the field by promoting gender equality. I have in mind committee structures in national organizations, departmental rewards and responsibilities, journal coverage, curricula balance, etc. But whatever the main features of the coalition, a case has to be made for why the idea of an all out effort should be seriously considered. This is the real purpose of this article.

Why Promote Gender Equity?

I argue first that our ability to overcome obstacles to the creation of a true Africana intellectual community will depend on an adequate understanding of the nature of our position and conditions that make for male chauvinistic gender ideology either to flourish or to subside, including the conditions that have contributed to less inclusiveness and visibility for women. What contributes to men according value to the study of Black women? To what extent have Black women published in areas that did not deal specifically with Black women? Have Black women developed a considerable body of scholarship in areas outside of a focus on their own gender? And, if so, to what extent can this work be universally relevant? For example, when Africana scholars focus on Black lives, how is the case being made as to the universality of the scholarship?

In sociology, for example, Du Bois' and Cox's theories have been seen as particularist, while studies on families, lives, race, caste, and capitalism by non-

Blacks have been seen as revolutionary and providing critical theory relevant for all. In the future, Africana women scholars might be persuaded to choose broader themes of study and to develop more theories to explain human phenomena as it relates to Black people and the world. In explaining my own perspective of Africana womanism, for example, I contend it is one where women are at the center of creating the discourse and not necessarily the focus of the phenomenon being set forth. Put another way, women create theoretical and empirical work, but such work may or may not center solely, or at all, on the lives of women. This also suggests women will be at the center of creating policies and directives that are positive for black men, women, and children. This perspective does not worry itself with bashing men, white women, or those who disagree with it. It is consumed with being at the center of framing issues, developing institutions, and implementing policies. It encourages continued development of scholarship by and about Africana women, particularly with increased focus on the social and behavioral sciences, the natural sciences, professions, and policy studies such as work done by Marimba Ani with her ground breaking book, *Yurugu, An African-Centered Critique of European Culture, Thought and Behavior* (1994). Work of those who have already published in these areas must be sought, studied, and cited to facilitate greater visibility. Men must both study issues surrounding women's lives as well as cite women scholars' work.

On the other hand, in pursuing scholarship Africana women scholars might advocate the promotion of their work in a number of structural arrangements within the academy. They might opt to have joint appointments with Women Studies and Africana Studies, or develop scholarship within longer standing disciplines while affiliating as associates or joint appointments in Africana Studies units as the discipline develops a broader vision of Africana scholarship—one that is inclusive placing value on its women's scholarship.

Toward Common Grounds of Male and Female Scholars

The need for such a vision is made apparent in my second argument. Perceptions of gender tension obscure the fact that both Black men and women suffer from many common problems, including the lack of respect for their work with the lesser visibility given to it. So while little value has been placed on women's scholarship outside of their own circles because of the direction that much of their scholarship has taken, *neither* has a great deal of value been placed on scholarship by and about Black men. Thus, there exist commonalities for all to forge ahead together.

Beginning in 1968, Black Studies programs and departments were formed at many colleges and universities—they were the academic structures that emerged from the various "Black Power" movements. Many of these programs were established as a result of nonviolent (and sometimes violent) protests launched on college and university campuses by Black and white students around the country. African American women fully participated in these protests and enrolled in the new courses in large numbers. Black women expected there to be common ground, but did not fully appreciate gender biases among men and also those women who had been socialized in a patriarchal society that placed greater value on men and their work than on women and their work. Despite women's participation in and support for Black Power and their enrollment in large numbers in Black Studies courses, African American women were met with male chauvinism and sexism. A perusal of the course listings for Black Studies programs between 1967 and 1970 reveals that there were few (if any) courses devoted to the history, literature, and experiences of African American women (Hull, Scott, and Smith, 1974).

In their introduction to *All the Women Are White, All the Blacks Are Men, but Some of Us Are Brave: Black Women's Studies*, Hull and Smith noted that "according to *Who's Who and Where in Women's Studies*, published by the Feminist Press in 1974, out of a total of 4,658 Women's Studies courses, approximately forty-five (less than one percent) of the courses listed a focus on Black women." Interestingly, it also was reported that "the largest number of courses on Black women was in Afro-American and Black Studies departments." More recently, in a study sponsored by the National Council for Black Studies in 1992, in surveying course offerings throughout the United States, I found there had been an increase in course offerings focusing on women, but no substantive changes in the inclusion of work by and about women that was outside of courses that carried women titles. And still, the majority of such courses were in Africana Studies units. This and many other observations precipitated concern for moving toward common ground and thus the idea of *Out of the Revolution: The Development of Africana Studies*. In this text by Aldridge and Young (2000), two women dared to frame intellectual thought and provide historical and quantitative data for the discipline. This was novel, for such an effort had almost totally been the domain of men.

The commonality of skills and ideas were put forth under one cover; the text allowed women to do equal time with men. Importantly, Africana women can never lose sight of the fact that they are Black and women, and it is easier to identify "Black" than "sexuality" or "gender," whatever the physical place or the nature of discrimination.

External Forces Impinging upon the Destiny of African Peoples and Their Scholarship

Thirdly, I argue that despite African America's understandable focus on racial discrimination, our fate is inextricably connected with the structure and functioning of the global economy, for there are external forces impinging upon the destiny of African peoples and their scholarship. In 1994 I wrote: "Placing diversity in historical context is important because obscuring the roots of this issue negates the contributions and importance of African Americans. The Civil Rights Movement and subsequent efforts to present African American life as a legitimate subject of academic study, are defining moments in our nation's consciousness of its diverse makeup" (p. ii). In that same year I also wrote "Toward Womanist Perspectives in Africana Studies." In retrospect, it seems a very timely overlap. I argue that Africana Studies, more than any other field, will benefit from reinforcing gender cohesion for strength in numbers in developing its craft. I wish to highlight the fact, however, that globalization of curriculums is not only being accompanied by new constraints on university funds and other private and federal funds, it is also occurring at a time when so many other competing demands exist.

Increasingly, European interdisciplinary studies are coming into the academy reaffirming and expanding commitment to white Western civilization. Africana women and men do not have the luxury of competing against each other—resources are too limited, and understanding bureaucracies and how they work makes this clear (Young, 2000). With limited resources, can bureaucracies accommodate another segment, such as Black Women Studies, as an independent unit? It has taken over thirty years for Africana Studies units to become institutionalized and they still are not fully accepted. What makes us think Black Women Studies as a separate entity would be funded and supported? When competing for scarce resources, choices have to be made. If this is a realistic assessment, then if the question is forced as to what should stay or go, what is going to be our response? The true tragedy would be a circumstance where there is increased funding for Black Women Studies with the rationale of need for enhanced emphasis on women's issues, but with a resulting decrease of funding of African Studies due to limited resources.

Therefore, the need for gender cooperation is imperative to generate programs that emphasize the lives of all Black people. But here I want to also spell out the conditions that I feel facilitate the formation of such a union. Take for example the newly emerging Africana Studies Department at Clark Atlanta University—an institution where I sit on the Board of Trustees. This department proposes to demonstrate how two separate and long standing units can merge into one with both becoming stronger as a result of the marriage. This merger is coming about as a result of much deliberation at various management levels and constituencies across the campus. While there is no reluctance of females to take all courses, males tend to question whether it is necessary for them to take courses with women listed titles or whether these courses are simply frills? This will necessitate a change in collective consciousness and makes it necessary to have courses focusing on women in the tract be required for completion of a degree.

Integrating Black Women into an Africana Studies Curriculum

The previous section as outlined allows us to now address an important question that emerges from the approach of Clark Atlanta University: whether the divisive issue of a women's tract should be included within a department. Building on the perception of tension, academic content equity, reward systems, and visibility, I would like to attempt to show how a distinct women's track can be a part of the gender equity agenda without becoming divisive. This track can be developed as we understand how Black women's realities have not been addressed in the academy historically and when we convincingly argue for the need, as was initially done for Africana Studies units themselves. Moreover, the intellectual togetherness can lay the foundation for mending the tension in our daily male-female lives as I articulate in my LENS Theory in works on Black Male-Female Relationships. Just as there have been divides between Africana men and women, so have there been divides over scholarship where white women scholars are concerned. Understandably, Black women are frustrated with both Black men and white women. Consequently, some Black women have responded to the insensitivity to their scholarship by indicating white women are "clueless" as to the need or desire to understand and promote work on or by Africana women. How have Black women responded?

One result of the "cluelessness" of white academic feminists about the history, culture, and experiences of African American women was the coining of the term "womanism" by novelist Alice Walker to highlight the differences in strategies and objectives between Black and white feminists. In her book, *In Search of Our Mothers' Gardens: Womanist Prose* (1983), Walker defined "womanist" as one who is committed to the survival and wholeness of an entire people. Walker placed her emphasis on distinct cultural practices and the need for African American men, women, and children to work together for survival and advancement. Clenora Hudson-Weems in her book, *Africana Womanism: Reclaiming Ourselves* (1993), grounded her concept in the cultures and experiences of people of African descent worldwide, and sought to build bridges between Africana men and women to end sexism and racism and to work for the liberation of all African people. Both Walker and Hudson-Weems, as well as Anna Julia Cooper and Ida Wells-Barnett, pointed to the unity of males and females as the future of the race. Thus, not only should courses focus solely on women, but they should also focus on intergroup relations between Black males and females. Or, at least seminars might be provided that allow for Black male-female issues to be aired. Africana Studies units are appropriate venues for such discourse to take place.

Marilyn Boxer (1998) argued that "recognizing differences" and "embracing diversity" became major objectives of the Women's Studies movement only in the 1980s and 1990s in the face of the challenges coming from lesbians and women of color. And by the 1990s, courses on women of color were offered in the vast majority of Women's Studies Programs. But did this change address the issues raised by African American women scholars? Did this move to the kind of inclusiveness they sought? Given the inequalities between African American and European American women in American society, as well as the impact of institutionalized racism and the subsuming of African American women's experiences under the rubric of "women of color" within Women's Studies programs, many African American feminist and womanist scholars called for the creation of academic programs devoted to "Black Women's Studies" and "Africana Womanism."

I would like to emphasize that I advocate that systematic tracts be built into Africana Studies programs as well as infused throughout the entire Africana Studies curriculum with scholarship by and about Black women, as well as scholarship on Black women by Black men, a number of whom already have embarked on this path (see for example, Matthews, 1979; Franklin, 2002). It is crucial that work by Black women on Black women be integrated into the curriculum so that we are taken seriously. For example, in sociology so much work on and by Blacks is included primarily, if at all, only in social problems and race and ethnic relations courses. To be taken seriously and to feel that Black women are critical to the enterprise, we must be included everywhere as are the men. It easily could be argued that a full tract on women is necessary for the long oversight, and for allowing students to catch up on the other half of those who hold up the sky.

Now, lest we delude ourselves, this means women have to do double time in producing solid scholarship. And, statistics suggest that there are now more Black women pursuing terminal degrees than men. So, the opportunity is there to be seized. The recent increased number of Africana women scholars in the academy has yielded an increase in scholarly research about them. Prior to their significant presence, Africana men and others had largely written from their own interests and perspectives, which excluded, minimized, or distorted the reality of Africana women. This, then, has been a major factor in the absence of Africana women in Africana Studies curricula—the lack of a critical mass of Africana women scholars equipped to provide both quality and quantities of work about Africana women. With the flowering of scholarly contributions, the future is encouraging for bridging the divide throughout curricula, programming, and academic appointments at all levels.

Summary

In summation, what I will attempt to do is to restate and integrate the main arguments on how to bridge the gender divide and how to promote and build support for a truly unified Africana Studies discipline and ensure its future survival. I believe how one group sees and behaves toward another group based on gender or identity by sex determines gender unity or division, and if women do not participate in issues that are at the center of discipline development, they, and their scholarship, will remain marginal. Women must be active at every level of the academy: committees, professional organizations, editorial boards, etc. They must help in the framing of the discourse as well as examining and presenting subsets of it. While some schools of thought within the field may be more or less intent upon counterbalancing the traditional "Eurocentric" bias characteristic of traditional American scholarship, the central tendency of Africana Studies is to investigate, illuminate, and celebrate the African world experience, in its own right (Hare, Stewart, Young, and Aldridge, 2000, 126). That cannot happen without the female gender being thoroughly a part of the enterprise.

As in any dynamic field, there are various schools of thought in Africana Studies. It is commonly agreed that the diversity of perspectives in the field is critical to its vitality and creativity. For example, there is an ongoing debate as to whether Africana Studies is a field of study, a discipline, or something else. Some scholars declare Africana Studies a discipline in which, like sociology, scholars look at different areas of the human experience, be it history, politics, family, etc., through the same lens. Such advocates call the discipline Africology. Some scholars consider Africana Studies to be an interdisciplinary field of focused study to which, like the field of education, scholars bring a variety of disciplinary lenses, be they anthropological, historical, etc., to study the African world experience. Still others would argue for a multi-disciplinary or non-disciplinary label (for a discussion of the implication of terms, see Stewart, 1992). Is there any reason why Africana womanism could not be raised to the level of a school of thought within Africana Studies. How have Africology or Afrocentrism been elevated to these levels? There have been individual spokespersons who have written, developed, and promoted the focus of the "new schools." The point is that labels have to be assigned in the academy as in the larger world to garner attention and move towards entrenchment. Our visible space will be created in much the same way.

Some have chosen the term "post disciplinary" as useful for describing the developmental trajectory of the field of Africana Studies. It expresses a view of Africana Studies as more than a territory to which scholars bring disciplinary lenses. It rather describes an evolving intellectual enterprise focusing upon traditional, traditionally ignored, contemporary, and future ways of knowing. For example, one characteristic of the field's approach is the recognition of indigenous cultural knowledge that lies outside the traditional boundaries of humanistic and scientific discourse, such as that attainable through visual and oral accounts (Hare, Stewart, Young, and Aldridge, 2000, 126–127). What better time for Africana women scholars and their scholarship to expand.

There exists a positive "creative tension" within the field, within the units, and between the units even as Africana Studies scholars share both the pursuit of scholarly knowledge and social responsibility as the dual goal of the Africana Studies enterprise. While we generally agree on the ends, there is great variation in the means by which these dual goals are pursued. Given the change-agent mission characteristic of many Africana Studies units, this tension perhaps becomes inevitable. This positive paradox may have been best expressed by Martin Luther King, Jr. when he declared that no change is possible without "creative tension" (Hare, Stewart, Young, and Aldridge, 2000, 127). So it is with Black women's scholarship. The fuller recognition and incorporation into Africana Studies should be seen as a creative tension, but one that can be overcome as we bridge the divide.

The continuing advancement of Africana Studies requires—in addition to a well-managed interface with traditional disciplines—a well-developed intellectual core that both differentiates the enterprise from and connects it to traditional disciplines. I concur with Stewart (1992), who identifies seven useful developmental thrusts for the field:

1. Development of a theory of history.

2. Articulation of a theory of knowledge and social change.

3. Delineation of a theory of "race" and culture.

4. Expansion of the scope of inquiry encompassed by the disciplinary matrix.

5. Expanded examination of the historical precedents to modern Africana Studies.

6. Increased emphasis on applications of theoretical work.

7. Strengthened linkages to interests outside academe to minimize misappropriation of knowledge and improve information dissemination.

If, indeed, women could become central to each of these thrusts from their women centered perspectives, while also focusing on women's lives, then many of the concerns of women could be dealt with as Africana Studies ensures its survival and development. It is imperative that Africana Studies understand its vision in order to know what to reject and what to accept in it—discipline-analysis is only meaningful if it liberates Africana Studies to choose its own destiny. It has the capacity to dream ever better dreams. Africana Studies has the capacity to build a finer discipline than it has ever before succeeded in building. The 21st Century is ours to shape. Ultimately, answers must be given to the questions: What is the vision of the future? What is in the best interest of Africana women? Africana men? Africana people? How do we liberate the village? Do we travel separately? Or together? And, if together, how?

References

Aldridge, D. P. (1984). "Toward a New Role and Function of Black Studies in Historically White and Black Institutions," *Journal of Negro Education*, Vol. 53, 359–367.

_____. (1989). Guest Editor, "Black Women in the American Economy," *The Journal of Black Studies*, Vol. 20, No. 2.

_____. (1992). "Womanist Issues in Black Studies: Towards Integrating Africana Women into Africana Studies," *The Afrocentric Scholar: The Journal of the National Council for Black Studies*, Vol. 1, 167–182.

_____. (1994). "Status of Africana Studies in Higher Education in the USA" (Mimeo).

_____, and Carlene Young (2000). *Out of the Revolution: The Development of Africana Studies*. Lanham, Maryland: Lexington Books.

Anderson, T. (1993). *Introduction to African American Studies: Cultural Concepts and Theory.* Dubuque, Iowa: Kendall Hunt.

Ani, M. (1994). *Yurugu, An African-Centered Critique of European Culture, Thought and Behavior.* Trenton, N.J.: Africa World Press.

Asante, M. (1990). *Kemet, Afrocentricity, and Knowledge.* Trenton, N.J.: Africa World Press.

Azibo, D. (1992). "Selected Issues in Black Women's Studies from the Perspective of the African Worldview: Toward African Women's Advancement" (Unpublished).

Boxer, M. J. (1998). *When Women Ask the Questions: Creating Women Studies in America.* Baltimore: John Hopkins University Press.

Franklin, V. P. (2002). "Hidden in Plain View: African American Women, Radical Feminism, and the Origins of Women's Studies Programs, 1967–1974," *The Journal of African American History,* Vol. 87, 433–445.

Gordon, V. V. (1987). *Black Women, Feminism, Black Liberation: Which Way?* Revised Edition. Chicago: Third World Press.

Hare, B. R., J. B Stewart, A. Young, and D. P. Aldridge (2000). "Africana Studies: Past, Present, and Future," in *The Disciplines Speak: A Continuing Conversation: Rewarding the Scholarly Professional and Creative Work of Faculty,* Robert M. Diamond and Broynyn E. Adam (eds.). Washington, D.C.: American Association of Higher Education.

Harris, R. (1990). "The Intellectual and Institutional Development of Africana Studies," in Robert Harris, Darlene Clark Hine, and Nellie McKay, *Black Studies in the United States, Three Essays.* New York: Ford Foundation, 15–19.

Hawken, P. (1999). "Corporate Futures," *Yes! A Journal of Positive Futures,* Summer (Http://www.futurenet. org/10citiesofexuberance/corporatefutures.html)

Henry, C., and F. Foster (1982). "Black Women's Studies: Threat or Challenge?" *The Western Journal of Black Studies,* Vol. 6, No. 1, 15–21.

Hooks, B. (1984). *Feminist Theory: From Margin to Center.* Boston: Southend.

Hudson-Weems, C. (1989). "Cultural and Agenda Conflicts in Academia: Critical Issues for Africana Women's Studies," *The Western Journal of Black Studies,* Vol. 13, No. 4, 185–189.

_____. (1993). *Africana Womanism: Reclaiming Ourselves.* Detroit/Troy, Michigan: Bedford.

_____. (1997). "Africana Womanism and the Critical Need for Africana Theory and Thought," *The Western Journal of Black Studies,* Vol. 21, No. 2, 70–84.

Hull, G., P. B. Scott, and B. Smith (1982). *All the Women Are White, All the Blacks Are Men. but Some of Us Are Brave: Black Women's Studies.* Old Westbury, N.J.: Feminist Press.

Matthews, M. D. (1979). "'Our Women and What They Think,' Amy Jacques Garvey and the Negro World," *The Black Scholar,* Vol. 10, Nos. 8, 9.

Stewart, J. B. (1992). "Reaching for Higher Ground: Toward an Understanding of Black/Africana Studies," *The Afrocentric Scholar,* Vol. 1, 1–63.

Walker, A. (1983). *In Search of Our Mothers' Gardens: Womanist Prose.* San Diego: Harcourt Brace Jovanovich.

Young, C. (2000). "The Academy as an Institution: Bureaucracy and African-American Studies," in *Out of the Revolution: The Development of Africana Studies,* Delores P. Aldridge and Carlene Young (eds.). Lanham, Maryland: Lexington Books.

_____, and G. Martin (1984). "The Paradox of Separate and Unequal: African Studies and Afro-American Studies," *The Journal of Negro Education,* Vol. 53, 257–267.

27

Will the Revolution be Digitized?
Using Digitized Resources in Undergraduate
Africana Studies Courses

James B. Stewart

Dr. James Stewart is a Professor of Labor Studies and Industrial Relations and African and African American Studies at Penn State University where he has also served as Vice Provost for Educational Equity and Director of the Black Studies Program. He is author, coauthor, editor, or coeditor of eight monographs and over fifty articles in professional journals. Dr. Stewart has served two terms as Vice Chair as well as two terms as Chair of the National Council for Black Studies for which he directed the organization's Summer Faculty Institute from 1989 to 1991. He has served as editor of The Review of Black Political Economy *and President of the National Economic Association.*—The Western Journal of Black Studies, *Fall 2003, Vol. 27, No. 3*

Abstract

Reviewed here are selected Internet resources for potential use as supplemental sources in the undergraduate Black/Africana Studies curriculum. It is argued that resources are available via the Internet that can, if used appropriately, provide new types of opportunities for students to access and engage valuable information at no additional expense to instructors and students. A brief overview of selected efforts to develop basic Africana Studies instructional resources since the late 1960s is used to provide a context for the discussion. The original curriculum design for majors in Africana Studies developed by the National Council for Black Studies (NCBS) is used to suggest how selected digitized resources can be effectively accessed. The relationships among Internet-based resources and various computer-based digitized resources are discussed in the concluding section, along with the importance of greater engagement by Africana Studies specialists in the development of additional digitized Africana Studies sources.

Introduction

This analysis reviews selected Internet resources for possible use for acquiring supplemental sources in undergraduate Black/Africana Studies courses (hereinafter referred to as Africana Studies). Most existing courses rely heavily on traditional print scholarship supplemented by various audio and visual materials in analog formats. The title of this analysis is a takeoff on Gil Scott Heron's classic song, "The Revolution Will Not Be Televised," with the intention of implying that creative and focused use of digitized resources in collegiate instruction, linked to well-designed social change advocacy strategies, may in the long run help achieve the type of social transformation envisioned by activists of the 1960s.

Looking at the world through a narrower lens, there is no question that resources are available via the Internet that can, if used appropriately, provide new types of opportunities for students to access and engage valuable information at no additional expense to instructors and students. While traditional print sources will continue to constitute the bedrock of Africana Studies instruction, there are several potential benefits that can be derived from expanding the repertoire of instructional resources and pedagogical approaches.

The learning styles of traditional-age college students today are generally more tactile and visually oriented than earlier generations. At the same time, Africana Studies courses disproportionately attract students from digitally-underserved populations. As a consequence, using digitized resources in Africana Studies classes can enhance these students' comfort level with information technologies and contribute to bridging the so-called "digital divide." In addition, given the proliferation of digitized misinformation spread through e-mail and various websites exemplified in a myriad of "urban myths," use of digitized resources can help students develop critical electronic literacy skills for making informed judgments about the accuracy of digitized information. Developing these skills serves the long-term individual and collective long-term social survival and empowerment objectives of Africana Studies.

Consistent with the general empowerment objectives of Africana Studies, use of digitized resources in instruction should be designed to encourage students to think of themselves as potential knowledge producers, rather than function simply as passive information consumers. Moreover, instructors must ensure that neither the technology itself, nor digitized content, induce undesired shifts in overall philosophical orientation or instructional goals. The most functional efforts to introduce digitized resources into Africana Studies courses will be closely aligned with the historical mission and trajectory of the field and with the orientation of existing printed sources that have demonstrated their instructional value.

The next section presents a brief overview of selected efforts to develop basic Africana Studies instructional resources since the late 1960s. The original curriculum design for majors in Africana Studies developed by the National Council for Black Studies (NCBS) is used in the third section as a template for evaluating the potential use of selected digitized resources. The relationships among Internet-based resources and various computer-based digitized resources are discussed in the concluding section. The importance of greater engagement by Africana Studies specialists in the development of additional digitized Africana Studies resources is also emphasized.

Instructional Resources in Africana Studies

The development of instructional materials to support undergraduate classroom instruction in Africana Studies has evolved through several distinct stages. When the contemporary Africana Studies movement gained momentum in the late 1960s and early 1970s there were no field-specific introductory texts available to instructors. In addition to the newness of the field, the development of introductory texts was hampered by disagreements about the contours of the field and appropriate course content.

Two of the earliest efforts to develop introductory textbooks reflected the wide diversity of approaches. In the monograph, *An Interdisciplinary Introduction to Black Studies* (Bright, et al., 1977), Africana Studies was described as "the study of what black people have been, what they are, and in what they will become alone or in concert with others." The role of the text in this effort was defined as exposing "the student to a variety of ideas from the arts, letters, history, and social sciences without any attempt at being exhaustive." In contrast, the claim advanced in *Introduction to Afro-American Studies* (People's College Press, 1977, 3) was that "the essence of Afro-American Studies is study and struggle...[such that] not only do we have to understand the problems faced by Black people, but we must grasp hold of the solutions to those problems." These two views differ, in part, in the relative importance attached to the mastery of basic knowledge and ideas, versus the cultivation of skills that enable the application of knowledge to foster social change.

These two texts were succeeded by the first edition of Maulana Karenga's *Introduction to Black Studies*, which reflected over a decade of active struggle for Black Studies and ongoing dialogue among practitioners about the nature of the enterprise. One of the features that distinguishes Karenga's text from its predecessors was the use of a systematic discussion of the origins of the enterprise of Africana Studies as the text's point of departure. Africana Studies was defined as "the scientific study of the multidimensional aspects of black thought and practice in their current and historical unfolding" (Karenga, 1982, 33). Karenga also used a variety of other terms and metaphors to elaborate on this basic definition, including "social science," "interdisciplinary social science," "interdisciplinary discipline," "particular and general social science," and "specialized and integrative."

Introduction to Black Studies has become the most popular introductory text in use today and is now in its third edition.

Talmadge Anderson's *Introduction to African American Studies* (Dubuque, Iowa: Kendall-Hunt, 1993) is another popular introductory text. Its organization is designed to "adhere closely to the curriculum guidelines of the National Council for Black Studies" and enable "students who may pursue an academic degree or career in any one of the traditional disciplines...[to] be prepared to apply or relate a Black perspective to a particular field" (pp. vii–ix). Anderson's comments are important because the development of Africana Studies curricula has focused on developing sequences of courses for majors in the discipline recognizing, of course, that non-majors also will enroll in upper-division courses.

Africana Studies courses are often included in general education curricula, increasing the numbers and variety of students in classes. The best pedagogical approaches associated with Africana Studies instruction at the undergraduate level expose students to the ideas, philosophical orientations, and benefits of the variety of schools of thought. Instructional strategies are designed to transmit critical analytical skills that allow students to make their own sense of the world. Courses are usually offered through organized units—usually departments, programs, centers, or institutes using faculty with various types of affiliations to the unit with the overall responsibility for the curriculum. The range and orientation of the curriculum generally reflect the mission, faculty expertise, and general focus of the sponsoring academic unit, e.g., African American or Diasporic Studies.

The original curriculum design advocated by the National Council for Black Studies is depicted in Figure 1. The introductory course, in which the textbooks discussed above are typically used, provides the foundations for further study by majors in three possible areas of concentration: History, Social and Behavioral Sciences, and Cultural Studies. Instruction in upper division courses in each area of concentration is expected to be complementary to the treatment of the topical areas in the introductory course. The introductory texts support this curriculum design by providing a variety of bibliographic references at the end of each chapter that can be used as sources in upper division courses. In addition, several edited volumes are available as resources in upper division courses, including: *Black Studies: Theory, Method, and Cultural Perspectives*, edited by Talmadge Anderson (1990), and *A Turbulent Voyage: Readings in African American Studies*, edited by Floyd Hayes (1992). There are also several specialized journals that constitute important sources of material for upper division courses, including: *The Journal of Black Studies*, *The Western Journal of Black Studies*, and the *International Journal of Africana Studies*.

The preceding overview provides the foundation for consideration of how specific digitized resources can be used in Africana Studies classroom instruction. Each of the three general areas comprising the NCBS curriculum model for majors will be discussed separately.

Figure 1. NCBS Interdiciplinary Curriculum Model.

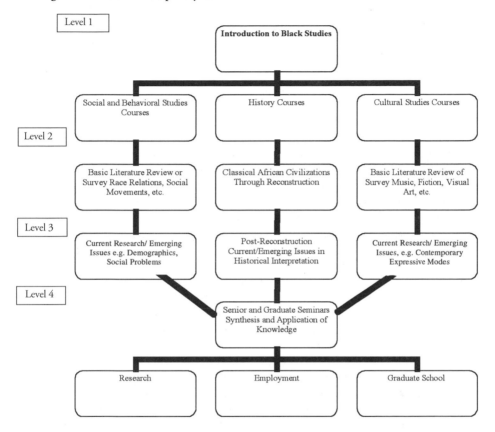

Integrating Digitized Resources into Africana Studies Curricula

It is well established that the study of history has a privileged status within Africana Studies. Karenga (1993, 69) insists that "the core task of Black Studies…is the rescue and reconstruction of Black History and humanity." In addition, he maintains that Black History is "indispensable to the introduction and development of all other subject areas. Black History places them in perspective, establishes their origins and development, and thus aids in critical discussion and understanding of them" (Karenga, 1982, 43).

Both the Anderson and Karenga texts include detailed narrative treatments of African history before the Atlantic slave trade. However, visuals supporting these narrative discussions are sparse. For example, the Karenga text includes only a few rudimentary maps of classic African empires, and there are no visuals related to classical African civilizations in the Anderson text. Digitized resources can enhance the presentation of this material in both introductory and advanced courses. One of the most comprehensive and interesting websites containing information about classical African civilizations is "African Timelines," developed by Cora Agatucci at Central Oregon Community College. The site includes separate timelines for Ancient Africa (web.cocc.edu/cagatucci/classes/hum211/timelines/htimeline.htm), and for the period from the 1st to 15th centuries A.D. (web.cocc.edu/cagatucci/classes/hum211/timelines/htimeline2.htm). Each time-line includes links to other sites that provide a variety of perspectives on classical African civilizations. Both Afrocentric and traditional interpretations of ancient Egyptian culture are presented. History Link 101's "West African Kingdoms" webpage (www.ucalgary.ca/HIST/tutor/imageislam/westAfrica.gif) is another useful resource. This page consists of an overlapping visual representation of the areas included in the 11th century Ghana, 14th century Mali, and 15th century Songhai empires. This representation enables students to understand the conti-nuity of cultural developments over time in West Africa.

Both the Karenga and Anderson texts provide extensive treatments of the Atlantic slave trade, but the use of visual material is limited. To illustrate, the Anderson text includes one comprehensive map showing the various Atlantic slave trade routes, but the time period during which each route was important is not indicated. "The Atlantic Slave Trade and Slave Life in the Americas: A Visual Record," based at the University of Virginia (gropius.Virginia.edu/Slav-ery), contains four separate maps illustrating the extension of Atlantic slave trade routes over time (adapted from Curtin, 1969). There are also visual images and diagrams of slave ships and European forts and trading posts in Africa.

One of the challenges associated with examining the Atlantic slave trade in Africana Studies courses is helping students understand the resulting devastation on African societies. The narrative in the Karenga text does an excellent job of conveying this information. The World History Center at Northeastern Uni-versity offers a web-based simulation that allows students to explore the range of magnitude of impacts caused by the slave trade on African societies. This is accomplished by determining varying assumptions about population growth rates and other factors (www.whc.neu.edu/whc/research/simulations/afrintro/afrform2.html).

As would be expected, both the Anderson and Karenga texts provide exten-sive discussions of the history of Africans in the United States. In both cases there is much more use of visual materials than in other portions of the texts. However, even greater access to images could further enhance students' learning. The website "The Atlantic Slave Trade and Slave Life in the Americas: A Visual Record," mentioned previously, contains a large number of visual representations of plantation scenes, domestic servants and free people of color, family life among enslaved Africans, brutality associated with enslavement, and other topics.

Other websites can further increase instructors' pedagogical options. The "Underground Railroad" webpage of the National Geographic Society website (www.nationalgeographic.com/features/99/railroad) includes a rudimentary simulation of the decision, and the consequences of choosing or not choosing, to escape enslavement via the Underground Railroad. The "St. Louis Court Historical Records Project" website contains detailed information about freedom petitions and suits filed by enslaved Africans (stlcourtrecords.wustl.edu/resources.cfm). The African American Mosaic website (www.loc.gov/exhibits/african/afam002.html) of the Library of Congress offers materials related to abolition and colonization.

Information about free Blacks and various forms of resistance is especially critical for insuring that the presentation of material about the era of enslavement reflects an appropriate Africana Studies emphasis on the agency of people of African descent. A number of the digital images available on the "NYPL Digital Schomburg Images of African Americans from the 19th Century" website (digital.nypl.org/schomburg/images_aal9/main.html) highlight resistance to slavery.

Upper division courses examining the literary culture of the antebellum period can also be invigorated by using several websites. Narratives by enslaved and formerly enslaved Africans are available on several sites, including the "Documenting the American South" website at the University of North Carolina at Chapel Hill (docsouth.unc.edu/dasmain.html), the Library of Congress website, and the "American Slave Narratives: An Online Anthology" website at the University of Virginia (xroads.virginia.edu/~hyper/wpa/wpahome.html). The University of Virginia also has a very interesting collection of Aframerindian slave narratives (www.people.Virginia.edu/~pnm3r/afram). These narratives can broaden students' understanding of the complex interplay between African American and Native American cultures.

The Digital Schomburg website has a digital collection of 52 published works by 19th century African American women writers on the "African American Women Writers of the 19th Century" web page (149.123.1.8/schomburg/writers_aa19/intro.html). This material can be especially useful in insuring that the experiences of Africana women are appropriately reflected in historical discussions. It would support the important contributions to reversing the traditional invisibility of women's voices in Africana Studies that have been made by scholar/activists involved in the development of Africana Women's Studies (e.g., Aldridge 1989, 1991, 1992; Gordon, 1987; Hudson-Weems, 1989, 1993, 1997) and Black Feminist Studies (e.g., Guy-Sheftall, 1995; Hill-Collins, 1991; Hull, et al., 1982).

The wide range of potential topics spanning the post-war and Jim Crow eras (1866–1954) obviously poses a challenge for any introductory course. Suggestions for the use of on-line resources are currently limited to Reconstruction, all-Black towns, Jim Crow segregation, major figures of the early 20th century, the Great Migration, and the Harlem Renaissance.

The website sponsored by *Harper's Weekly*, "Toward Racial Equality: *Harper's Weekly* Reports on Black America, 1857–1874" (blackhistory.harpweek.com/4Reconstruction/ReconLevelOne.htm) offers a variety of interesting information about the Reconstruction period based on material published in the magazine. In addition to detailed treatments of important topics, there also is a Reconstruction Convention simulation exercise. Use of this resource can allow instructors to combine the exploration of literary and historical themes.

The formation and legacy of efforts to found post-Civil War all-Black towns, primarily in the Mid-West, are especially important topics in Africana Studies. These efforts to achieve self-determination reinforce the theme of agency among people of African descent. There are two particularly interesting websites that offer extensive information about this phenomenon. "Black Towns in the West: A Case Study of the Exodusters" (www.ssecinc.org/less/Pg_1s_black.htm) is built around a detailed high school lesson plan. "African Towns and Settlements of Indian and Oklahoma Territories" (www.african-nativeamerican.com/6-towns.htm) includes information about both "African Ghost Towns" and "African Towns Today."

The origins, institutionalization, and operation of Jim Crow segregation is a complex topic. The Public Broadcasting System (PBS) website titled "The Rise and Fall of Jim Crow" constitutes a valuable resource for delving into the nuances of this era (www.pbs.org/wnet/jimcrow). Much of this material was included in the PBS documentary of the same title. The segment of the Library of Congress website titled "The Progress of a People" (memory.loc.gov/ammem/aap/aapexhp.html) is a useful starting point for examining the political responses by Blacks to growing oppression under Jim Crow. For example, the site allows visitors to "attend" an 1898 meeting of the Afro-American Council in Washington, D.C., that was called to evaluate the status of African Americans. "'Art [and History] by Lightning Flash': *The Birth of a Nation* and Black Protest" (chnm.gmu.edu/features/episodes/birthofanation.html) is another website that engages a similar theme.

In considering the contributions of well-known figures to the political, social, and economic uplift of African Americans in the early 20th century, instructors could consider an assignment requiring students to cull available information solely from several websites. Examples of sites containing information about seven major figures are suggested below in Table 1.

The leadership activities of the major leaders highlighted in Table 1 were inextricably interwoven with changes in Black America associated with the Great Migration from the Southern states to the North. This topic can be treated at several levels—national, regional, or local. At the national level, charts and maps showing the size and geographical distribution of the Black population from

Table 1.
Selected Websites Containing Information about Major Early 20th Century African American Leaders.

Name	Website Title/URL
Ida B. Wells Barnett	"Ida B. Wells-Barnett and Her Passion for Justice" www.duke.edu/~ldbaker/classes/AAIH/caaih/ibwells/ibwbkgrd.html
Mary McLeod Bethune	"Explore DC: African American Heritage Biographies" www.exploredc.org/index.php?id=42
Nannie Helen Burroughs	"Special Presentation, Nannie Helen Burroughs" lcweb.loc.gov/loc/kidslc/sp-burroughs.html
W.E.B. Du Bois	"W.E.B. Du Bois Virtual University" members.tripod.com/DuBois/index.htm
Marcus Garvey	"The Marcus Garvey and Universal Negro Improvement Association Papers Project" www.isop.ucla.edu/mgpp
Mary Church Terrell	"Explore DC: African American Heritage Biographies" www.exploredc.org/index.php?id=42
Booker T. Washington	"The Booker T. Washington Papers" www.historycooperative.org/btw

1790 to 1890, and from 1940 to 1970, are available on the Library of Congress Website, "Migration: African American Mosaic Exhibition" (www.loc.gov/exhibits/african/afam008.html). That same site also features in-depth information about Black migration to Chicago, on the "Chicago Destination for the Great Migration" webpage (www.loc.gov/exhibits/african/afam011.html).

Typically, the Harlem Renaissance is explored primarily as a literary movement. As a consequence, most web-based resources focusing on art and literature of the Harlem Renaissance are generally embedded in websites examining broader patterns of Black cultural activity. Examples include "African American Literature: Voices of Slavery and Freedom" (www2.worldbook.com/features/aawriters/html/intro.html), "Poets of the Harlem Renaissance and After" (www.poets.org/exh/Exhibit.cfm?prmID=7), and "Rhapsodies in Black" (www.iniva.org/harlem/home.html).

Non-digitized resources examining the Civil Rights and Black Power movements and the more recent historical experiences of African Americans are abundant. One obvious example is the PBS documentary series, *Eyes on the Prize*. Given the large amount of resources available for this era, some instructors may perceive less benefit from attempting to integrate digitized resources into discussions about this period. Nevertheless, there are several interesting websites that are valuable resources. "Malcolm X: A Research Site" (www.brothermalcolm.net) offers an abundance of information and links to other web sites. The site can be used to allow students to conduct in-depth research on this cultural icon. Enlightening perspectives on the government's efforts to monitor Malcolm X, as well as other major political figures of the 1960s and earlier, including W.E.B. Du Bois, can be garnered by traversing the FBI's website and accessing the "Freedom of Information Act—Electronic Reading Room" (foia.fbi.gov/room.htm). The material is heavily edited to shield the identity of informants, but the contents of the reports still provide illuminating perspectives on federal surveillance activities.

The previous discussion about the Harlem Renaissance highlighted several websites containing material that can be used to supplement traditional upper division cultural studies instruction in Africana Studies. However, there are several additional interesting sites that instructors may also wish to consider. The "Database of African-American Poetry, 1760–1900," website (etext.lib. Virginia.edu/aapd.html), includes over 2,500 poems. "The Development of an African-American Musical Theatre 1865–1910" (memory.loc.gov/ammem/ award97/rpbhtml/aasmsprs3.html) describes and tracks the musical/theatrical motifs that were dominant during each encapsulated decade. As an example, shifts in the traditional minstrel format to incorporate elements of vaudeville occurred during the 1890–1900 decade. The "Special Collections" page of the Archives of African American Music and Culture at Indiana University (www.indiana.edu/~aaamc/special.html) covers the spectrum of musical genres, including popular music, religious music, and classical music; Black radio is also extensively examined.

While jazz occupies a special status in the pantheon of Black cultural genres, it is sometimes difficult to cultivate an appreciation for the art form among students, who are patterned to contemporary hip-hop music. One of the more innovative websites that can be used to introduce students to major jazz figures is "Jazz History@harlem.org A Great Day in Harlem" (www.harlem.org/greatday. html). This site uses a famous 1958 photograph of 57 jazz artists in Harlem as its platform. Students can click on each individual's face and obtain biographical and discographical information about that artist.

In discussions about contemporary popular culture, instructors may find that assignments requiring students to analyze the lyrics of contemporary songs may enhance their broader understanding of the role of popular culture in disseminating values and cultivating culturally-grounded behaviors and collective self-awareness. The lyrics of many contemporary African American popular songs can be found on the "African American Song Lyrics" website (www.straightblack. com/music/Artists.html).

Africana Studies scholar/activists should be able to make especially good use of the "Black Arts Movement" website (www.umich.edu/~eng499). The introduction to the site notes: "Sometimes referred to as 'the artistic sister of the Black Power Movement,' the Black Arts Movement stands as the single most controversial moment in the history of African-American literature—possibly in American literature as a whole." This site can help students explore the extent to which art can be a political instrument and still be valued for its purely aesthetic qualities.

Upper-division instruction in the social and behavioral sciences concentration of Africana Studies should be designed to impart an understanding of the information conveyed by various social indicators, and by trends in the value of such indicators over time. Students should be assisted in developing skills in identifying factors influencing changes in indicators, determining the strength of relationships between influences and indicators, as well as the interrelationships among indicators. Students should also be cautioned not to be mesmerized by quantitative indicators, and be helped to appreciate the value of qualitative research for understanding how individuals, families, and communities confront their life circumstances and are affected by public policies. They should also receive in-depth information about the origin, organization, and operation of social and political institutions developed by African Americans. Students should also be assisted in evaluating policy alternatives, consistent with the social change objectives of Africana Studies.

Ideally, the foundations for the type of upper division instruction in the social and behavioral sciences outlined above will be established in the introductory course. In this regard, the Anderson textbook does a better job than the Karenga text. Both address the issues of the organizational structure of African communities adequately, but treatments of social indicators are limited, especially in the Karenga book. In the Anderson text, students are exposed to data about family composition in the chapter focusing on sociology, about demographic trends and voting behavior in the chapter about Black politics, and income and household characteristics in the section titled "Black Economic and Entrepreneurial Concepts." The principal problem that arises in attempting to incorporate social indicators into traditional texts is that the indicators are constantly changing, and this is where on-line resources can be of special benefit.

However, a totally satisfactory "one-stop-shopping" site for social indicators has not really been identified. The closest approximation may be "Changing America, Indicators of Social and Economic Well-Being by Race and Hispanic Origin," available on the Internet in a PDF format (www.access.gpo.gov/eop/ca/index.html). This document was prepared by the Council of Economic Advisors as part of former President Clinton's President's "Initiative on Race." The eighty page document can be downloaded or obtained in traditional print format. Instructors may want to consider this volume as a supplemental text in either an introductory course, or in the first social and behavioral sciences course in the Africana Studies major sequence.

Suggestions of websites that provide social indicators of various types are listed below in Table 2 in alphabetical order.

Students will develop useful skills if assigned to use the federal government's websites. Users must specify some combination of population groups, gender,

Table 2.
Selected Websites Containing Social Indicators.

Indicator	Website Title/URL
Business Ownership	"The Black Population in the United States" www.census.gov/population/www/socdemo/race/black.html Located on the Bureau of the Census website.
Crime and Criminal Justice Statistics	"Demographic Trends in Correctional Populations" www.ojp.usdoj.gov/bjs/gcorpop.htm Located on the Bureau of Justice website
Community Economic Development	"Tour the Urban EZ/ECs" www5.hud.gov/urban/tour/statestour.asp Located on the Department of Housing and Urban Development website. Identifies areas designated as Renewal Communities, Empowerment Zones, and Enterprise Zones.
Education Statistics	"National Education Statistics & other Equity Indicators" maec.org/natstats.html The site contains information about educational achievement, school safety, parental involvement, and technology access and use.
Elected Officials	"Black Elected Officials: A Statistical Summary, 2000" jointcenter.org/whatsnew/beo-2002 This is part of the Joint Center for Political and Economic Studies website. Data for previous years are currently available only in a traditional print format.
Employment/ Unemployment	"Geographic Profile of Employed and Unemployed, 2001" www.bls.gov/opub/gp/laugp.htm Located on the Bureau of Labor Statistics website. Data are available for previous years.
Health Statistics	"Race/Ethnicity" www.prb.org/template.cfm?template=InterestDisplay.cfm&InterestCategoryID=244 Located on the Population Reference Bureau website.
Housing/ Homeownership	"Race/Ethnicity" www.prb.org/template.cfm?template=InterestDisplay.cfm&InterestCategoryID=244 This is part of the Population Reference Bureau website. "The Black Population in the United States" www.census.gov/population/www/socdemo/race/black.html Located on the Bureau of the Census website
Income	"Income" www.census.gov/hhes/www/income.html Located on the Bureau of the Census website.
Population	"The Black Population in the United States" www.census.gov/population/www/socdemo/race/black.html Located on the Bureau of the Census website
Poverty	"U.S. Families in Poverty: Racial and Ethnic Differences" www.prb.org/Template.cfm?Section=PRB&template=/ContentManagement/ContentDisplay.cfm&ContentID=7873
Voting	"Voting and Registration" www.census.gov/population/www/socdemo/voting.html Located on the Bureau of the Census website

geographical areas, and time frames to generate tables containing the desired information. There also are more visually oriented databases that allow the same type of data tailoring, using map interfaces and Geographic Information System (GIS) databases. One example is "Windows on Urban Poverty" (www.urbanpoverty.net). This is an interactive website where users can select a city or metropolitan area to view high-poverty census tracts and observe the growth of high poverty areas over the 1970–2000 period. This type of site is useful for orienting students toward a focus on public policies contributing to entrenched poverty in certain areas.

Conclusion

The preceding discussion has focused on identifying existing web-based resources available for supplementing instruction in Africana Studies. The suggestions offered are meant to be illustrative, rather than exhaustive. New digitized resources are becoming available daily, while others disappear as websites are not maintained and updated. Instructors and researchers will be increasingly challenged to maintain current knowledge about the available digitized resources.

Many of the websites introduced in this analysis have not been produced by Africana Studies specialists, nor have they been designed with Africana Studies-specific instructional objectives in mind. In addition to paying close attention to the explicit and implicit philosophical and ideological orientations embedded in website designs, it is also important that users recognize important distinctions among types of web-based resources that can affect how particular resources can best be used in instruction. These distinctions are also important for guiding efforts to produce additional web-based resources specifically designed to support Africana Studies instruction.

Many of the websites discussed in this study include multi-media digitized resources, including links to other websites, searchable full-text databases, bibliographies, digitized images of visual and narrative materials, interactive GIS-based maps and databases, non-GIS searchable databases, video and audio clips, and specially prepared introductory and other narrative material that helps guide users.

"E Black Studies" (www.eblackstudies.org) is one of the few examples of an effort to develop a website specifically designed to serve the interests, concerns, and needs of Africana Studies. The project's mission is identified as allowing "one stop shopping for everyone in the field of Africana Studies" with respect to providing "information…in all academic fields that focus primarily on Africa and the African Diaspora." The wealth of material focusing on Malcolm X through this venue was discussed previously. The site also supports upper-division instruction via the extensive links provided to Africana Studies journals, which too often are overlooked as potential supplemental resources for upper-division instruction (www.eblackstudies.org/journals.html).

Although this analysis has focused specifically on web-based resources, it is important to keep in mind that computer-based software packages also constitute a means to integrate digitized information into classroom instruction. The most well-known package is *Microsoft Encarta Africana* (Appiah and Gates, 2000). This two CD-ROM resource contains a virtual storehouse of information. The available information is, in fact, not restricted to what is stored on the CD-ROMs, per se. Some inquiries activate links to various websites. One of the downsides of computer-based software packages, compared to Internet resources, is the cost associated with acquiring the software. The web-based resources discussed in this study are free, which is not the case for *Microsoft Encarta Africana*, although the cost is reasonable.

In some cases, purchasing software CD-ROM based resources is absolutely essential to gain access to important resources that can enhance Africana Studies instruction. As an example, instructors in upper division history courses may want to make use of *The Trans-Atlantic Slave Trade Database* on CD-ROM developed under the auspices of the W.E.B. Du Bois Institute at Harvard (Eltis, Behrendt, Richardson, and Klein, 1999). The database includes the records of over 27,000 trans-Atlantic slave ship voyages between 1595 and 1866.

As in the case of web-based resources and textbooks, issues related to ideology and orientation are relevant in making decisions about the use of software packages. To illustrate, *Black Studies 101*, a CD-ROM based software package being developed by Norman Harris, includes an Afrocentric interpretation of ancient civilization that differs markedly from the more traditional interpretation reflected in *Microsoft Encarta Africana*.

Harris's efforts constitute a model that other instructors and researchers can follow in becoming more proactive in developing digitized resources. As instructors' comfort levels and expertise with information technologies increase, students could be assigned to work on projects involving the development of digitized materials as part of the capstone seminar in Africana Studies depicted in Figure 1. And, as Africana Studies instructors and researchers continue to explore new opportunities to use information technologies we may produce a new generation of scholar/activists for whom the revolution will be digitized!

Published References

Aldridge, D. (ed.) (1989). "Black Women in the American Economy," special issue of *The Journal of Black Studies*, Vol. 20, No. 2.
_____. (1991). *Focusing: Black Male-Female Relationships*. Chicago: Third World Press.
_____. (1992). "Womanist Issues in Black Studies: Towards Integrating Africana Women into Africana Studies," *The Afrocentric Scholar*, Vol. 1, No. 1, 167–182.
Anderson, T. (ed.) (1990). *Black Studies: Theory, Method, and Cultural Perspectives*, Pullman: Washington State University Press.
_____. (1993). *Introduction to African American Studies*. Dubuque, Iowa: Kendall-Hunt.
Bright, A., et al. (1977). *An Interdisciplinary Introduction to Black Studies*. Dubuque, Iowa: Kendall/Hunt.
Gordon, V. (1987). *Black Women, Feminism, Black Liberation: Which Way?* rev. ed. Chicago: Third World Press.
Guy-Sheftall, B. (ed.) (1995). *Words of Fire: An Anthology of African-American Feminist Thought*. New York: New Press.

Hayes, F. (ed.). (1992). *A Turbulent Voyage: Readings in African American Studies*. San Diego: Collegiate Press.

Hill-Collins, P. (1991). *Black Feminist Thought: Knowledge, Consciousness, and the Politics of Empowerment.* New York: Routledge.

Hudson-Weems, C. (1989). "Cultural and Agenda Conflicts in Academia: Critical Issues for Africana Women's Studies," *The Western Journal of Black Studies*, Vol. 13, No. 4, 181–189.

_____. (1993). *Africana Womanism: Reclaiming Ourselves.* Troy, Michigan: Bedford.

_____. (1997). "Africana Womanism and the Critical Need for Africana Theory and Thought," *The Western Journal of Black Studies*, Vol. 21, No. 2, 70–84.

Hull, G., P. Scott, and B. Smith. (1982). *All the Women Are White, All the Blacks Are Men, but Some of Us Are Brave: Black Women's Studies*. Old Westbury, New York: Feminist Press.

Karenga, M. (1982). *Introduction to Black Studies*, 1st ed. Los Angeles: University of Sankore Press.

_____. (1993). *Introduction to Black Studies*, 2nd ed. Los Angeles: University of Sankore Press.

People's College Press. (1977). *Introduction to Afro-American Studies*, 4th ed., Vols. 1 and 2. Chicago: Peoples College Press.

Electronic Resources
(available as of Fall 2003)

Aframerindian Slave Narratives: www.people.Virginia.edu/~pnm3r/afram

African American Literature. Voices of Slavery and Freedom World Book Encyclopedia: www2.worldbook. com/features/aawriters/html/intro.html

(The) African American Mosaic. Library of Congress: www.loc.gov/exhibits/african/intro.html

African American Song Lyrics: www/straightblack.com/music/Artists.html

African American Women Writers of the 19th Century: 149.123.1.8/schomburg/writers_aa19/intro.html

African Towns and Settlements of Indian and Oklahoma Territories: www.african-nativeamerican.com/6-towns.htm

Agatucci, C. (n.d.). *African Timelines, Part I*: retrieved November 17, 2003, from web.cocc.edu/cagatucci/classes/hum211/timelines/htimeline.htm

_____. (n.d.). *African Timelines, Part II*: retrieved November 17, 2003, from web.cocc.edu/cagatucci/classes/hum211/timelines/htimeline2.htm

American Slave Narratives: An Online Anthology: xroads.virginia.edu/~hyper/wpa/wpahome.html

Appiah, K., and H. Gates. (2000). *Microsoft Encarta Africana*. CD-ROM.

Archives of African American Music and Culture. Special Collections: www.indiana.edu/~aamc/special.html

"Art [and History] by Lightning Flash": The Birth of a Nation and Black Protest. Center for History and New Media: chnm.gmu.edu/features/episodes/birthofanation.html

Baker, L. (n.d.). *Ida B. Wells-Barnett and Her Passion for Justice*. Retrieved November 19, 2003, from www.duke.edu/~ldbaker/classes/AAIH/caaih/ibwells/ibwbkgrd.html

Black Arts Movement: www.umich.edu/~eng499

Black Elected Officials: A Statistical Summary, 2000 (n.d.). Joint Center for Political and Economic Studies: jointcenter.org/whatsnew/beo-2002

(The) Black Population in the United States. U.S. Census Bureau: www.census.gov/population/www/socdemo/race/black.html

Black Towns in the West: A Case Study of the Exodusters: www.ssecinc.org/less/Pg_1s_black.htm

(The) Booker T. Washington Papers. University of Illinois Press: www.historycooperative.org/btw/

Chicago: Destination for the Great Migration (n.d.); retrieved November 19, 2003, from www.loc.gov/exhibits/african/afam011.html

Council of Economic Advisors. *Changing America, Indicators of Social and Economic Well-Being by Race and Hispanic Origin*: www.access.gpo.gov/eop/ca/index.html

Curtin, P. (1969). *The Atlantic Slave Trade: A Census* [electronic resource]: name umdl umich edu/HEB01348. Madison: University of Wisconsin Press.

Database of African-American Poetry, 1760–1900. Chadwyck-Healey: etext.lib.Virginia.edu/aapd.html

Demographic Trend in Correctional Populations. Bureau of Labor Statistics: www.ojp.usdoj.gov/bjs/gcorpop.htm

(The) Development of an African-American Musical Theatre, 1865–1910. Library of Congress: memory.loc. gov/ammem/award97/rpbhtml/aasmsprs3.html

Documenting the American South. University of North Carolina Academic Affairs Library: docsouth.unc. edu/dasmain.html

eBlack Studies. Twenty-first Century Books: www.eblackstudies.org

Eltis, D., et al. (1999). *The Trans-Atlantic Slave Trade: A Database on CD-ROM*. New York: Cambridge University Press.

Explore DC: Mary Church Terrell: www.exploredc.org/index.php?id=42

Explore DC: Mary McLeod Bethune: www.exploredc.org/index.php?id=42

Eyes on the Prize: America's Civil Rights Years (1987) [video-recording]. Alexandria, Virginia: PBS Home Video.

Freedom of Information Act—Electronic Reading Room. Federal Bureau of Investigation: foia.fbi.gov/room. htm

Geographic Profile of Employed and Unemployed, 2001. Bureau of Labor Statistics: www.bls.gov.opub/gp/ laugp.htm

Handler, J. S., and M. L. Tuite. (n.d.). *The Atlantic Slave Trade and Slave Life in the Americas: A Visual Record*: gropius.lib.Virginia.edu/Slavery

Harris, N. *Black Studies 101*. CD-ROM.

History Link 101. *West African Kingdoms*: www.ucalgary.ca/HIST/tutor/imageislam/westAfrica.gif

Income: U.S. Bureau of the Census: www.gov/hhes/www.income.html

Jazz History@harlem.org A Great Day in Harlem: www.harlem.org/greatday.html

Malcolm X: A Research Site: www.brothermalcolm.net

(The) Marcus Garvey and Universal Negro Improvement Association Papers Project. James S. Coleman African Studies Center: www.isop.ucls.edu/mgpp

Migrations: African American Mosaic Exhibition. Library of Congress: www.loc.gov/exhibits/african/ afam008.html

National Education Statistics and other Equity Indicators. Mid-Atlantic Equity Consortium: maec.org/nat-stats.html

NYPL Digital Schomburg Images of African Americans from the 19th Century: digital.nypl.org/schomburg/ images_aa19/main.html

Poets of the Harlem Renaissance and After. The Academy of American Poets: www.poets.org/exh/Exhibit. cfm?prmID=7

(The) Progress of a People. Library of Congress: memory.loc.gov/ammem/aap/aapexhp.html

Race/Ethnicity. Population Reference Bureau: www.prb.org/template.cfm?template=InterestDisplay.cfm& InterestCategoryID=244

(The) Rise and Fall of Jim Crow. Public Broadcasting System: www.pbs.org/wnet/jimcrow

St. Louis Court Historical Records Project: stlcourtrecords.wustl.edu/resources.cfm

Special Presentation—Nannie Helen Burroughs. Library of Congress: lcweb.loc.gov/loc/kidslc/sp-burroughs. html

Tour the Urban EZ/ECs. U.S. Department of Housing and Urban Development: www5.hud.gov/urban/ tour/statestour.asp

Toward Racial Equality: Harper's Weekly Reports on Black America, 1857–1874: blackhistory.hrpweek. com/SlaveryHome.htm

(The) Underground Railroad. National Geographic Society: www.nationalgeographic.com/features/99/rail-road

U.S. Families in Poverty: Racial and Ethnic Differences. Population Reference Bureau: www.prb.org/Tem-plate.cfm?Section=PRB&template=/ContentManagement/ContentDisplay.cfm&ContentID=7873

Voting and Registration. U.S. Bureau of the Census: www.census.gov/population/www/socdemovoting. html

W.E.B. Du Bois Virtual University: members.tripod.com/DuBois/index.htm

Watkiss, C. (1997). *Rhapsodies in Black*. Institute of International Visual Arts: www.iniva.org/harlem/hone. html

Windows on Urban Poverty. Brookings Institution Center on Urban and Metropolitan Policy: www.urban-poverty.net

World History Center at Northeastern University: www.whc.neu.edu/whc/research/simulations/afrintro/ afrform2.html

Afterword

E. LINCOLN JAMES

Washington State University

The preceding collection of articles is representative of the theoretical paradigms and philosophical perspectives presented in articles published in *The Western Journal of Black Studies* between 1977 and 2003. The fact that the readings are organized by specific decades does not suggest abrupt shifts or sudden directional changes or the demise of a particular orientation, rather they are meant to be representative samples of theoretical approaches used by intellectuals of those time periods. As the reader would note, they include *all* of the utilized multiple theoretical paradigms. The theoretical approaches seen in the early writings of Black Studies scholars still serve as the framework for modern-day research. There are no paradigms lost, as new theoretical and methodological applications augment our store of knowledge.

On a very macro level the common theme of these articles, and one could argue, of all Black Studies, is identity. Identity discussions embrace race, racial identity, and the consequence of race—racism. First are those articles and essays addressing questions about "race" as a construct and how the European view has disavowed and distorted the contributions of Africa to the development of Western thought. These essays and articles examine the social, economic, biblical, and political motivations behind the construction of the idea of race and the connection between these constructions, colonization, slavery, and the African diaspora. Chukwuemeka Onwubu's analysis, for example, notes the distortion of Africa's contribution to Western civilization and how this distortion by European intellectuals has been instrumental in creating stereotypes and racism. Also note Betty Collier and Louis Williams' examination of Marxism and the African American condition. Other works in this anthology representative of this paradigm are John Clarke's treatise on the University of Sankore, Dona Richards' piece on the ideology of European dominance, and Jacqueline Wade on race and raceness.

A second orientation is represented by those articles that argue about the appropriate methodology for framing issues about Africa and Africans in the diaspora. Included in this category are the Pan African, Afrocentric, and Africana

Womanism paradigms. Some articles illustrative of this perspective are James Turner's essay on Black Nationalism, Molefi Asante on applying the Afrocentric approach to the analysis of drama, and Clenora Hudson-Weems on Africana Womanism. Other of these types of articles include those studies that raise issues of pedagogy, such as, What should be the focus of Black Studies and the appropriate orientation for effective teaching/learning? Karla Spurlock suggests an interdisciplinary approach to Black Studies. Johnnella Butler considers the interaction between identity and pedagogy. Victor Okafor proposes an Africological pedagolocical approach. Gordon Morgan philosophizes about Afrocentricity in Social Science. Delores Aldridge looks at expanding Black Studies curricula to include gender equity studies, while Arthur Lewin traces the evolution and direction of Black Studies.

A third kind of approach that is reflected in this collection is the examination of what may be called "correlates of the Africana Identity," as exemplified by James Turner's piece on the Black Nationalist movement; also Clovis Semmes on Black health, Delores Aldridge's discussion of gender relationships as a function of differential socialization, Clyde Franklin on Black masculinity, and Richard Davis on Neo-Conservatism.

Finally, two other philosophical orientations generally consider a variety of identities and realities from within a framework of a kind of critical race theory: (1) studies proposing identity as a dependent variable affected by factors such as slavery, culture, etc.; see Amuzie Chimezie on theories of Black Culture, and Robert Perry on Black on Black crime, and (2), studies that treat identity as an independent variable that could predict a variety of attitudes, opinions, and behaviors; e.g., Rudolph Cain on perception of power control.

Thus, the articles in this collection reflect a number of traditional and emerging paradigms. The examples presented here are not exhaustive; neither are they mutually exclusive in terms of orientation. It is hoped that the reader would come away with a sense of the very distinct yet very eclectic nature of the theoretical paradigms in Black Studies articles that have appeared in *The Western Journal of Black* Studies over the past three decades.